HERESY AND THE PERSECUTING SOCIETY
IN THE MIDDLE AGES

STUDIES IN THE HISTORY
OF
CHRISTIAN TRADITIONS

FOUNDED BY HEIKO A. OBERMAN †

EDITED BY

ROBERT J. BAST, Knoxville, Tennessee

IN COOPERATION WITH

HENRY CHADWICK, Cambridge
SCOTT H. HENDRIX, Princeton, New Jersey
PAUL C.H. LIM, Hamilton, Massachusetts
ERIC SAAK, Indianapolis, Indiana
BRIAN TIERNEY, Ithaca, New York
ARJO VANDERJAGT, Groningen
JOHN VAN ENGEN, Notre Dame, Indiana

VOLUME CXXIX

M. FRASSETTO

HERESY AND THE PERSECUTING SOCIETY
IN THE MIDDLE AGES

HERESY AND THE PERSECUTING SOCIETY IN THE MIDDLE AGES

ESSAYS ON THE WORK OF R.I. MOORE

EDITED BY

MICHAEL FRASSETTO

BRILL

LEIDEN · BOSTON

2006

This book is printed on acid-free paper.

Library of Congress Cataloging-in-Publication Data

Heresy and the persecuting society in the Middle Ages : essays on the work of R.I.
    Moore / edited by Michael Frassetto.
        p. cm. — (Studies in the history of Christian traditions, ISSN 1573-5664 ; v. 129)
    Includes bibliographical references and index.
    ISBN 90-04-15098-6 (alk. paper)
        1. Moore, R. I. (Robert Ian), 1941- 2. Heresies, Christian—History—Middle Ages,
    600-1500. 3. Persecution—Europe—History—To 1500. I. Frassetto, Michael.
    II. Series.

BT1319.H475 2006
273'.6—dc22

                                                                                    2005058259

ISSN   1573-5664
ISBN-13: 978-90-04-15098-0
ISBN-10: 90-04-15098-6

CONTENTS

ACKNOWLEDGEMENTS

The origins of this volume can be traced to a session at Kalamazoo, but for many of the volume's contributors the origins can be traced to their first meeting with the work of R.I. Moore. I wish to thank Professor Moore particularly for his involvement in this volume as well as his support for the work of all those involved. His insights into medieval heresy and society have formed the basis for much of the work of many of those involved in this volume, and it is the purpose of this volume to recognize his contributions and to continue the investigations he began. I should also thank the contributors to this volume, who have given their time and efforts to make this volume a success. Thanks are owed to Hendrik van Leusen, Robert Bast, and the many fine people at Brill for their support and assistance in bringing this work to its fruitful conclusion. My colleague and friend, Sarah Orwig, has offered much encouragement and has been a helpful sounding board for many of the ideas that appear in my own contribution to this volume. Finally, I owe my deepest thanks to Jill and Olivia, who have helped me in more ways than they know.

LIST OF CONTRIBUTORS

Malcolm Barber BA, PhD (Nottingham), FRHistS. Professor of History. Director of the Graduate Centre for Medieval Studies, 1986–1989. British Academy Research Readership, 1989–1991. Leverhulme Research Fellowship, 1997–1998. Senior Fellowship, National Humanities Center, North Carolina, 1998–1999. Author of *The Trial of the Templars* (1978), *The Two Cities: Medieval Europe, 1050–1320* (1992), *The New Knighthood: A History of the Order of the Temple* (1994), *Crusaders and Heretics, 12th to 14th Centuries* (1995), *The Cathars* (2000) and many articles on the Templars, the Cathars, the crusader states, popular crusading movements, the lepers in medieval society, western attitudes to Latin Greece, and the reign of Philip the Fair. Editor, *The Military Orders. Fighting for the Faith and Caring for the Sick* (1994). General editor of *A History of Medieval Europe*, published by Routledge. Editor of *The Journal of Medieval History*.

Daniel Callahan, Professor of History at the University of Delaware received his Ph.D. in 1968 from the University of Wisconsin, Madison, where his major professor was David Herlihy. He has published articles on tenth- and eleventh-century spirituality, with a concentration on the writings of Ademar of Chabannes. His most recent pieces include "The Cult of St. Michael the Archangel and 'The Terrors of the Year 1000,'" in *The Apocalyptic Year: Religious Expectations and Social Change, ca. 950–1050*, eds. R. Landes and D. Van Meter. He is currently working on the book *The Making of a Millennial Pilgrim: Jerusalem and the Cross in the Life and Writings of Ademar of Chabannes*.

Michael Frassetto is an independent scholar and adjunct instructor at the University of Delaware. He has earned degrees from LaSalle University (BA), Michigan State University (MA), and the University of Delaware (Ph.D.). He edited *Medieval Purity and Piety: Essays on Medieval Clerical Celibacy and Religious Reform* (New York, 1998), *The Year 1000* (2002) and co-edited (with David Blanks) *Western Views of Islam in Medieval and Early Modern Europe: Perception of Other* (1999).

James Given is professor of history at the University of California Irvine. He is the author of *State and Society in Medieval Europe, Society and Homicide in Thirteenth-Century England,* and *Inquisition and Medieval Society Power, Discipline, and Resistance in Languedoc.* His research focuses on heresy and society in Europe as well as how various societies in Afro-Eurasia interacted.

Bernard Hamilton is Emeritus Professor in Crusading History at the University of Nottingham. He is the author of numerous articles on the Crusades, the Inquisition, and other topics concerning the history of the medieval church. He has also published *Religions in the Medieval West, The Medieval Inquisition, The Leper King and His Heirs: Baldwin IV and the Crusader Kingdom of Jerusalem,* and edited, with Janet Hamilton and Yuri Stoyanov, *Christian Dualist Heresies in the Byzantine World, c. 650– c. 1405.*

Carol Lansing is Professor of History at the University of California, Santa Barbara, and earned her Ph.D. at the University of Michigan. The author of numerous articles, she has also published *The Florentine Magnates: Lineage and Faction in a Medieval Commune* and *Power and Purity: Cathar Heresy in Medieval Italy* and *The Lament for the Dead* (forthcoming).

Laurence W. Marvin is associate professor of history at Berry College. He has published articles in *The Journal of Medieval History* and *The Historian,* and is the author of the forthcoming *The Occitan War: A Military and Political History of the Albigensian Crusade, 1209–1218.*

R.I. Moore was educated at Oxford University and has taught medieval history at the Universities of Sheffield and Newcastle upon Tyne, where he is presently Professor of Medieval History, and was a visiting professor at the University of Chicago in 1989. He is the author of *The Birth of Popular Heresy, The Origins of European Dissent, The Formation of a Persecuting Society,* and *The First European Revolution, c. 970–1215.* He is also Editor of the Blackwell History of the World.

Mark Pegg is associate professor of History at Washington University in St. Louis. He is the author *The Corruption of Angels: The Great Inquisition of 1245–1246* and *The Albigensian Crusade.*

Edward Peters is the Henry Charles Lea Professor of History and Curator of the Lea Library at the University of Pennsylvania. He is the author of *The Shadow King* (1970), *The Magician, the Witch, and the Law*

(1976), *Torture* (1985), and *Inquisition* (1988). A volume of essays, *Limits of Thought and Power in Medieval Europe* appeared in 2001.

Arthur Siegel earned his Ph.D. in 2003 at the University of Delaware. His dissertation is "Heresy, Reform, and Regional Power in Eleventh-Century Italy: A Re-Evaluation of the Monforte Sect."

Susan Taylor Snyder is assistant professor of history at Benedictine College. She earned her Ph.D. at University of California, Santa Barbara, where she completed her dissertation, "Woman as Heretic: Gender and Lay Religion in Late Medieval Bologna," under the direction of Carol Lansing.

Claire Taylor, Ph.D. University of Nottingham (Awarded unconditionally) 1999, is a lecturer in medieval history as University of Nottingham. Publications include "The Letter of Heribert of Périgord as a source for dualist heresy in the society of early eleventh-century Aquitaine," *Journal of Medieval History* (2000), and "Innocent III, King John and the Albigensian Crusade (1209–1216)," in ed. J. Moore, *Pope Innocent III and his World* (1999), 205–228, "The year 1000 AD and 'those who labour'" in *The Year 1000 Problem: Social and Religious Responses to the Turning of the First Millennium*, and *Dualist heresy in Aquitaine and the Agenais, c. 1000–c. 1249.*

INTRODUCTION

Michael Frassetto

Since its publication in 1977, R.I. Moore's *The Origins of European Dissent* has been one of the seminal works of medieval religious and social history.[1] Moore's argument that "the habit of dissent was formed and expressed substantially, though not exclusively, in association with the dissemination of popular heresy in the Europe of the eleventh and twelfth centuries" has greatly influenced a generation of scholars.[2] Moore himself has further explored the implications of his observation as have others, including some who have questioned its teleological perspective.[3] Moore's efforts to understand the motivations that drove the heretics of the Middle Ages moved beyond the traditional debate over whether heresy was primarily caused by social conditions or religious concerns. For Moore, expressions of religious dissent were a manifestation of deep-seated anxieties. Although cloaked in religious garb, heresy, for Moore, is an expression of profound dissatisfaction with the church, one of the most important institutions in medieval society, and, at times, with the state that supported the church. Beyond that, Moore's work explored the social dynamic that existed between the heretics and orthodox leaders of church and society, and the insights he provided into the development of medieval and modern European civilization continue to shape how scholars understand medieval society.

The Origins of European Dissent not only offered a unique methodological approach to the study of medieval heresy and society but also established the main outlines of contemporary understanding of

---

[1] Published originally by Allen Lane, a corrected edition was published (Oxford: Basil Blackwell, 1985) that included a new appendix, replacing Bernard Hamilton's discussion of the Cathar council of St-Félix de Caraman, that assessed recent scholarship on 11th-century heresy.

[2] *Origins of European Dissent*, ix.

[3] Along with numerous articles on medieval heresy, Moore continued his examination of heresy and society in two noteworthy volumes, *The Formation of a Persecuting Society* (Oxford: Blackwell, 1987), and *The First European Revolution, c. 970–1215* (Oxford: Blackwell, 2000). See Edward Peters, "Moore's Eleventh and Twelfth Centuries: Travels in the Agro-Literate Polity," below for a full assessment of Moore's work and influence. See also Professor Moore's epilogue for his reflections on his work.

the resurgence of heresy in the eleventh and twelfth centuries and the church militant's reaction to it. Although he was not the first to reject Bogomil influence on the origins of medieval heresy, Moore offered the most persuasive case against foreign influence on the revival of heresy around the year 1000.[4] A generation of scholars has taken Moore's arguments as a starting point for their understanding of heresy in the early eleventh century. Accepting his premise that medieval heresy was *sui generis*, a broad range of scholars have sought the reasons for heresy's sudden appearance. Among the issues explored by scholars such as Richard Landes and Brian Stock are the relationship of heresy to reform, heresy as a millennial phenomenon, and heresy and the rise of literacy in medieval society.[5] In the process, scholars have built upon Moore's work, examining religious dissent in the broader social context.

---

[4] Raffaello Morghen, *Medioevo cristiano* (Bari: Laterza, 1953) was perhaps the first to challenge the prevailing view that Balkan dualist missionaries inspired the revival of heresy. Jeffrey Burton Russell, *Dissent and Reform in the Early Middle Ages* (Berkeley and Los Angeles: University of California Press, 1965) did not reject completely the possibility of Bogomil influence but did challenge the established view that they were the cause of the origins of heresy. The standard view of the time is best presented in Antoine Dondaine, "L'origine de l'hérésie médiévale," *Rivista di storia della chiesa in Italia* 5 (1951): 47–78; and Steven Runciman, *The Medieval Manichee: A Study in the Christian Dualist Heresy*, 2nd ed. (New York: Viking Press, 1961). A recent argument in favor of Bogomil influence on western European heresy in the 11th century is Claire Taylor, "The Letter of Heribert of Périgord as a Source for Dualist Heresy in the Society of early Eleventh Century Aquitaine," *Journal of Medieval History* 26 (2001): 313–349. See also the articles by Daniel Callahan and Bernard Hamilton in this volume, and Malcom Barber, *The Cathars: Dualist Heretics in Languedoc in the High Middle Ages* (London: Longman, 2000), 21–33, and Malcolm Lambert, *Medieval Heresy: Popular Movements from the Gregorian Reform to the Reformation*, 3rd ed. (Oxford: Blackwell, 2002), 37–40, who also recognize the possibility of Bogomil influence. A forceful statement of the view asserted by Moore is Mark Pegg, "On Cathars, Albigenses, and Good Men of Languedoc," *Journal of Medieval History* 27 (2001): 181–195. See also Pegg's provocative *The Corruption of Angels. The Great Inquisition of 1245–1246* (Princeton: Princeton University Press, 2001), as well as his chapter below, "Heresy, Good Men, and Nomenclature," for a greater challenge to traditional approaches to medieval heresy.

[5] These matters, and others, are considered in Richard Landes, "La vie apostolique en Aquitaine en l'an mil: paix de Dieu, culte des reliques, et communauté hérétiques," *Annales ESC* 46 (1991): 573–593; and Brian Stock, *The Implications of Literacy: Written Language and Models of Interpretation in the Eleventh and Twelfth Centuries* (Princeton: Princeton University Press, 1983). R.I. Moore, "The Birth of Popular Heresy: A Millennial Phenomenon?" *Journal of Religious History* 24 (2000): 8–25, and Richard Landes, "The Birth of Popular Heresy: A Millennial Phenomenon," *ibid.*, 24–43 offers an interesting debate between these two scholars on the origins of medieval heresy. And Moore's scholarship surely pervades such recent works as Scott L. Waugh and Peter D. Diehl, eds., *Christendom and its Discontents: Exclusion, Persecution, and Rebellion, 1000–1500* (Cambridge: Cambridge University Press, 1996); and Monique Zerner, ed., *Inventer l'hérésie? Discours*

Similarly, his examination of heresy in the early twelfth century has proved influential, both in terms of his approach and his conclusions. He argued that the Gregorian Reform influenced the birth of heresy in the early twelfth century because of the successes and failures of the Gregorians. Indeed, the papal reform movement itself offered critiques of the church that had previously been made by the heretics, themselves inspired by a broader reform movement, of the early eleventh century.[6] The papal reformers thus made the earlier heterodox challenge to the church its own, and a subsequent generation of heretics in turn attacked the shortcomings of late eleventh-century reform efforts. Moore's work on early twelfth century heresy emphasized further the connection between religious dissent and the broader social and cultural developments of the time. His arguments that the Cathar, or Albigensian, heresy emerged only after the mid-twelfth century has been persuasive for most medievalists, including Malcom Lambert, who once argued for the arrival of the Bogomils in the early eleventh century.[7] But again, the influence of the Bogomils can only be understood in the broader social context for Moore and most subsequent scholars of medieval history.

Moore has continued to examine the themes raised in *The Origins of European Dissent* in numerous articles as well as in another highly influential work, *The Formation of a Persecuting Society*, whose central theme formed the focus of a collection of essays.[8] In this book, Moore explores the reaction of the religious and secular institutions that responded to the emergence of dissent. He examined the creation of mechanisms

---

polémiques et pouvoirs avant 'inquisition (Nice: Centre d'Études Médiévales, Faculté des Lettres, Arts et Sciences Humaines, Université de Nice Sophia-Antipolis, 1998).

[6] Richard Landes, "Between Heresy and Aristocracy: Popular Participation in the Limousin Peace of God, 994–1033," in Thomas Head and Richard Landes, eds., *The Peace of God: Social Violence and Religious Response in France around the Year 1000* (Ithaca, NY: Cornell University Press, 1992), 184–218, and elsewhere has examined the relationship between heresy and reform in the early eleventh century.

[7] In *Medieval Heresy: Popular Movements from Bogomil to Hus* (New York: Homes and Meier, 1977), Lambert argued that Bogomil missionaries were active in western Europe in the early eleventh century. In *Medieval Heresy: Popular Movements from the Gregorian Reform to the Reformation*, 2nd ed (Oxford: Blackwell, 1992), he rejected any Bogomil influence on western heresy before the mid-twelfth century. In the third edition of the work (Oxford: Blackwell, 2002), however, Lambert accepts the possibility of some Bogomil influence in the first decades of the eleventh century.

[8] John Christian Laursen and Cary J. Nederman, eds., *Beyond the Persecuting Society: Religious Toleration Before the Enlightenment* (Philadelphia: University of Pennsylvania Press, 1998).

intended to suppress dissent. Moreover, and more importantly, he considered the emergence of a mentality that sought to eliminate and demonize the "other." In this work, Moore explored the ways in which European society created an enemy and sought to destroy it. The creation of stereotypes for various dissident groups had, of course, been explored by other scholars,[9] but Moore offered a compelling case that the leaders of society created a uniform image of these minority groups that transformed them into one unified enemy of society that needed to be suppressed. It was not the appearance of great throngs of heretics, whose number he suggests has been exaggerated, that led the religious and secular hierarchies to establish various mechanisms of persecution. Rather, medieval society evolved in such a way that it could not tolerate dissent or difference and, consequently, lumped heretics, Jews, homosexuals, and lepers together as enemies of society who, because of perceived differences, came to be persecuted. Indeed, the clerical, especially, and temporal elites of society created these categories and imposed certain characteristics on various out groups, which thus created the perception of a vast conspiracy against society. In this way institutions like the inquisition can be seen as a manifestation of society's efforts to preserve itself and its fundamental values against real or imaginary enemies.

As important and influential as his book-length studies have been, Moore's shorter works have also left an important mark on medieval scholarship and demonstrate his continued engagement with contemporary debates. Perhaps most notable is his description of heresy as a disease, which has shaped the understanding of medieval responses to heresy.[10] His works on heresy and medieval religion during the Gregorian reform movement provide valuable insights into key developments

---

[9] Christian attitudes toward various minority groups have been examined in John Boswell, *Christianity, Social Tolerance, and Homosexuality* (Chicago: University of Chicago Press, 1980); Robert Chazan, *Medieval Stereotypes and Modern Antisemitism* (Berkeley and Los Angeles: University of California Press, 1997); Norman Cohn, *Europe's Inner Demons: The Demonization of Christians in Medieval Christendom*, rev ed. (Chicago, 1993); and Joshua Trachtenberg, *The Devil and the Jews: The Medieval Conception of the Jew and Its Relation to Modern Anti-Semitism* (Philadelphia: The Jewish Publication Society, 1943). See also Dominque Iogna-Prat, *Ordonner et exclure: Cluny et la société chrétienne face à l'hérésie, au judaïsme et à l'islam, 1000–1150* (Paris: Aubier, 1998).

[10] "Heresy as a Disease," in W. Lourdaux and D. Verhelst, eds., *The Concept of Heresy in the Middle Age (11th–13th C.)* (Leuven and The Hague: University Press The Haque, 1976), 1–11.

during a pivotal time in European history.[11] More recently, Moore has debated the importance of apocalyptic sentiment on the emergence of heresy in the early eleventh century with Richard Landes and has reflected on the growing perception that heretics and heresy were constructed as much by orthodox commentators as alleged heretics.[12] He has also explored the development of anti-Semitism in the Middle Ages, and he has written insightful treatments of important religious figures such as Guibert of Nogent and Christina of Marykate. And many of the themes raised in *The Origins of European Dissent* and other works have been examined anew in his consideration of *The First European Revolution, c. 970–1215*, which treats the profound changes in medieval society during the eleventh and twelfth centuries that led to the emergence of European civilization.[13]

Moore's work has clearly exercised a pronounced impact on scholarship since the appearance *The Origins of European Dissent*, and it is the purpose of this volume to consider that influence and to explore further the issues Moore raised in his many publications, which have shaped much of the modern debate on medieval dissent and its repression. Taking an essentially chronological approach, the essays in this volume address matters of foreign influence on heresy, the relationship between heresy and social power, and societal response to the appearance and expansion of religious dissent from the eleventh to the fourteenth century. These essays, reflecting primarily on Moore's seminal work, demonstrate the continued vitality of the approach he took and the arguments he made originally in 1977. They also seek to expand the boundaries of Moore's original efforts, which did not consider events in Italy, for example, as fully might have been possible.

---

[11] "Family, Community and Cult on the Eve of the Gregorian Reform," *Transactions of the Royal Historical Society*, 5th ser., 30 (1980), 49–69; and "Heresy, Repression and Social Change in the Age of the Gregorian Reform," in Scott J. Waugh and Peter Diehl, eds., *Christendom and Its Discontents* (Cambridge: Cambridge University Press, 1996), 19–46.

[12] "The Birth of Popular Heresy. A Millennial Phenomenon," *Journal of Religious History* 24 (2000): 8–25; and "Postface," in Monique Zerner, ed., *Inventer L'Hérésie? Discours Polémiques avant L'Inquisition* (Nice: Centre d'Études Médiévales, Faculté des Lettres, Arts et Sciences Humaines, Université de Nice Sophia-Antipolis, 1998), 263–269.

[13] Oxford and New York: Blackwell, 2000. See Edward Peters' assessment below and John O. Ward, "Cereals, Cities, and the Birth of Europe: R.I. Moore's *First European Revolution, c. 970–1215*: A Review," *Journal of Religious History* 26 (2002): 250–263, for further comments on this work.

Beyond the matter of the origin and nature of religious dissent in the Middle Ages, the matter of the persecution and stereotyping of heresy is considered. The development of secular and religious institutions that played a central role in the suppression of dissent, in Moore's view, are also addressed. This volume, it is hoped, will provide an appreciation of Moore's impact on medieval scholarship as well as a broader understanding of the role of heresy and persecution in the Middle Ages.

The volume opens with Edward Peters' thorough evaluation of Moore's major works and their importance to our understanding of medieval social and religious history. This is followed by a series of chapters that assess what has emerged in recent years as one of the more controversial arguments of Moore's work: the rejection of Bogomil influences on the emergence of heresy after the turn of the year 1000.[14] Daniel Callahan and Bernard Hamilton argue for the appearance of Bogomil missionaries in western Europe a full century before Moore and most other scholars now believe. These chapters, in part, drawing on new sources and offering a broader understanding of heresy in the eastern Mediterranean offer a challenge to one of Moore's more important contentions that is answered in Arthur Siegel's evaluation of heresy and reform in Italy in the eleventh century. Michael Frassetto's examination of the sermons of Ademar of Chabannes asks how well eleventh-century ecclesiastics understood the religious dissent facing them, and thus questions one of the fundamental assumptions of many scholars who contend that Ademar and others understood contemporary heresy as a result of their reading of St. Paul and St. Augustine of Hippo.

The essays by Malcolm Barber and Claire Taylor examine the development of heresy in regions that have attracted less attention than the great centers of medieval heresy. Barber, whose recent work includes a study of the Cathars of Languedoc, addresses the matter of the northern expansion of the Cathar heresy in the twelfth and thirteenth

---

[14] Claire Taylor, "The Letter of Heribert of Périgord as a Source for Dualist Heresy in the Society of the early Eleventh Century Aquitaine," *Journal of Medieval History* (2000): 313–349, has argued for the earlier appearance of Bogomil missionaries; and Macolm Lambert, *Medieval Heresy*, 3rd ed., has allowed for the possibility of Bogomil missionaries in Aquitaine in early eleventh century. The most dramatic assertion of the early appearance of the Bogomils is Jean-Pierre Poly and Erich Bournazel, trans. C. Higgitt, *The Feudal Transformation 900–1200* (New York: Holmes and Meier, 1991), 272–309.

centuries.[15] As Moore did in his seminal work,[16] Barber surveys the accounts of the appearance of heretics in Cologne and other northern towns. Drawing from a variety of sources—including histories, letters, and inquisitorial records—Barber charts the activities of heretics in northern Europe and observes that they had little success. As Moore did in *Origins of European Dissent*, Barber contends that heresy was imported from Bulgaria and the Byzantine world and notes the importance of religious and social conditions for the failure of heresy, specifically dualist heresy, in the north.[17] Claire Taylor focuses on regions of northern Languedoc in her essay and considers Moore's understanding of the relationship between heresy and social power and his contention that accusations of heresy do not always correspond to the existence of heresy. In this way, she addresses issues raised in Moore's works on the origins of dissent and on the persecuting society and demonstrates how the Albigensian Crusade and efforts at suppression of heresy in parts of northern Languedoc contributed to support of the Cathars by their Catholic neighbors.

The reaction to and understanding of heresy is the focus of the essays by Laurence Marvin and Mark Pegg. Marvin challenges the prevailing opinion on the nature of the massacre at Béziers during the Albigensian Crusade. Although not denying the brutality of the event, Marvin argues that the massacre was not that distinct from standard military practice at the time. The importance of the massacre, Marvin contends, is not that it was unusually severe but that it demonstrated to the victors that theirs was God's way, thus confirming the validity of the use of force against heresy—a component of the persecuting society. Drawing from one of Moore's recent essays, as well as the general tenor of much of his work, Pegg questions the facile way in which the terms "Cathar" and "Catharism" have been used by scholars. His study of inquisitorial records offers a nuanced understanding of religious and social practices in the Toulousain in the thirteenth century. Pegg argues that Catharism is a modern construct that bears little connection with the reality of medieval belief and practice. Like the inquisitors before them, most historians, according to Pegg, have formed the beliefs of the "heretics"

---

[15] *The Cathars: Dualist Heretics in the Languedoc in the High Middle Ages* (London: Longman, 2000).

[16] *Origins of European Dissent*, 186–196.

[17] *Origins of European Dissent*, 170–171. The importance of considering both religious and social conditions, is, of course, one of the strengths of Moore's book.

into what they believed they should have been. Citing Moore's insights into medieval social customs, Pegg attempts to provide a picture of medieval practices unburdened by the conventional understanding of "Catharism."

The next three chapters address heresy, orthodoxy, and persecution in the late thirteenth and early fourteenth centuries. In their studies of developments in Italy, Susan Taylor Snyder and Carol Lansing assess the narrow boundaries between heresy and orthodoxy.[18] Snyder demonstrates the fluid boundaries between Catholic and Cathar communities in Bologna. She notes how both communities shared interests in local confraternities and demonstrates that Cathars participated in urban religious rituals associated with the Catholic church. The Cathars of Bologna recognized the value of religious practices whether these practices were promoted by a Cathar perfect or Catholic priest. Carol Lansing extends the ideas raise by Moore in his works on heresy and persecution to examine a unique inquisitorial record concerning the pious fraud of certain Italians. She reveals the contours of popular religious beliefs, and their abuse, in later thirteenth-century Italy and raises the issue of how contemporaries interpreted these beliefs. And in the penultimate chapter of the volume, James B. Given develops themes raised by Moore's persecuting society.[19] Given describes the creation of stereotypes by the French king Philip IV and how these stereotypes of the religious other shaped royal policy in the late thirteenth and early fourteenth centuries.

The volume concludes with R.I. Moore's own reflections on the origins of his influential work on religious dissent and its impact on subsequent scholarship. Offering a brief intellectual biography, Moore provides insights into the development of his approach to medieval dissent and its persecution as well as his understanding of medieval society as a whole. Moore also responds to the themes raised throughout this volume, engaging in debate with arguments with which he disagrees and challenging those with whom he agrees to further refine their arguments with characteristic generosity and humanity.[20] In so

---

[18] A good introduction to the Cathars of Italy is Carol Lansing, *Power and Purity: Cathar Heresy in Medieval Italy* (Oxford: Oxford University Press, 1998).

[19] See also James B. Given, *Inquisition and Medieval Society: Power, Discipline, and Resistance in Languedoc* (Ithaca, NY: Cornell University Press, 1997).

[20] His generosity of spirit is perhaps no better demonstrated than when he commented to a rather nervous graduate student following his first, and admittedly very poor, conference presentation was "very interesting indeed".

doing, he continues the dialogue he initiated with the publication of his book in 1977.

It is the intention of this volume, therefore, to maintain that conversation and to further consider Moore's understanding of religious dissent and persecution in the Middle Ages. Although not always in agreement with Moore, the authors of the essays in this volume have found Moore's work to be consistently thoughtful and provocative. Indeed, even those who disagree with him recognize the importance of his work and the generosity of his intellect. Quoting Spinoza, Moore once noted that it is our responsibility not to judge those in the past but to understand them; it is the hope of the contributors to this volume that in furthering the discussion on heresy and persecution begun by Moore we can follow the example he has set.[21]

---

[21] *Origins of European Dissent*, 20, where Moore cites Spinoza's advice: "humanas actiones non ridere, non lugere, neque detestari, sed intelligere."

MOORE'S ELEVENTH AND TWELFTH CENTURIES:
TRAVELS IN THE AGRO-LITERATE POLITY

EDWARD PETERS

It is now just over thirty years since R.I. Moore published his first article on medieval heresy.[1] After reviewing a number of earlier explanations of both the emergence of popular heresy in a small number of
sources from the late tenth and the first half of the eleventh century
and its continuous history after the early twelfth, Moore argued that
the interests of the earlier dissenters had paralleled the interests of many
ecclesiastical reformers of the period and that the triumph of the latter
at the end of the eleventh century had led to compromises and doctrines that many of their former fellow-critics found unpalatable:

> If, on the one hand, the severest and most vigorous critics of the church
> and the clergy no longer found their opinions echoed and their action
> sympathetically viewed by the papacy, it is not difficult to understand
> why they carried their enthusiasm elsewhere…. Whatever the orthodoxy
> of their proposals, it is difficult to find a criticism made of the church
> by a twelfth-century heretic which had also not been made by a papal
> reformer.[2]

That article, its argument elaborated in greater detail and substantially
expanded, has been followed by several dozen others and by three
major books: *The Origins of European Dissent* (1977), *The Formation of a
Persecuting Society: Power and Deviance in Western Europe, 950–1250* (1987),
and *The First European Revolution c. 970–1215* (2000).[3] As is usually the
case with intelligent, thorough, and adventurous scholars, Moore's later

---

[1] R.I. Moore, "The Origins of Medieval Heresy," *History* 55 (1970), 21–36.

[2] Moore, "The Origins of Medieval Heresy," 35. A later restatement of the thesis is
Moore's "Heresy, Repression, and Social Change in the Age of Gregorian Reform,"
in *Christendom and Its Discontents: Exclusion, Persecution, and Rebellion, 1000–1500*, Scott
L. Waugh and Peter D. Diehl, eds. (Cambridge: Cambridge University Press, 1996),
19–46.

[3] *Origins of European Dissent* (London, 1977; 2nd ed. Oxford-New York, 1985; rpt.
Toronto: University of Toronto Press, 1994) throughout this essay I cite the Toronto
reprint; *The Formation of a Persecuting Society* (Oxford-New York: Blackwell, 1987); *The First
European Revolution* (Oxford-New York: Blackwell Publishers, 2000). Moore's collection
of annotated documents in translation is *The Birth of Popular Heresy* (London: Edwin

articles not only supplement, elaborate, and fill in occasional points of detail in his original field of interest (on the uses of literacy, for example, on changes in the patterns of miracles in saints lives, and on heresy and the millennium), but in Moore's case some very recent work also indicates a new direction of interest—on early western European history as a component of the history of the wider Eurasian world.[4] His new interest is already adumbrated in *The First European Revolution*, in which he applies the anthropologists' and development economists' model of the agro-literate polity to both western Europe in the eleventh and twelfth centuries and briefly to other parts of Eurasia, with promises of more to come. Such a lively sequence of scholarly interests deserves serious consideration.

I

The sequence of Moore's books begins with a tight focus on a particular eleventh- and twelfth-century phenomenon—the appearance of heresy practiced and conceptualized by clerics and layfolk as a form of dissent from an increasingly precisely articulated orthodoxy—and

---

Arnold, 1975; rpt. Toronto: University of Toronto Press, 1995). I cite the Toronto reprint throughout.

[4] R.I. Moore, "Heresy and the Making of Literacy, c. 1000–1150," in Peter Biller and Anne Hudson, eds., *Heresy and Literacy in the Middle Ages* (Cambridge: Cambridge University Press, 1994), 19–37, rpt. in Lester K. Little and Barbara Rosenwein, eds., *Debating the Middle Ages* (Oxford: Blackwell Publishers, 1998), 363–375; "Between Sanctity and Superstition: Saints and Their Miracles in the Age of Revolution," in Miri Rubin, ed., *The Work of Jacques Le Goff and the Challenges of Medieval History* (Woodbridge: Boydell Press, 1997), 63–75 (cf. *The First European Revolution*, 23–29); "Medieval Europe: Religious Enthusiasm in the 'Millennial Generation,'" in Abbas Amanat and Magnus Bernhardsson, eds., *Imagining the End: Visions of Apocalypse from the Ancient Middle East to Modern America* (London-New York: I.B. Tauris, 2002), 129–147; on his geographically wider interests, "The Birth of Europe as a Eurasian Phenomenon," *Modern Asian Studies* 31 (1997), 583–601, rpt. in Victor Lieberman, ed., *Beyond Binary Histories: Re-imagining Eurasia to ca. 1830* (Ann Arbor, MI: University of Michigan Press, 1999), 139–159, and his lecture at Duke University in March, 2001, entitled, "The Eleventh Century in Eurasian History.". Moore is the general editor of the Blackwell History of the World series and was elected a Fellow of the Royal Asiatic Society in 1992. He has also not coincidentally written the article on the great historian of Europe in Eurasia, W.H. McNeill in J. Cannon, ed., *Blackwell's Dictionary of Historians* (Oxford: Blackwell, 1988), 325–326. Moore has also written lucidly and generously on one of his major influences, Georges Duby: "Duby's Eleventh Century," *History* 69 (1984), 36–49, an essay whose title and opening sentences I have appropriated and modified for this essay.

moves from that point outward in a widening focus to the character of the wielders of power in a society that defined heresy and other conditions and activities as offences in ways that compelled their persecution, and finally to a comprehensive picture of the entire western European society in the eleventh and twelfth centuries in which the first two phenomena become components of larger-scale social, economic, and political change, that is, how everything falls into place. In a sense, *The First European Revolution* is Moore's challenge to his own earlier work: if the larger history does not convince, can his earlier interpretation of some of its key components be entirely reliable?

It is possible, of course, for a cagy and unscrupulous historian on a similar errand to arrange the larger and later picture so as to accommodate easily the smaller and earlier, but Moore is neither cagy nor unscrupulous, and *The First European Revolution* is aimed at and acknowledges responsibility to a general readership. It draws upon both original sources and the best recent scholarship, with most of whose consensus it is entirely consistent and whose debates and impasses it acknowledges frankly. The book also reflects another striking characteristic of Moore's work, his ability to treat themes that are subjects of considerable scholarly and ideological dispute without taking profitless partisan sides. In the case of his particular subjects, this is no mean feat. For example, he has made a very strong case for the importance of the social, political, and economic context of eleventh-century heresy without participating in the old and unfruitful debate as to whether heresy was a spiritual *or* a materialist phenomenon.[5] He has also written of the religious character of his persecuting society without echoing the venomous Protestant and later secular anti-Catholic (and particularly anti-Inquisition) polemics of the late nineteenth and early twentieth centuries. He has always been his own historian and not the spokesman of a particular ideology, old or new.[6]

---

[5] The debate is very well described in Robert Lerner, "Introduction to the Translation," in Herbert Grundmann, *Religious Movements in the Middle Ages*, trans. Steven Rowan (Notre Dame-London: University of Notre Dame Press, 1995), ix–xxv, and by Moore, "Heresy, Repression, and Social Change." The most comprehensive study is that of John Van Engen, "The Christian Middle Ages as an Historiographical Problem," *The American Historical Review* 91 (1986), 519–552. Moore, who cites French and Italian scholarship abundantly, nowhere cites Grundmann and rarely German historical scholarship.

[6] E.g., "But what has led most medievalists to express themselves more cautiously on persecution is not any indication to condone it, but the honourable and proper struggle to which serious historians of all religious persuasions and none are con-

Such criticism as Moore's first two books have encountered has not been for one or another expression of partisanship in academic debates, although some disagreement with one or another of his views is reflected in the essays in this volume, but rather for a perceived teleology that implies, as their titles suggest (*The Origins of European Dissent*; *The Formation of a Persecuting Society*), the emergence in the eleventh and twelfth centuries of cultural-political features that have structurally characterized Europe and European-influenced societies ever since.[7] Perhaps the most severe criticism of this aspect of the approach of Moore (and others) is that expressed by David Nirenberg.[8] Nirenberg's own work emphasizes the particular historical specificity of certain Christian-Jewish conflicts in southern France and Aragon in the early fourteenth century, and he argues strongly against the teleological approach of Moore and others:

> [Such historians as] Robert Moore, emphasize processes of historical change up to a point. They allow contingency during the gestation of intolerance, but after its birth the persecuting mentality seems to transcend particularities of time and place.[9]

Writing in the 1970s and 80s, Moore and other historians certainly experienced features of their own time that appeared to bear strong similarities to features of earlier periods, experience that Nirenberg fully

---

demned, to achieve a sympathetic comprehension of a distant civilization and its institutions. They have strenuously striven, with Spinoza, not to ridicule men's actions, or bewail them, or despise them, but to understand" (*Formation of a Persecuting Society*, 2–3). Moore takes Spinoza's dictum seriously; he had cited it earlier in *The Origins of European Dissent*, 20.

[7] Other remarks of Moore echo the teleology of the titles. For example, in the introduction to his collection of translated documents on heresy, *The Birth of Popular Heresy*, he observes (p. 7), "Heresy and the disposition towards it are an integral part of the European inheritance, not an optional extra." And in the introduction to *The Origins of European Dissent*, he points out that his subjects are, "the pioneers of dissent" (p. 20).

[8] David Nirenberg, *Communities of Violence: Persecution of Minorities in the Middle Ages* (Princeton: Princeton University Press, 1996), esp. 1–17, repeated in a different context in Nirenberg, "The Rhineland Massacres of the Jews in the First Crusade: Memories Medieval and Modern," in Gerd Althoff, Johannes Fried, and Patrick J. Geary, eds., *Medieval Concepts of the Past: Ritual, Memory, Historiography* (Cambridege: Cambridge University Press, 2002), 279–309.

[9] Nirenberg, *Communities of Violence*, 5. It is worth pointing out that Moore's work has had considerable influence on the continent, not least in the detailed study of Cluny by Dominique Iogna-Prat, *Ordonner et exclure: Cluny et la société chrétienne face à l'hérésie, au judaïsme et à l'Islam, 1000–1150* (Paris: Aubier, 1998). Esp. 30–31. Moore cites the work in *The First European Revolution*, 154–156.

acknowledges. But one may argue that the teleological/structuralist aspects of Moore's work can be considered separately from his discussions of the historical contingencies that form its basis and that at the very least the former may hold until the end of the *ancien régime* and thus support the argument for a "long Middle Ages." Moore has also been criticized for erecting the institutions of his persecuting society into monolithic, homogeneous abstractions, less than fully attentive to local variations in the extent and function of ecclesiastical and secular power.[10] But in neither instance does Moore read the future back into the eleventh- and twelfth-century past—he reads that past into a particular and still debatable future.

Since *The First European Revolution* deploys the earlier work as details in a much larger canvas, the remainder of this essay will consider Moore's work from the perspective of that book.

II

Moore's eleventh and twelfth centuries are first and foremost centuries of a revolution, one that brought Europe into being. Moore can make this argument more readily, perhaps, than might another historian writing on the same subject, since *The First European Revolution* is the second in a series of studies called "The Making of Europe," edited by Jacques Le Goff. The book that precedes Moore's in the series, Peter Brown's *The Rise of Western Christendom*, is a characteristic tour de force that focuses on the spread of Christianity across all of Eurasia and then concentrates on the distinctive forms of Latin Christianity shared by Mediterranean and northwest Europe:

> For the Jarrow and Monkwearmouth of the Venerable Bede (died 735) and the spectacular foundations of bishop Wilfrid (died 709), far from being miraculous oases of "Roman" culture perched at the furthest ends of the earth, lay, rather, close to the center of a whole new world of their own—a northwestern world, where the Irish and North Seas came closest, around the slender neck of northern England. They stood out as centers of learning in a new cultural zone that stretched from Mayo

---

[10] Cary J. Nederman, "Introduction: Discourses and Contexts of Tolerance in Medieval Europe," in *Beyond the Persecuting Society: Religious Toleration Before the Enlightenment*, John Christian Laursen and Cary J. Nederman, eds. (Philadelphia: University of Pennsylvania Press, 1998), 13–24; cf. 4, 24. Laursen and Nederman deliberately borrow—and subvert—Moore's title.

to Bavaria. By 800, the emergence of Frankish power under Charlemagne joined this new "Middle Ground" to Italy and the Mediterranean. For good or ill, a peculiarly determined form of Catholic Christianity became the mandatory common faith of all the regions, Mediterranean and non-Mediterranean alike, that had come together to form a post-Roman western Europe.[11]

Western Christendom, then, forged out of a host of "microchristendoms," preceded western Europe, leaving what Moore calls "an essential stock of materials," for later use:

> The argument of this book, that Europe was born in the second millennium of the Common Era, not the first, is far from seeking to minimize or devalue the achievements of the classical or patristic eras, or to deny their indispensability to our Europe. But that is not the same thing as saying that they were European achievements, or that their history was European history. Above all, it is not the same thing as saying, what is often said, that these legacies shaped or formed Europe. They did not. They provided an essential stock of materials, certainly—social, economic and institutional as well as cultural and intellectual—but from that stock, as we shall see repeatedly, the men and women of the eleventh and twelfth centuries took what they wanted for their own intricate and highly idiosyncratic construction and discarded what they did not want.[12]

Moore's book is an account of the shaping of that "intricate and highly idiosyncratic construction" that became Europe in the eleventh and twelfth centuries. Between them, Brown and Moore have effectively redated to an earlier period the old chronological distinction between Christendom and Europe once formulated by Denys Hay, on the basis of their reappraisals of the evidence, their application of different criteria, the influence of a substantial, if not unanimous, recent scholarly consensus, and the literature on *le tournant de l'an mil*.[13]

---

[11] Peter Brown, *The Rise of Western Christendom: Triumph and Diversity AD 200–1000*, The Making of Europe, Series Editor, Jacques Le Goff (Oxford-Malden, Massachusetts: Blackwell Publishers, 1996), 16–17. Moore praises Brown's volume in *The First European Revolution*, 187. See also below, n. 50.

[12] *The First European Revolution* (hereafter, FER), 1–2; cf. "Heresy, Repression, and Social Change," 37: "For perhaps the only time in European history we are dealing with a world which constructed far more of itself than it inherited."

[13] Denys Hay, *Europe: The Emergence of an Idea* (Edinburgh: University Press, 1957). The Hay thesis had been reconsidered by Karl Leyser, "Concepts of Europe in the Early and High Middle Ages," *Past and Present* 137 (1992), 25–47; rpt. in Leyser, *Communications and Power in Medieval Europe: The Carolingian and Ottonian Centuries*, ed. Timothy Reuter (London-Rio Grande: Hambledon Press, 1994), 1–18, and by Basileios Karageorgos, "Der Begriff Europa im Hoch- und Spätmittelalter," *Deutsches Archiv* 48 (1992): 137–164, as well as the collection of essays edited by August Buck, *Der Europa-Gedanke*

Pointing to the spiritual anxieties of the tenth century that produced both the eleventh-century papal reformers and later dissidents, the concurrent remarkable intensification of cereal agriculture, the substantial rate of population growth that did not outrun productivity, the resulting diversification of labor, the intensification of local (rather than long-distance) exchange, and the emergence of a "citied civilization" (Moore takes the expression from Marshall Hodgson, but it can be traced back at least as far as Werner Sombart) not based on Roman remains, Moore argues that the eleventh and twelfth centuries witnessed a reorganization of the countryside by the remnants of an old, but necessarily reconfigured and defined nobility, and the transformation of the aristocracy and its power in order to subordinate the peasantry, in cooperation with ecclesiastical institutions, including the great monastic network of Cluny, and the imposition of the parish system, the tithe, and the ecclesiastical calendar throughout rural Europe. Briefly, the revolution defines one version of the transformation of the agro-literate polity of early western Europe.

Moore adapts his very engaging model of the agro-literate polity from the Islamicist, anthropologist, and philosopher Ernest Gellner, who, if he was not the first to name it, laid it out articulately in his book *Nations and Nationalism*.[14] But neither Moore nor Gellner was the first to apply it to early European history. In 1944, Karl Deutsch used an early version of the model to explain the appearance of new economic networks, compact political units, and new ruling elites in the late twelfth and thirteenth centuries.[15] Deutsch's essay responded critically to the distinctive wartime attitude that led some historians and others who

---

(Tübingen: Niemeyer, 1992). An eloquent version of the older thesis of Hay has recently been used by John Hale, *The Civilization of Europe in the Renaissance* (New York-London: HarperCollins, 1993), 3–50. But Hale discusses a changing kind of awareness of Europe, rather than its foundation.

[14] Oxford, 1983, 9–13, although Moore regrettably does not reproduce the useful graphic printed by Gellner, he does verbally clarify Gellner's occasionally obscure description. The model and the graphic are often used by both anthropologists and economists dealing with developing societies.

[15] Karl W., Deutsch, "Medieval Unity and the Economic Conditions for an International Civilization," *Canadian Journal of Economics and Political Science* 10 (1944): 18–35; rpt. in Sylvia Thrupp, ed., *Early Medieval Society* (New York: Appleton-Century-Crofts, 1967), 247–260. Moore rightly indicates the current interests in the European Economic Community and the European Union in a similar idea of Carolingian "internationalism" (2), including the Charlemagne Prize awarded by the Council of Europe since 1950.

bitterly opposed the consequences of nineteenth- and twentieth-century unchecked nationalism to idealize the alleged "internationalism" of Carolingian and general medieval Europe. For Deutsch, that idealization was entirely misplaced: "So far as the economic factor is concerned, much of the internationalism of the Middle Ages was rooted in a scarcity of goods and services, and in the scarcity of skilled persons."[16] This is very much the situation in Gellner's and Moore's argument for "laterally insulated communities of agricultural producers," essentially alike, producing similar and hence unexchangable agricultural products, and requiring a widely, but thinly spread set of layers of various kinds of elites, small in number and characterized by a low rate of entry, over considerable areas and distances.[17] Deutsch focused primarily on trade and merchants, the former in the early period small in volume, but necessarily covering long distances. The merchants needed a mutually comprehensible language and a universally accepted set of rules for their exchanges and, like later university personnel, local protection, or at least protection from rapacious locals. The same conditions applied to Latin learning as well as to technological and administrative skills, of which there was also "an international blanket spread over a host of primitive local economies."[18] Once the number of new entrants into those elites grew too large, according to Deutsch, their "international" character was lost, and more and more layers of elites were localized.

In Gellner's and other economists' version of the model, however, what changes is not the increased pressure from new entrants, but the material ability on the part of smaller geographical areas to support more and more layers of elites locally, however the term "locally" may be defined, and to control the rate of entry to them. As the number of contiguous areas required to support the necessary elites is reduced, the "international" character of those elites diminishes, and they become localized, in areas that gradually develop into sufficiently productive, ruleable or otherwise manageable territories, eventually in the case of western Europe, territorial monarchies and, for a time, independent city-republics and princely states. The end point of this process for Moore is the consolidation of social rank and political

---

16 Deutsch (in Thrupp), 248.
17 FER, 188–189.
18 Deutsch (in Thrupp), 254.

power expressed in the three orders of *oratores, bellatores,* and *laboratores* of which Duby has written.[19] I will return to Moore's reading of Gellner below.

Sylvia Thrupp's inclusion of Deutsch's essay in her intelligent and useful anthology, *Early Medieval Europe,* in 1967 ought to have circulated the idea and the model more widely than it did, but it was not until 1971 that the image was taken up again, this time with considerable imaginative expansion, by H.G. Koenigsberger.[20] Koenigsberger rephrased Deutsch's view of the early period:

> In the first half of the Middle Ages, from the fifth to the eleventh or twelfth century, Europe was a continent of peasant societies, each clinging tenaciously to its local customs and languages. Above this mass of the peasantry, with its very rudimentary skills, there was a thin crust of men highly skilled in the production of sophisticated commodities or in the performance of complex services. This upper crust was international in education, attitudes, and often, physical mobility; for this was the only way it could function.[21]

Koenigsberger cites the example of the bell-founder, whose skill was far beyond that of the average village blacksmith, but whom no single town or group of nearby towns could sustain and whose craft therefore could only be supported by the economic resources of a very large territorial area.

But Koenigsberger's most original and imaginative addition to Deutsch was his application of the model to ecclesiastical and devotional history: "It seems to me more useful to shift the emphasis from the problem of the assimilation of new entrants into the international crust to an analysis of the functional suppression of this crust by other, more regionally based and oriented, crusts."[22] Citing the examples of the increasing variety of styles within Gothic architecture compared

---

[19] Georges Duby, *The Three Orders: Feudal Society Imagined,* (Chicago: University of Chicago Press, 1980); cf. Moore, "Duby's Eleventh Century," 42–46.

[20] H.G. Koenigsberger, "The Unity of the Church and the Reformation," *Journal of Interdisciplinary History* 1 (1971): 407–447; rpt., in Koenigsberger, *Politicians and Virtuosi: Essays in Early Modern History* (London-Ronceverte: Hambledon Press, 1986), 169–178. Koenigsberger used the model again in his *Early Modern Europe, 1500–1789* (London-New York: Longman, 1987), 13–14, 59–61, and also in his *Medieval Europe, 400–1500* (London-New York: Longman, 1987), 142–148, although in both in a very minor key. Koenigsberger also redefines in a useful way the particular universal character of Roman Catholicism that survived the Reformations of the sixteenth century.

[21] Ibid. 411.

[22] Ibid. 413.

to the widely standardized Romanesque, Koenigsberger turns to other
features of the Latin Christian church that also became localized—
including appointments to higher ecclesiastical office, the increasing
localization of universities and students, and the emergence of "national" churches bound to Rome by concordats, in the direction of an
explanation of the Reformations of the sixteenth century by his virtuoso application of Deutsch's model. Koenigsberger might have added
the adaptation of the universal idea of crusade to individual territorial monarchical and princely agenda, e.g., those of the Dukes of
Burgundy. It is doubtful that Gellner and Moore knew of Koenigsberger's virtuoso use of the Deutsch model, but both versions remain
extraordinarily stimulating, not only for the long view of European history from the fifth to the seventeenth centuries, and perhaps for the
idea of a "long Middle Ages," but also as the basis for a comparison of western Europe with other civilizations in Eurasia and Saha-
rasia.[23]

III

Moore begins with the tenth-century peace movements which arro-
gated to clergy and people a responsibility for peace which had once
belonged exclusively to kings, but had been lost or neglected by them,
only to be reassumed by their stronger and better advised successors
toward the end of Moore's period, but not until after some regional

---

[23] Moore does not cite Koenigsberger's illustration of the bell-founder where one
might expect it (FER, 34–35), nor would he seem to agree with Koenigsberger on
the varieties of Gothic architecture constrasted with Romanesque (FER, 121). For the
larger Eurasian world, esp. FER, 188–198, but frequently elsewhere, e.g., 66–67, 80–81.
Not only does Moore's survey draw in comparable—and alternative—movements in
India, China, and the Muslim world, drawing on the best recent historical scholarship
in these areas, but it also draws intelligently on the work of social scientists: Weber,
Skocpol, Fox, Douglas, Malinowski, Gluckman, and Sahlins, among others. Research
on other aspects of Eurasian and Afro-Eurasian history from various viewpoints is
found in the lively numbers of *The Medieval History Journal* (New Delhi, 1998–) and often
in *The Journal of World History*. Pioneering works were James Muldoon, *The Expansion
of Europe: The First Phase* (Philadelphia: University of Pennsylvania Press, 1977); idem,
Popes, Lawyers, and Infidels: The Church and the Non-Christian World, 1250–1550 (Philadelphia:
University of Pennsylvania Press, 1979); J.R.S. Phillips, *The Medieval Expansion of Europe*
(Oxford: Oxford University Press, 1988, 2ⁿᵈ ed. 1998); Archibald R. Lewis, *Nomads and
Crusaders, A.D. 1000–1368* (Bloomington-Indianapolis: Indiana University Press, 1988),
not cited by Moore.

groups of prelates in peace councils had in a sense raised the crowd against the ambitious and ruthless castellans and other lordlets on the make:

> Thus the history of the Peace of God represents, in one of its many aspects, the central theme of this book—how in the eleventh century power which had leaked away from the established institutions of an old [i.e., late Carolingian] world was used by a bizarre but temporarily effective alliance of church and people to construct a new one, before being brought once more under control, to uphold the newly established social and political order of western Europe for many centuries to come.[24]

Moore's key here is the alliance of church and the *pauperes*, the formerly powerless, both in a moral campaign to restore the imagined lost purity of clerical status (particularly in the matters of clerical celibacy and freedom from the rights of laymen in appointment to priestly office) and to reacquire lost ecclesiastical property, on the one hand, and to harness the energies of the predatory warriors who had usurped control over both by arrogating to themselves the old *ban* of the Carolingian kings. The first purpose succeeded, creating a new kind of clergy defined by the Gregorian reformers and their successors, culminating in the emergence and articulation of papal authority and reflected in the canons of the Fourth Lateran Council in 1215. The second did not. The predatory warriors of the late tenth century begat a newly reconfigured western European aristocracy and created a dynastic consciousness which eventually came to collaborate with the new churchmen in imposing their rule throughout Europe until they, too, were marginalized by the growing power of the centralized monarchical state.

In addition, many people argued that the alleged restoration of the purity of clerical status and ecclesiastical authority was not the restoration of apostolic norms, but rather a novelty. They

> did not think that all that this transformation entailed was right, in theory or in practice, and ... did not see the replacement of the old world, in which the combination of secular and spiritual office and its rewards

---

[24] FER, 8–9. A recent, eloquent study of the consequences of the leaking away of power is Thomas N. Bisson, *Tormented Voices: Power, Crisis, and Humanity in Rural Catalonia, 1140–1200* (Cambridge, MA-London: Harvard University Press, 1998). On the general subject, see *The Peace of God: Social Violence and Religious Response in France around the Year 1000* (Ithaca-London: Cornell University Press, 1992), eds. Thomas Head and Richard Landes, particularly Moore's own essay in that volume, "The Peace of God and the Social Revolution," 308–326, as well as the cautionary review by Janet L. Nelson in *Speculum* 69 (1994), 163–169.

provided a secure and frequently harmonious basis for regional and local
hegemonies, as either desirable or virtuous, much less inevitable.[25]

The ecclesiastical reformers, including Gregory VII, had raised the
crowd, and some of the crowd's members would not be put to rest
by the course and results of ecclesiastical reform, particularly when
the results of reform in the twelfth century seemed to bog down in a
polluting and sacrilegious compromise. And there, at the beginning of
the book, is Moore's location of *The Origins of European Dissent* in the
larger historical picture. But it is there by way of introduction only. It is
taken up later as a fugal theme, but other things have to be said first.[26]

Those other things are described and analyzed over two chapters,
each of which concludes with a return to the circumstances and set-
tings of dissent. Chapter Two analyzes the transformation of the undy-
namic Carolingian mixed agricultural economy of *ager* and *saltus*, as
well as tribute and plunder, to the end of expansion and the affluence
it had brought to churchmen and nobles alike, and their turning to
the more intensive development of agricultural enterprise, making the
"transition from living on the profits of plunder to living on those of
agriculture, from booty to tax and rent."[27] That transition entailed the
vast restrictions on the former personal freedom of the peasantry in
order to increase cereal cultivation and lordly control, the inaugura-
tion of widespread serfdom. The chapter concludes with a section entitled "The Little Community," an astute description of the new social
organization of the now-immobile village and the parish, its local affec-

---

[25] FER, 13. Cf. *Origins*, 46–81.

[26] Pp. 101–111. The delay is for tactical reasons; indeed, Moore's design of the book
is one of its significant virtues. See below, pp. 24–26. Moore had elaborated on the
character and functions of the crowd in his essay, "Family, Community and Cult on the
Eve of the Gregorian Revolution," *Transactions of the Royal Historical Society*, 5th Series 30
(1980), 49–69.

[27] FER, 42. Moore thus comes down firmly on the side of a particular view of the
early European economy identified with the early work of Duby and others. Very
recent research, however, would locate the restructuring of that economy a century
or more earlier than do Duby and Moore. The most detailed reconsideration is now
that of Michael McCormick, *Origins of the European Economy: Communications and Commerce,
300–900* (Cambridge: Cambridge University Press, 2001). But there is also much valuable discussion in Peregrine Horden and Nicholas Purcell, *The Corrupting Sea: A Study
of Mediterranean History* (Oxford-Malden, MA: Blackwell Publishers, 2000) and in the
extensive review article by Brent D. Shaw, "Challenging Braudel: a new vision of the
Mediterranean," *Journal of Roman Archaeology* 14 (2001): 419–453, and my own "*Quid nobis
cum pelago?* The New Thalassology and the Economic History of Europe," *Journal of
Interdisciplinary History* 34 (2003): 49–61.

tions, with its church, patron saint, churchyard, and cemetery and its increasingly indispensable priest. In the Little Community the grounds of villagers' protests against clerical marriage and simony were,

> not so much that they were thought spiritually objectionable in them-
> selves as because they represented ties which bound the priest to his lord
> and family at a time when the community more and more felt the need
> of his services as a free and independent leader and arbitrator.[28]

The formation of the Little Community did not take place by chance; it was imposed by lords who themselves were reconfigured into patri-lineages that assured security of tenure and the intact disposition of an entire familial property to a single, most often male, member of the next generation. But such changes in family structure also entailed both a closer association with ecclesiastical establishments, especially promi-nent local monasteries, and also the exclusion of people who might once have expected a share in family property. Moore traces the former in his analysis, following Rosenwein, of the properties of Cluny and the relations of their donors to the monks. He traces the latter in his analysis of changing marriage patterns, including the possibility of no marriage at all for some of the excluded, including those generations of younger, landless sons whom Duby has made famous. The cooper-ation and reciprocal legitimation of heirs, knights, and celibate clerics raised knighthood to a sufficiently dignified status for the designation *miles* to be shared by the highest aristocracy and the meanest fighting man—and established an absolute gulf between that fighting man and any, even the most prosperous, peasant:

> In this way the alliance which religious benefaction represented between
> the eldest son and those of his siblings who enjoyed the benefits of the
> family patronage was sealed by the role of the monasteries as family
> shrines. In a parallel movement of the twelfth century, families of the
> lesser aristocracy, or those who made their way towards social position
> by way of royal service, acquired their burial places through the less
> expensive patronage of the new monasticism and of canons regular.[29]

---

[28] FER, 55–69, at 62. Throughout the book, Moore's use of the parish, church-building, and related ecclesiological and devotional themes gives the book a social depth often absent in studies of the period and processes. His arguments here are influenced by the work of Barbara Rosenwein, especially her *To Be the Neighbor of Saint Peter: The Social Meaning of Cluny's Property, 909–1049* (Ithaca-London: Cornell University Press, 1989).

[29] FER, 100. On the ruthless and categorical distinction between fighting men and peasants, see Paul Freedman, *Images of the Medieval Peasant* (Stanford: Stanford University Press, 1999). Freedman has also written a perceptive critical analysis of Duby's (and

But those new social creations—the Little Community and the new ecclesiastical and secular aristocracy—proved mutually antagonistic. Chapter Three concludes with Moore's second, indeed fugal, reconsideration of the origins of European dissent, a section called, "Apostacy and Betrayal." The success of the movement for ecclesiastical reform, which had once appealed against *raptores* to a wide public in the name of common Christian brotherhood, had ended by legitimating those very *raptores* and made peasants' complaints against the latter implicitly complaints against the former:

> Against this background it is not difficult to understand why the accusation of heresy should have been transferred from those within the ranks of the privileged who resisted the "reforms" promoted by the princes and great abbots to spokesmen of the less privileged who began to query whether the game of Peace was worth their candle.[30]

Hence the ecclesiological—antisacerdotal and antisacramental—focus of so much early twelfth-century dissent: the new church buildings and their permanently attached property, infant baptism, the eucharist, clerical status and authority, new controls over marriage (and virginity), original sin, saints and relics, prayers for and to the dead—the entire papal, priestly, sacramental, and disciplinary apparatus that had arrived in the wake of ecclesiastical reform and been represented by the reformers as authentic tradition.

Hence, the origins, in two fugal stages separated by a very impressive and wide-ranging account of many aspects of social and economic change, enriched by abundant and well-chosen concrete examples for illustration. How did the new clerical and secular rulers respond? How did they face "the necessity of forcing back into the bottle the genie of popular power whose release had been necessary to oust its predecessor"?[31] By transforming the nature of power and status to create "The Ruling Culture," the title and subject of Chapter Four, and eventually, but in a refigured way, the Persecuting Society.[32]

---

to a large extent Moore's) treatment of peasants: "Georges Duby and the Medieval Peasantry," *Medieval History Journal* 4 (2001): 259–271.

[30] FER, 101–111, at 105.

[31] FER, 168.

[32] Cf. FER, 3: "The argument of this book is that the character and consequences of that revolution were profoundly influenced by the nature of the political processes which brought it about, though not necessarily, as I shall be compelled to insist repeatedly, through the conscious intentions of the people involved in them."

At the outset, however, the operative term is "culture." Using Heloise and Abelard as an introduction, Moore surveys the emergence of twelfth-century higher learning in the three generations from Guibert of Nogent to John of Salisbury, its need for linguistic precision in Latin, its respect for and dependence on the study of logic, and its attitude toward earlier *auctoritates*. The scholars—*magistri*, not new men, but "men of a new sort"—transformed the organization of knowledge, invented the university both to protect and to replicate themselves, and gradually made themselves indispensable to ecclesiastical and lay authorities, not least in the study and articulation of theology and law.[33] In schools and courts, academic masters and royal servants systematized and intensified the powers of governance, and governance in turn marginalized those whom it could not or would not assimilate, even the warrior aristocracy, "by the long and unrelenting assimilation of power to the institutions of the state."[34]

But the nobles were the last to be marginalized. Chapter Five, "Order Restored," is a kind of *Persecuting Society redux*—and rethought. The first to be marginalized were thinkers—the excluded alternative sources of intellectual authority and cultural prestige that might challenge the legitimacy of the new masters: Byzantines, the old northern and Celtic world cited by Peter Brown, Arabs, and Jews. Such an argument had not been made in *The Formation of a Persecuting Society*. Now, only the second to be marginalized are the heretics, but most emphatically after 1160 the secret heretics, the little foxes, the malignant and invisible enemy within. Next are the visible and excluded aliens—Jews, lepers, sodomites, and later witches.

But persecution is less Moore's theme here than the means by which *magistri* and royal servants acquired a monopoly on definition of who was and was not a Christian and exercised it against the Little Community by removing that community's control over some of the most conspicuous signs of its identity and authority: the abolition of clerical (and community) participation in the judicial ordeal; arrogating to the monopoly the right of canonization of saints; subordination of preachers and holy men to episcopal and ultimately papal authority. "Justice belonged either to the neighbourhood or to the lord, either to the little community of custom, tradition, and face-to-face authority,

---

[33] FER, 115, cf. 119–120, 144–146. The question of law is considered below.
[34] FER, 177. The inclusion of the nobility among the marginalized is an original and considerable extension of the original argument of *The Formation of a Persecuting Society*.

or to the large one of written law, literacy, and the clerks."[35] In some sense, Moore has transformed the persecuting society into a function of the larger centralizing and monopolizing society. Even mob violence against heretics may be seen, not necessarily as the expression of the locals' hatred of heresy and heretics, but as their exercise of local jurisdiction in lieu of that of outsiders.[36] This shift in emphasis and context greatly strengthens the original argument, while modifying it.

For Moore, two events in 1214 and 1215 sum up the victory of the centralizing society. The first is the depiction of the three orders in Guillaume le Breton's revision of the *Philippiad* which includes the third estate, but no longer as the *laboratores* of earlier convention and the famous dream of Henry I of England, but as the *plebiani* of Andreas Capellanus, the *negotiatores* who work with their intelligence and money rather than their hands.[37] The brutish peasantry is now excluded from society itself, and its parish and potential *superstitio* become almost as suspect as the sects of the heretics. The second is the Fourth Lateran Council:

> From 1215 onwards our sources describe an entirely different world—a world pervaded and increasingly moulded by the well-drilled piety and obedience associated with the traditional vision of "the age of faith," or of medieval Christianity. All the practices and rituals which we have encountered as mechanisms for the articulation and expression of communal sentiment were firmly suppressed.[38]

And this revolution was exported—to Iceland and Scandinavia, Iberia, Sicily, briefly to the Crusader states, and to the Slavic world, following the model and supporting the argument of Robert Bartlett's fine study.[39]

---

[35] FER, 170. Cf., FER, 172: "If any single aspect of the twelfth-century revolution in government was of decisive importance for the future it was the capacity developed by both secular and ecclesiastical powers to penetrate communities of every kind vigorously and ruthlessly, overriding the restraints of custom, and enlisting, or destroying, men of local standing and influence in the name of order, orthodoxy, and reform."

[36] FER, 168–169.

[37] Here Moore follows closely Georges Duby's *The Three Orders*, esp. 322–356. See the critical review article by Otto Gerhard Oexle, "Perceiving Social Reality in the Early and High Middle Ages: A Contribution to a History of Social Knowledge," in Bernhard Jüssen, ed., *Ordering Medieval Society: Perspectives on Intellectual and Practical Modes of Shaping Social Relations* (Philadelphia: University of Pennsylvania Press, 2001), 92–143.

[38] FER, 174.

[39] Robert Bartlett, *The Making of Europe: Conquest, Colonization and Cultural Change, 950–1350* (Princeton: Princeton University Press, 1993). Moore's support of the Bartlett argument is evident in his review of Richard Fletcher, *The Conversion of Europe: From*

And this brings Moore to the model of the agro-literate polity, the economic and governmental details of which he has been filling in all along. The last section of the final chapter is "The Europe of the New Regime." But Deutsch's and Gellner's economic model is here replaced by an *imaginaire*, their laterally insulated communities of agricultural producers by Moore's "*rustici, illiterati, pagani, heretici*, etc."[40] Moore has shifted the character of the model from a descriptive economic, social, and political one to a classificatory one, based on the social perception of intellectual and social elites rather than economic development. But not all of the excluded were the same. The Little Community was, I suggest, considerably tougher than Moore allows. If both hatred of bondage and fortunate economic circumstances led to the rapid breakdown of serfdom in western Europe as early as the thirteenth century, can the perception have been entirely in touch with reality?[41] And may not the more significant interpretation of the model of the agro-literate polity be precisely the development of relatively smaller societies developing the means of sustaining more and more of the elites they required—somewhere between Moore's rather bleak contrast between a relentless universal monopolism and his admirable, if sentimental affection for the Little Community?

If Koenigsberger could extend the Deutsch model to include ecclesiastical and devotional matters, might we not also extend it so some of the other results of the transformation/revolution, for example, to law? In *The Formation of a Persecuting Society*, Moore said rather little about law, and what he said was based largely on Durkheim and Weber.[42] In *The First European Revolution* he is obliged, perhaps wishes, to say rather more, and he does. To be sure, there is the familiar, dismissive, functionalist anthropological echo, but there is also a fine appreciation of Gratian's *Decretum* and the brilliant research of Anders Winroth, as well as one of Glanvill's *Treatise on the Laws and Customs of England* and the case of Becket.[43] This is a considerable expansion of an important topic, for another function of the transformation of the agro-literate polity, as

---

Paganism to Christianity, 371–1386 AD (London: HarperCollins, 1997), in the *Times Literary Supplement*, February 6, 1998, 24.

[40] FER, 188–189.

[41] Freedman, *Images*; William Chester Jordan, *From Servitude to Freedom: Manumission in the Sénonais in the Thirteenth Century* (Philadelphia: University of Pennsylvania Press, 1986).

[42] *Formation of a Persecuting Society*, 106–112.

[43] For the functionalism, FE, 162. Anders Winroth, *The Making of Gratian's Decretum* (Cambridge: Cambridge University Press, 2000), FER, 119. For Glanvill, FER, 144–145.

Manlio Bellomo has shown, was to create a set of *iura propria*, which
worked in tandem with, rather than opposition to the universal learned
laws.[44] Nor was canon law entirely the monopoly of the central ecclesiastical authority.[45] In addition, the late eleventh and twelfth centuries
may be said to have virtually invented criminal law as it is now understood, first in discussions of ecclesiastical discipline and coercion in the
late eleventh century.[46] Learned jurists of the universal laws could also
perform theoretical wonders for some little communities.[47] Well before
the persecuting society there were prosecuting societies, and perhaps
Moore's persecution is more clearly understood in this context.

The First European Revolution, because of, rather than in spite of its
nature as a survey and its consequent editorial constraints, has proved
extremely helpful in assessing Moore's own ideas about his work nearly
thirty years later. The arguments in *Origins* become more persuasive
when set in a broader historical context; those in *Persecuting Society* are
intelligently modified by the same context. If there is rather more
French, English, American, and Italian scholarly influence in the book
than German, so be it. Karl Leyser and I.S. Robinson are reliable
transmitters in many of Moore's areas.[48] *The First European Revolution*

---

[44] Manlio Bellomo, *The Common Legal Past of Europe, 1000–1800*, trans. Lydia G. Coch-
rane (Washington, DC: Catholic University of America Press, 1995). For the earlier
period, Maurizio Lupoi, *The Origins of the European Legal Order*, trans. Adrian Belton
(Cambridge: Cambridge University Press, 2000).

[45] James A. Brundage, *Medieval Canon Law* (London-New York: Longman, 1995), and
especially Richard H. Helmholz, *The Spirit of Classical Canon Law* (Athens, GA-London:
University of Georgia Press, 1996).

[46] Eg. Richard M. Fraher, "IV Lateran's Revolution in Criminal Procedure: The
Birth of *Inquisitio*, the End of Ordeals, and Innocent III's Vision of Ecclesiastical
Politics," in *Studia in Honorem Eminentissimi Cardinalis Alphonsi M. Stickler*, ed. Rosalio
Iosepho Card. Castillo Lara (Rome: LAS, 1992), 97–111, with a review of the relevant
literature. Fraher, too, would argue for a "prosecuting society" (100). I sketched out a
rudimentary outline of the problem in "The Prosecution of Heresy and Theories of
Criminal Justice in the Twelfth and Thirteenth Centuries," in Heinz Mohnhaupt and
Dieter Simon, eds., *Vorträge zur Justizforschung. Geschichte und Theorie*, Vol. II (Frankfurt:
V. Klostermann, 1993), 25–42. More recently, Kathleen G. Cushing, *Papacy and Law in
the Gregorian Revolution: The Canonistic Work of Anselm of Lucca* (Oxford: Clarendon Press,
1998), 122–141; Nicole Gonthier, *Le châtiment du crime au Moyen Âge, XIIe–XVIe siècles*
(Rennes: Presses universitaires de Rennes, 1998).

[47] Magnus Ryan, "Bartolus of Sassoferrato and Free Cities," *Transactions of the Royal
Historical Society*, 6th series 10 (2000), 65–90.

[48] Leyser cited above; I.S. Robinson, *Henry IV of Germany, 1056–1106* (Cambridge:
Cambridge University Press, 1999). See also Stefan Weinfurter, *The Salian Century: Main
Currents in an Age of Transformation*, trans. Barbara M. Bowlus (Philadelphia: University
of Pennsylvania Press, 1999). A recent and impressive collection of essays on related

is also a book that springs to mind on other occasions. In a recent and highly critical review of another study of the same period, Marcia Colish contrasted it unfavorably with Moore's version:

> Moore covers many of the same themes in an account rich in pertinent concrete detail, wide-ranging in geographical and comparative sweep, inclusive both of intellectual history and of subaltern groups, and lucid and economical in exposition. Further, Moore sees the new society emerging by the thirteenth century as the seedbed of the *ancien régime*.[49]

This is not casual praise, and it is gratuitously bestowed by a great and highly respected scholar whose research interests are quite different from Moore's.

Moore's first European revolution created Europe. And other revolutions, which Moore also dates from the eleventh century, created China, India, the Islamic World, and Byzantium, the other great components of the Saharasian world. Far too few historians of early (as we should now term it, rather than the anachronistic "medieval") Europe consider these revolutionary constructions, but Europe only becomes fully intelligible if we do.[50] Moore concludes *The First European Revolution* with a series of brief, but highly illuminating comparisons among them in much the same categories in which he has just described the making of Europe:

> By around 1200 the building blocks of modern world history were in place. What turned out to be lasting citied civilization had extended not only to northern and western Europe, including Russia, as we have seen, but to the entire Yangtze basin, to Japan, south India and both mainland and island Southeast Asia, into central Asia, to the African coast of the Indian Ocean, and the valley of the Niger.[51]

Now there is a fine scope for a historical project, and if Moore has touched on it only lightly, he suggests that it should represent one future direction of European medieval studies.

---

topics by German and American medieval historians is *Medieval Concepts of the Past: Ritual, Memory, Historiography*, eds. Gerd Althoff, Johannes Fried, and Patrick J. Geary (Cambridge: Cambridge University Press, 2002). To these must now be added Vol. IV of *The New Cambridge Medieval History*, Parts 1 and 2, *c. 1024–c. 1198* (Cambridge: Cambridge University Press, 2004), especially the chapters on the church and papacy by I.S. Robinson (1: 9 and 11: 2, 13) and on law by Peter Landau (1: 5), among others.

[49] Marcia L. Colish, review in *Renaissance Quarterly* 55 (2002): 734–737, at 737.

[50] Timothy Reuter, "Medieval: Another Tyrannous Construct?" *The Medieval History Journal* 1 (1998): 25–45, an article which Moore knows and admires. Reuter cites Moore on Peter Brown again, 34, n. 20.

[51] FER, 196.

ADEMAR OF CHABANNES AND THE BOGOMILS*

Daniel F. Callahan

In his chronicle the Aquitanian monk of the early eleventh century Ademar of Chabannes wrote, "Shortly thereafter [ca. 1018] Manichaeans arose throughout Aquitaine, seducing the people, denying holy baptism and the power of the Cross and whatever was of sound doctrine, abstaining from food as if monks, and pretending to be chaste but among themselves engaged in all forms of excess. They were messengers of the Antichrist, and made many deviate from the faith."[1] These words provide exceptionally early information on the rise of heresy in the medieval West at the turn of the millennium.[2] Noting that he was the first to use the term Manichaeans to designate these heretics, schol-

* I wish to express my gratitude to the University of Delaware for several research grants which allowed me to work on this piece at the Deutsche Staatsbibliothek and to the Institute for Advanced Studies in Princeton, New Jersey where I wrote an early draft. I also owe a large debt of gratitude to the three readers for *Studies in Medieval and Renaissance History*, where an extended version was to have appeared before that journal ceased publication, and especially to Professors Elizabeth A.R. Brown and Michael Frassetto for their many helpful suggestions for revisions.

[1] Ademar of Chabannes, *Chronicon*, P. Bourgain et al., eds., in Corpus Christianorum Continuatio Mediaevalis, vol. 129, Pars I of Ademari Cabannensis Opera Omnia (Turnhout: Brepols, 1999), iii, 49, p. 170. "**Pauco post tempore per Aquitaniam exorti sunt** manichei, seducentes plebem, **negantes baptismum sanctum et crucis virtutem**, et quidquid sane doctrine est, abstinentes a cibis quasi monachi et castitatem **simulantes**, sed inter se ipsos omnem luxuriam **exercentes**; **quippe ut** nuncii Antichristi, **multos** a fide exorbitare fecerunt." Later insertions by Ademar, corrections or other marginalia to the basic text are in bold type, just as the material appears in the new edition.

[2] See especially W.L. Wakefield and A.P. Evans, *Heresies of the High Middle Ages* (New York and London: Columbia University Press, 1969), 73–74; R.I. Moore, *The Birth of Popular Heresy* (New York: St. Martin's Press, 1975), 8–10; H. Fichtenau, *Heretics and Scholars in the High Middle Ages, 1000–1200*, D. Kaiser, tr. (University Park, PA: Pennsylvania State University Press, 1998, first pub. in German in 1992 by C.H. Beck), 30–35; M. Lambert, *Medieval Heresy*, 2nd ed. (Oxford and Cambridge, Mass., Blackwell, 1992), 20–22; R. Landes, "Between Aristocracy and Heresy: Popular Participation in the Limousin Peace of God, 994–1033," in *The Peace of God: Social Violence and Religious Response in France around the Year 1000*, T. Head and R. Landes, eds. (Ithaca, NY: Cornell University Press 1992), 184–218; idem, "La vie apostolique en Aquitaine au tournant du millenium: Paix de Dieu, culte de reliques et communautés hérétiques," *Annales E.S.C.* 46 (1991), 573–593 and idem, "The Birth of Heresy: A Millennial Phenomenon,"

ars have scrutinized this statement and several other references in the same chronicle, especially to heresy in Toulouse and Orléans. They have questioned if Ademar understood the meaning of Manichaean, whether these heretics were indeed dualists and if so, whether they were eastern Bogomils or influenced by Bogomil ideas.[3]

That Ademar did understand the nature of Manichaean dualism is evident from his knowledge of the writings of St. Augustine, as for example the list of heresies he copied from the bishop of Hippo's *De haeresibus*.[4] What Malcolm Lambert has written on the connection between Augustine and the designation of the new heretics is very much on target for Ademar, "Writers used the term [Manichaean] solely because they smelt dualism in the outbreaks, and Manichaeanism was the most famous form of dualism for Western writers, owing to the experience of Augustine."[5] Yet Ademar says little about the nature of the heresy in his chronicle, and nothing about its origins or its success. Even when one compares his accounts with others on these specific episodes, especially the outbreak at Orléans, or examines other contemporary or nearly contemporary outbreaks of similar heresy, such as that concerning Leutard c. 1000, Arras c. 1025, Monforte in northern Italy c. 1028 or Châlons-sur-Marne c. 1044–1048, little consensus has developed about the nature of this heresy or heresies.[6] Prior to the Second World War many historians of medieval heresy took Ademar at his word and saw the outbreak as a revival of Manichaeanism. See, for example, the presentation in Steven Runciman's classic *The Medieval Manichee*, a fine synopsis of this earlier view.[7]

The *Journal of Religious History*, 24, 1 (2000), 26–43 and in the same issue of that journal, R.I. Moore, "The Birth of Popular Heresy: A Millennial Phenomenon?", 8–25.

[3] See e.g. J.B. Russell, *Dissent and reform in the Early Middle Ages* (Berkeley and Los Angeles: University of California Press, 1965), 35; R.I. Moore, *The Origins of European Dissent* (London: Allen Lane, 1977), 9, 30, 164–165 and 244; Lambert, *Medieval Heresy* 2nd ed., 20, 22, and 31; and B. Stock, *The Implications of Literacy: Written Language and Models of Interpretation in the Eleventh and Twelfth Centuries* (Princeton: Princeton University Press, 1983), 97 and 116. See also the thoughtful overview of Christopher Brooke in the essay "Heresy and Religious Sentiment: 1000–1250," in his book *Medieval Church and Society* (New York, 1971), 139–161.

[4] B.N., Ms. Lat. 2400, 130ʳ–131ʳ. Michael Frassetto has a forthcoming article on Ademar's copy of the *De Heresibus*.

[5] Lambert, *Medieval Heresy*, 1st ed., 33. He uses similar wording in the 2nd ed., p. 31.

[6] See the English translations of the accounts of these episodes in Wakefield and Evans, *Heresies*, 72–93 and R.I. Moore, *Birth of European Dissent*, 9–24.

[7] S. Runciman, *The Medieval Manichee* (Cambridge: Cambridge University Press, 1949). On the importance of Runciman's work, see J.B. Russell, "Interpretations of

The contemporary historiography on the problem traces its roots back to Father Antoine Dondaine's reaction to Raffaello Morghen's book *Medioevo cristiano* (Rome, 1951).[8] Morghen had stressed that the rise of heresy in the West in this period was not Manichaean, did not have external roots, had occurred in a number of places independently as a reaction to local conditions and was seeking a return to the purity of the gospels. Morghen's thesis has generally triumphed, especially in the English-speaking world, as is evident in the writings of Jeffrey Russell, R.I. Moore, and Brian Stock, among others.[9] Even Malcolm Lambert came around to this view in the second edition of his work *Medieval Heresy*.[10]

Dondaine criticized Morghen's ideas and emphasized on the contrary that the heresy came from without and was the result of the efforts of Bogomil missionaries to prosyletize their dualist version of the Christian observance which had originated in Bulgaria in the early tenth century.[11] To prove his case he used a letter written by an orthodox Bulgarian clergyman named Cosmas c. 972 against the Bogomil teachings to show the many similarities to the Western developments.[12] Dondaine noted that the accounts of the activities of the Western heretics mentioned many of the same beliefs as those of the Bogomils. Among the

---

the Origins of Medieval Heresy," *Mediaeval Studies*, 25 (1963), 36 and R.I. Moore, "The Origins of Medieval Heresy," *History*, 55 (1970), 21–22.

[8] A. Dondaine, "L'origine de l'hérésie médiévale," *Revista di Storia della Chiesa in Italia*, 6 (1952): 47–78.

[9] See fn. 3.

[10] In the second edition of his book Lambert moved much closer to the position of those who do not see evidence for a Bogomil presence and seems to have been especially influenced by the writings of Moore and Stock on the subject. He also makes use of the work of Richard Landes on heresy in Ademar's early writings, essays which make little reference to the material on the heretics in this monk's later manuscripts which are the basis for the present study. For a recent restatement of Moore's position, see R.I. Moore, "Literacy and the Making of Heresy, c. 1000–c. 1150," in *Heresy and Literacy, 1000–1530*, P. Biller and A. Hudson, eds., (Cambridge: Cambridge University Press, 1994), 19–37.

[11] On the Bogomils and their origins see esp. D. Obolensky, *The Bogomils* (Cambridge, Eng.: Cambridge University Press, 1948). For more summary examinations see J. Hussey, *The Orthodox Church in the Byzantine Empire* (Oxford: Clarendon Press, 1986), esp. 157–166 and J.V.A. Fine, Jr., "Bogomilism," in *Dictionary of the Middle Ages*, J. Strayer, ed., vol. 2 (New York: Scribner, 1983), 294–297. Also of value by Fine, "The Bulgarian Bogomil Movement," *East European Quarterly*, 11 (1974): 385–412.

[12] On the letter of Cosmas, the standard edition and commentary is that of H.C. Puech and A. Vaillant, *Le Traité contre les Bogomiles de Cosmas le prêtre* (Paris: Imprimerie nationale, 1945).

most prominent were a denial of the Trinity (at Orléans and Monforte); rejection of the Old Testament (by Leutard and at Arras); rejection of the ecclesiastical hierarchy and institutions (Arras); aversion to
the cross (Leutard, Aquitaine, Arras, and Monforte); denial of baptism
(Aquitaine, Orléans and Arras); denial of a number of other sacraments, including the Eucharist (Orléans and Arras), confession (Orléans
and Arras) and marriage (Leutard, Aquitaine, Orléans, Monforte, and
Châlons); denial of the cult of the saints and relics (Arras) and abstinence from meat (Aquitaine, Orléans, Monforte and Châlons).[13] Jeffrey
Russell nicely sums up the importance of Dondaine's piece, especially
the comparative listing, thusly:

> In the first place, the evidence of the chart [the comparative listing]
> is overwhelming only if all the Catharists of the eleventh century are
> lumped together as one group. If they were in fact one group, the almost
> exact correspondence of the doctrines of this group to those of the
> Bogomils would indeed leave little room for doubt. But the Catharists
> did not have, especially as early as the eleventh century, any unified body
> of doctrine, and each of the groups called Catharists must, it seems to
> me, be treated separately.[14]

What Dondaine did through his review essay was to establish the two
poles of contemporary thought on the origins of popular heresy in the
central Middle Ages. The diversity of opinions produced by so small
an amount of material has been extraordinary. Reviewing the great
variety of scholarship generated by Morghen's book and Dondaine's
response, Christopher Brooke in an elegant essay on the historiographical responses to "a Bogomil iceberg" refers to the creation of "a sort
of Enigma variations".[15] Malcolm Lambert agreed when he suggested
that the only way out of the problem is the finding of new materials.[16]

Important new evidence has appeared and strongly suggests that
Bogomils were indeed active in the West in the eleventh century and
were Ademar's Manichaeans. Before the presentation of the data from
Ademar's manuscripts, it is necessary to consider some recently redated
material. Guy Lobrichon discovered in a mid-eleventh century manuscript from Auxerre a copy of a letter of a certain Heribert recounting
the appearance of heretics in Périgord.[17] It is an earlier and more com-

---

[13] Dondaine, "L'origine de l'hérésie médiévale," 60–61.
[14] Russell, "Interpretations," 37.
[15] Brooke, "Heresy and Religious Sentiment," 140.
[16] Lambert, *Medieval Heresy*, 1st ed., 36.
[17] G. Lobrichon, "The Chiaroscuro of Heresy: Early Eleventh-Century Aquitaine as

plete version of a piece which historians have usually indicated placed the heretics in Périgord in the middle of the twelfth century.[18] After an initial greeting to Christians everywhere, Heribert declares that a new heresy has arisen in the world begun at this time by pseudo-apostles and that from their very origins they were ministers of all iniquity.[19] Many heretics had appeared in Périgord who were thoroughly perverting Christianity yet were claiming to lead an apostolic life.[20] They do not eat meat nor do they consume wine, except possibly a little every third day.[21] And there is much additional descriptive material. For a closer scrutiny of this piece see the recent articles by Michael Frassetto and Claire Taylor.[22]

A number of features of Heribert's account deserve special attention. He states that it was a new heresy in his region at this time. The adherents practiced an apostolic life, but he viewed them as false apostles because of their denial of the Church and the sacraments. He describes them as a perverse and secretive sect whose teachings lead many astray, including those in religious life. Yet not only the educated were endangered but even the simple rustics. What the heretics imparted seems to have been a spiritual gnosis that could enervate even the simplest individual so that he could overcome with his new-found knowledge those who would oppose him. This inner power enabled them to work wonders. Finally, and very importantly, they were spreading to other regions.

If the teachings of these heretics in Périgord are compared to those of the Bogomils, interesting similarities certainly do exist, as R.I. Moore

---

Seen from Auxerre," in *The Peace of God*, Head and Landes, eds., 80–103. The document is found on pp. 347–348. For more on this piece, see M. Frassetto, "The Sermons of Ademar of Chabannes and the Letter of Heribert," *Revue Bénédictine*, 109 (1999), 324–340. See also Claire Taylor, "The Letter of Heribert of Périgord as a Source for Dualist Heresy in the Society of Early Eleventh-Century Aquitaine," *Journal of Medieval History*, 26 (2000), 313–349.

[18] See e.g. Moore, *Origins of European Dissent*, 197–198. "His scraps of information include genuine novelties which are suggestive of Bogomilism."

[19] Lobrichon, "Chiaroscuro of Heresy," 347. "Nova heresis horta est in mundo, incipiens hoc tempore a pseudo apostolis: ab ipso sui exordio sunt ministri totius iniquitatis."

[20] Lobrichon, "Chiaroscuro of Heresy," 347. "Surrexerunt igitur sicut veritas rei se habet nostri tempore in petragorensem regionem quamplurimi heretici, qui pro eo ut christianitatem radicitus pervertant. Dicunt se apostolicam vitam ducere."

[21] Lobrichon, "Chiaroscuro of Heresy," 347. "Carnem non comedunt, vinum non bibunt nisi per modicum tertio die."

[22] See note 17.

has noted.[23] Both groups had no use for the Mass or sacraments, especially the Eucharist. Both groups abstained from meat and wine. Each had a strong aversion to the cross or depiction of the human Christ. Both were averse to entering churches as places of worship. Both condemned worldly wealth. Both could make simple rustics intellectually able to defend their new beliefs.[24] Another similarity is the use of the formula *quoniam tuum est regnum* in place of the *Gloria patri*.[25] An argument, therefore, can unquestionably be made for the parallels. Moreover, if they indicate likely Bogomil derivation for the Western heresy when the document was attributed to the mid-twelfth century, they do so when it is dated as early eleventh century. In some ways it is even more the case when viewed in the context of the other episodes of heresy in the same time period elsewhere in Western Europe and especially in the light of the writings of Ademar of Chabannes, who says in his chronicle that it was a *rusticus* from Périgord who brought the heresy to Orléans.[26]

As valuable as the letter of Heribert is in throwing new light on the heretics of Aquitaine, so the sermons of Ademar, most still unpublished, provide much additional new material on the topic. These sermons, among Ademar's last writings, are found in several manuscripts he left at the monastery of Saint-Martial of Limoges when he left for Jerusalem in 1033. Today they are listed as Lat. Ms. 2469 at the B.N. in Paris and Lat. Ms. 1664 at the D.S. in Berlin. The Paris manuscript contains a cycle of forty-six sermons promoting the apostolicity of St. Martial. The Berlin manuscript contains many of the writings he prepared just before leaving on his pilgrimage. In addition to its support of the apostolicity of St. Martial, its two principal themes are the need for orthodoxy and the proximity of the Apocalypse; themes very much interrelated in the sermons. For Ademar the heretics were a sign that he was living in the last days.

---

[23] Moore, *Origins of European Dissent*, 198.

[24] Compare to the description of the simple peasants at Châlons, Wakefield and Evans, *Heresies*, p. 90, "If it happened that any ignorant tongue-tied persons were enrolled among the partisans of this error, it was stoutly asserted that at once they became more eloquent than even the most learned Catholics, so that it almost seemed as if the really true eloquence of the wise could be overcome by their garrulity."

[25] On the importance on the use of this Eastern formula see Dondaine, "L'origine de l'hérésie médiévale," 71–74 and Moore, *Origins*, 198.

[26] Ademar, *Chronicon*, iii, 59, 180. "Nam ipsi decepti a quodam rustico **Petragoricensi**, qui se dicebat facere virtutes, et pulverem ex mortuis pueris secum deferebat, de quo si quem posset communicare, mox manicheum faciebat…"

The pieces in these two manuscripts provide many insights into the items on the heretics in the chronicle and in Heribert's letter. The remainder of this article will examine what Ademar has to say in his sermons about the heretics' attitudes toward the sacraments, particularly baptism, the Eucharist, and matrimony, but also the cross. His words will strengthen the case that for this monk of Angoulême the heretics were dualists. Michael Frassetto and I will present this material in much greater detail in our forthcoming book on Ademar's writings and the origins of heresy in the West in the tenth and eleventh centuries.

Most basic is baptism. In the chronicle when he first mentions the appearance of the heretics in Aquitaine c. 1018, he immediately states that they denied baptism.[27] Reference to their denial of baptism also appears in several places in the sermons.[28] In an insertion into the Pseudo-Isidore collection in Ms. 1664, he refers to ten heretics, undoubtedly those at Orléans, and specifically mentions their rejection of baptism.[29] The fact that he copied Theodulf of Orléans' tract on baptism in the same manuscript additionally demonstrates his preoccupation with the topic at this time.[30]

---

[27] *Chronicon*, iii, 49, 170. "...**negantes baptismum sanctum**..." He began his earlier version in a similar way. On p. 13, "**Suadebant** negare baptismum..."

[28] D.S., Ms. Lat. 1664, 75ʳ. In a lengthy segment on the communion of saints and the attack on them by the heretics, Ademar states, "Ideo cavete ab haereticis, qui dicunt nihil prodesse communionem sancti altaris. Et sicut haec sancta abnegant, ita baptismum, et crucem, et Ecclesiam abnegant, quia repleti sunt diabolo et nuntii sunt Antichristi, et seducere volunt oves Domini usque in damnationem aeternam sicut ipsi sunt damnati." The connection between the appearance of the heretics and the proximity of the Last Days is absolutely central in this manuscript and was explored in great detail in the expanded version of this piece which was to have appeared in *Studies in Medieval and Renaissance History*. A similar reference to the heretics appears on 114ᵛ, " ... et de haereticis qui modo latenter inter nos surgunt, qui negant baptismum..."

[29] D.S., Ms. Lat. 1664, 168ʳ. "Quod autem significaverunt consulendo nos episcopi Galliarum quod decem versis haereticis fieri debuisset sciant nos eos qui in sanctae Trinitatis fide baptizati sunt per impositione manus suscipere."

[30] D.S., Ms. Lat. 1664, 64ᵛ–78ᵛ. On the origins and importance of Theodulf's tract see S.A. Keefe, "Carolingian Baptismal Expositions: A Handlist of Tracts and Manuscripts," in *Carolingian Essays: Andrew W. Mellon Lectures in Early Medieval Studies*, U.-R. Blumenthal, ed. (Washington, D.C.: Catholic University of America Press, 1983), 174–175 and more recently P. Cramer, *Baptism and Change in the Early Middle Ages, c. 200–c. 1150* (Cambridge and New York: Cambridge University Press, 1993), 151–156. See also H.B. Porter, "The Rites for the Dying in the Early Middle Ages. I: St. Theodulf of Orleans," *Journal of Theological Studies*, N.S. 10, pt. I (1959), 43–62. For the denial of

This same emphasis also appears in the defense of the Eucharist against the new heretics. Although he does not specifically refer to the denial of the Eucharist in his chronicle, Ademar does indicate in several places in the sermons their attack on this sacrament. In a long section on the heretics, in which he comments on the idea of the communion of saints, he quotes Christ on the necessity of eating his flesh and drinking his blood, the bond of the Christian life. He then states, "Therefore beware the heretics who say that the communion of the altar is not beneficial."[31] Ademar further emphasizes this in another sermon, one of his most apocalyptic and most important, when he states, "...but no one can come to eternal life unless he receives in food and drink the body and blood of the Lord." This idea he then connects with the following passage, "We have to speak to you concerning other things which pertain to the synod and concerning the heretics who now secretly arise among us, who deny baptism, the Mass ..."[32] In still another sermon he defends the Eucharist against heretics and associates them with the unbelieving Jews.

> "I am the living bread" says the Lord, "who came down from heaven. If anyone eats from this bread he will live forever. And the bread which I will give you is my flesh for the life of the world." (John 6:51–52) Just as the Jews were murmuring nor believed concerning this since the Lord was saying, "I am the bread which came down from heaven," and angered were saying, "How can he give to us his flesh for eating?" (John 6:53), so now the heretics and those who do not believe in the Christian faith murmur and allege in their hearts, not believing that the sacrifice of Christians is so great mystery.

---

baptism by the heretics in this period both in the West and the East, see the accounts on the heretics at Orléans (Lambert, *Medieval Heresy*, 1st ed., appendix A, 344–345; Rec. des Hist. des Gaules, x, 537 and 539; and John of Fleury, ibid., 498), at Arras (PL 142: 1270B, 1271C, 1272B, 1273–1278, and 1311C-2A), Cosmas (Puech-Vaillant ed., *Traité contre les Bogomiles*, 69, 81, 86 and Puech's comments on 223–226), Euthymius of Peribleptos (Ficker ed., 28 and 74) and Euthymius Zigabenes (PG 130: 1311-2B-D).

[31] D.S., Ms. Lat. 1664, 75ʳ. The section quoted in fn. 28 is preceded by these words, "Credimus ergo qui per sanctorum communionem, in Deo manemus et Deus manet in nobis. Sicut ipse Dominus ait, 'Qui manducat meam carnem et bibit meum sanguinem, in me manet et ego in eum.' (John 6:57) Quicumque ergo non credit per sanctorum communionem pervenire ad vitam aeternam, totus per omnia haereticus est."

[32] D.S., Ms. Lat. 1664, 114ᵛ. "... sed ad vitam aeternam nemo potest pervenire nisi acceperit in aescam et potum corpus et sanguinem Domini. Dicere habemus vobis de aliis rebus quae pertinent ad sinodum, et de haereticis qui modo latenter inter nos surgunt, qui negant baptismum, missam..."

He continues, as he did in the last-mentioned sermon on fol. 114ᵛ, and emphasizes the connection between the Eucharist and eternal life, setting the linkage into an apocalyptic context. "Who eats my flesh and drinks my blood has eternal life and I will revive him on the last day." (John 6:55)[33]

The last of the three sacraments which the Bogomils so strongly rejected and which is also recorded as being condemned in a number of the accounts of the outbreak of heresy in the West is matrimony. The entrapment of spirit by the material order went to the very heart of the dualist beliefs of this period. Ademar in an early version of the chronicle lists among the errors of the Manichaeans appearing in Aquitaine the denial of legitimate marriage.[34] He repeats this in one of his sermons but also charges that these heretics secretly among themselves perform all sorts of lascivious actions in the fashion of swine.[35]

---

[33] D.S., Ms. Lat. 1664, 107ᵛ. "'Ego sum panis vivens,' dicit Dominus, 'qui de caelo descendi. Si quis manducaverit ex hoc pane vivet in aeternum. Et panis quem ego dabo caro mea est pro mundi vita.' Sicut Judei murmurabant nec credebant de hoc quia dicebat Dominus, 'Ego sum panis qui de caelo descendi,' et irati dicebant, 'quomodo potest hic nobis carnem suam dare ad manducandum,' ita nunc haeretici et hi qui in fide Christiana non credunt murmurant et causantur in cordibus suis non credentes tam manum esse misterium sacrificium Christianorm… 'Qui manducat meam carnem et bibet meum sanguinem habet vitam aeternam et ego resuscitabo eum in novissimo die.'" Other sources in the West indicating that the heretics attacked the sacrament of the Eucharist include Erbertus (Lobrichon, "Chiaroscuro of Heresy," 348), John of Fleury (Rec. des Hist. des Gaules, x, 498), Paul of Saint-Père of Chartres (ibid., 537 and 539), the account of the synod of Arras (PL 142:1271D, 1278–1284, and 1311D–2B), the account of the episode at Monforte (MGH SS viii, 66) and Guibert of Nogent (PL 156: 951B). For the Bogomil attacks on the Eucharist, see the letter of Theophylact to the Bulgar ruler Peter (Obolensky, 113, fn. 5), Cosmas (Puech-Vaillant ed., *Traité contre les Bogomiles*, 61–63), Euthymius of Peribleptos (Ficker ed., 74–75), Anna Comnena (*The Alexiad*, Dawes, tr., xv, ch. 8, 413) and Euthymius Zigabenes(PG 130: 1313–1314A).

[34] Ademar, *Chronicon*, p. 13. "**Suadebant** negare… **coniugia laegitima, aesum carnium**…"

[35] D.S., Ms. Lat. 1664, 75ʳ. Immediately following the passage quoted in fn. 28 we find, "Et ideo ut possint seducere Christianos simplices profunditatem divinorum non intelligentes, fingunt se ieiunare a cibis quos Deus creavit abstinere, nulli maledicere, pecuniam saeculi relinquere, honores pro nihilo ducere, nuptias damnare, occulte tamen scelera turpissima perpetrant, quae nefas est dicere, et cunctas voluptates corporis more porcorum latenter inter semetipsos agunt." The amount of information on the attack on matrimony by the heretics both in the West and in the East is lengthy and detailed. The accounts of the activities of the heretics at Orléans, Arras and Châlons (John of Fleury in Rec. des Hist. des Gaules, x, 498; Andrew of Fleury in *Vie de Gauzlin*,

As for the cross, in an early version of his chronicle Ademar stated that the heretics who arrived in Aquitaine were persuading the people to deny the cross and the Redeemer of the world himself.[36] The same denial is underlined when he says that the heretics at Orléans secretly rejected Christ.[37] He repeats these ideas in several places in the sermons. One reiterates the Manichaean denial of the cross.[38] In another sermon, this one on the Lord's prayer in the Mass, he mentions again the heretics who now secretly appear and deny the cross.[39] The close identification in his mind between the cross and the humanity of Christ is also seen in another sermon in which after discussing the importance of Christ as a man he states, "Therefore, since the Son of God who according to his divinity is unknowable assumed the human figure when he was made a man, and on account of the victory which the Lord made through his cross, etc."[40]

Especially important is Ademar's emphasis that his Manichaean ministers specifically urged that the cross not be adored. They claimed that God would not wish to recall the cross of his passion, just as a brigand who had been snatched from the gibbet would not wish to see further the pulleys by which he was suspended. The sermon claimed that the heretics as the devil's minions speak in this fashion because they

---

Bautier and Labory ed., ch. 56, 9. 98; on Arras: PL 142: 1270B, 1271D, 1299–1301, 1311D and 1312C and for Châlons: MGH SS, vii, 226). See also Guibert of Nogent (PL 156: 951C). On the Bogomil rejection of marriage as a central feature of their beliefs, see the observations of Patriarch Theophylact (Obolensky, 114, fn. 3), Cosmas (Puech-Vaillant ed., *Traité contre les Bogomiles*, 77) and Zigabenes (PG 130: 1325-6B-D).

[36] Ademar, *Chronicon*, 13. "**Suadebant** negare... **signum sanctae** crucis [found in the later version as **crucis virtutem**, p. 170], **ecclesiam, et ipsum redemptorem seculi, honorem sanctorum Dei...**"

[37] *Chronicon*, iii, 59, 180. "... penitus Christum latenter respuerant..."

[38] D.S., Ms. Lat. 1664, 75^r. "Et sicut haec sancta abnegant, ita baptismum, et crucem, et Ecclesiam abnegant..."

[39] D.S., Ms. Lat. 1664, 114^v. "... et de haereticis qui modo latenter inter nos surgunt, qui negant baptismum, missam, crucem, Ecclesiam, qui precursores Antichristi sunt."

[40] D.S., Ms. Lat. 1664, 92^r. "Ideo quia filius Dei qui secundum divinitatem incogitabilis est, assumpsit figuram humanum, quando homo factus est, et propter victoriam quam fecit Dominus per crucem suam, signum crucis circa caput in omni majestate debet exprimere pictor." This is only one example of the emphasis on the humanity of Christ in the sermons. It appears in many places, in particular with analyses of the creed. On the creed see D. Callahan, "The Problem of the 'Filioque' and the Letter from the Pilgrim Monks of the Mount of Olives to Pope Leo III and Charlemagne: Is the Letter Another Forgery by Adémar of Chabannes?", *Revue Bénédictine*, 102 (1992), 75–134.

have power everywhere except where the sign of the cross is found.[41] Once again the triumph of God through the cross is emphasized.[42]

This article has sought to make the case that the Bogomils or individuals influenced by Bogomil ideas arrived in Aquitaine by the early eleventh century and that they were Ademar of Chabannes' Manichaeans. Yet it will take the book on heresy that Michael Frassetto and I are writing to offer a more detailed case. At the very least, even if the argument of this article that the heretics were dualists, most likely the Bogomils, is not wholly convincing because of its brevity, one must admit that a very real possibility of their presence in the West around the turn of the millennium exists and that the rise of heresy is unlikely to have been completely indigenous. Or as Bernard Hamilton stated several years ago, "Although most recent scholarship is sceptical about the influence of Bogomilism on Western heretical movements in the eleventh century the question seems to me by no means closed."[43] The Bogomil iceberg may yet be melted.

---

[41] D.S., Ms. Lat. 1664, 72ᵛ. "Observate autem vos ab haereticis diaboli ministris, qui blasphemant non debere adorari crucem, loquente diabolo in cordibus eorum. Non vult inquiunt Deus meminisse crucem passionis suae, sicut latro a patibulo suspendu ereptus, non vult ultra videre trocleas suspensionis suae. Ideo ista loquitur diabolus per ministros suos qui vocantur Manichei quia in omni loco virtutem habet nisi ubi viderit signum crucis." This material on the cross is included in a very long piece on the faith, which Ademar attaches to the tract of Theodulf of Orléans on baptism.

[42] The opposition of the heretics to Christ the redeemer and the cross occurs in a number of sources, both West and East, in this period. See in particular the Docetist conception of Christ at Monforte (MGH SS viii, 66. "... animus est hominis a Deo dilectus...Iesum Christum... est animus sensualiter natus ex Maria virgine, videlicet natus est ex sancta scriptura... et vere Filium Dei, qui natus est ex Maria virgine secundum carnem crederet...") and in the account of Paul of Saint-Père of Chartres of the heretics at Orléans (*Gesta synodi Aurelianensis*, in Rec. des Hist. des Gaules, x, 537). "Christum de Virgine Maria non esse natum, neque pro hominibus passum, nec vere in sepulchro positum, nec a mortuis resurrexisse..." For the Docetic Christianity of the Bogomils in the East, see Obolensky, 113, 211 and 238. For the denial of the Cross by the heretics, see Erbertus (Lobrichon, "Chiaroscuro of Heresy," 348), the heretic Leutard in northern France in the early eleventh century (Glaber, *Historiarum*, France ed., ii. 11 (22), 90–91), the synod of Arras (PL 142:1304–1306, 1312D), the heretics at Monforte (MGH SS viii, 66), Cosmas (Puech-Vaillant ed., *Traité contre les Bogomiles*, 59–61, and esp. 55 where the Bogomils are described as the enemies of the cross of Christ), Euthymius of Peribleptos (Ficker ed., 74) and Euthymius of Zigabenes (PG 130:1309–1312).

[43] B. Hamilton, "Wisdom from the East: the Reception by the Cathars of Eastern Dualist Texts," in *Heresy and Literacy, 1000–1530*, Biller and Hudson, eds., 39.

ITALIAN SOCIETY AND THE ORIGINS
OF ELEVENTH-CENTURY WESTERN HERESY

ARTHUR SIEGEL

During pastoral rounds made of the diocese of Milan in 1028, Archbishop Aribert of Milan discovered a heresy at the *castellum* of Monforte, located near Turin.[1] Questioning Gerard, the leader of this sect, about the tenets of this heresy, Aribert learned that the sectarians were communalistic, dedicated to poverty and chastity, unwilling to eat meat, anticlerical, and generally literate. More than this, they had crafted a theology based upon an allegorical, and quite independent, interpretation of Scripture—one which challenged the basic authority and doctrines of the Catholic Church. The heretics at Monforte were not alone in their challenge to the Church, for theirs was just one of a number of similar heresies which were rooted out and condemned in western Europe during the late-tenth and early-eleventh centuries.[2]

The last period of widespread heresy in the West occurred during the fourth century, a period in which Christianity was still fairly young and in which the Church attempted to create a coherent and unified dogma *e pluribus*. As such, dissenting voices and those forms of Christianity which deviated even slightly from orthodoxy were condemned as heretical, and eventually either snuffed out or forced underground. Except for the threat of Adoptionism in the eighth century and the condemnation of Gottschalk for his predestinarian ideas in the ninth century, there was little deviant religious behavior of any significance in the West in the period between the sixth and eleventh centuries.

---

[1] The two primary sources for the Monforte heresy are Rodulfus Glaber's *Historiarum libri quinque*, ed. and trans. John France (Oxford: Clarendon Press, 1989), 176–181 and Landulf Senior's *Historia mediolanensis*, Bk 2 ch. 27.

[2] Glaber claims that heresy had become a widespread problem throughout Italy and the Mediterranean region: "Plures etiam per Italiam tunc huius pestiferi dogmatis sunt reperti, qui et ipsi aut gladiis aut incendiis perierunt. Ex Sardinia quoque insula, que his plurimum habundare solet, ipso tempore aliqui egressi, partem populi in Hispania corrumpentes, et ipsi a viris catholicis exterminati sunt." See *Historiarum libri quinque*, IV. 12, p. 92.

Where, then, did the Monforte sectarians acquire such strange and troubling ideas, and why did heresy reemerge at this time after centuries of relative quiescence? These questions have long been a source of controversy to medievalists. Some recent scholarship has attributed the reemergence of heresy in the eleventh century to the presence of Bogomil preachers in the West, whose apparent influence on heretics was seen in their theology and rituals. Scholars such as Bernard Hamilton, Daniel Callahan, and Claire Taylor have rested this assumption on the writings of Ademar of Charbannes and a letter of Heribert of Périgord (only recently re-attributed to the early eleventh century), both of whom claimed that Manichees were living and preaching in Aquitaine.[3]

---

[3] The debate over the Bogomil issue is treated in Ilarino da Milano, "Le Eresie populari del secolo XI nell'Europa occidentale," *Studi Gregoriani*, ed. G.B. Borino, II (Rome: Abbazia di San Paolo, 1947): 43–89, and Antoine Dondaine, "L'origine de l'hérésie médiévale," *Revista di storia dell chiesa in Italia* 5 (1951): 47–78. For more recent work in support of the Bogomil theory, see Claire Taylor, "The Letter of Heribert of Périgord as a source for dualist heresy in the society of early eleventh-century Aquitaine," *Journal of Medieval History* 26 (2000): 313–349; Daniel Callahan, "The Manichaens and the Antichrist in the Writings of Ademar of Chabannes: The Origins of Popular Heresy in the Medieval West and 'The Terrors of the Year 1000'," in *Studies in Medieval and Renaissance History*, 15 (1995): 163–223; Daniel Callahan, "Ademar and the Bogomils," in this volume; and Bernard Hamilton, "Wisdom from the East: the reception by the Cathars of eastern dualist texts," in *Heresy and Literacy, 1000–1530*, ed. Peter Biller and Anne Hudson (Cambridge: Cambridge University Press, 1994). Taking a deconstructionalist and quite controversial approach to Heribert's text, Guy Lobrichon counters that the Aquitanian heresy described therein was merely a matter of politics within Cluniac monastic circles, rather than of heretical doctrine. See Guy Lobrichon, "The Chiaroscuro of Heresy: Early-Eleventh Century Aquitaine as Seen from Auxerre," in *The Peace of God: Social Violence and Religious Response in France around the Year 1000*, ed. Thomas Head and Richard Landes (Ithaca, NY: Cornell University Press, 1992), 84–103, which also includes a transcription of Heribert's account. Some historians have even dismissed eleventh-century heresy entirely, viewing only heresy from the twelfth century onwards as barometers of the religious and spiritual temper of western culture. For example, Marie-Dominique Chenu focuses on the religious association of laymen, their insistence upon poverty, and their dependence upon the authority of Scriptures—to the point where they came to question basic Church institutions. Yet, Chenu sees these heretical communities as being the result of the canonical movement of the twelfth century: "The Evangelical Awakening," in *Debating the Middle Ages: Issues and Readings*, ed. Lester K. Little and Barbara Rosenwein, (Malden, Mass: Blackwell, 1998), 311–314. Malcolm Lambert sees these eleventh-century heresies as relatively isolated and uninfluencial phenomena: *Medieval Heresy: Popular Movements from the Gregorian Reform to the Reformation*, (Oxford: Blackwell, 1992), 9–32. Herbert Grundmann all but ignores the heresies of the eleventh century, focusing his attention instead on the period after 1100—from which time he views the heresies as constituting a reaction against the centrist tendencies of the post-Gregorian Church: *Religious Movements in the Middle Ages*, trans. Steven Rowan (Notre Dame, Ind: University of Notre Dame Press, 1995).

By focusing solely on this influence, however, like-minded historians have neglected to place Western heresy in the broader context of the political, economic, and social developments that were to shape Western culture, and which first came to fruition in eleventh-century Italy.

It is not my intention to dismiss outright the possibility of Bogomil teaching forming a basis for the practices and beliefs of western heresies in the eleventh century, but only to offer an alternate possibility—one perhaps more mundane but equally valid. The proliferation of heresy in the West during the tenth and eleventh centuries likely resulted from several simultaneous developments: the stirrings of communalism in Italian towns, the reform movement, and the rise of lay literacy.[4] Thus, far from being a manifestation of outside influence, the heresy at Monforte, as well as those occurring north of the Alps, arose out of the larger religious and cultural milieu that had begun to take shape within Italy and thereafter spread to other parts of Europe. Reading contemporary accounts of eleventh-century heretical sects, it is not difficult to establish connections between their religious beliefs and practices and

---

[4] The work of R.I. Moore, one of the leading proponents of this view, has been integral in framing heresy in the context of the larger religious and social movements of the period, particularly the reform movement; *The Origins of European Dissent*, (London: Allen Lane, 1977). Taking more of a socio-political approach to the question of heresy rather than a doctrinal one, Moore sees eleventh-century heretical sects as localized centers of deviance from the universal cultural standards which the Catholic Church was attempting to create—a characteristic which provided a common link to later heresies as well. See also Brian Stock, *The Implications of Literacy: Written Language and Models of Interpretation in the Eleventh and Twelfth Centuries*, (Princeton: Princeton University Press, 1983); H. Taviani, "Naissance d'une hérésie en Italie du nord au XIe siecle," *Annales ESC*, 29 (1974): 1224–1252; Raffaelo Morghen, "Problemes sur l'origine de l'hérésie au moyen age," *Revue Historique* 236 (1966): 1–26; and Cinzio Violante, *La società milanese nell'età precommunale*, (Bari: Laterza, 1953) have rejected the Bogomil argument, examining instead many of the social and political aspects of these heretical groups. Heinrich Fichtenau believes that Bogomil influence among eleventh-century heretics was possible, but that the beliefs and practices of these sectarians are more attributable to contemporary social conditions and theological traditions within western Catholicism, *Heretics and Scholars in the High Middle Ages, 1000–1200*, trans. Denise A. Kaiser (University Park, PA: Pennsylvania State University Press, 1998). The Milanese Pataria, as well as other movements of popular spirituality, are examined in Cinzio Violante and H. Taviani. For a brief overview on some of the contemporary sources and modern Italian scholarship regarding eleventh- and twelfth-century heretical movements in Italy, see Pierre Toubert, "Hérésies et réforme écclesiastique en Italie au XIe et au XIIe siècles: a propos de deux études récentes," *Revue des Études Italiennes*, 8 (1961): 58–71.

socio-political developments occurring within Italy.[5] Indeed, an especially strong link can be made to the reform movement in Italy, which was marked by anti-clericalism, a reliance on scriptural authority, and a politicization of the Italian religious environment. Combined with a marked increase in the importance of lay literacy, it seems as if heresy at this time merely reflected a culture beginning to redefine its spiritual temper.

Yet, the study of eleventh-century western heresy has often been relegated merely to assessing the context of this heresy in the larger question of western Manichaeism. Though this is an important question to consider, much of the doctrinal content of these sects has been inadequately recorded (either through lack of interest or lack of understanding by contemporaries), and the fragmentary nature of evidence makes it difficult to assess them accurately and fully. Moreover, the contemporary source material may be inherently flawed to begin with, as writers frequently referred to heretics as "Manichees" in the most general sense—again, because they frequently failed to comprehend the doctrinal positions of individuals whose beliefs were foreign to their own.[6] Use of the term "Manichee" did not necessarily convey a recognition by contemporary writers of the similarities between eleventh-century heresies and that of (ancient) Manichaeism, but rather displayed, through use of a standard rhetorical device, the authors' overall ignorance and fear of these heresies.

This is not to suggest that there was absolutely no justification for their suspicions. After all, wandering preachers, both eastern and western, were certainly common throughout Europe, and a free cultural exchange between East and West existed in this very open period of the early eleventh century.[7] Yet, it seems as likely that the lead-

---

[5] Tellingly, the first recorded incidence of heresy in this period came from Italy, specifically Ravenna, in the middle of the tenth century. See *Historiarum libri quinque*, Bk. II, 12.

[6] *Medieval Heresy*, 30–31. Indeed, Moore argues that the "myth of the medieval manichee" was not even fully developed in the West until after the middle of the twelfth century, *Origins of European Dissent*, 243–246.

[7] This was especially true of monastic houses like Monte Cassino. See Patricia McNulty and Bernard Hamilton, "Orientale Lumen et Magistra Latinitas: Greek Influences on Western Monasticism (900–1100)," in Bernard Hamilton, *Monastic Reform, Catharism, and the Crusades, (900–1300)*, (London: Variorum Reprints, 1979). See also *Vita S. Nilus*, I.19 and XI. 126–127; Peter Damian, *Life of the Blessed Romuald*, LXIV, in *The Mystery of Romuald and the Five Brothers: Stories from the Benedictines and Camaldolese*, (Trabuco Canyon, CA: Source Books, 1994); Herbert Bloch, *Monte Cassino in the Middle Ages*, vol. 1

ers of heretical sects could have been numbered among those unregulated preacher-hermits from Italy about whom Peter Damian and
others complained, and who were considered to be potentially dangerous social agitators.[8] This type of danger was presented by the sectarians at Monforte, for example, who offered biblical instruction to
curious onlookers even after they were taken into custody by Archbishop Aribert of Milan. Violante suggests that there was an element
of anti-Patarene sentiment in Landulf Senior's account of the Monforte

---

(Cambridge, Mass: Harvard University Press, 1986); Silvano Borsari, *Il monachesimo
bizantino nella Sicilia e nell'italia meridionale prenormanna*, (Napoli: Nella sede dell'Istituto,
1963). Monte Cassino was unique in that many of its eleventh-century abbots, raised
on the Latin rite, had spent time in religious houses in the East, and brought back with
them an appreciation and openness for Greek spirituality, which itself was translated to
those who took the habit there. One such abbot was John III (997–1010), a monk of
the abbey who left for the East after the ascension of Abbot Manso, spending several
years on Mt. Athos and in the Mt. Sinai community: "... atque in monte Syna per sex
continuos annos commoratus. Inde vero in Grecia in monte qui Agionoros vocatur, per
aliquot temporis spatia conversatus est." See *Chronica Monasterii Casiensis, MGH SS* VII
(1846) ed. W. Wattenbach, II.22. Abbot Desiderius (1058–1087) summoned a number
of artists from Constantinople to work on several buildings at the abbey, including
the basilica of St. Benedict. See *CMC*, III.27. "Legatos interea Constantinopolim ad
locandos artifices destinat, peritos utique in arte musiaria et quadrataria, ex quibus
videlicet alii absidam et arcum atque vestibulum maioris basilicae musivo comerent,
alii vero totius ecclesiae pavimentum diversorum lapidum varietate consternerunt." At
one time, Monte Cassino was even headed by a Greek abbot, Basil (1036–1038), who
was forced upon the monks of the abbey (over their own candidate for abbot) by the
despised Pandulph III of Capua. *CMC*, II.61. As Hamilton suggests and the sources
seem to bear out, that Greeks and Greek culture could be so readily assimilated and
accepted in the West implies that both sides were rather familiar and comfortable with
each other's traditions.

[8] In a letter to the Florentine hermit Teuzo, Damian stresses the dangers of an
undisciplined preacher: "you decided to live an eremetical life, not in the wilderness,
but within the walls of a densely populated city, where anything that is said by a man of
such great reputation, is seized upon as if it were some oracular prophecy proceeding
from a Sibylline source..." If not properly instructed in the faith, this could lead to
heresy or even social unrest, and could undermine the spiritual authority of the local
clergy: "[n]or do you judge yourself by the testimony of your own conscience, but
rather according to the opinion of a flattering mob, with whom slave-like pallor on the
face and just hearing the word fasting cause them to go out of their mind." *The Letters of
Peter Damian*, #44, p. 225. Tuezo had in his younger days himself publicly admonished
simoniacs in the Florentine marketplace *[h]ic publice simoniam damnabat*, while years
later encouraging John Gualbert to continue the practice: *Vita Johannes Gualberti*, ed.
F.Baethgen, MGH SS XXX, v. 2, p. 1081, ch. 8. Damian believed in the importance
of social responsibility, discipline, and obedience for young monks, and felt that such
freelance preaching posed a serious threat to public order as well as to the souls of the
populace. Such fears were to play themselves out in the popular riots associated with
the Milanese Pataria.

heretics, particularly regarding their preaching to the masses in Milan.[9] Indeed, writing as he did at the end of the eleventh century, Landulf could—in his own mind—make connections between the encouragement of religious and political dissent by these heretics, and the same type of preaching on a much more dangerous scale by Ariald and the Patarene leadership several decades later. What is perhaps more significant is Landulf's remark that though the bishop had every last heretic rounded up from Monforte in an effort to reconvert them, certain wicked individuals (*nefandissimi*) had come from other parts of Italy to Milan to proselytize among the humble folk.[10] This pervasive and unregulated spread of "heretical" ideas would undoubtedly have alarmed the authorities, and must have seemed to Landulf a precursor to the Pataria.

Though there were *apparent* doctrinal similarities between these heretical sects and the teachings of the Bogomils, such as the rejection of various sacraments and the refusal to eat meat, these similarities do not necessarily mean that the heresies grew out of Bogomil teaching.[11] Indeed, though the weight of combined evidence towards a Bogomil presence seems compelling, many of the similarities with the practices and beliefs of heretics were, upon close examination, superficial, generalized, and ambiguous. One of the fundamental similarities claimed by supporters of the Bogomil theory is the dualism of western heretics. Yet, this dualism has been overstated—after all, was there not an element of dualism inherent in Western religious thought as well? Frequent was the outcry against the secular life and an interest in worldly affairs, a moral preference given to the more spiritual life of the hermit or monk. In fact, the dualistic theology that was such an integral component of Bogomilism seems to be lacking in all but the most rudimentary of forms among most western heretical sects in the eleventh century.[12]

---

[9] Violante, *La società milanese*, 108.

[10] *Historia mediolanensis*, II. 27, p. 66, 27–28: "At ipsi nefandissimi et a qua orbis parte in Italia fuissent eventi inscii, quasi boni sacerdotes cottidie tamen privatim rusticis…"

[11] Fichtenau dismisses the connection between eleventh-century heretics and the Bogomils outright, and even maintains skepticism about Bogomil influence on later sects like the Cathars: *Heretics and Scholars*, 17–29 and 77–78.

[12] Glaber states that the Orleans heretics did not believe that carnality was a sin: "in hoc tamen Epicureis erant hereticis similes, quoniam voluptatum flagitiis credebant non recompensari ultionis vindictam." *Historiarum libri quinque*, III. 27, p. 142. For a contrary view, see *Medieval Heresy* (1st ed.), 26–33. Lambert makes a compelling claim that Western heretics engaged in a type of "proto-dualism"—a theology that could not be easily integrated into either the thrust of Western reform dissidence or Bogomil

Hamilton argues that this is not surprising, since dualistic beliefs were not even fully developed among eastern Bogomils at this time, and that works such as the Sermon of Cosmas focus generally upon the "moral and social aspects of the heresy," instead of on its theology.[13] Nevertheless, he insists that there was a connection between Bogomils and western heretics in the eleventh century, based on the "presumptive evidence" that both groups shared many doctrinal and social elements in common.[14]

One tenet often attributed to Bogomil teaching is the rejection of infant baptism. Yet, the idea of rejecting baptism, and especially infant baptism, could very well have derived from socio-political developments in Italy and from a reliance on ancient Christian texts. The heretics at Arras (1025), whose leader Gundulfo allegedly came from Italy, provide an apt illustration of this. For them, the rejection of the sacrament of infant baptism was predicated on three notions: that the sacrament may be contaminated by a corrupt cleric, thus rendering it useless; that sins washed away at the baptismal font are likely to be committed again in later life; and that children possess neither an understanding of the faith nor the sacrament in which they are involved, and thus cannot truly consent to becoming a member of the Catholic community.[15] The origins of the first point can be easily traced in contemporary circles to the anti-simony sentiments of many Italian reformers. Men like Ariald and John Gualbert denied the validity of any sacrament performed by simoniacal clergy. Though some, like Peter Damian, refuted this idea and believed it set a dangerous precedent, the linkage of simony to the actual sacrament was a popular notion that could easily have been carried to the Arras sect by its founder. Moreover, that Gundulfo came from Italy might explain why the religious ideas of this trans-

---

dualism. This may explain why some heretical sects held beliefs that were very similar to Bogomilism and had no foundation in Western thinking, like the refusal to eat meat, but why the overall belief system of these sects was unique.

[13] Taken from D. Obolensky, *The Bogomils. a Study in Balkan Neo-Manichaeism* (Cambridge: University Press, 1948), 126.

[14] "Wisdom from the East," 39.

[15] The rejection of infant baptism by the Arras community stemmed from their belief that only an adult can take responsibility for his spiritual life, and can fully comprehend the significance of the rite: "ad parvu[tum] non volentem neque currentem, fidei nescium saeque salutis atque utilitatis ignarum, in quem nulla regenerationis petitio, nulla fidei potest inesse confessio, aliena voluntas, aliena fides, aliena confessio nequaquam partinere videtur." *Acta Synodi Atrebatensis in Manichaeos*, PL 142.1272 B-C.

Alpine heresy seem to reflect elements of the Italian evangelical reform movement.

The origins of the second and third points pertaining to rejection of infant baptism by the Arras sectarians are less easy to deduce, though they may reflect larger notions of personal responsibility and consent that arose from within the communal movements of eleventh-century Italy. For example, a breakdown in traditional social relationships necessitated the development of larger societal mechanisms as compensation for this—such as the creation of social and religious confraternities and other care-based institutions. This sense of responsibility carried over to the spiritual realm as well, in the changing opinions towards *caritas* and in the marked assumption of personal responsibility for one's own sins. The notion of consent also arose from communal politics—in Milan, for example, as a result of the struggle of the citizenry against the imposition of foreign, imperially-appointed bishops. Though no direct evidence is available to tie Italian socio-political developments to heretical doctrines and social practices in this way, there is—in Hamilton's words—a great deal of this type of "presumptive evidence" to suggest that there may have been a larger connection. Perhaps important too was a recognition by the sectarians of the growing relevance of literacy to spirituality (particularly lay spirituality), and the understanding that to be fully responsible, one had to be literate—or at least able to grasp the tenets of the faith. Finally, and perhaps most fundamentally, they rejected infant baptism because its practice is not actually described anywhere within the New Testament—the primary text upon which the spirituality of the Arras sectarians was based.

The allegorical view of the Trinity, and of Christ in particular, as held by the Monforte sectarians has generally been attributed to Bogomil influence as well. For example, the Monforte heretics, like the Bogomils, maintained that the Virgin Mary is merely an allegory for the Scripture.[16] Thus, when it is written that Jesus was born of Mary, the meaning was understood to be that he was actually born of Scripture. In this way he becomes merely a figurative vehicle for the dissemination of the Word of God.[17] Yet here again, the importance of

---

[16] "Jesum Christum quem dicis est animus sensualiter natus ex Maria Virgine, videlicet natus est ex sancta scriptura." in *Historia mediolanensis*, II. 27. p. 66, 5–6.

[17] This sounds quite similar to the writings of John Scotus, who said "animus itaque id est intellectus omnium, dei filius est. Ipse est enim ut ait sanctus Augustinus intellectus omnium, immo omnia." *Commentary on St. John the Evangelist*, ed. E. Jeauneau, (Paris: Sources chértiennes, 1972), I. XXVIII, pp. 138–139.

literacy, rather than Bogomil influence, is apparent, as it seems evident that these ideas of the Monforte heretics were based on their own interpretations (or misinterpretations) of Scripture, perhaps combined with some ideas from the works of writers like Augustine and Eriugena.[18] Taken as a whole, members of the group (or at least its leadership) must have been educated enough to craft a theology based on allegory, an allegory in which the divine mysteries are textually-based.

If one examines the Gospel according to John, it is easy to envision how the Monforte sectarians could have formulated their ideas regarding the Trinity independent of Bogomil preaching. The concept that Jesus was born of Scripture is one that is fundamental to John, for it is this book alone, of all the Gospels, in which there is a distinct implication that the Virgin and Scripture may be one and the same. This idea centers around the term "Word"—which is the Word of God, or the Scriptures ("in the beginning was the Word, and the Word was with God, and the Word was God").[19] The text continues, that "the Word became flesh and dwelt among us, full of grace and truth."[20] This could only refer to the incarnation of the figure of Christ, and yet it is implied that he was born not of the "Virgin" but of the Word itself. This allegory and line of reasoning is further supported towards the end of the text when Christ, dying on the cross, tells his disciple "Behold, your mother," referring in a literal sense to the Virgin. The text continues by stating that "from that hour the disciple took her into his own home."[21] In an allegorical sense, though, John could also mean that, inspired by

---

[18] Huguette Taviani, "Naissance d'une hérésie en Italie du nord au XIe siècle," *Annales ESC* 29 (1974), 1236 #66: "Animus itaque, id est intellectus omnium, Dei filius est. Ipse est enim, ut ait sanctus Augustinus, intellectus omnium, immo omnia." Indeed, the works of Eriugena may have played a particularly important role in the neoplatonic and allegorical elements of scriptural hermeneutics as practiced by Monforte and other sectarians. See Henry Bett, *Johannes Scotus Erigena: A Study in Medieval Philosophy*, (New York: Russell & Russell, Inc., 1964), who finds clear elements of Eriugena's influence on heresies of the twelfth and thirteenth centuries, as well as on the writings of the eleventh-century Berengar of Tours. It is also evident that at least his *Periphysion* was being copied in the early eleventh century; see Andre Vernet, "Fragment d'un manuscrit du 'Periphyseon' de Jean Scot (XIe siecle)" in *Jean Scot Erigene et l'Histoire de la Philosophie*, (Paris: Centre nationale de la recherche scientifique, 1977), 101–107.

[19] John I. 1: "In principio erat Verbum et Verbum erat apud Deum et Deus erat Verbum."

[20] John I. 14: "et Verbum caro factum est et habitavit in nobis et vidimus gloriam."

[21] John XIX. 27: "ergo Iesus matrem et discipulum stantem quem diligebat dicit matri suae mulier ecce filius tuus deinde dicit discipulo ecce mater tua et ex illa hora accepit eam discipulus in sua."

the Word, the disciple took the Scripture into his heart. Given the context of the Gospel, as well as the fleeting, almost amorphous, references to the Virgin contained therein, such scriptural evidence seems to belie the need for Bogomil influence.

Neither Rodulfus Glaber nor Landulf Senior, whose writings provide the two primary sources for information regarding this heresy, give any indication that the Monforte sectarians were influenced by an outside force. In his chapter discussing the Monforte sect, Glaber uses the heading *De heresi in Italia inventa*.[22] The term *inventa*, however, is an ambiguous one, and could mean either "discovered" or "invented," a subtle but very important difference in the context of the Bogomil argument. Elsewhere, in discussing the heresy of Vilgard in Ravenna, Glaber uses the chapter heading *De herese in Italia reperta*.[23] *Reperta* is an equally ambiguous word that could mean "discovered" or "invented" as well. He does, however, provide a helpful clue within the text itself, claiming that Vilgard's heresy originated (*exortum*) in Ravenna.[24] The term *exortum*, then, suggests that *reperta* may mean "invented" rather than "discovered," and thus implies that it was an indigenous heresy. The same then may be said for the term *inventa* in conjunction with the Monforte heresy. What is more, Landulf lends credence to this assumption by stating that the heresy at Monforte had been previously unheard-of (*inaudita*)—an unlikely claim if their beliefs and practices had derived from those of a known sect.[25]

In addition, Bogomils denied the validity of the Old Testament, claiming that it was associated with the Devil, whereas the sectarians at Monteforte embraced that text along with the New Testament and the works of the Church Fathers. Fichtenau suggests, quite plausibly, that many of the tenets of these western heretics that appear to have been derived from Bogomil teachings could have just as easily been derived from reading the works of men like Origen and Augustine— hardly heretical authors.[26] Moreover, these works would have been

---

[22] *Historiarum libri quinque*, IV, 176.

[23] *Historiarum libri quinque*, II, 92.

[24] *Historiarum libri quinque*, II, 92. "Ipso quoque tempore non impar apud Ravennam exortum est malum."

[25] *Historia mediolanensis*, II.27, p. 65, line 28. Glaber makes a similar claim for the Orleans heresy: "continuo palam exposuerunt omnium antiquarum stultissimam ac miserrimam, nempe sui deceptricem heresem," suggesting that there was no relation to manicheism. *Historiarum libri quinque*, III. 27, p. 140.

[26] *Heretics and Scholars*, 29 and 105–107.

readily accessible to literate Christians of the period. Indeed, men like Romuald, very influential preachers who were not connected to either heresy or Bogomilism, encouraged the reading of these ancient texts, even among laymen. With the preponderance of such reformist preachers throughout Italy in the eleventh century, there can be no question of their direct influence upon heretical sects.

Needless to say, the question of doctrinal influence and the position of the heretics in the context of Western theology is a speculative one at best, as are their ties to Bogomils. And though the doctrinal aspects of heresy seem to have held the most interest for contemporary writers, in actuality a more serious problem for heretics was one not overtly expressed—specifically their lack of conformity to the strict institutionalism of the Church, in a period when the Church was attempting to set a uniform standard for religious dogma, law, and practice. Interactions between the institutionalism of the Church (based on ritual, canon law, and, increasingly standardized dogma), and more mystical, diverse manifestations of popular piety (characterized by a strong sense of intellectual and spiritual independence) created a dynamic tension from the tenth century onwards. It is within this dynamic that the reemergence of heresy must be viewed, for it was one manifestation of a larger process whereby western culture was in the midst of redefining its religious character. Indeed, most chroniclers of the eleventh century tended to see in these sects an unleashing of unregulated (and thus subversive) spiritual forms and scriptural exegesis, in much the same way as they saw this danger arising from the reform movement in Italy.

A minutely fine line existed between heresy and reform, in that the very same trends which led to evangelicalism and the reform movement in the tenth and eleventh centuries could, if misdirected, easily lead to heresy.[27] Indeed, many of the ideas among heretical sects flowed from

---

[27] According to Moore, "reformers and heretics [were] moved by the same indignations, the same impatience and frustration, the same ideal of apostolic purity..." *The Origins of European Dissent*, 264. Many of the same eccentric tendencies which led to heresy were also prevelant within Italian voluntary religious communities, and under more catholic direction these tendencies gave birth to such orders as Vallombrosa and the Camaldoli. *The Origins of European Dissent*, 31. See also *Historia mediolanensis*, II.35, 70–71. Landulf contrasts the *canonica* and the radical nature of the reform movement to the traditions of the Ambrosian church in Milan—in which the laity enjoyed a relatively healthy degree of participation in its affairs. Both sides of the struggle, in defense of their cause, claim that they are returning to the ideas of St. Ambrose and the *primitiva ecclesia*, but Landulf clearly believes that the Patarenes have abandoned tradition and twisted the saint's original intentions. Interestingly, Obolensky sees reformist tendencies

the currents of Italian reform—including a reliance upon the moral
and spiritual authority of Scripture, the necessity of textual interpretation (which implied at least an ideological basis for literacy), and the
practice of an apostolic lifestyle based on chastity, charity, and poverty.[28]
The Milanese *canonica*, established in 1057 by leaders of the Pataria,
was similar to these earlier heresies in that it represented the efforts of
reformers to separate themselves from the body of a Church that was
perceived to be corrupt and unresponsive to the spiritual needs of the
Christian populace. In this case, evangelical reformers attempted to set
themselves apart from the traditional clergy through the formation of
a separate and, in their eyes, a more legitimate source for their own
authority—one that flowed from scriptural and other sacred texts. The
hagiographer of radical reformer and Pataria leader Ariald points to
the importance of scriptural authority: "God chose those to whom he
gave the knowledge of Scripture to be his ministers, so that they might
live in the light of his word and ordained that their life should be your
book…"[29] From the very beginning, the *canonica*, which viewed itself
as the legitimate spiritual authority in Milan, addressed far more than
the issue of simony and other clerical abuses, but religious power and
authority as well—specifically, who would wield it.

Followers of the *canonica* sought to remove themselves from a tainted
church which they believed had lost all moral authority—segregating
themselves, according to Andrew of Sturmi, "from the false *consortia* of sinful priests."[30] It is interesting to note that Andrew uses the
term *falsorum consortio* in this text when referring to a Milanese clergy
guilty of simony. Since one's rejection from a *consortium* connoted, in
religious terms, a form of excommunication from the brotherhood of
the Church, such terminology implied not only that these simoniacal

---

in the tenth-century Eastern Church as a prime catalyst for Bogomilism: "an analysis
of Bogomilism reveals the presence in it of two basic trends, the one doctrinal the other
ethical. The first is a dualistic cosmology of foreign origin, imported into Bulgaria from
the Near East; the other, largely autochthonous, is a revolutonary attempt to reform
the Christian Church, based on the dissatisfaction with its existing state and a desire
to return to the purity and simplicity of the apostolic age. These two trends together
produced Bogomilism." *The Bogomils: a Study in Balkan Neo-Manichaeism*, 139.

[28] *Vita Johannes Gualberti*, pp. 1082–1083.

[29] Andrew of Sturmi, *Vita Sancti Arialdi*, MGH SS XXX, vol. 2, p. 1052, 14–17.

[30] "Quapropter ut veritate, quae Deus est, perfrui perfecte valeatis, per ipsum vos
obsecro, ut a falsorum consortio sacerdotum penitus vos segregetis, quoniam luci cum
tenebris, fidelibus cum infidelibus, Christo cum Belial nulla esse debet conventio aut
pars sive societas." See *Vita Sancti Arialdi.*, p. 1057, 18–21.

priests were illegitimate, but that an entire Church community mired in such abuses was illegitimate as well. For Andrew, the only true *consortium* was that established by Ariald and his followers. This attitude was fairly widespread in numerous Italian towns, and the *canonica* became very popular, attracting large numbers of individuals not only from Milan but from the surrounding region as well.[31]

Separation from the body of the Church and reliance upon the moral authority of sacred texts was a defining characteristic of the heresies of the early-eleventh century. Yet, this separation was not unusual in the context of the early-eleventh century; the Church had yet to achieve the level of standardization that it would reach in later centuries, leaving local churches to pursue their own independent practices.[32] Seen in this light, then, heresy was not a sporadic, isolated phenomenon, but rather one of many potential manifestations of the evangelical reform movement and the traditional independence of localized religious communities.

As a way to counter this trend and to bolster their own power, many clerics took to writing invective and fashioning a world-view that legitimized their traditionally-held position, but which did not reflect the reality of a changing religious environment. The inability of eleventh-century authors to place the heretics in a familiar frame of reference was translated into an overt hostility in their writings—a hostility which often led to exaggeration and misrepresentation of the heretical sects. That hostility was equally the result of the clergy's latent uneasiness over lay literacy, and the importance which the written word had assumed in lay spiritual discourse.

The case of Vilgard of Ravenna, as documented by Rodulfus Glaber, provides an example of this phenomenon. It is clear that this tenth-century heretic was educated and literate (having studied in Italian schools and mastered the art of grammar), and he seems to exemplify Philip Jones's point that Italian lay schools in the tenth and eleventh centuries were home to teachers with great interest and competence in classical studies.[33] This led to uneasiness by men like Atto, Bishop

---

[31] H.E.J. Cowdrey, "Pope Gregory VII and the Chastity of the Clergy" in *Medieval Purity and Piety: Essays on Medieval Clerical Celibacy and Religious Reform*, ed. Michael Frassetto (New York: Garland Publishing, 1998), 271.

[32] Richard F. Gyug, "The Milanese Church and the Gregorian Reform," *Scintilae*, v. 2–3 (1985–1986), 29–65.

[33] Philip Jones, *The Italian City-State: From Commune to Signoria* (Oxford: Clarendon

of Vercelli (d. 961), who harbored a distrust of rhetoric, dialectics, and with the merits of secular learning in general. Indeed, Atto believed that there was a strong connection between an interest in secular learning and the emergence of heresy.[34] Vilgard was condemned by both Archbishop Peter of Ravenna (927–971) and Rodulphus Glaber, who painted him as a deranged instrument of the Devil (*depravatus*). Similarly, the chronicler Landulf deemed Ariald, the erudite and well-educated leader of the Milanese Pataria, to be perverse as well.[35] Clearly these were exaggerations, though not surprising ones, as they underscore the Church's fear of these individuals. Indeed, by portraying the

---

Press, 1997), 113. Also Ronald G. Witt, "Medieval Italian Culture and the Origins of Humanism" in *Renaissance Humanism: Foundations, Forms, and Legacy* vol. 1, ed. Albert Rabil Jr. (Philadelphia: University of Pennsylvania Press, 1988), 38–44. According to Glaber, "Is enim cum ex scientia sue artis cepisset inflatus superbia stultior apparere, quadam nocte assumpsere demones poetarum species Virgilii et Oratii atque Juvenalis, apparentesque illi fallaces retulerunt grates quoniam suorum dicta voluminum carius amplectens exerceret, ..." and in terms of the focus on grammar in Italian schools, "sicut Italicis mos semper fuit artes negligere ceteras, illam sectari." *Historiarum libri quinque*, II. 12, p. 92. See also R.I. Moore, *The Origins of European Dissent*, 31. Damian did not think very highly of the arts of the "secular grammarians," which amounted to little more than hollow rhetorical exercises which almost completely ignored the sacred texts. In a letter written sometime before 1047 to the advocate Bonushomo, Damian elaborates: "I am quite aware that when my letter gets into the hands of secular grammarians, they at once try to discover whether it contains the grace of an artistic style or the luster of rhetorical elegance, and they search carefully for a necessarily deceptive charm of syllogisms and enthymemes." *The Letters of Peter Damian*, trans. Owen J. Blum (Washington DC: Catholic University of America Press, 1989–1998), vol. 1, #21, p. 197. Peter Damian expounded at length against the influence and worldly wisdom of the ancient philosophers Plato, Euclid, Pythagoras, and Nicomachus—those "nudist philosophers [who] forever shiver in their nakedness for love of wisdom, and the peripatetics [who] seek truth at the bottom of a well." *The Letters of Peter Damian*, vol. 1, #28, p. 257. He then continues with a cry against poets, rhetoricians, and orators. It was not only in secular schools but also within monasteries that such learning was becoming increasingly popular, due in large part to an interest in and influence of Greek learning. This interest in the classics was also fostered within monastic *scriptoria*—Monte Cassino in the eleventh century was a center for the study of the liberal arts, and under Abbot Desiderius were copied works of Cicero, Ovid, Seneca, Virgil, and others. See B. Lawn, *The Salernitan Questions* (Oxford: Clarendon Press, 1963); Cowdrey, *The Age of Abbot Desiderius: Montecassino, the Papacy, and the Normans in the Eleventh and Early Twelfth* Centuries (Oxford: Clarendon Press, 1983), 20–22.

[34] Suzanne Fonay Wemple, *Atto of Vercelli: Church, State, and Christian Society in Tenth-Century Italy*, (Rome: Edizioni di storia e letteratura, 1979), 162–165.

[35] *Historia mediolanensis*, III. 9, p. 79, 36. As Ariald was inciting his Milanese supporters against the clergy, Landulf says that he acted "quasi insanus contra vesanum sine mora."

views of a threatening group as radical, paganistic, and stemming from the manipulation of demons, the Church was better able to delegitimize them.[36]

Like some forms of eremitism, heretical movements were perceived as a threat to the hegemony of the clergy. The clergy believed that it possessed a monopoly on understanding and interpreting ancient Christian texts, a highly-coveted monopoly that gave them great power. By contrast, they tended to view the laity with scorn, thinking them *illiterati* incapable of attaining divine wisdom of their own accord. Yet, the reality was somewhat different. Brian Stock, for example, has examined the heresies of the late-tenth and early-eleventh centuries and found common features among them—including a rejection of clericalism and a strong component of literacy.[37] Though literate laity made up a very small percentage of the general population, among whom were the emergent *ceto medio* of the eleventh century, many of them began to take an interest in Scripture and religious texts.

Even more problematic was the increasing involvement of the laity in religious affairs. The wide range of heretical sects and confraternities provided an outlet for the manifestation of lay spirituality to a degree that was denied even through a reform movement that tended to view the laity as a weapon in its own quasi-political agenda. Some of the more progressive evangelical communities, like Vallombrosa, were generally modeled after monastic communities, and maintained only a peripheral role for laymen—usually as *conversi*.[38] Even the *canonica* in Milan insisted upon a separate and lesser role for the laity, despite its appeal to a laity which could "hear God's word with free minds and

---

[36] Glaber says of the heretics of Monforte that "[c]olebant enim idola more pagano-rum." *Historiarum libri quinque*, IV. 2, p. 176. From Landulf Senior's account of the Mon-forte sect, however, this was clearly not the case. See *Historia mediolanensis*, II. 27, pp. 65–66. Glaber claims that Leutard was *Satanae legatus* and the heretics of Orleans were seduced by a woman possessed of the devil ("ut erat diabolo plena"). He insists upon similar demonic origins for the other heresies he discusses—*Historiarun libri quinque*, III.8, p. 138; II.11, p. 90; IV. 2, p. 178. Indeed, his view of heresy fits nicely into his overall millennialist vision of the world: "Quod presagium Iohannis prophetie congruit, quia dixit Sathanam soluendum, expletis mille annis." II. 12, p. 92.

[37] *The Implications of Literacy*, 92–150. See also *Medieval Heresy*, 31.

[38] For an examination on the phenomenon of *conversii*, generally believed to have begun with the Vallumbrosians, see K. Hallinger, "Woher kommen die Laienbruder?" *Analecta Sacri Ordinis Cisterciensis* 12 (1956): 1–104; Ernst Werner, *Pauperes Christi: Studien zu social-religiösen Bewegungen im Zeitalter des Reformpapsttums* (Leipzig: Koehler and Amelag, 1956); Bede K. Lackner, *The Eleventh-Century Background of Citeaux* (Washington, DC: Cistercian Publications, 1972).

partake of the sacraments," and despite the fact that it was born of a movement which relied upon the support and leadership of the laity for its success.[39] The heretical sects, however, were generally more inclusive of laymen, and often offered leadership roles to them. Unlike the more typical lay confraternity, moreover, these heretical sects were, almost by definition, independent from the main body of the Church and thus posed a threat to it.

The voraciousness with which the heretical movements were persecuted, and the invective unleashed in portraying the laity as unlettered, only lends credence to the assumption that the laity were more literate and more genuinely threatening than the clergy would readily admit. Indeed, the existence of religious associations of literate and intellectually-curious laymen were deeply troubling to many within the clergy. In an age when the written word possessed an authoritative and almost numinous character, those who had access to it had access to power—a power which the clergy sought to keep within its own hands exclusively.[40]

It is important also to keep in mind the place that these heretical sects maintained within the larger context of the Italian social and political environment. They exhibited a strong sense of community, of a collective spiritual association. Such *fraternitas*, a concept that was only just beginning to gain currency among the laity, went beyond the reform movement and was heavily influenced by the communal spirit emerging within Italian towns.[41] The term *fraternitas* connoted more than simply a life in common, for it also implied a unique bond among the members of a community as well. John Gualbert, founder of Vallombrosa, was an important proponent of fraternal bonds within

---

[39] *Vita Sancti Arialdi*, c. 12, p. 1058.

[40] For a fuller exposition on this point, see *Implications of Literacy* and Moore, "Literacy and the making of heresy," 22–25.

[41] Grundmann sees no connection between heretical movements and towns. Indeed, he denies any connection between urban centers and the evangelical movement altogether. *Religious Movements in the Middle Ages*, 232. Peter Damian expressed reservations about the value of evangelical preaching in towns when he criticized the hermit Teuzo for dwelling and preaching to the populace of Florence; see *The Letters of Peter Damian*, #44. This, however, was largely rhetorical and was not reflective of the very real connection between the evangelical movement and Italian urban centers—a reality acknowledged by more recent historians. J.B. Russell, *Dissent and Order in the Middle Ages: The Search for Legitimate Authority* (New York: Twayne Publishers, 1992), 28, for example, makes the connection between the rise of towns and the rise of heresy in the eleventh century, largely by means of evangelical preachers and increased literacy.

a spiritual community. Seeing in Vallombrosa more than simply a community of monks, Gualbert espoused the fostering of sentiments of brotherly love—a congregation based on the moral precepts of *caritas* and *fraternitas*.[42]

It is possible that heretical sects, like lay confraternities and other lay religious-oriented communities, arose in part as a result of the spirit of economic associations seen in Italian *consortia*. Indeed, in the eleventh century it was often difficult to make a clear distinction between these religious communities and guilds or other professional associations.[43] Fichtenau suggests that the heretics of Arras were craftsmen, which in turn suggests something of a spiritual guild—a religious association of laymen based on occupation.[44] He says that the Arras sectarians were wandering craftsmen, suggesting that their "community" was not so much a physical one but rather a "brotherhood" that united individuals of a similar social and occupational station.[45] They lived according to the precepts of the Bible, and Fichtenau also states that much of the focus of their spiritual self-identity came from a comparison to the apostles—who, for the most part, had also been simple craftsmen. Again, that this and other trans-Alpine heretical movements shared elements of religious thought with Italian urban evangelicalism may be explained by the Italian origins of their leaders.[46]

---

[42] *Vita S. Johannis Gualberti*, 80, pp. 1100–1101.

[43] Citing the work of Pierre Michaud-Quantin who discusses this possibility (especially for northern France and the Netherlands) in *Expressions du mouvement communautaire dans le Moyen Âge latin*, L'Église et l'État au Moyen Âge, 13 (Paris: J Vrin, 1970), Vauchez says that "[t]hese corporations often doubled as mutual aid societies and sometimes put themselves under the protection of a patron saint ..." *The Laity in the Middle Ages: Religious Beliefs and Practices*, trans Margery J. Schneider (Notre Dame, IN: University of Notre Dame Press, 1997), 110. Meersseman, too, points out that there was often little difference between lay confraternities and guilds—in that mutual assistance was provided to members. *Ordo Fraternitas*, 8.

[44] *Heretics and Scholars*, 22. Moore believes that they were more likely peasants—though relatively prosperous ones; "Literacy and the making of heresy," 26.

[45] They were taught charity, but only for those "who are gripped with zeal for our *propositum*"—that is, for the brothers of the community only. Mansi, *Sacrorum Consiliorum Nova et Amplissima Collecto*, c. 1, 19:425D. English translation is from *Heretics and Scholars in the High Middle Ages*, 23.

[46] See *Acta Synodi Atrebatensis*, PL142 1269–1312. This was also true of the Orleans sect (1022), of which Glaber states: "Fertur namque a muliere quadam ex Italia procedente hec insanissima heresis in Galliis habuisse exordium." in *Historiarum Libri Quinque*, 138. Viewing this in light of the establishment of Italianate scholasticism north of the Alps by men like Anselm and Lanfranc, eleventh-century heresy should be seen as merely part of a larger intellectual and religious migration from Italy. The early

Sentiments of *fraternitas* did not arise from, but were certainly enhanced by, political struggles within eleventh-century Italian cities. In
many cases, citizens banded together in opposition to royal or episcopal authority.[47] Indeed, it is no coincidence that these lay spiritual
communities began to flourish at just the time when nascent communal
associations of citizens were wresting town governments and institutions
from the hands of bishops and emperors. This sense of fellowship was
a notion that acquired greater significance and developed with greater
energy in the eleventh century, and this mindset influenced the way in
which individuals viewed their own personal relationship with God and
their spiritual vocabulary in general.[48]

---

career of Lanfranc of Bec is a perfect example of this phenomenon. Born in Pavia
c. 1010, his father was a *judex* (possibly among the newly-emergent *ceto medio*). Lanfranc was educated in the law schools of northern Italy. This legal education—which
was becoming a common pursuit for middle class sons—was crucial in the development of a tradition of Scriptural hermeneutics, whereby the same type of criticism and
attempt to view the law in a rationalistic manner was applied to religious texts. Lanfranc left Italy around 1030, perhaps as a result of the endemic unrest in late-tenth
and early eleventh-century Italy resulting from the conflicts between the emperor and
Italian towns. This was a common phenomenon. Kathleen Cushing and H.E.J. Cowdrey suggest that both Anselm I of Lucca (later Pope Alexander II) and his nephew
Anselm II of Lucca were sent to Bec to study with Lanfranc, as did both Anselm of
Besate and Anselm of Aosta. *Papacy and Law in the Gregorian Rvolution*, 46; Cowdrey,
"Anselm of Besate and Some North-Italian Scholars of the Eleventh-Century," *Journal of Ecclesiastical History*, 23 (1972), 115–124. Landulf Senior tells of the large number of Milanese clergy who traveled north of the Alps to study: "In tantum enim
in clericali habitu saeculi vetustate ac visitatione, multis transactis temporibus, vultu,
habitu, incessu erant nutriti, ut si aliquem chori Ambrosiani totius in Burgundia aut
in Teutonica aut in Francia literarum studiis deditum inveniares, etiamsi non ultra
vidisses, de hujus ecclesiae usibus aliquantulum notus sine mora huius esse ecclesiae
affirmares." II. 35. Damian laments that a certain Walter, an assistant to Ivo Bishop
of Piacenza (1040–1045), "sought an education throughout western Europe, moving
from one kingdom to another, and traveling to the cities, burghs, and regions not
only of Germany and France, but even to those of the Saracens in Spain." (#117,
325). These individuals were part of a "diaspora" of Italian intellectuals north of the
Alps.

[47] When in 1037, for example, the citizens of Milan learned that Emperor Conrad
was coming to attack their city, they banded together in a sworn association (*conventio*)
the aim of which was to defend themselves and their liberties: "Cumque plocamarent
assidue clerus populus atque miles, facta est de absolutione conventio, datis obsidibus
augusto." Arnulfi, *Gesta archiepiscoporum mediolanensium*, MGH VIII, Bk.II.12, p. 15, 9–10.
See also Landulf Senior, *Historia mediolensis*, II. 22, p. 59.

[48] These types of associations were not limited to Italy: in the wake of political
collapse in France during the eleventh century, groups of peasants gathered together
for mutual protection. Robert Fossier, *Paysans d'Occident: XIe–XIVe siècles* (Paris: Presses
universitaires de France, 1984).

Such is exemplified by the Monforte sectarians. They were organized communally within the fortress of that town.[49] Their unique bond, or *fraternitas*, was based upon an apostolic lifestyle: they practiced chastity (though many were married), called themselves brothers and prayed constantly, did not eat meat, fasted often, and held all of their property in common.[50] They engaged in daily readings from Scripture and, more importantly, regulated their lives according to the precepts of this text. In many ways, the Monforte sect was akin to the type of spiritual community more common (and, from the standpoint of the Church, more accepted) during the thirteenth century, such as the mendicant communities of the Franciscans. Monforte might also be seen as a precursor to communities such as the Beguines and *Umiliati*.[51] Indeed, according to Becker, heresies like that at Monforte were manifestations of the same impulse which inspired accepted religious orders such as the Vallombrosians and Camaldoli.[52]

Yet, a fine line existed between those communities deemed acceptable and those which were viewed as heretical by the Church. Aside from questions of religious belief, perhaps the most important aspect separating the "acceptable" from the "heretical" was the relation between the sect and society. "Acceptable" sects were akin to mutual-aid associations that existed within the larger Catholic community, whereas "heretical" sects sought to separate themselves from accepted social

---

[49] *Historiarum libri quinque*, 176.

[50] *Historia mediolanensis*, 2. 27, 39–44. "Virginitatem prae ceteris laudamus; uxores habentes, qui virgo est virginitatem conservat, qui autem corruptus, data a nostro maiori licentia castitatem perpetuam conservare liceat. Nemo nostrum uxore carnaliter utitur, sed quasi matrem aut sororem diligens tenet. Carnibus numquam vescimur; ieiunia continua et orationes indesinenter fundimus; semper die ac nocte nostri maiores vicissim orant, quatenus hora oratione vacua non praetereat. Omnem nostram possessionem cum omnibus hominibus communem habemus."

[51] See C.H. Lawrence, *The Friars: The Impact of the Early Mendicant Movement on Western Society* (London: Longman, 1994). It was only from the middle of the thirteenth century that the *laicus religiosus* was recognized and accepted by the canonists. The *Umiliati*, a penitential movement of artisans, was the culmination of a desire to lead an evangelical life and the need to remain active in one's secular profession. See Vauchez, *Laity in the Middle Ages*, for a general overview of the lay penitential movement and of Meersseman's work on lay confraternities, 107–127. Fichtenau says that similar communal groups, espousing a life of poverty and a common ownership of property, began to emerge among southern German villages at the end of the eleventh century, *Heretics and Scholars*, 43.

[52] Marvin B. Becker, *Medieval Italy: Constraints and Creativity* (Bloomington, IN: Indiana University Press), 72–74.

hierarchies in obedience to scriptural authority—thus posing a threat
to the hegemony and authority of the Church.[53]

Italian confraternaties like those at Modena, Ivrea, and Valdelsa provide good examples of the lay religious organization deemed acceptable
by the Catholic Church. The confraternity at Modena, established in
the late tenth century, was organized to redeem the souls of its members
and to provide a means for their illumination by the light of Christ.[54]
This group, like others, was subsidized by annual payments (one denar-
ius) which its members placed into a common fund. Like many Italian
urban centers and lay confraternities, the individuals of the Modena
congregation found unity in a patron saint—in this case Saint Gemini-
ani, through whose intervention they could succor spiritual assistance
from God.[55] The late-eleventh century community of S. Appiano of
Valdelsa was a community of clerics and laymen, brought together in
emulation of the monastic lifestyle.[56] The elected leader was called *magister et abbas,* and though it is uncertain whether he was a layman or
a member of the clergy, his eligibility for leadership of the community
evidently rested on his piety and his intimate knowledge of scripture
(*doctus in scripturis*). A focus on purity is evident in the community's rule,
as expulsion was the punishment for a host of sins, including adultery,
usury, and perjury. The clergy within the community was held to a very
high standard, and their behavior was to be an example for the rest of
the community.[57] Significantly, this focus on morality and knowledge of

---

[53] See Giles Constable, *The Reformation of the Twelfth Century* (Cambridge: Cambridge
University Press, 1996), 5, who postulates that to contemporaries a substantial distinction was made between orthodoxy and heresy only when established social and political
interests were threatened. For similar views see Robert Fossier, "Les mouvements pop-
ulaires en Occident au XIe siècle," in *Comptes rendus de l'académie des inscriptions,* (1971):
257–269; and Tadeusz Manteuffel, *Naissance d'une hérésie: les adeptes de la pauvrété volontaire
au moyen âge,* trans. Anna Posner (Paris and The Hague: Mouton, 1970).

[54] The constitution of this confraternity, as well as those at Ivrea, Valdelsa, and
Tours are reprinted in Gerard Meersseman, *Ordo fraternitatis,* 97–99.

[55] The Virgin Mary was invoked as well, providing an early example of her role
as intercessor—a role that would be more prominent from the twelfth century. See
Carolyn Walker Bynum, *Jesus as Mother: Studies in the Spirituality of the High Middle Ages*
(Berkeley: University of California Press, 1982), esp. 136–137; Hilda Graef, *Mary: A
History of Doctrine and Devotion,* 2 vol. (London: Sheed and Ward, 1963).

[56] *Ordo fraternitatis* ibid., 60, ch. I, 1, 55–65.

[57] idem., ch. VIII, 21. "Sit (sacerdos) castus et humilis, misericors, pacificus et hele-
mosinarius; non sit avarus, non turpis lucri cupidus, non iracundus, non violentus; non
sit detractor[em], non desideret otiosa verba; provideat ut in omnibus det exemplum
bonum." Expulsion from the community was punishment for failure to abide by certain moral standards, in language not unlike that found in the Rule of St. Benedict. In

sacred texts echoes tenets held by members of both the reform movement and various heretical sects.

What made these communities palatable to the Church was their
designation to laymen of accepted religious roles and their deference to
Church authority. For example, among the members of the Ivrea community, established in the tenth century, religious participation by the
laity was limited to prayer, the recitation of the canonical offices, and
the distribution of alms—rituals which defined the traditional boundaries of lay participation within the mainstream Church.[58] Yet, when
these mainstream boundaries were crossed, authorities were apt to portray these offending individuals as heretics. Such was the case with the
twelfth-century confraternity of the Capuciati, a radical and militant
association of peasants who were deemed heretical by the Church only
after challenging the legitimacy of the local feudal hierarchy.[59] There
are clear parallels here to the movements of eleventh century heresy,
where the label of heretic was given to those who threatened the social
order.

These boundaries were evidently crossed by the Monforte community, the foundation of which was based in the interpretation of the
Scriptures. Fichtenau calls its adherents "laypeople who regulated their
lives according to biblical precepts and wished to form a strong com-

---

the Rule of St. Benedict, a monk is to be excommunicated (which in this case amounts
to physical segregation from the rest of the community) only after refusing to make
amends for his sins: "If a brother is found to be stubborn or disobedient or proud, if he
grumbles or in any way despises the holy rule and defies the orders of his seniors, he
should be warned twice privately by the seniors in accord with our Lord's injunction.
If he does not amend, he must be rebuked publicly in the presence of everyone. But
if even then he does not reform, let him be excommunicated, provided that he understands the nature of this punishment." *The Rule of St. Benedict in English*, ch. 23, pp. 49–
50. Compare this to Valdelsa: "Ut omnes oboedientes sint suo magistro et abbati. Que
ipsos predicaverit, et lex Domini precipit, custodiant. / Si vero neglegentes fuerint, et
predicati non se correxerint, excommunice⟨n⟩tur a canonica sententia." ch. VI, 17–18.
Indeed, much in the Valdelda statutes, as well as those of the other lay confraternities,
is modeled after the Benedictine Rule—from the activities of the congregants to the
focus on obedience to the leader of the community. These similarities do seem to lend
credence to Grundmann's assertion that the monastery was the model for the lay confraternity throughout the eleventh century. However, it is important to note that, unlike
the strict focus on the lack of obedience as the primary cause for excommunication in
the Rule, the statutes of Valdelsa also point to uncorrected moral lapses as a cause for
expulsion as well. See ch. VIII, 21–22.

[58] *Ordo fraternitas*, 95–97.
[59] Vauchez, *Laity in the Middle Ages*, 110.

munity ... the people of Monforte were 'Bible exegetes' who had developed the rudiments of a unique theology."[60] Clearly literate, the members of this sect read religious texts for themselves: "[w]e follow the Old and New Testaments, together with the sacred canons, which we read daily."[61] Gerard, one of the *maiores* who led the community, was particularly erudite, and seems to have had the benefit of a good religious education. His answers to the inquiries of Archbishop Aribert of Milan tend to mirror the vocabulary of patristic theological debate, which suggests that he was familiar with the writings of the Church Fathers.[62] With the ability to go directly to the original sources, and to achieve divine illumination through the Word, the Monforte sectarians see no need for a priesthood.[63]

Though the rejection of priests was a Bogomil concept, it could also have followed from the influence of certain elements within the Italian reform movement. Some members of the Italian reform movement peddled anticlericalism as part of their political and religious agenda, and these ideas may have been taken further by such sectarians as those at Monforte. This anticlericalism was most virulently expressed in the total rejection of simoniacal clergy and the sacraments which they ministered, as well as a total disdain for the interest in wealth shown by many monks and clerics.[64] More subtly, anticlericalism manifested itself in the seemingly ubiquitous practice of laymen abandoning their clergy to seek confession and penance from local holy men, often unordained, who were perceived as carrying greater moral, and thus spiritual, authority.[65] Reformers like John Gualbert and Ariald also insisted upon the necessity of a priestly figure, though he need not be ordained.

---

[60] *Heretics and Scholars*, 46.

[61] "Vetus ac novum testamentum ac sanctos canones cottidie legentes tenemus." Landulf, Bk. II, p. 65.

[62] *Medieval Heresy*, 18.

[63] For the Monforte sectarians, divine illumination is the holy spirit imparted to man from God, through which divine matters can be understood. This was achieved through Scripture. *Historia mediolanensis*, II.27, 66: "divinarum scientiarum intellectus, a quo cuncta discrete reguntur." According to Brian Stock, "[t]exts are the justification for eliminating any intermediary between God and man. Man achieves salvation not through God's love, sacrifice, and goodwill but through reason, understanding, and illumination." *The Implications of Literacy*, 145.

[64] In the *Vita* of John Gualbert there is a story of a noble donation to one of his monasteries, and Gualbert's angry reaction to this donation. He was so upset, in fact, that he personally destroyed the deed of gift and cursed the very house which accepted it. *Vita Johannes Gualberti*, ed. F. Baethgen, MGH SS XXX v. 2, 44. 1089.

[65] In the *Life of Romuald*, for example, Damian says that "[f]rom every part men and

The Monforte sectarians echoed these beliefs. In questioning the leader of this heretical movement, Archbishop Aribert asks: "[i]n whom lies the responsibility for absolving our sins, the pope, the bishop, or the priest?" To this Gerard responds: "we do not acknowledge the Roman pontiff but another, who daily visits our dispersed brethren throughout the world. When God acts as minister through him, remission from our sins is devoutly granted."[66] He later adds: "[t]here is no priest beyond our priest, although he lacks tonsure and mystery."[67] This lack of "tonsure and mystery" might imply that such an individual was not ordained, and leaves open the possibility that he might even have been a layman.[68] Terms like "priest" may even have represented the spirit (*animus*) of the Word present within the soul of man, and this would be consistent with the allegory upon which the spirituality of this sect was based.[69] For those at Monforte, the priest was not necessary because remission from sin was achieved solely through the spirit of the Word, and an understanding of this spirit which could be achieved by the individual on his own. This belief was common to other heresies as well. For example, the Italian Gundolfo, leader of the Arras community, believed that the individual was responsible for his own salvation, and that priests were not necessary as intermediaries between man and God.[70] It is important to remember that even conservative writers such as Peter Damian stressed that divine illumination, spiritual mysticism,

---

women came to him for confession and penance, while he distributed their offerings to the poor." *Life of the Blessed Romuald*, XXXV, p. 229.

[66] *Historia mediolanensis*, II.27, p. 66, 10–13.

[67] *Historia mediolanensis*, II.27, p. 66, 21–22.

[68] Indeed, as in other cults, terms like "priest," "abbot," or "elders" could denote more of a social position within the community rather than an actual religious function. Fichtenau, *Heretics and Scholars*, 42.

[69] According to Landulf, they behaved "quasi boni sacerdotes"—perhaps not unlike the notion of the priesthood of all believers that gained wide acceptance among the Protestants of the sixteenth century. *Historia mediolanensis*, II. 27, p. 66, 28.

[70] *Acta Synodi Atrebatensis*, 1272A-B. Gundolfo may have brought with him similar ideas current among the Italian evangelical reformers. His followers' explanation of the sect's beliefs to the authorities is rife with allusions to imitation of the life of Christ as well as independent religious thought: "lex et disciplina nostra, quam a magistro accepimus, nec evangelicis decretis, nec apostolicis sanctionibus contraire videbitur, si quis eam diligenter velit intueri. Haec namque hujusmodi est: mundum reliaquere, carnem a concupiscentiis frenare, de laboribus manuum suarum victum parare, nulli laesionem quaerere, charitatem cunctis, quos zelus hujus nostri propositi teneat, exhibere; servata igitur hac justitia nullum opus esse baptisimi; praevaricata vero ista, baptisimum ad nullam proficere salutem." Thus, not only is there is a strong element of anticlericalism and precepts of the reform movement, but it is clear that

and thus, by extension, one's salvation could be achieved by the individual penitent through contrition and by personal reflection on the sacred texts.[71]

The Monforte sectarians also crossed accepted boundaries in the way that they exhibited quasi-political behavior. This reflected a politicization that existed within the Italian reform movement, but was even more clearly articulated in the power struggles between emergent communal associations and traditional forms of hierarchical authority. According to Landulf, once the heretics had been questioned and brought to Milan, the magistrates of that city offered the heretics the option of embracing the cross or being burned at the stake. Many of them chose the flames over the cross. Given the language of the text and the political environment of Italy at the time, it seems possible that they were not rejecting the cross per se, but rather the magisterial power which that symbol may have represented.[72] Independent-minded and confident in their own moral rectitude, the Monforte sectarians would have felt themselves subject to no authority other than the Scriptures. From an official standpoint, such a position would have been unacceptable, especially as the heretics were preaching to the Milanese populace. Thus, in order to minimize the risk of inflaming popular sentiment, it would have been necessary to bring the heretics into line.[73]

Both Moore and Taviani take a somewhat different stance, viewing the confrontation as one which pitted the rural *castellum* (Monforte) as a bastion of resistance against the encroachment of an archbishop eager to augment his power. According to George Dameron: "[t]hese

---

through living life in a certain way and performing good works, one can actively achieve salvation.

[71] *The Letters of Peter Damian*, #17, pp. 145–158.

[72] Glaber states flatly that the heretics preferred death over the saving grace of Christ, making no mention of the magistrates and their ultimatum. *Historiarum libri quinque*, IV. 2, p. 176. Framing the episode strictly in religious terms like this effectively demonized the heretics and made it much easier to dismiss their movement as an aberration concocted by a demon-inspired sect.

[73] Malcolm Lambert would be inclined to agree, for he insists that "[f]ew heresy accusations were ever launched out of pure concern for purity of doctrine ..." *Medieval Heresey*, 15. Tadeusz Manteuffel also sees heresy defined in the eleventh century not so much in terms of deviance from standard dogma but rather as the political challenge which a particular sect posed to local authorities: *Naissance d'une hérésie*. There was no such universal condemnation of the Pataria from the secular leaders of Milan, largely because many within the urban nobility were complicit in that rebellion themselves. This, then, brings back the argument that only those movements lacking in some sort of official sanction (primarily within the Church) were deemed to be heretical.

castelli and their surrounding properties ... became the centers of economic and jurisdictional power in the countryside in the tenth century ... Indeed, the *castello* and the administrative district around it (the *curia*) became the fundamental economic and political unit in the countryside."[74] *Castelli* were important centers for control in a region, and thus would have elicited intense competition among bishops, monasteries, and the local nobility for possession of them. R.I. Moore, in fact, suggests that the sect was labeled heretical by the Archbishop of Milan because he hoped to extend his authority over Monforte, and found this accusation an expedient means of eliminating a potential rival for power.[75]

An episode of heresy several decades earlier, involving the peasant Leutard, from Vertus near the river Marne, may be viewed in a similar light. In that case, however, the cross likely represented to him the power of the Church over the local populace.[76] Though Glaber's accounting of details and motivation for these events are incomplete and even formulaic, it is quite possible that Leutard's "heresy" was little more than an abortive peasant uprising against the secular domination of the Church in that locale.[77] Leutard claimed to have received a revelation from God, which led him to question both the legitimacy of tithes and the very *raison d'être* of the clergy.[78] As a result of this revelation he entered the church of Châlons-sur-Marne and broke the image of the crucifix. This action could be interpreted as a challenge to the

---

[74] George W. Dameron, *Episcopal Power and Florentine Society, 1000–1320* (Cambridge, Mass: Harvard University Press, 1991), 43.

[75] *The Formation of a Persecuting Society: Power and Deviance in Western Europe, 950–1250* (Oxford: Blackwell, 1987), 116. According to Moore, this heresy was more of a political issue than a doctrinal one, and came to light really only because the sect was comprised of laymen from one of two rival political factions in the region—with members of the other faction seeking to expose them. In this way, a literate, spiritually-oriented community of laymen provided a vehicle for a larger political agenda, and the charge of heresy could be used as a powerful political weapon. Indeed, Moore sees buried within such episodes, episodes which greatly increased in number during the twelfth and thirteenth centuries, the emergence of the modern state—whereby official violence was legitimized and institutionalized for the sake of political expediency.

[76] Glaber places this heresy "circa finem millesimi anni." *Historiarum Libri Quinque*, 2, p. 88.

[77] Unlike other heresies, Leutard's found followers only among the common people (*vulgi*)—suggesting a movement of limited social interest. *Historiarum Libri Quinque*, 2, p. 90.

[78] *Historiarum libri quinque*, II.11, p. 90: "Nam decimas dare dicebat esse omnimodis superfluum et inane." Moore also believes that Leutard's rebellion was more socially than religiously motivated; *The Origins of European Dissent*, 45.

authority of the Church, and perhaps as an attempt to deprive it of a means, however symbolic, to exert control.

Like Leutard, some individuals viewed the Church as an oppressive force, and saw the payment of the tithe (highly-coveted and upon which the Church relied for financial support) as a burdensome tax and just another way for an ecclesiastical lord to exact money from his peasants.[79] In the case of Leutard, there was an explicit social and economic component to the heresy, and its seemingly unsophisticated ideas and goals (though perhaps made to seem more "simple" by a hostile Glaber) bespeak both this and the fact that such heresy was a fairly new phenomenon that had more of an air of a peasant revolt than a coherent religious cult. Therefore, it is important to recognize the hidden social dimension of these heretical movements. It was perhaps easier for the authorities to justify their persecution by painting these agitators as religious heretics, rather than to recognize that their actions may have been based to some degree on social and economic discontent.

In this context, then, the cross can be viewed as more than just a religious symbol, but one of overt power by those who could wield it. Moreover, if the Scripture and the events described therein were merely allegorical to the Monforte sectarians, then the cross would also have been viewed as an allegory—and therefore not as a literal object to be venerated.[80] If the cross as a religious symbol was stripped of meaning, then, in this context, what other significance could it have held for them than as a symbol of temporal power? The fact that Gerard at no time explicitly mentions an opposition to the cross in his testimony is telling, and leaves the impression that the sect maintained a benign

---

[79] The tithe had been an instrument of local power even in the Carolingian period; Patricia Skinner, *Family Power in Southern Italy: the Duchy of Gaeta and its Neighbors, 850–1139* (Cambridge: Cambridge University Press, 1995), 93. Violante says that the tithe was an essential part of the initial motivation of all religious movements of the eleventh century—which, in his opinion, is why so many *rustici* were attracted to heresy, *La società milanese*, 105. To them, the tithe was merely a symbol of ecclesiastical power and authority, and its onerous nature, combined with a rising consciousness of clerical abuses, made the tithe a focal point for rebellion. Rather of Verona recognized the potential for abuse when he stated that the tithe frequently provided deacons and priests "the wherewithal also to get wives for their sons and husbands for their daughters, and vineyards and fields, and finally so that they can serve the mammon of iniquity without intermission ..." *The Complete Works of Rather of Verona*, 356–357, letter #28.

[80] See Henry Bett, *Johannes Scotus Erigena*, 88–149.

attitude towards this symbol. This is rather different in tone from the outright scorn for the cross held by Bogomils, who viewed it as an offense to God.

It may be helpful here to view the rejection of the cross, with all of its political as well as spiritual implications, in a similar light to the rejection of saints' relics.[81] Some historians have argued that the rejection of saints' relics and their associated miracles by Western heretics can be attributed to the dualist nature of Bogomil teaching, which held that the Devil was behind the working of miracles as a means of tricking the faithful into false devotion. Yet, given the fact that fraud was not infrequently perpetrated by the peddlers of these relics, it should come as no surprise that there were those who rejected the authority and sanctity of those objects. Glaber relates a vivid illustration of this phenomenon. In France there lived a cunning peddler, known variously as Stephen, Peter, or John, who had taken to digging up the bones of ordinary Christians and passing them off as the relics of saints, selling them to unsuspecting believers.[82] This man had won a great following from the *rusticane plebis*, who flocked to the relics of his false martyrs for cures and to witness miracles. What was worse, according to Glaber, was that local bishops not only were aware of the deception and did nothing about it, but that they actually capitalized on it—taking money from the people who were eager to see the saints.[83]

As Glaber admits that such deception was not all that uncommon, is it any wonder that some individuals would openly scorn the authority and sanctity of relics that may not even have been authentic? Furthermore, the rejection of relics and their associated miracles takes an even greater importance when one considers that the power and authority of the clergy was based, at least in part, on the authority of the local saint.[84] The Florentine bishop Ildebrand (1008–1024), for example, sought to expand his property and authority throughout the dio-

---

[81] On the rejection of relics by the Orleans heretics, see *Cartulaire de l'abbaye de St.-Père de Chartres*, ed. B. Guerard, vol. 1 (Paris: Crapelet, 1840), 111.

[82] *Historiarum Libri Quinque*, IV, 180.

[83] *Historiarum Libri Quinque*, IV, 182. "Nec tamen Morianne vel Utzetice seu Gratinone urbium presules, in quorum diocesibus talia profanabantur, diligentiam huius inquirende rei adhibuere; quin potius conciliabula statuentes, in quibus nil aliud nisi inepti lucri questum a plebe, simul et favorem fallacie exigebant."

[84] Monasteries, for example, largely relied on the power of their saint's relics to defend their property, often through the process of quitclaiming, sometimes through sheer intimidation, and always through the medium of local hagiography. This coersive authority of the abbey rested on the belief of the local population in the validity and

cese, and determined that fostering the local cult of St. Minias was an effective way to better secure this end.[85] If the Florentine or any other church was perceived to be in possession of a false saint, however, the authority of that church might be viewed with suspicion by those subjected under it. This risk was famously demonstrated in the challenge successfully made to the apostolicity of St. Martial by the Italian Benedict of Chiusa in 1029, effectively ending Ademar of Chabannes' efforts (through forgeries) to enhance the prestige and authority of his abbey.[86]

Claire Taylor claims that the Bogomils "ridiculed saints and those who prayed to them," as did most heretics, and she uses this fact as part of her overall evidence to prove a Bogomil influence in the West.[87] Yet, given the false claims made in regards to saint's relics and their frequent socio-political use, a Bogomil presence need not be inferred, for the heretics' rejection of relics may simply stem from indigenous anti-clericalism and skepticism. Moreover, it must be noted that "heretics" were not the only ones to ridicule saints' relics and those who worshipped them.[88] Indeed, the fact that the *rustici* often blindly followed these "martyrs" would have undoubtedly been met with scorn by those who felt they knew better. Bernard of Angers, whose writings on St. Foy Taylor uses as evidence to establish a Manichean presence in Aquitaine in the early-eleventh century, had also ridiculed the *rustici* of Conques for worshipping their local saint. He believed that such devotion was simple-minded and contrary to *reason*.[89]

---

retributive power of the saint's relics. Without this, monastic property would be easy prey for neighboring and land-hungry *castellans*.

[85] *Episcopal Power and Florentine Society*, 28–37.

[86] See Richard Landes, *Relics, Apocalypse, and the Deceits of History: Ademar of Chabannes, 989–1034* (Cambridge, MA: Harvard University Press, 1995). It is perhaps noteworthy that Benedict of Chiusa was an Italian (in fact, from Lombardy), for his venomous denunciation of the cult of relics and of local clerical practices in general contained strong ideological elements from both the radical reform and heretical movements. For the role of the Peace movement in the development of the legend of St. Martial see H.E.J.Cowdrey, "The Peace of God in the Eleventh Century" *Past and Present* 46 (1970), 51–52.

[87] "The Letter of Heribert of Périgord," 343.

[88] See *Historia mediolanensis*, III.9, p. 80, 10–13. The Patarene leader Landulf Cotta insisted that the martyrs no longer be venerated: "Igitur cum huius rei fama ad Landulfum volitasset, et ut magis ac magis, quod in obscuro dixerunt, super tectum divulgaretur, martyris veneratione relicta, cui omnes devote convenerant, ac antiquorum veneratione omissa, arrepto manibus Arialdo, furiose ac pessime vociferando cum paucis ad theatrum pervenit."

[89] A Bouillet, *Liber Miraculorum Sancte Fides* (Paris: A. Picard, 1897), XIII, I.13, 46–49.

Talk of challenges to established authority should not detract, however, from the fact that the members of the Monforte sect apparently had a strong sense of the spiritual benefits of martyrdom, and thus may have ended their lives out of genuine religious conviction. According to Landulf, "[Gerard] was completely prepared for martyrdom and was eager to end his life with the most severe torments."[90] In this sense, perhaps, antagonism of the magistrates provided the perfect means by which to achieve their goals (not unlike the way Christ hastened his martyrdom through radical preaching and antagonism of the Roman leadership). Indeed, this analogy would not have been lost on a group whose members studied the Bible, and closely modeled their lives upon this sacred text.

Monforte and other eleventh-century heresies cannot be considered isolated phenomena. Rather, they comprised part of a larger spiritual and social movement in the West that began in Italy during the later tenth century and swept rapidly across Europe. Though these heresies shared many similarities with the preaching of Bogomils, these similarities were in large measure incidental. In actuality, these tendencies were more likely to have arisen from contact with the Italian reform movement, independent scriptural interpretation, and the socio-political environment of pre-communal Italian cities. The heretics at Monforte espoused many of the same tenets of social and religious reform encouraged by Italian evangelicals (namely chastity, communalism, a reliance on Scriptural authority, and a marked anticlericalism). What made them particularly "heretical," though, was their threat to the authority of the Milanese bishop and magistrates as much as their interpretation of the Scriptures—one that clashed with established Catholic dogma. In Milan, there had been no incidence of officially-condemned heresy, despite the avid preaching of similar "radical" social ideals. The difference, of course, lay in the fact that this radical preaching in Milan had been politically expedient for those who supported it, including some of the clergy, much of the nobility, and even the pope.

Clearly, eleventh-century heresies were the result of an increasingly literate lay population, one which possessed the self-confidence, intellectual curiosity, and spiritual hunger to form religious associations outside of traditional Church authority. Noted for their anticlerical-

---

[90] *Historia mediolanensis*, II. 27.

ism, rejection of outward forms of devotion, and an invalidation of key tenets of the Catholic faith, the basic moral tenets they espoused were found within and inspired by the pages of Scripture. Literacy, and access to sacred texts which it thus provided, offered a sense of spiritual *empowerment*, perhaps because those who relied upon it were denied this power through more mainstream channels. Moreover, this power was a means to reject traditional social hierarchies while simultaneously embracing a sense of spiritual independence, and arose from the conviction that these heretics were personally infused with divine illumination through the Word of God.

PAGANS, HERETICS, SARACENS, AND JEWS IN THE SERMONS OF ADEMAR OF CHABANNES

MICHAEL FRASSETTO

The origin of medieval heresy in the eleventh century has been one of the more contentious issues of the last half century. It has been argued that heresy was a purely domestic phenomenon that emerged because of changing social, religious, and cultural conditions or because of the intervention of Balkan missionaries or some combination of the two.[1] More recently, the rhetorical strategies of eleventh-century ecclesiastics have been considered and the very existence of heresy at that time has been questioned.[2] At the heart of debate over the origins of heresy is the assertion made by Ademar of Chabannes, writing in the late 1020s, that the heretics in his native Aquitaine in 1018, in Orleans in 1022, and elsewhere in the West in the 1020s were Manichaeans.[3] Indeed, as R.I. Moore notes, it was Ademar who created the confusion that has plagued modern scholars concerning the origin and nature of the medieval heresy or dissent.[4] As a result, historians have either taken

---

[1] The two sides were argued in R. Morghen, *Medioevo Cristiano* (Bari: Laterza, 1953) and Antoine Dondaine, "L'Origine del'hérésie médiévale," *Rivista di storia e letteratura religiosa* 6 (1952): 43–78 respectively. See also the discussion in Malcolm Lambert, *Medieval Heresy: Popular Movements from the Gregorian Reform to the Reformation*, 3rd ed., (Oxford: Blackwell, 2002), 3–40.

[2] See, for example, the essays in Monique Zerner, ed., *Inventer l'hérésie? Discours polémique et pouvoirs avant l'inquisition* (Nice: Centre d'Études Médiévales, Faculté des Lettres, Arts et Sciences Humaines, Université de Nice Sophia-Antipolis, 1998).

[3] *Ademari Cabannensis Chronicon*, eds. R. Landes and G. Pon (Turnhout: Brepols, 1999): 3:49, p. 170. "Pauco post tempore per Aquitaniam exorti sunt manichei, seducentes plebem, negantes baptismum sanctum et crucis virtutem, et quidquid sane doctrine est, abstinentes a cibis quasi monachi et castitatem simulantes, sed inter se ipsos omnem luxuriam exercentes; quippe ut nuncii Antichristi, multos a fide exorbitare fecerunt." He repeats the reference in chapters 59 and 69, pp. 180, and 189. For discussion of these passages see Richard Landes, "Between Aristocracy and Heresy: Popular Participation in the Limousin Peace of God, 994–1033," in *The Peace of God: Social Violence and Religious Response in France around the Year 1000*, ed. Thomas Head and Richard Landes (Ithaca, NY: Cornell University Press, 1992), 184–218; and Michael Frassetto, "The Sermons of Ademar of Chabannes and the Letter of Heribert: New Sources Concerning the Origins of Medieval Heresy," *Revue Bénédictine* 109 (1999): 324–340.

[4] R.I. Moore, *The Origins of European Dissent*, rev. ed. (Oxford: Blakwell, 1985), 30.

Ademar at his word, accepting that the "Manichaeans" held to dualist teachings or have rejected Ademar's assertion, arguing that he applied the lessons of St. Augustine to the alleged heretics of the eleventh century.[5] The latter view is the current scholarly consensus, even though some students of the issue have voiced reservations.[6]

Unfortunately, few scholars have sought to understand Ademar's vocabulary in any meaningful way and thus the issue has been confused even further. However, Ademar himself has provided the information necessary to resolve this dilemma. In two great collections of sermons, Ademar addressed in extensive detail the fundamental questions of orthodoxy and heterodoxy in his day. These sermons, written near the end of his life and now held in Paris and Berlin, provide the means to discern the underlying assumptions with which Ademar approached religious dissent and to understand the terminology he would use to define heresy and heretics.[7] It is not my intent to attempt to address the broader debate over the origins of medieval heresy, but rather to provide the context of Ademar's usage of various terms to define the enemies of the faith—a discussion, I hope, that will be relevant to both the origins of heresy and the formation of the persecuting society. Indeed, Ademar's concern throughout the sermons was to define who and what was essentially Christian and orthodox and who and what was not. In his many sermons, Ademar used a number of terms to describe the enemies of the faith, including pagan, Saracen, heretic, and Jew.[8] And it is the purpose of this study to consider the use of these

---

[5] Guy Lobrichon, "The Chiaroscuro of Heresy: Early Eleventh-Century Aquitaine as Seen from Auxerre," in *The Peace of God: Social Violence and Religious Response in France around the Year 1000* (Ithaca, NY: Cornell University Press, 1992), 100. "Ademar sedulously accumulated a set of commonplaces from Augustine's *De haeresibus*, polished and refined at length by tradition."

[6] Moore's *Origins of European Dissent* and related articles greatly influenced the direction of scholarly opinion in this matter. There has, however, been some recent dissent from the prevailing view; see Malcolm Barber, *The Cathars: Dualist Heretics in the High Middle Ages* (London: Longman, 2000), 28–33; Claire Taylor, "The Letter of Heribert of Périgord as a Source for Dualist Heresy in the Society of the early Eleventh Century Aquitaine," *Journal of Medieval History* (2000): 313–349; and Daniel Callahan in this volume.

[7] Paris, B.N. MS. Lat. 2469, fols. 1ʳ–112ᵛ and Berlin, Deutsche Staatbibliothek, Phillipps MS. Lat. 1664, 68ᵛ–170ᵛ.

[8] Indeed, there are times throughout the sermons in which Ademar will use these terms together in a series, suggesting that each of them held slightly different meanings for him but also that they were equally opposed to the orthodox faith. For example, D.S. MS. 1664, fol. 74ᵛ, "... congregationem Christianorm qui veriter fidem credunt

terms and their possible implication for the broader issue of the origins of medieval dissent.[9]

The sermons themselves were written after Ademar's defeat in the controversy over the apostolicity of St. Martial of Limoges with the Italian monk Benedict of Chiusa, who humiliated Ademar on the day that the apostolic liturgy for Martial—written by Ademar himself—was to be proclaimed for the first time.[10] The sermons he wrote in the late 1020s and early 1030s were part of a larger corpus of forgeries designed to prove Ademar's victory and were written to give the impression that they were delivered at various church councils.[11] They contain the details of the life of St. Martial as well as his miracles and appear to provide church sanction of the saint's apostolic status through the implicit approval of the councils where the sermons were putatively delivered. Indeed, Ademar sought to demonstrate his own orthodoxy by creating the appearance of the orthodoxy of the apostolicity of St. Martial. The focus of the sermons, therefore, is on Martial, but the

---

et inter congregationem Iudeorum, paganorum, Sarracenorum et omnium haereticorum." See also MS. 1664, fols. 97ʳ, 102ʳ, 112ʳ.

[9] The model for this paper is the very excellent Robert Markus, "Gregory the Great's Pagans," in *Belief and Culture in the Middle Ages: Studies Presented to Henry Mayr-Harting*, Richard Gameson and Henrietta Leyser, eds. (Oxford: Oxford University Press, 2001), 23–34.

[10] Ademar recorded the debate in *Epistola de Apostolatu s. Martialis*, PL, 141. 87–112, but, of course, in this version Ademar won. See also Louis Saltet "Une discussion sur Saint Martial entre un Lombard et un Limousin en 1029," *Bulletin de litterature ecclesiastique* 26 (1925): 161–186, 279–302; and Landes. For an introduction to the sermons see Daniel Callahan, "The Sermons of Ademar of Chabannes and the Cult of St. Martial of Limoges," *Revue Bénédictine* 86 (1976): 251–295; Leopold Delisle, "Notice sur les manuscrits originaux d'Adémar de Chabannes," *Notice et extraits des manuscrits de la Bibliothèque nationale* 35 (1896), 241–385; and Michael Frassetto, "The Sermons of Ademar of Chabannes and the Origins of Medieval Heresy" (University of Delaware: Ph.D. dissertation, 1993).

[11] On Ademar's career as a forger, see Daniel Callahan, "Ademar of Chabannes and His Insertions into Bede's *Expositio Actuum Apostolorum*," *Analecta Bollandiana* 111 (1993): 385–400; Michael Frassetto, "The Art of Forgery: The Sermons of Ademar of Chabannes and the Cult of St. Martial of Limoges," *Comitatus* 26 (1995): 11–26; Herbert Schnieder, "Ademar von Chabannes und Pseudoisidor—der 'Mythomane' und der Erzfälscher," *Fälschungen im Mittelalter*, vol. 2 Gefälschte Rechtstexte der bestrafte Fälscher (Hanover: Hahnsche Buchhandlung, 1988), 129–150; and, especially, the series of articles in by Canon Saltet, in the *Bulletin de litterature ecclesiastique* "Une discussion sur Saint Martial entre un Lombard et un Limousin en 1029;" "Une pretendue lettre de Jean XIX sur Saint Martial fabrique par Ademar de Chabannes," 27 (1926): 117–139; "Les faux d'Ademar de Chabannes. Pretendues decisions sur Saint Martial au concile de Bourges du 1er novembre 1031," 27 (1926): 145–160 and "Un cas de mythomanie historique bien documente: Ademar de Chabannes (988–1034)," 32 (1931): 149–165.

sermons also contain extended discussions of the sacraments, church doctrine, and the lives of other saints. The Paris manuscript concludes with accounts of the councils of Bourges and Limoges in 1031, and the Berlin manuscript contains Ademar's copies of works by Theodulf of Orleans and the Pseudo-Isidorean decretals, both organized in the form of sermons and much altered by Ademar, as well as works by Bede and Jerome.[12] All of which were intended to emphasize the essential orthodoxy of Ademar's defense of St. Martial and Ademar himself.

One group, therefore, that gets attention from Ademar is the pagans, even though it is unlikely that any real pagans lived in southwestern France in Ademar's time. He does, however, often denounce the *pagani* in the sermons of the Berlin manuscript and clearly distinguishes them from other non-Christian or heretical enemies of the faith. He notes in one passage that no "Jew, Saracen, pagan, or heretic" will be saved unless they believe in the faith of St. Peter.[13] In another passage, he notes that Saracens are worse than pagans, because the former worship idols but the latter blaspheme the true God.[14] In other sermons in ms. 1664, Ademar identifies the pagans along with Saracens, Jews, and heretics, as enemies of the faith, or impious men opposed to God.[15]

Even though the sermons in the Berlin manuscript focus more clearly on Ademar's own day, references to *pagani* throughout the collection clearly refer to the opponents of St. Martial. Although he sometimes links the pagans with contemporary enemies of the faith, Ademar generally understood pagans to be non-Christian opponents of the faith from antiquity who could one day convert to the Christian faith. He places pagans in antiquity on several occasions in the collection, noting in one sermon that St. Augustine converted from paganism to Chris-

---

[12] The material from Bede includes his commentaries on the Acts of the Apostles (fols. 2^r–17^v) and on the book of the Apocalypse (fols. 17^v–37^r). Jerome's commentary on Daniel (fols. 40^r–57^r). The Theodulfan material, a capitulary and treatise on baptism, is on fols. 58^r–78^v, but much of the material after fol. 68^v was written by Ademar even though it purports to be from Theodulf. The decretals, in the form of sermons and with numerous insertions from Ademar, are on fols. 116^r–170^r. For further discussion of the Paris and Berlin codices see Frassetto, "The Sermons of Ademar," 164–229 and Delisle, "Notice sur les manuscrits originaux d'Adémar," 244–296.

[13] D.S. MS. Lat. 1664, fol. 83^v. "Inpossibile enim est ut nullus Iudeus, Sarracenus, paganus, haereticus umquam salvus fiat nisi tantum illi qui in fide Sancti Petri credunt."

[14] D.S. MS. Lat. 1664, fol. 90^r.

[15] D.S. MS. Lat. 1664, fol. 102^r. "… et impii homines Iudei, Sarraceni, pagani, haeretici qui Deo contrarius sunt." And fol. 97^r, "Iudeorum atque Sarracenorum et paganorum et haereticorum et antichristi."

tianity under the influence of St. Ambrose, and in another that Constantine fought against the pagans after his conversion and that the pagans sometimes joined with the Arians against Catholic Christians.[16] The *pagani* were those in ancient times who "adored demons and idols of dead men and women"; they were also those who refused to await the one foretold by the prophets and instead adored the false gods in temples.[17] Ademar also addressed the life of Martial in the sermons in ms. 1664 and further associated the *pagani* with non-Christians in earlier times. Martial, according to the monk of Limoges in his sermon on the Eucharist, offered the pagans baptism and through it the remission of sin. In a later sermon, Ademar describes Martial's activities in Aquitaine, including the saint's preaching and denunciation of temples and idols, and then notes that the pagans adore created things and idols of dead men and women. The pagan can, however, be converted to Christianity, unlike the Saracen, because the pagan can come to understand that he worships nothing.[18] In general, the pagans were those living in earlier times, who worshipped idols and false gods, but could be converted to Christianity.

Pagani most likely served a specific purpose for Ademar, distinct from the other Christian enemies he attacked throughout the sermons. By identifying them as those who opposed Martial, or at the least were the focus of the "apostle's" mission, Ademar separates them from Christians and other non-Christians. Although he recognized that they could ultimately accept the true faith, Ademar places them outside the church. Pagans not only worship idols and demons but reject the truth and are, therefore, not to be counted among the saved. The *pagani* who worshipped Mercury and Diana surely no longer existed by Ademar's day, but there were those in the early eleventh century who rejected the truth as Ademar saw it. They were the new pagans who rejected the truth of Martial's apostolicity, just as the pagans of antiquity rejected the truth of Martial's preaching. Ademar most likely drew the parallel

---

[16] D.S. MS. Lat. 1664, fols. 108ʳ and 85ʳ respectively.

[17] D.S. MS. Lat. 1664, fol. 90ᵛ. "Similiter pagani per universorum mundum cum primo ab antiquitate Deum creatorem cognovissent nimiis peccatis involuti pro Deo coeperunt adorare daemonia et idola mortuorum virorum et mulierum." And fol. 91ʳ. "Illum antiqui iusti expectabant illum prophetae praenuntiabant illum ipsi pagani ignoranter adorabant ipsi templum fabricaverant inter suos falsos deos."

[18] D.S. MS. Lat. 1664, fol. 91ʳ. "Paganus per praedicatorem Christi facili intelligat quia nihil prodest quod adorat creaturam; Sarracenus in tantum errorem blasphemiae ingurgitatus est."

between ancient and contemporary "pagans" as a means to enroll
his opponents in the congregation of the enemies of the faith. In his
attempt to confirm his orthodoxy and that of Martial's apostolicity,
Ademar made reference to the pagans of antiquity, suggesting at the
same time that his contemporaries were no better than the ancient
pagans were.

Ademar's concerns in the sermons, however, were focused most
immediately on the contemporary enemies of the faith, especially Jews,
Muslims, and heretics, whom Ademar believed formed a conspiracy
against Christians. Indeed, in the history, he describes the coordination
between the Jews of the West and the Muslims in the Holy Land
in the year 1010, when the Egyptian leader al-Hakim persecuted the
Christians and destroyed several churches.[19] Both Jews and Muslims, or
Saracens as Ademar calls them, receive attention in the sermons.[20] The
Jews denied the truth, Ademar alleges, even though there is sufficient
testimony in the Hebrew Scriptures, but the Jews refuse to accept this
truth through willful ignorance.[21] In other words, they have access to
the truth, which is plainly revealed to them, but they choose not to
accept it. Moreover, he notes further that the Jews and heretics alike
reject one of the central teachings of the faith, explaining that just as
the Jews in Jesus' day refused to believe that Jesus was the living bread
the heretics of Ademar's day refuse to accept the Eucharist. As a result

---

[19] *Chronicon*, 3:47, pp. 166–167. A similar tale is told by Rodolphus Glaber in *Rodulfi Glavri Historiarum Libri Quinqui*, ed. John France (Oxford: Clarendon Press, 1989), 3:7.24–25, pp. 132–137, who also dates the events, erroneously to 1010 rather than 1009. See also Marius Canard, "La Destruction de l'église de la resurrection par la calife Hakim et l'histoire de la descente du feu sacre," *Byzantion* 35 (1965): 16–43; Michael Frassetto, "The Image of the Saracen as Heretic in the Sermons of Ademar of Chabannes," in *Western Views of Islam in Medieval and Early Modern Europe: Perception of Other*, eds. David R. Blanks and Michael Frassetto (New York: St. Martin's Press, 1999), 84–85; and Richard Southern, *Western Views of Islam in the Middle Ages*, 2nd printing (Cambridge, MA: Harvard University Press, 1978), 28.

[20] For fuller consideration of Ademar's attitudes toward Muslims and Jews see my "The Image of the Saracen as Heretic in the Sermons of Ademar of Chabannes," 83–96, and "Heretics and Jews in the Writings of Ademar of Chabannes and the Origins of Medieval Anti-Semitism," *Church History* 71 (2002): 1–15.

[21] D.S. MS. Lat. 1664, fol. 84[r]. "Iudei tam in suis libris inveniunt trinitatem atque ascensionem Domini in omnia quae de Domino Ihesus Christo credimus ispi inveniunt praedicta a prophetis in suis libris sed non credunt quia non praedestinati ad vitam aeternam." For a general discussion of the Jews' rejection of their Scriptures, see Joshua Trachtenberg, *The Devil and the Jews: The Medieval Conception of the Jew and Its Relation to Modern Anti-Semitism*. (Philadelphia: The Jewish Publication Society, 1983; reprinted with a forward by Marc Saperstein), pp. 15–18.

of this, it is argued in the sermons, the Jews are guilty of numerous crimes against the church. Most notably for Ademar, the Jews killed Christ. In one of his synodal sermons, Ademar calls Christ the "true and living bread" who was crucified by the Jews.[22] In his sermon on the mystery of the mass, Ademar again defines the Jews as Christ-killers, asserting that their impiety and desire to remove his name from earth led the Jews to crucify Christ.[23] The Jews continued their opposition to the faith and persecution of Christ by their denial of the cross. Like the heretics mentioned in Ademar's history, the Jews denounce the cross as an idol of wood.[24] Even worse, the Jews perform acts of violence against the cross. They abused the cross on one occasion by wounding the figure of Jesus; their blows led to a miraculous effusion of blood and water from its side.[25]

Ademar expresses a more negative view of the Jews than he did of the pagans, adopting several antisemitic commonplaces, because of the Jews' continued existence and perceived opposition to Christianity. Similarly, Ademar adopts the developing stereotypical view of Muslims and Islam. In the sermons, he indulges in gross caricatures of Muslims. He expounds on Muslim ritual in most detestable fashion, describing one rite in which a sacrificial offering is made and devoured and desecrated by black dogs. In another passage, Ademar contends that the Saracens "do not believe in the true God, who is true peace, and thus never give the kiss of peace."[26] Instead, he alleges, they turn the Christian rite upside down and indulge in a ritual anal kiss. The Limousin monk also believed that the Saracens were heretics who failed to accept the true Catholic faith. In his *Sermo ad Sinodum de Catholica Fide* (fols. 83^r–96^r), the longest and most complex of the sermons, Ademar defends

---

[22] D.S. MS. Lat. 1664, fol. 108^v. "Quia in passione Domini corpus eius immolatum est in cruce et sanguinis eius confusses est et ille verus et vivus panis qui de caelo descendit in terram quando natus est qui etiam angelos ante saecula pascebat in caelo postquam a Iudeis crucifixus est."

[23] D.S. MS. Lat. 1664, fol. 97^v. "Quia Iudei pro impietate Dominum crucifixerunt ut delerent nomen eius de terra."

[24] D.S. MS. Lat. 1664, fol. 73^r.

[25] D.S. MS. Lat. 1664, fol. 73^r. "Et quem multocies Iudei zelantes imagines crucifixi ... lanceis vulnerarunt et sanquine et aqua ex eis profluit tamquam quondam ex latere Domini."

[26] D.S. MS. Lat. 1664, fol. 91^r. "Et sicut in verum Deum, qui vera pax est, non credunt ita alter alteri numquam dat osculum pacis." See also Daniel Callahan, "Ademar of Chabannes, Millenial Fears and the Development of Western Anti-Judaism," *The Journal of Ecclesiastical History* 46 (1995): 19–35, especially 29.

the fundamental teachings of the faith and repudiates the errors of all heretics. After defending the Catholic definition of the Trinity, Ademar argues that the Saracens lie when they claim to believe in one God and insult Christians when they accuse them of worshipping three gods. Although the Saracens assert belief in one God, they reject the Trinity and thus both deny God and provoke his wrath by their blasphemy. Their error is compounded, according to Ademar, because they also reject the Incarnation and are thus like the Jews and heretics.

Ademar thus had a well-defined understanding of pagans, Jews, and Muslims. His view of the latter two was shaped by the developing stereotypical view that would come to dominate among medieval Westerners.[27] This understanding differed from his perception of the pagans, in part, because Jews and Muslims offered an on-going challenge to Christians and their faith that the pagans did not, in part because the Jews and Muslims did not convert to Christianity as the pagans had. As a result, Jews and Muslims received much worse treatment than the pagans and were joined with the heretics as enemies of the faith and disciples of Satan.

Although Ademar fervently opposed the heretics of his day, his understanding of them was not conditioned by the ignorance that it seems shaped his understanding of Muslims and Jews. Indeed, throughout the sermons Ademar displays considerable knowledge of the heresies that have challenged the church during its history. He reveals at least passing familiarity throughout both collections of sermons with the lesser and greater heresies from church history and fashions extensive discussion of them in the sermons of ms. 1664. Perhaps motivated by the notion that there is nothing new under the sun, Ademar denounced these ancient heresies in order to repudiate contemporary heresies and demonstrate his own pronounced orthodoxy. At the same time, however, the choice of heresies and heretics he made cannot be without significance.

Drawing from his knowledge of the fathers, notably Isidore of Seville whose list of heresies he copied into the Paris ms. 2400, Ademar con-

---

[27] For a good, general introduction to the phenomenon see R.I.Moore, *The Formation of a Persecuting Society: Power and Deviance in Western Europe, 950–1250* (Oxford: Blackwell, 1987). For the development of Jewish stereotypes see Gavin Langmuir, *Toward a Defintion of Antisemitism* (Berkeley and Los Angeles: University of California Press, 1990); and Trachtenberg, *The Devil and the Jews*. On anti-Muslim stereotypes, see Norman Daniel, *Islam and the West: The Making of an Image*, rev. ed. (Oxford: Oneworld Publications, 1993); and Richard Southern, *Western Views of Islam*.

sidered a number of better and lesser known heresies in his sermons.[28] Although the earlier collection of sermons focuses more on the life and miracles of St. Martial, it has a number of references to heresy. Indeed, in ms. 2469 his concerns with heresy and St. Martial came together in the denunciation of the Hebionites, members of an early Jewish-Christian sect that lived ascetically and rejected the virgin birth.[29] They also rejected the apostolicity of St. Paul, which provided Ademar a model for his opponents who rejected the apostolicity of St. Martial. He declared that those who do not accept as true apostles anyone other than the original twelve act against the true Catholic faith and is a Hebionite.[30] He further provided conciliar support for his position by including discussions of the matter in his versions of the councils of Bourges and Limoges in 1031. In this way, the church fathers of Ademar's day condemned the opponents of Martial's apostolicity just as the ancient church fathers condemned the opponents of Paul. According to Ademar's account of the council of Limoges, Odolric, abbot of St. Martial of Limoges, and Isembert of Poitiers declared that they were not Hebionite heretics and accepted Martial's true rank. Those who denied that Martial was an apostle were declared heretics and schismatics by the council.[31]

The sermons of the Paris manuscript address other heresies as well, including iconoclasm. In a sermon commemorating the dedication of the church of St. Peter of Limoges, Ademar attacks Leo the Isaurian and the Iconoclasts of the eighth century. Criticizing Leo's rejection of holy images, Ademar notes that Leo's actions brought about a sentence of excommunication over the emperor and empire from the pope.[32] His discussion of the Byzantine iconoclasts is part of a broader discussion in the sermon, which covers several folios, on the use of images in the

---

[28] It is commonly assumed that Ademar's understanding of heresy, especially Manichaeanism, was dependent on the works of Augustine. This view is somewhat difficult to maintain in the absence of any of Augustine's work from Ademar's corpus and the lack of any Augustinian texts on heresy from the monastery of the library at St. Martial of Limoges.

[29] B.N. MS. Lat. 2469, fols. 6^r, 6^v, 30^r, 79^r, and others.

[30] B.N. MS. Lat. 2469, fol. 11^r. "Contra fidem enim agit Catholicam qui non credit apostolos esse praeter XII. Qui, enim, sic credit Hebionita est, non Catholicus."

[31] "Concilium Lemovicense," Mansi, v. 19, cols. 512 and 525.

[32] B.N. MS. Lat. 2469, fol. 42^v. "Quam impietatem Anastasius et Leo Augusti edictis suis adiuverunt quo usque a papa Romano totam Greciam sub anathemate excommunicationem sentirent diu sicque inviti sacras imagines iterum eclesiae erectas restitui permitterent."

decoration of churches.[33] In defense of the use of images, Ademar cites the precedents of St. Martial of Limoges; he also argues that icons inspire true piety among people and are not the false idols of the pagans.[34] As he did with the denunciation of the Hebionites, Ademar mixes contemporary and historical concerns. His denunciations were most likely motivated by the ancient errors and the contemporary rejection of the cross by the heretics of Aquitaine.[35] Although he does not mention this group explicitly, it is not unlikely that they inspired Ademar's vigorous defense of the orthodox view of images.

That his concerns in ms. 2469 with orthodoxy and heresy were inspired by contemporary events is suggested by his attention to the issues of nicolaitism and simony, the two great issues of reform in the eleventh century.[36] Ademar offers commentary on these two matters in the accounts of the peace councils of Bourges and Limoges that form the conclusion of the Paris collection.[37] According to Ademar, the fathers of the council of Bourges rejected the practice of clerical mar-

---

[33] B.N. MS. Lat. 2469, fol. 40ᵛ–43ᵛ.

[34] B.N. MS. Lat. 2469, fol. 42ᵛ. "Certes priores piisimi imperatores effigies Domini nostri Christi, crucifixas vel in sede maiestatis residentes, ex auro vel qualibet materia compositas, imagines etiam Dei Genitricis et archangelorum nec non et quorum libet sanctorum non pro idolis Mercurii et Iovis aliorumque daemonum deputabant."

[35] *Chronicon*, 3:49, p. 170, where Ademar notes that the heretics "negantes baptismum et crucis virtutem." Indeed, there seems to have been an iconoclastic tendency among the heresies of the early eleventh century. One of the earliest involved the destruction of the cross by the peasant Leutard of Vertus. On Leutard see Rodolphus Glaber in *Historiarum Libri Quinqui*, ed. France; 2:9.22, pp. 88–91; Heinrich Fichtenau, *Heretics and Scholars in the High Middle Ages, 1000–1200*, trans. Denise A. Kaiser (University Park, PA: Pennsylvania State University Press, 1998), 16–19; Lambert, *Medieval Heresy*, 3rd ed., 35–36; Moore, *Origins*, 35–36; and Brian Stock, *The Implications of Literacy: Written Language and Models of Interpretation in the Eleventh and Twelfth Centuries*, (Princeton: Princeton University Press, 1983), 101–106.

[36] Uta-Renate Blumenthal, *The Investiture Controversy: Church and Monarchy from the Ninth to the Twelfth Century* (Philadelphia: University of Pennsylvania Press, 1988); Augustin Fliche, *La réforme grégorienne*, 3 vols. (Paris, 1924–1937); Michael Frassetto, ed., *Medieval Purity and Piety: Essays on Medieval Clerical Celibacy and Religious Reform*, (New York: Garland Publishing, 1998); and Gerd Tellenbach, *The church in western Europe from the tenth to the early twelfth century*, trans. Timothy Reuter (Cambridge: Cambridge University Press, 1993), provide useful introductions to the issues associated with the Gregorian Reform of the eleventh century.

[37] B.N. MS. Lat. 2469, fols. 97ʳ–112ᵛ. *Consilium Bituricense*, Mansi, 19: cols. 501–508 and *Consilium Lemovicense*, Mansi, 19: cols. 509–548. For fuller discussion of the Peace of God movement see the essays in *The Peace of God: Social Violence and Religious Response in France around the Year 1000*, eds. Thomas Head and Richard Landes (Ithaca, NY: Cornell University Press, 1992); Dominique Barthélemy, *L'an mil et la paix de Dieu: La France chrétienne et féodale, 980–1060* (Paris: Aubier, 1999); Daniel Callahan, "Ademar de

riage, recognizing the number of problems caused by the children of priests and incontinent priests. The fathers at Bourges declared that, in accordance with canon law, no priest, deacon, or subdeacon may have a wife or concubine.[38] They proclaimed further that all members of the higher clergy must renounce their wives or be forsaken by the church, and that no member of the lower clerical orders may advance in rank if they are married. The leaders of the council, according to Ademar, also denounced the equally grave practice of simony, forbidding the clergy to accept payment for the performance of spiritual duties. Canon twelve of the council specifically decreed that no gift may be accepted by the clergy in exchange for the performance of baptism, penance, or burial unless it is freely offered by the faithful.[39] Moreover, these canons were approved at the council of Limoges, in Ademar's record of the affair, and were supported by further arguments by the various church leaders at that council.[40]

Although Ademar addresses the matter of heresy and orthodoxy in the sermons of ms. 2469, he provides much greater attention to it in the sermons of the Berlin manuscript. Along with his concern with proving the truth of the apostolicity of St. Martial, the issues of affirming orthodox belief and denouncing heterodox belief are the primary concerns of the sermon. To demonstrate his own orthodoxy, Ademar bound the sermons with works by Bede, Jerome, and Pseudo-Isidore, and based the opening sermons, even if very loosely, on Theodulf's work on baptism. The sermons themselves focus on issues including baptism, the Eucharist, gifts of the Holy Spirit, and several were given titles that indicate that they were delivered before church councils. His sermons routinely upheld the basic tenets of the faith as taught by the church in his day, and they also repeatedly warn of the appearance of heresy and

---

Chabannes et la Paix de Dieu," *Annales du Midi* 89 (1977): 21–43; and Bernhard Töpfer, *Volk und Kirche zur Zeit der beginnenden Gottesfriedensbewegung im Frankreich* (Berlin, 1957).

[38] Mansi, vol. 19, col. 503. "Ut presbyteri, et diacones, et subdiaconi, sicut lex canonum praecipit, neque uxores neque concubines habent: et qui eos modo habent, ita eas sine mora peracto hoc concilio derelinquant, ut nunquam ulterius ad eo accedant: qui vero derelinquere eas noluerint, a proprio gradu et officio cessent, et inter lectores et cantores permaneant. Similiter nulli de clero permittimus deinceps uxorem neque concubinam habere." See also Michael Frassetto, "Heresy, Celibacy, and Reform in the Sermons of Ademar of Chabannes," in *Medieval Purity and Piety: Essays on Medieval Clerical Celibacy and Religious Reform*, ed. Michael Frassetto (New York: Garland Publishing, 1998), 131–148.

[39] Mansi, vol. 19, cols. 504–505.

[40] B.N. MS. Lat. 2469, fols. 107ᵛ–108ʳ, and Mansi, vol. 19, cols. 536 and 545.

denounce the errors of heretics. Indeed, throughout the sermons, Ademar makes broad denunciations of heretics and, as noted, pagans, Jews, Saracens, Antichrists, and the like.[41] In his sermon on the Catholic faith he calls on the "priests of the true God" to preach zealously in defense of the faith against "all heretics, antichrists, and pseudo-apostles" who pollute the teachings of Christ.[42] And in that same sermon he calls on the support of the Church Fathers who denounced as heretics all those who held false teachings on the creation of humans.[43]

These general denunciations are complimented, on several occasions in the sermons, by specific warnings about the activities of heretics, whose beliefs and practices echo those of the Manichaeans described in Ademar's history. Aware of the dangers of heresy in his own day, Ademar, in his *Sermo ad Sinodum de Catholica Fide*, records that the bishop of Poitiers advised a council held in 1031 that it should not discuss the nature of the Holy Trinity or other higher doctrines in front of the laity lest they lapse into blasphemy.[44] Although he does not mention heresy by name in this passage, Ademar clearly recognizes the possibility that the laity would fall into error, and therefore heresy, when exposed to the mysteries of the faith, and he also provides a possible dynamic for the formation of heresy in the early eleventh century.[45] That Ademar's fears about the laity lapsing into blasphemy reveal his concerns with heresy is confirmed by other comments in the sermons. At the end of

---

[41] D.S. MS. Lat. 1664, fol. 102^v, for example, where Ademar notes "... et ipse diabolus qui Deo contrarius est et ipsi impii homines Iudei, Sarraceni, haeretici qui Deo contrarii sunt."

[42] D.S. MS. Lat. 1664, fol. 90^v. "Videte, o sacerdotes veri Dei, quantum zelare debetis pro Catholica fide contra omnes haereticos, antichristos, et pseudo-apsotolos si illi sacerdotes vilissimae creaturae zelum habebant pro pollutione erroris sui contra apostolos Christi."

[43] D.S. MS. Lat. 1664, fol. 93^r.

[44] D.S. MS. Lat. 1664, fol. 94^r. "In concilio episcoporum quod fuit hesterno anno, ille grammaticus qui faciebat sermonem de altitudine Sancte Trinitatis exposuit breviter hunc psalmum usque ad hunc versum; et cum praetermisset, quia perfecte non eius recordabatur, et episcopus Pictavensis iuberet ei hunc versum exponere, dixit alii secrete, propter laicos principes qui ibi aderant sermonem audientes, 'Non debet quis audientibus laicis de misterio Sanctae Trinitatis profunditatem investigare, meliusque ut taceatur quam in cordibus laicorum, qui discrete nesciunt cogitare, nescantur inlicite cogitationes quae exeant ad blasphemiam.'"

[45] This model for the emergence has been suggested by a number of scholars, and for Ademar and Aquitaine by Richard Landes, "Between Aristocracy and Heresy: Popular Participation in the Limousin Peace of God, 994–1033," in *The Peace of God: Social Violence and Religious Response in France around the Year 1000*, eds. Thomas Head and Richard Landes (Ithaca, NY: Cornell University Press, 1992), 184–218.

his sermon on the Lord's Prayer, Ademar proclaims that he has things to tell the synod concerning "heretics who secretly rise among us, who deny baptism, the mass, the cross, the church, and who are messengers of Antichrist."[46] His awareness and concerns with heresy are revealed also in one of the early sermons in ms. 1664, which is drawn from Theodulf's treatise on baptism. In this sermon, *De Eucharistia*, Ademar condemns heretics or ministers of the devil who blaspheme, rather than adore, the cross.[47] And in one of the later sermons, entitled simply *In Sinodo Sermo*, Ademar observes that there are heretics who reject the church's teachings on the mystery of the Eucharist.[48]

His concerns with heresy were clearly motivated by his own personal condition, but also by the existence of religious dissidents in his own time and place. To further distinguish himself from them and to place them in the company of the church's traditional opponents, Ademar discusses a number of historical heresies in the sermons of ms. 1664. Motivated, perhaps, by his understanding that the heretics of Aquitaine rejected "all sane doctrine," Ademar focused his attention in the sermons on several ancient heresies that erred on basic doctrinal matters.[49] Among the more important concerns for the monk of Limoges, as indeed for the entire church, was the definition of the nature of Christ. Although it had been concluded by the church by the fifth century, the debate over nature of the person of Christ had been a heated one in the early church, and unorthodox understanding of Christ's person was not unknown in the early eleventh century.[50]

---

[46] D.S. MS. Lat. 1664, fol. 114ᵛ. "Dicere habemus vobis de aliis rebus quae pertinent ad sinodum et de haereticis qui modo latenter inter nos surgunt qui negant baptismum, missam, crucem, ecclesiam, qui praecursores Antichristi sunt."

[47] D.S. MS. Lat. 1664, fol. 72ᵛ. "Observate, autem, vos haeretics diaboli ministris qui blasphemant, non adorari crucem, loquente diabolo in cordibus eorum."

[48] D.S. MS. Lat. 1664, fols. 107ᵛ–108ʳ. "Ita nunc haeretici, et hi qui in fide Christiani non credunt, murmurant et causantur in cordibus suis non credentes tam magnum esse misterium sacrificium Christianorum."

[49] *Chronicon*, 3:49. "Pauco post tempore per Aquitaniam exorti sunt manichei, seducentes plebem, negantes baptismum sanctum et crucis virtutem, et quidquid sane doctrine est."

[50] The best known example of this involves the heretics at Orleans in 1022 who taught a docetist Christology. On the heresy at Orleans, see Robert Bautier, "L'hérésie d'Orléans et le mouvement intellectuel au début du XIe siècles," in *Actes du 95e Congrès national des sociétés savantes, Reims 1970* (Paris: Bibliothèque nationale, 1975), 63–88; Fichtenau, *Heretics and Scholars*, 30–41, and "Die Ketzer von Orléans (1022)," in *Ex ipsis rerum documentis: Festschrift Harald Zimmermann* (Sigmaringen: Thorbecke, 1991), 417–427; Lambert, *Medieval Heresy*, 3rd ed., 14–21; Moore, *Origins*, 25–30; and Stock, *Implications of Literacy*, 106–120. It is possible that Ademar believed that the heretics of Aquitaine

Responding, perhaps, to both the contemporary and historical manifestations of Christological heresy, Ademar described a number of ancient
errors about Christ's person. In his sermon on the Catholic faith, Ademar repudiates the heresy of the *Thimotiani*. These heretics failed to
make the proper distinction between the two natures of Christ, human
and divine in one person, but combined the two so that there is only
one substance.[51] Ademar also denounces the blasphemy of Apollinaris
of Laodicea (c. 310–390), who rejected the two natures defined by the
orthodox by denying the full humanity of the Son incarnate. Apollinaris, Ademar explains, did not accept the existence of a human soul
in the body of Christ because human depravity prohibited the full con-
joining of God and man.[52] Clearly, Ademar's concerns were not merely
to repudiate ancient heresies, but to denounce Christological errors in
his own day. Indeed, that he was concerned with both historical and
contemporary errors is suggested by his condemnation of the errors of
the Saracens and the warning of the bishop of Poitiers that is recorded
in this sermon.

Ademar's concern with theology also includes discussion of Trinitarian heresies, and once again he examines the great heresies of the

---

held an unorthodox Christology. As noted by Richard Landes, "Between Heresy and
Aristocracy," p. 207, a composite of the various versions of Ademar's history includes a
reference to the heretics's rejection of "the Redeemer of the World." See also *Chronicon*,
3:59, p. 180. "Eo tempore decem ex canonicis Sanctae Crucis Aurelianis, qui vide-
bantur aliis religiosiores, probati sunt esse manichei. Quos rex Rotbertus, cum nollent
alicatenus ad fidem reverti, primo a gradu sacerdotii deponi, deinde ab ecclesia elimi-
nari, et demum igne cremari jussit. Nam ipsi decepti a quodam rustico Petragoricensi,
qui se dicebat facere virtutes, et pulverem ex mortuis pueris secum deferebat, de quo si
quem posset communicare, mox manicheum faciebat, adorabant diabolum, qui primo
eis in Etyopis, deinde angeli lucis figuratione apparebat, et eis multum cotidie argen-
tum deferebat. Cujus verbis obedientes, penitus Christum latenter respuerant, et abom-
inationes et crimina quae dici etiam flagitium est in occulto exercebant, et in aperto
christianos veros se fallebant."

[51] D.S. MS. Lat. 1664, fol. 96^r. "Et ipsa naturae non sunt in eo confuse neque
inmixtae, sicut Thimotiani haeretici blasphamaverunt, sed sunt duae natuare in una
societate unite sicut duae naturae, naturae auri et gemmarum, sunt societate in una
corona regali." It is possible that Ademar refers to the Monophysite patriarch of
Egypt, Timothy IV (518–535). For Timothy IV, see W.H.C. Frend, *The Rise of Christianity*
(Philadelphia: Fortress Press, 1984), 840.

[52] D.S. MS. Lat. 1664, fol. 95^r. "Fuerint haeretici, qui vocatis Apollonaristae, qui
praedicabant populo talem blasphemiam de Domino Ihesu Christo, dicentes qui Dominus factus homo non habuerit in sua carne anima rationalem, sicut omnes homines
habent, sed in loco animae rationale fuerit deitas eius, nec in corpore suo aliam
habuerit anima nisi solam deitatem." For Apollinaris, see Frend, *Rise of Christianity*, 634–
635.

past, which had been denounced by the fathers, in order to repudiate the possible errors of contemporaries who reject sane doctrine. Ademar wrote that whoever believes that God exists in only one person, and not in three, is a Sabellian heretic and not an orthodox Catholic.[53] The Sabellians, he explains, erred by emphasizing the essential unity of God at the expense of his triune nature, unlike the Arians, who emphasized the trinity at the expense of unity. The Arians, as Ademar states in his sermon on the Catholic faith, believed correctly that the godhead is made of three persons but were not content with three persons of one substance. They believed that God exists in three separate substances that are neither coequal nor coeternal.[54] Ademar also discusses the Macedonian heresy, which emerged at the time of the Emperor Theodosius I (378–395). These heretics believed in the Father and the Son just as Catholics did, but they denied that the Holy Spirit is equal to the other persons of the Trinity or of the same substance.[55] Ademar also refers to heretics from the time of St. Theophilus of Alexandria who spread their teaching to many people and plagued the church with "a diabolical fantasy" that God had the form of a man and that the Trinity existed in the from of three men, a belief that Ademar attacks vehemently because it makes God a sort of horrible giant.[56]

Ademar's concerns in the sermons are not limited to Christological and Trinitarian errors but include sacramental matters as well. Clearly at the core of Catholic Christianity in his day, the sacraments

---

[53] D.S. MS. Lat. 1664, fol. 84ʳ. "Ideo Deus neque confundentes personas, neque substantiam separantes. Sunt haeretici qui dicuntur non Catholici, sed Sabelliani qui credunt male, ut una sit tantum persona in Deo et non tres sicut est una persona in uno homine."

[54] D.S. MS. Lat. 1664, fol. 84ʳ. "Sunt haeretici Arriani qui bene credunt tres personas distinctas, sed non credunt unam substantiam et illis substantia separant. Et sic Sabelliani non dividunt tres personas, sed de tribus personis unam personam esse credunt; ita Arriani unam substantiam Dei separant in tres substantias... Et ita Arriani male credunt, ut Deus Pater de altera substantia sit et Filius Dei de altera et Spiritus Sanctus de altera."

[55] D.S. MS. Lat. 1664, fol. 86ʳ. "Congregavitque ipsum concilium propter illos haereticos alios qui sunt Macedoniani qui in Patre et Filio bene credunt, sicut et nos Catholici, sed non credunt in Spiritu Sancto, ut ipse sit Deus aequalis Patre et Filio et separant substantiam eius a substantia Patris et Filii."

[56] D.S. MS. Lat. 1664, fol. 92ᵛ. "In tempore, ergo, Sancti Theophili surrexerunt haeretici qui dicuntur antropomorfitae et coeperunt popolo praedicare quia Deus hominis forma haberet et Pater et Filius et Spiritus Sanctus simili figura essent quasi homines."

represented the operation of divine grace through material substances. Acceptance of the church's teaching on the sacraments was an essential sign of orthodoxy, and Ademar intended to confirm his own orthodoxy by his defense of the sacraments. At the same time, his concerns with the sacraments, including baptism, were likely inspired by their rejection by the heretics of Aquitaine. As noted in the *Chronicon*, the Manichaeans of Aquitaine "denied baptism" (*negantes baptismum*), and Ademar's commentary on baptism was intended to demonstrate the heretics' error.[57] Moreover, in one of the sermons from Theodulf's treatise on baptism Ademar denounces as heretics those who use the wrong type of chrism to administer the sacrament or who usurp the rite to perform the sacrament from the bishop.[58] Consequently, Ademar focused his attentions on the defense of baptism and condemnation of those who erred in the past on this sacrament, most notably the Arians. Indeed, just as they erred on theological matters, the Arians, according to Ademar, erred on sacramental matters. In the sermons of ms. 1664, Ademar comments on the errors of the Arians in the practice of baptism. Indeed, the Arians seem to represent all heretics who baptize improperly. The Arians, according to Ademar, pronounced the blessing incorrectly, thus rendering the rite worthless. Even more, they denied Catholic baptism in this way and therefore disturbed the church itself.[59] These ancient heretics denied true baptism and the true church and thus separate themselves from all true Christians and from the possibility of obtaining salvation.

Ademar understands that the heretics' failure to accept baptism isolates them from the church and that acceptance of the truth of baptism by the church makes it the faithful representative of Christ; the sacrament of baptism joined the believing Christian to the true church of Christ. In contrast to the baptism of the Arians, the Catholic Christian accepts the sacrament according to apostolic tradition as Jesus

---

[57] *Chronicon*, 3:49, p. 170.

[58] D.S. MS. Lat. 1664, fol. 69ʳ. "Hoc ideo memoramus quia sancta catholica ecclesia valde execratur haereticos qui, per quasdam regiones et provintias orbis, non curant conficere chrisma de balsamo." And fol. 69ᵛ, "Apud Romanos autem solis episcopi reservatum est quia in tanta multitudine presbiterorum haersis oriebatur et iste aliter ille aliter tantum sacramentum chrismate depravabat."

[59] D.S. MS. Lat. 1664, fol. 84ᵛ. "Arriani autem haeretici non sic baptizabant sed perverse ita baptizabant in nomine Patris per Filium in Spiritu Sancto et per talem baptismum haeretici eorum tota ecclesia per orientem erat turbata et habebat in se magna discordiam et omnes qui sic erant baptizati nullo modo poterant esse salvi."

intended. Ademar suggests that it is the very act of baptism that makes one a Christian, asserting that "by the name from the Lord Christ himself, we are called Christians, we who believe in Christ and receive the holy chrism of baptism."[60] Indeed, by the sacrament of baptism Christians repeat an event from the life of Christ himself. As Ademar explains, Jesus was anointed, made the Christ, by the Holy Spirit in the womb of the Virgin Mary.[61] It is this anointing of Christ that is repeated by all Christians at the baptismal font when they receive the chrism and are immersed in the water. At baptism, the material anointing with water and oil is accompanied by the spiritual consecration of the Holy Spirit. Although couched in conventional language, Ademar's defense of baptism demonstrates his engagement over the issue as the result of both historical and contemporary controversy concerning the sacrament.

The sacrament of the Eucharist receives similar treatment by Ademar as does the Creed and the cross. Indeed, the crucifix is of great importance to Ademar, and heretics from the history of the church and Ademar's own day attacked its veneration.[62] In his defense of the image during the discussion of the creed in the sermon De Eucharistia, Ademar's contemporary and historical concerns are most clearly merged. In this sermon, Ademar denounces the Manichaeans and explains that because Christ suffered crucifixion for us, the instrument of his death is a sign of victory over the devil has power over the devil and is adored by Christians.[63] He continues with a warning concerning heretics or ministers of the devil who blaspheme rather than adore the symbol and keep the devil in their hearts. These heretics, recalling the sectaries described in the Chronicon who reject the power of the cross, are Manichaeans; they teach that God does not wish the passion of the cross to be remembered because it is a symbol of the punishment of a criminal.[64] This was no sign of victory for the heretics, but a sign of

---

[60] D.S. MS. Lat. 1664, fol. 72ʳ, "Et ab eo nomine quo ipse Deus Christus nos appellamur Christiani qui in Christum credimus et chrismate sacro in baptismo." The idea is repeated at various points in the sermons, including fols. 68ᵛ, 69ʳ, and 79ʳ.

[61] D.S. MS. Lat. 1664, fol. 68ᵛ–69ʳ. "Sicut autem a chrismatis unctione appellabantur Christi, ita Dominus noster Ihesus Christus ab illo invisibili, hoc est Spiritu Sancto, a quo unctus sive consecratus est in utero virginies, nunc appellabatur proprie et singulariter Christus."

[62] Chronicon, 3:49, 170.

[63] D.S. MS. Lat. 1664, fol. 72ᵛ.

[64] D.S. MS. Lat. 1664, fol. 72ᵛ. "Observate, autem, vos haereticis diaboli ministris qui blasphemant, non adorii crucem, loquente diabolo in cordibus eorum. Non vult,

humiliation and suffering unworthy of God. Moreover, Ademar recognizes the seriousness of the rejection of this important Christian symbol by asserting that baptism, communion, and the whole church are sanctified and cleansed by the sign of the cross.[65] As he does throughout his sermons, Ademar once again draws from his not insubstantial knowledge of church history to denounce an error that is at once both a contemporary concern and an ancient problem.

Ademar's sermons thus provide the broader context necessary for ending the confusion he caused and for gaining a better understanding of his assertion that the heretics of Aquitaine were Manichaeans. At the very least, the common assumption that Ademar merely applied what he learned from Augustine to the sectaries of his own day can be challenged. Indeed, even if he identified the heretics as Manichaeans because of what he learned from Augustine, the sermons make clear that this was no simple choice. It should now be abundantly clear that Ademar had at least basic knowledge of a wide range of heretics from the history of the church as well as well-formed attitudes toward pagans, Jews, and Muslims. The author of two works of history and a copyist of the *Liber Pontificalis*, Ademar surely had a deep understanding of the history of the faith and the many dissidents who challenged the church's teaching of the faith. This knowledge was reinforced by the copy of Isidore of Seville's list of heresies and their beliefs. From this extensive list of heresies, Ademar obtained a basic introduction to a sizeable number of heresies from the church's past. He could have used any of Isidore's heresies to label contemporary sectaries if his sole intent were to demonize them by association with the church's ancient enemies or to distinguish himself from those holding unorthodox views. What the sermons in ms. 2469 and, especially, ms. 1664 demonstrate clearly is that Ademar adapted his knowledge of the ancient heresies to contemporary conditions. Just as he compared the ancient pagans to contemporary opponents of the apostolicity of St. Martial, he denounced ancient Arians, Macedonians, Sabellians, and others for various errors that contemporary heretics most likely held.

---

inquiunt, Deus meminisse crucem passionis suae sicut latra a patibulo suspendu eruptus, non vult ultra videre trocleas suspensionis suae. Ideo, iste loquitur diabolus per ministros vos haereticos, qui vocantur Manichei, quia in omni loco virtutem habet nisi ubi viderit signum crucis." *Chronicon*, 3:49, p. 170.

[65] D.S. MS. Lat. 1664, fol. 72ᵛ. "Baptismum, enim sacramentum altaris, et omnis ecclesia per signum crucis sanctificantur et muniuntur contra adversarias potestates."

His choice of the term Manichaean, therefore, must be seen in light of his general knowledge of heresy, and it must now be considered that he chose the term above all others specifically because it most suited the heretics who appeared in Aquitaine in the early eleventh century.

BOGOMIL INFLUENCES ON WESTERN HERESY

BERNARD HAMILTON

Bob Moore and I first met when I was taken ill in the middle of term in 1971 and with characteristic kindness Bob drove down to Nottingham from Sheffield each week and taught my Special Subject class on the Cathars in addition to his own academic commitments. He was then collecting material for *The Origins of European Dissent* and when discussing this we found that we radically disagreed about the authenticity of the Saint-Félix document. As the first edition of his book came out in 1977 while my article on the subject was still in press, he included an Appendix by me in which I briefly set out my reasons for supposing this document was a genuine source.[1]

Bob has a naturally skeptical turn of mind, and as people in the Middle Ages were aware, this can be a valuable stimulus to investigating truth more fully; Gregory the Great once said that the doubt of St. Thomas about Christ's resurrection was of more value to future believers than the faith of the other Apostles. Certainly Bob's critical approach to received opinion, and to the slender basis of evidence on which it rests, has made all of us working in the field of Cathar studies look more carefully at the sources, and this has been very beneficial to scholarship.

I think it is fair to say that since 1977 Bob and I have diverged in our views about the origins of Catharism. I have become more convinced that Western Catharism was a branch of Balkan and Byzantine dualism, while Bob has increasingly come to hold a minimalist view of the importance of the Balkan and Byzantine links and has also come to question whether the Cathar movement can in any meaningful sense be described as an organized Church. In this paper, I want to look again at the evidence for Balkan influence on Catharism, which itself has a bearing on how the Cathars perceived their own role in Christian history.

---

[1] I examined the evidence in more detail in "The Cathar Council of Saint-Félix reconsidered," *Archivum Fratrum Praedicatorum* (henceforth *AFP*) 48 (1978): 23–53.

The Eleventh Century

Bob always regarded as implausible the traditional view (which found classic expression in Steven Runciman's *The Medieval Manichee*), that the outbreaks of heresy in Western Europe in the late tenth and early eleventh centuries were offshoots of Bogomilism. In the last twenty-five years his view, that eleventh-century dissent was the product of indigenous Western reform movements, has become the new orthodoxy.[2] This view has the merit of satisfactorily explaining why these heterodox Western groups died out in the 1050s at precisely the point when the papacy took the lead in implementing a program of radical church reform, and why a new wave of dissent began in the first half of the twelfth century after papal reformers had reached a compromise with the secular establishment and their program had lost its vitality. Yet such an interpretation is not without problems.

Those who hold this view point out quite justly that when contemporary writers like Ademar of Chabannes and Rodulfus Glaber assert that Manichees were present in early eleventh-century France they cannot be taken literally. Manichaeism seems to have died out in the Mediterranean world by the end of the sixth century, although it survived in central Asia and China into the late Middle Ages.[3] When medieval writers in the Western or Byzantine worlds describe their contemporaries as Manichaeans, they are referring to groups which Obolensky called "neo-Manichaeans," but which I think Runciman more accurately described as Christian dualists.[4] These groups differed from each other in some matters of doctrine, but they all identified themselves as

---

[2] S. Runciman, *The Medieval Manichee. A Study of the Christian Dualist Heresy* (Cambridge: University of Cambridge University Press, 1947); R.I. Moore, *The Origins of European Dissent*, 1st ed. (London: Allen Lane, 1977), 23–45. The impact of the new approach is seen in the work of Malcolm Lambert, who in his second edition of *Medieval Heresy* (Oxford: Blackwell, 1992) writes: "I used to believe that the Byzantine dualist heresy of Bogomilism began to touch the West in [the eleventh century]. Fresh work...has caused me to retreat from that view." p. xiii; and in his more recent study, *The Cathars* (Oxford: Blackwell, 1998), he argues in more detail that dualist movements first appeared in the West in the twelfth century.

[3] S. Lieu, *Manichaesim in the Later Roman Empire and Medieval China, a Historical Survey* (Manchester: Manchester University Press, 1985). It is possible that William of Rubruck encountered Manichaean communities on his travels to the court of the Great Khan in 1253–1255, but did not recognize them, P. Jackson, "William of Rubruck in the Mongol Empire, Perception and Prejudices," in Z. von Martels, ed., *Travel Fact and Travel Fiction* (Leiden: E.J. Brill, 1994), 66–71.

[4] D. Obolensky, *The Bogomils: A Study in Balkan neo-Manichaeism* (Cambridge: Univer-

Christian, based their teachings on the canonical books of the New Testament and interpreted the Christian faith in a dualistic sense. Although they gave different explanations of why this was so, all Christian dualists agreed that the Good God had not created the phenomenal world in the form in which it now exists. It was this doctrine, which they shared with the followers of Mani, that led medieval theologians to label them Manichaeans.

The critics of the traditional view of eleventh-century heresy explain references to Manichees in contemporary sources by asserting that those writers used a technical theological vocabulary in an imprecise way. They argue that men like Ademar of Chabannes were simply applying the name Manichee, which they knew from the writings of St. Augustine of Hippo, to describe what they thought was a serious heresy, without considering whether the label was relevant to the teachings of the groups whom they were denouncing. This interpretation ignores one salient fact: that educated churchmen thought it important to diagnose heresies correctly. Bob Moore has frequently, and justly, pointed out the way in which medieval Catholic writers equated heresy and disease; yet it must follow from this that they considered it of vital importance to identify particular cases of heretical contagion correctly, since if they were wrongly diagnosed they could not be effectively treated. For this reason I think one should assume that when educated churchmen labeled a movement "Manichaean," they did so because it approximated to what they understood Manichaean beliefs to be like. The central tenet of the true Manichaeans, described by patristic writers like Augustine, and also of medieval Christian dualists, was that the material creation was not the work of the Good God.

If there really were Manichees in France in the early eleventh century, they must have been Christian dualists and were probably Bogomils. There is no evidence of Christian dualist thought in Western Europe in the early medieval centuries, but a new, popular dualist Christian movement had been initiated in Bulgaria in the reign of Tsar Peter (927–969) by the *pop* Bogomil.[5] If Ockham's razor is applied to this synchronicity, it seems highly probable that the West-

<hr />

sity Press, 1948). Christianity was first interpreted in a dualist sense by Constantine of Mananalis, an Armenian who lived in the reign of Constans II (641–668).

[5] *The Discourse of the Priest Cosmas against the Bogomils*, tr. Y. Stoyanov, in J. Hamilton and B. Hamilton, *Christian Dualist Heresies in the Byzantine World, c. 650–1450* (Manchester: Manchester University Press, 1998), 116.

ern "Manichees" had been influenced by the new Balkan dualist movement. Bob would no doubt object to this, noting that Ockham said: "Entia non sunt multiplicanda praeter necessitatem", and that in this case there is a necessity because there is no evidence of a Bogomil presence in France, or even in Western Europe at that time. The Byzantine monk, Euthymius of the Periblepton monastery, however, writing in c. 1045, reports that Bogomilism spread into the Greek-speaking Byzantine world by penetrating the monasteries; he found a group of Bogomil monks in his own community, which had been newly founded by the emperor Romanus III in 1030.[6] An unprecedentedly large number of Byzantine clergy, particularly monks, visited Western Europe in the late tenth and early eleventh centuries, and any Bogomils who came to the West at that time would not merely have looked like Orthodox monks, they would have been professed as Orthodox monks.[7] The lack of Bogomil sightings in Western Europe is therefore not in itself conclusive.

Some of the explanations which have been advanced to explain eleventh-century heretical movements in an entirely Western context seem to me far-fetched. An example of this may be seen in recent work on the heretics of Monforte, arrested in 1028 by Archbishop Aribert of Milan, which Malcolm Lambert has quite fairly summarized in this way:

> The phrases [used by the group to describe their faith] are reminiscent of Eriguena's commentary on St. John's Gospel, where he uses a mode of discussion of the doctrine of the Trinity based on analogies rather than on definitions, and there are echoes in Gerard's replies of Eriguena's double similitudes.[8]

Since the heretics of Monforte appear to have been all lay people, it is difficult to accept that they had succeeded in finding texts of Eriguena's work, or, even if they had done so, in reading his difficult Latin, or in understanding his Neoplatonist speculations. That kind of learned but eccentric interpretation of the Christian faith must have

---

[6] "Letter of Euthymius, monk of the monastery of the Periblepton," tr. in Hamilton and Hamilton, *Christian Dualist Heresies*, pp. 142–164.

[7] I have drawn attention to the presence of Byzantine monks in the West in the century 950–1050 in an article I wrote with P.A. McNulty, "*Orientale lumen et magistra latinitas*: Greek influences on Western Monasticism, 900–1100," in *Le Millénaire du Mont Athos, 963–1963. Études et Mélanges*, I (Chevetogne: Éditions de Chevetogne, 1963), 181–216. Paul Magdalino has told me how unusual this Byzantine interest in the West was.

[8] Lambert, *Medieval Heresy*, 18.

been mediated to them by a scholar trained in theology. He would have been more likely to have received that training in the Byzantine world where Neoplatonism remained a living tradition than in early eleventh-century Western Europe. It seems rash to assert that because the materials for heretical thought were availiable in Western Europe in the eleventh century they were therefore usable by any dissident group.

I would, however, agree with those scholars who say that there is no basis in the evidence that we have to consider the heretics of Monforte dualists, even though I do not find the alternative explanation they offer very convincing. There seems a determination on the part of some scholars to refuse to accept that any of the eleventh-century movements could have been influenced by dualism. The most egregious example of this is their reaction to the discovery of an eleventh-century exemplar of the Letter of Heribert of Périgord. Bob reflected the general scholarly consensus when he said of this letter in 1985 that: "Such scraps of information [as the letter contains] can hardly be alleged to amount to a systematic or irrefutable record of the appearance of Catharism in the Midi, but they do reflect... a more direct similarity to Bogomil belief and practice than had been noted in the region before."[9] He wrote this when the letter was thought to date from the 1140s, and his views were uncontroversial, but now that an early eleventh-century exemplar has been found, some scholars have sought to explain away the similarities between Catharism and Bogomilism and the heresy which it describes.[10] This does seem to me to reopen the whole question of a dualist, and almost certainly Bogomil, presence in early eleventh-century Aquitaine, as does Michael Frassetto's recent work on the sermons of Ademar of Chabannes.[11]

---

[9] Moore, *The Origins of European Dissent*, rev ed (Oxford: Basil Blackwell, 1985), 198.

[10] G. Lobrichon, "The Chiaroscuro of Heresy: Early Eleventh-Century Aquitaine as seen from Auxerre," and "The Latin texts of the 'Letter' of Heribert," in T. Head and R. Landes, eds., *The Peace of God: Social Violence and Religious Response in France Around the Year 1000* (Ithaca and London: Cornell University Press, 1992), 80–103, 347–350. See the critique of C. Taylor, "The letter of Heribert of Périgord as a source for dualist heresy in the society of early eleventh-century Aquitaine," *Journal of Medieval History*, 26 (2000): 313–349.

[11] M. Frassetto, "The Sermons of Ademar of Chabannes and the Letter of Heribert: New Sources Concerning the Origins of Medieval Heresy," *Revue Bénédictine*, 109 (1999): 324–340; "The Writings of Ademar of Chabannes, the Peace of 994, and the 'Terrors of the Year 1000,'" *Journal of Medieval History*, 27 (2001): 241–255.

But I would not wish to support the traditional view that all the heresies found in Western Europe from 1000–1050 were manifestations of dualism. I am coming to think that a whole range of Byzantine influences might have entered the West through the well attested and numerous monastic visitors and that not all of them were heterodox. I think it is possible, for example, that the canons of Orleans, burnt at the stake in 1022, had been influenced by the teachings of St. Symeon the New Theologian, although they had not shared his intention to work strictly within the Orthodox tradition.[12] Nevertheless, it would, in my view, be unnecessarily dogmatic to rule out the possibility of Bogomil influences in the West in the early eleventh century; indeed, to do so would be to produce a mirror image of the traditional view that all dissident outbreaks in that period were products of Bogomilism.

One further point needs to be remembered when considering eleventh-century evidence about heresy: if Bogomils were at work in the West at that time their teaching would have looked rather different from that of the Bogomils who influenced the Cathars in the twelfth century. The Bogomils described in Old Slavonic and Byzantine sources for the period c. 950–1050 had no formal organization and were only beginning to use a set liturgy at the end of that time. The hierarchy and rituals associated with twelfth-century Catharism would not therefore have been found among Western dissident groups influenced by Bogomilism in the eleventh century.

There were virtually no reports of dissident movements in the West in the second half of the eleventh century. In so far as these had been inspired by Eastern influences, this break is explicable in terms of the political conditions in southern Italy, where the Norman wars disrupted the normal pilgrim routes from Byzantium to the West, which ran along the Via Egnatia to the ports of Apulia and thence to Rome. I doubt whether the formal breach between Rome and Constantinople in 1054 was of great importance in this regard; it seems to me to have had political and diplomatic rather than religious consequences.

Bob's skepticism about the traditional, monolithic view of eleventh-century Western heresy has proved fruitful, because it has helped to make all of us working in this field look again at the evidence, and as a result of this a more nuanced picture is beginning to emerge.

---

[12] My wife, J. Hamilton, and I read a paper on "St. Symeon the New Theologian and Western dissident movements," to the XXe Congrès international des Études byzantines, held in Paris from 19–25 August 2001, which we intend to publish.

The Coming of the Cathars

Although Charles Schmidt thought that the dissident groups of the early eleventh century, driven underground by persecution, surfaced again in the Cathar movement of the twelfth century, few if any modern scholars would now defend this view.[13] The early years of the twelfth century were a period of religious ferment in Western Europe. Dynamic leaders, who wished to promote church reforms attracted large followings; some of them, like Bernard of Tiron, succeeded in working in harmony with the ecclesiastical authorities, but many of them came into conflict with bishops and seceded from the Church. Bob has shed much light on the activities of this group, particularly on the career of Henry of Le Mans.[14] Yet with the exception of that founded by Peter Valdès of Lyons, these new groups lacked organization and did not long outlast the deaths of their founders. A different kind of movement grew up during this time which proved far more resilient, that of Catharism.

Cathars are referred to in the sources in a variety of names. Cathars is in origin a Greek word, καθαροι. It was first applied to Western heretics in 1163 by Egbert of Schonau who had examined a group of them at Cologne. He wrote a set of sermons against them and was influenced in his description by what St. Augustine had said of the Manichaeans in the late Roman Empire, but was not influenced by Augustine in his choice of name for them. Augustine did not describe the Manichaeans as καθαροι, and Byzantine writers did not describe the Bogomils in that way either. In the Orthodox Church the name καθαροι referred to the Novatians, condemned by the First Council of Nicaea in 325 as schismatics, but unswerving in their adherence to the Catholic faith in a form which had been professed in Rome in c. 200 A.D.[15] Henri Grégoire pointed out that the Novatians and the Cathars both called themselves by the same Greek name, but no direct connection between them has ever been established. It is probable

---

[13] C. Schmidt, *Histoire et doctrine de la secte des Cathares ou Albigeois*, 2 vols. (Paris, Geneva, 1848–1849), vol. 1, pp. 53–54.

[14] On orthodox holy men and their impact see the unpublished Ph.D. thesis of J.M.B. Porter, "*Compelle intrare*. Monastic reform movements in twelfth-century northwestern Europe" (Nottingham, 1997). On heterodox leaders, R.I. Moore, "New Sects and Secret Meetings: Association and Authority in the Eleventh and Twelfth Centuries," in W.J. Sheils, ed., *Studies in Church History*, 23 (Oxford: B. Blackwell, 1986), 47–68.

[15] G.D. Mansi, *Sacrorum Conciliorum nova et amplissima collectio* (Florence, Paris, Venice, 1759–1927), III, p. 671.

that both groups used this name because they both claimed to hold
the Christian faith in its pure form.[16] Although Catholic theologians
frequently used this name to describe dualist heretics, it is most unlikely
that they invented it; it seems probable that the first generation of
dissidents, who had direct links with the Byzantine world, used it of
themselves. Certainly the heretical bishop and his companion, who
were examined and burnt at Cologne in 1143, were conscious of their
Byzantine roots, claiming that "this heresy has lain concealed from the
time of the martyrs even to our own day, and has persisted thus in
Greece and certain other lands."[17]

Throughout France the Cathars were popularly described as Bulgar-
ians. William of Tudela, at the beginning of the *Chanson de la Croisade
Albigeoise* (written, 1210–1213), describes a debate between the papal
legates and the Cathar leaders:

> Si que l'avesques d'Osma ne tenc cort aramia,
> E li autre legat, ab cels de Bolgaria,
> Lai dins e Carcassona, on mota gent avia,
> Que'l reis d'Arago y era ab sa gran baronia.[18]

In northern France the popular name for Cathars was *Bougres*, Bulgar-
ians, which became a term of abuse, passing into English as bugger,
because the Cathar perfects were each assigned a companion of the
same sex, and this led some of their opponents to make ribald comments.

In Italy, Dalmatia, and Bosnia, the Cathars were usually called Patarenes. This name had originally been given to the popular pro-papal
reform movement in eleventh-century Milan, whose members supported the archbishop appointed by Pope Gregory VII against the aristocratic candidate nominated by Henry IV. In the second half of the

---

[16] H. Grégoire, "Cathares d'Asie Mineure, d'Italie et de la France," *Archives de l'Orient
chrétien* 1 (1948): 142–151. Alan of Lille did not know what the word Cathar meant and
derived it from *cattus*, the Latin form of the German name for *felis domesticus*, claiming
that the Cathars worshipped Satan in the form of a cat. *De fide Catholica contra haereticos
sui temporis*, Bk. I, chap. 63, in J.P. Migne, *Patrologia Latina* [henceforth *PL*] 210, col.
366. No scholar except Duvernoy has taken this suggestion seriously because there
is no corroborative evidence in any other source: J. Duvernoy, *La Religion des Cathares*
(Toulouse: Privat, 1976), 302–304.

[17] Eberwin of Steinfeld, *Epistola ad S. Bernardum*, *PL*, 182, col. 679. I cite the translation of W.L. Wakefield and A.P. Evans, *Heresies of the High Middle Ages* (New York and
London: Columbia University Press, 1969), 132.

[18] *La Chanson de la Croisade Albigeoise*, ed. and tr. E. Martin-Chabot, 3 vols., 2nd ed.
(Paris: Société d'édition "Les Belles lettres," 1960), vol. 1, pp. 9–10.

twelfth century the name was applied to the Italian Cathars, as well as to those in the cities of the Dalmatian coast and those of Bosnia. The origin of this name is uncertain; some scholars have argued that it means people dressed in rags (an exact equivalent of the English word "the rag-tag") while others think that it has a Greek root.[19]

Occasionally groups of Western heretics in the twelfth century were called *publicani* or *populicani*. Although *publicani* normally meant tax-collectors to Western readers (the group of men singled out in the Gospels as the most notorious sinners), when applied to dissident groups it was an attempt to render the Greek word *Paulikianoi*, or Paulicians. These members of a dualist sect which antedated the Bogomils were well regarded as fighting-men and at the time of the First Crusade contingents of them served both in the Byzantine and north Syrian Muslim armies. The crusaders were aware of this sect because its members had a deeply rooted antipathy to the cross, which the crusaders, of course, wore on their clothing and held in great veneration.[20] Consequently, the word became part of Western vocabulary. There is no evidence that by the twelfth century the Paulicians were interested in making converts, and the references to *publicani* in western Europe should not be taken as referring to Paulicians, for whose presence there is no other evidence whatsoever.[21] In the course of the twelfth century the word came to mean "Eastern heretic." Thus the Old French translator of William of Tyre, writing in the early thirteenth century, describes the founder of the Maronite Church as "uns popeliquans qui avoit non Marons," but it could be used about Cathars and sometimes was.[22]

From 1184, when Pope Lucius III published the decree *Ad abolendam*, the names Cathar and Patarene were used interchangeably by the Catholic authorities to describe dualist heretics.[23] Yet except perhaps in their very early years these dissenters did not refer to themselves as Cathars. In the Languedoc the initiated members of their movement called themselves "good men" and "good women" and were often referred to as "the perfect." Yet these terms all mean the same as

---

[19] Wakefield and Evans, *Heresies of the High Middle Ages*, 701–702, n. 3.

[20] For instances of crusader encounters with Paulicians, N. Garsoian, *The Paulician Heresy* (The Hague: Mouton, 1967), 14–16.

[21] Hamilton and Hamilton, *Christian Dualist Heresies*, 22–25.

[22] *L'Estoire de Eracles empereur et la conqueste de la terre d'Outremer*, Bk 22, chap. 7, ed. P. Paris, *Guillaume de Tyr et ses continuateurs: texte français du XIIIe siècle*, 2 vols. (Paris: Firmin Didot, 1879–1880), vol. 1, p. 420.

[23] Text in Mansi, *Concilia*, 22, pp. 476–478.

Cathar, and refer to those who considered themselves to be practicing Christianity in its true form. Despite the variety of names by which they were known, these dissidents can be identified as part of a single religious movement because they all practiced their faith in the same way. I will consider this point further later in this article.

The names given to Western dualists show that they were perceived as coming from the Greek lands of Byzantium or from Bulgaria. The possible exception is the name Patarene, yet the Patarenes were the one group of Western dualists whose links with the Byzantine world are well documented. How far can this popular perception of Eastern origins be substantiated?

The Cathars do not seem to have been very interested in their own history. Moneta di Cremona, the learned Dominican whose treatise *Adversus Catharos et Valdenses* is the most detailed contemporary study of the movement, devotes a section of his work to Cathar origins, but had not been able to find out a great deal about them. The Cathars, he tells us, refused to accept the authority of the pope, saying that the church in Rome which Sts. Peter and Paul had founded had been destroyed in the age of persecution, and that the popes were the successors not of Peter but of Constantine the Great, who had given the western lands to Pope Sylvester I. Beyond that, Moneta had to fall back on giving a pedigree of the Cathars' religious beliefs, which they had drawn, he asserted, from Pythagoras the Greek, the Jewish Sadducees, the false teacher Mani, the heretic Tatian, and the Gnostic Valentinian.[24]

Evidence about how Catharism reached Western Europe is sparse. The Cathars were, of course, aware of recent history: those who were brought to trial at Oxford in Henry II's reign knew that they had come from Flanders or the Rhineland.[25] No Cathar community in Western Europe claimed an apostolic foundation, or even one dating from the early Christian centuries. Only the Cathars cross-examined at Cologne in 1143 claimed continuity with the church of the martyrs, and they traced their origins to the Byzantine world.

Unlike other Cathars, those of north and central Italy were very aware of and interested in their roots. This was because of schisms

---

[24] Moneta di Cremona, *Adversus Catharos et Valdenses libri quinque*, V, ii, 1, 2, ed. T.A. Ricchini (Rome: Ex Typographa Palladis, excudebant N. and M. Palearini, 1743), pp. 410–411.
[25] William of Newburgh, *Historia rerum anglicarum*, I, 13, ed. R. Howlett, Rolls Series, 82 (I) (London: Longman, 1884), pp. 131–134.

which at an early date split the Cathar church there, causing the perfect to seek assurance about the validity of their own spiritual line
of descent. That was what Cathars termed an *ordo*. It resembled the
Catholic doctrine of apostolic succession, and had the same function,
that of linking the contemporary church to the Apostles through an
unbroken chain of sacramental acts. The anonymous *De heresi Catharorum in Lombardia*, written soon after 1200, describes how the first Lombard Cathar bishop, Mark, had been consecrated in the *ordo* of Bulgaria, but had subsequently been persuaded by papa Nicheta of Constantinople to accept instead consecration in the *ordo* of Drugunthia.
After Mark's death, Petracius, a representative of the Bulgarian *ordo*,
came to Lombardy and persuaded some of the Cathars to return to
his sect. The long-term consequence of this was that the Lombard
Cathars became divided into three main groups, all of whom traced
their descent from Balkan and Byzantine communities:

> Bishop Garattus, ordained in Bulgaria, holds the see of Concorrezo...
> Bishop Caloiohannes of Mantua was ordained in Sclavonia [Bosnia/Dal-
> matia] ...Marchisius of Soiana is a bishop of the *ordo* of Drugunthia.[26]

This story is broadly confirmed by the account of the inquisitor, Anselm
of Alessandria, written in c. 1266/7. This is based on knowledge gained
during his examination of Cathars, and is independent of the *De heresi*,
which it contradicts in some points of detail. Anselm, for example,
calls papa Nicheta of the *ordo* of Drugunthia "episcopus...illorum de
Constantinopolim." He also reports that Bishop Mark received his
Bulgarian ordination from the Bishop of Francia (meaning northern
France), who was then living in Italy.[27]

There is no secure evidence about how or when Catharism first
reached northern France. Anselm of Alessandria, who was unusual
among inquisitors in being interested in Cathar history, wrote in
c. 1266:

> ...Frenchmen went to Constantinople to conquer land and found this
> sect [of Cathars] there, and, growing in number, they appointed a bishop
> who is called Bishop of the Latins...Later on (*postea*) the Frenchmen who
> had gone to Constantinople returned to their own land and preached,
> and growing in number appointed a Bishop of Francia. And because the

---

[26] *De heresi catharorum in Lombardi*, ed. A. Dondaine, "La hiérarchie cathare en Italie.
I.", *AFP* 19 (1949): 280–312 (citation, p. 312).
[27] Anselm of Alessandria, *Tractatus de hereticis*, ed. A. Dondaine, "La hiérarchie cathare. II.", *AFP* 20 (1950): 308–324.

Franks were first led into error in Constantinople by Bulgars, they call the heretics Bulgars throughout the whole of [northern] France.[28]

If this report is true, then the first western Cathar congregation to be founded would have been that of the Latins of Constantinople, listed as one of the sixteen Cathar churches by Rainier Sacconi writing in c. 1250. Anselm cannot be referring in this passage to the Fourth Crusade, because in his narrative the event described precedes other events, which, according to him, took place in 1174. I have argued elsewhere that Anselm is almost certainly talking about the First Crusade, whose armies met up in Constantinople in 1097 on their way to conquer the Holy Land. Anselm's claim that the members of this church were responsible for the initial introduction of Catharism into Western Europe is persuasive, because preachers trained in the Latin Church of Constantinople would have had no problems of communication as they were Westerners themselves. That would also explain why no exotic Bogomil preachers are reported as at work in the West during the first half of the twelfth century.[29]

It is not known how Catharism first reached Languedoc, though it is usually assumed that it did so from northern France. The Saint-Félix document asserts that Papa Niquinta (a variant phonetic spelling of Nicheta) presided at a council there in c. 1170 attended by Bishop Mark of Lombardy, Robert de Spernone, bishop of northern France, and Sicard Cellarier, bishop of Albi together with many Cathar perfect. If this source is accepted as authentic, it provides evidence that Papa Nicheta of Constantinople persuaded the Cathars of northern and southern France as well as those of Lombardy to accept ordination in his *ordo* of Drugunthia. Some scholars are skeptical about the authenticity of this text, chiefly because it is known only in what purports to be a thirteenth-century copy printed by Guillaume Besse in 1660. The manuscript that Besse used has never been seen since, and we only have his word for it that it ever existed. This case is very similar to that of the text of *The Fight at Finnesburg*, a fragment of an Old English

---

[28] Ibid., 308. The passage about Frenchmen going to Constantinople to conquer land cannot refer to the Fourth Crusade, since in Anslem's narrative it precedes events which he dates to 1174. It probably relates to the First Crusade, which assembled at Constantinople in order to conquer the Holy Land.

[29] Rainier Sacconi, *Summa de Catharis et Pauperibus de Lugduno*, ed. F. Sanjek, *AFP* 44 (1974): 50. I have discussed this possibility in "Wisdom from the East: The Reception of by the Cathars of Eastern Dualist Texts," in P. Biller and A. Hudson, eds., *Heresy and Literacy, 1000–1530* (Cambridge: Cambridge University Press, 1994), 44–46.

epic which is referred to in *Beowulf*. George Hickes, a non-juring clergyman, claimed to have found this fragment among the Anglo-Saxon
manuscripts in Lambeth Palace Library, and it was printed in 1705, but
the original has never been seen since. Hickes's text is now generally,
though not universally, accepted as authentic. I have nothing further
to add to what I have already written about the authenticity of the
Saint-Félix document. It is possible that the text that Besse published
had been forged in the thirteenth century, though I have never seen
any adequate explanation about why such a forgery would have been
necessary then; but I do not consider that it could have been forged
by Besse, because the document only makes sense if read with the
knowledge of Catharism which has only been made available through
the scholarship of the past fifty years. The quality of knowledge about
Catharism that the document displays was not available to a forger
in Besse's day. I therefore still maintain that this is a copy of a genuine twelfth-century document, and that it is proof of Byzantine dualist influence at work in the establishment of the Cathar churches of
Languedoc.[30]

Although in the twelfth century the Cathars became divided about
which *ordo* was valid, they all practiced their faith in the same way.
Their own writings, the works of Catholic polemicists and records of
Inquisition interrogation are all in agreement about what that practice
was. The central act in a Cathar's life, from which all other observances followed, was the reception of the *consolamentum*, baptism in the
Holy Spirit through the laying-on of hands. Those who received this
sacrament became full members of the Cathar church and were known
as the perfect, while sympathizers, who had not been consoled, were
known as *credentes*, or believers, and were not bound by the austere rules
of Cathar observance. The liturgy of the *consolamentum* is preserved in
two versions of the Cathar *Ritual*, one written in Occitan, the other, of
which only a fragment survives, in Latin. Although Christine Thouzellier, in her edition of the fragmentary Latin *Ritual*, argued that the text
was derived entirely from Western sources, Duvernoy pointed out that
she was only able to prove this in regard to the Gloss on the Lord's

---

[30] The Saint-Félix document is printed in G. Besse, *Histoire des ducs, marquis et comtes
de Narbonne...* (Paris: A. de Sommaville, 1660), 483–486. For my own views about this
see n. 1 above. Details of recent writing about it are given by M. Pegg, "On Cathars,
Albigenses and good men of Languedoc," *Journal of Medieval History* 27 (2001): 187–188
and n. 14. On the Fight of Finnesburg, see J.R.R. Tolkien, ed. A. Bliss, *Finn and Hengest.
The Fragment and the Episode* (London: Houghton Mifflin, 1982).

Prayer, which is a part of the service which the presiding minister was allowed to extemporize.[31] No rite of this kind is known to have been used in Western Europe before the Cathars appeared there, whereas the Byzantine Bogomils had an initiation rite in the early twelfth century that closely resembled the Cathar *consolamentum*, so it seems very likely that the Cathars received their *Ritual* from the Bogomils.[32] This cannot be affirmed with complete certainty because no text of the Bogomil *Ritual* is known, apart from that made in fifteenth-century Bosnia for Radoslav "the Christian." This contains an Old Slavonic version of the form of liturgical prayer with which the Provençal *Ritual* opens, but that is not in itself helpful because Radoslav's *Ritual* may have been translated from a Western exemplar.[33] Nevertheless, it seems likely that the Cathars who derived their power to confer the *consolamentum* from the Bogomil *ordines* of Bulgaria, Drugunthia, and Bosnia also received from them the service-book that they all used.

Unlike the Orthodox church of Byzantium and the Catholic church of the West, Bogomils and Cathars had no creed. The most succinct account of Cathar beliefs is that written in the mid-thirteenth century, when the movement was well established, by the Inquisitor for Lombardy, Rainier Sacconi. He was in a position to be well informed because he had been a Cathar minister for seventeen years before being converted to Catholicism. His account can be controlled by the Cathars' own writings as an epitome of their doctrines: Sacconi's account is accurate though incomplete, though it affords no insight into their spirituality.[34] In Sacconi's day there were deep divisions among the Cathars, and although these had probably originated over the question of the validity of the *consolamentum* conferred within particular *ordines*, the groups also differed about matters of belief. Sacconi lists the Cathar churches of East and West—he made no distinction between

---

[31] *Rituel Cathare*, ed. C. Thouzellier, Sources Chrétiennes, 236 (Paris: Éditions du Cerf, 1977), 182–184; Duvernoy, *La religion des Cathares*, "Addition au chapitre 'Le baptême'," unnumbered pages at the end of the book.

[32] Euthymius Zigabenus, *Against the Bogomils*, chap. 16, trans. in Hamilton and Hamilton, *Christian Dualist Heresies*, 189–190.

[33] Christine Thouzellier gives the Old Slavonic text with a French translation in the tables at the end of her edition of the *Rituel Cathare* and discusses the manuscript on pp. 63–70.

[34] I have examined the evidence for Cathar spirituality in "The Cathars and Christian Perfection," in P. Biller and B. Dobson, eds., *The Medieval Church: Universities, Heresy, and the Religious Life. Essays in Honour of Gordon Leff*, Studies in Church History, Subsidia, 11 (Woodbridge: Boydell, 1999), 5–23.

Cathars and Bogomils—and concludes: "The Church of Bulgaria. The Church of Druguuithie. They all trace their origin from the last two named."[35]

The church of Bulgaria was a moderate dualist church whose members believed in one God who had created Heaven and the angels, including Lucifer who had then either created the physical universe or fashioned it from the four elements that God had created. Sacconi relates that the moderate dualists among the Western Cathars interpreted the Christian faith as set out in the New Testament in a cosmological context identical to that used by the Byzantine Bogomils in c. 1100 described by Euthymius Zigabenus.[36] In Sacconi's day the majority of Italian Cathars, together with the Cathars of northern France who were living in exile in Italy, were moderate dualists.

Like the Bogomils the moderate dualists rejected the historical books of the Old Testament, and this presented them with a theological dilemma. Since they believed that the world in which they lived had been brought into being by an evil demiurge, who had inspired the book of Genesis in which he falsely claimed to be the true God, they had to explain why human souls were part of the creation of the Good God and therefore needed liberating from material bodies. It would otherwise have been logical to suppose that the demiurge had made men's souls as well as their bodies, yet if that had been so the Cathar faith would have had no raison d'être. They therefore used apocryphal works, attributed to biblical figures, which gave accounts of how the comsos had come to be as the Cathars described it. The Cathars learned to do this from the Bogomils, who had built up a literature of Christian mythology, derived chiefly from early Christian Gnostic works preserved in Byzantine libraries, which they had copied and sometimes altered to meet their needs.[37]

Among the texts that they obtained from the Bogomils was the *Vision of Isaiah*, a Greek Gnostic text of the first century A.D., which presented a cosmic view of the creation that was in conformity with dualist beliefs. The Cathars did not use the partial Latin translation made in late antiquity, but commissioned a new Latin translation from

---

[35] Sacconi, *AFP* 44 (1978), 50.

[36] Euthymius Zigabenus, *Against the Bogomils*, tr. Hamilton and Hamilton, *Christian Dualist Heresies*, 180–207.

[37] J. Ivanov, *Livres et légendes bogomiles*, trans. M. Ribeyrol (Paris: Maisonneuve et Larose, 1976); Y. Stoyanov, *The Other God. Dualist Religions from Antiquity to the Cathar Heresy* (New Haven and London: Yale University Press, 2000), 157–158, 260–274.

the Old Slavonic text, a version which the Bogomils had amended to
conform with their own teachings.[38]

The moderate dualist Cathars also had a Latin translation made of
the *Secret Book of St. John*, which the Bogomils had written. It is cast in
the form of a dialogue between Christ and St. John at the Last Supper
in which Christ reveals to the Apostle the truth about the creation of
the universe and the ongoing struggle between the powers of good and
evil. The Inquisition copy of this text preserved at Carcassonne has this
colophon:

> Here endeth the *Secret* of the heretics of Concorezzo, brought from
> Bulgaria by Nazarius their bishop. It is full of errors.[39]

The Cathars of Concorezzo formed the largest moderate dualist church
in Lombardy.

The Cathar source that has been most neglected by scholars is the
New Testament in Occitan translation. This has been available in litho-
graphic reproduction since 1887, yet it has not been transcribed, translated, or, to any significant extent, commented upon.[40] M.R. Harris has
rightly pointed out that the New Testament texts used by the Cathars
in their other writings should be collated with the Lyons text to see
whether there are specific variant readings that diverge from the Vul-
gate text but which all Cathars use. He described this objective as trying
to discover whether the Cathars had their own "authorized version" of
the Bible. Stuart Westley, acting on this suggestion, made some preliminary soundings in this field, which suggest that the Cathars may indeed
have preferred certain variants, but much more work needs to be done
on this before any firm conclusions can be reached. Such a project
might help elucidate whether the Cathar text of the New Testament
was dependent in any significant way on Byzantine or Old Slavonic
biblical manuscripts.[41]

---

[38] The medieval Latin version exists only in a text printed at Venice in 1522 by Anto-
nio de Fantis and reprinted by A. Dillmann, *Ascensio Isaiae Aethiopice et Latine* (Leipzig:
F.A. Brockhaus, 1877), 76–83. It was read by the moderate dualists of Lombardy, Moneta di Cremona, II, ix, 4, ed. Ricchini, p. 218. For the full edition of the texts in all
versions: R.H. Charles, *The Ascension of Isaiah* (London: Adam and Charles Black, 1900).

[39] *Le Livre secret des Cathares, Interrogatio Iohannis. Apocryphe d'origine bogomile*, ed. and
trans. E. Bozóky (Paris: Beauchesne, 1980).

[40] L. Clédat, *Le Nouveau Testament traduit au xiiie siècle en langue provençale, suivi d'un Rituel
Cathare* (Paris: E. Leroux, 1887).

[41] M.R. Harris, "The Occitan Epistle to the Laodiceans: Towards an edition of
MS. PA 36," in A. Cornagliotti et al., eds., *Miscellanea di Studi Romanzi offerta a Giu-*

solute
dualis

Sacconi's second group of Cathars, those who traced their origins to the *ordo of Drugunthia*, comprised the Cathars of Desenzano in Lombardy, also known as the Albanenses, and the Cathars of Languedoc. All the sources describe the members of this *ordo* as absolute dualists, and that is borne out by their own writings. Drugunthia is an attempt to Latinize the Slav name Dragovitia, which was in the Rhodope Mountains near Philippopolis. The members of this *ordo* combined an acceptance of absolute dualist theology of a kind traditionally associated with the warlike Paulicians, with the ascetic way of life and the religious observances of the Bogomils. I have argued that this syncretism occurred when a group of Paulicians from Philippopolis, where they had a strong presence in the twelfth century, was converted to Bogomilism.[42] Papa Nichetas/Niquinta was a member of this church and converted some western Cathars to that *ordo*. The Albanenses renewed contact with the headquarters of this church a generation later, for the *De heresi* relates that during the schisms which occurred among the Cathars of Lombardy following the death of Bishop Mark, "certain men from Desenzano, having formed a congregation, chose a man called John the Fair as their bishop and sent him across the sea to Drugunthia so that he might be ordained bishop there."[43]

The absolute dualists among the Cathars tried to dispense with dependence on myths. Although they accepted the *Vision of Isaiah*, and while some of them may have read *The Secret Book of St. John*, they did not use them as substitutes for the account of creation in the Book of Genesis.[44] Their own account of the creation was based on the authority of the twelfth chapter of the Book of Revelation, which describes the war in Heaven between St. Michael and the heavenly

---

liano Gasca Queirazza, 2 vols. (Alessandria: Edizioni dell'Orso, 1988), 1, pp. 428–446; S. Westley, "Quelques observations sur les variantes presentées par le Nouveau Testament cathare occitan, le MS de Lyon (PA 36)," *Heresis* 26–27 (1996): 7–21.

[42] I. Dujčev, "Dragvista-Dragovitia," *Revue des études byzantines* 22 (1964): 215–221; B. Hamilton, "The Origins of the Dualist Church of Drugunthia," *Eastern Churches Review* 6 (1974): 115–124.

[43] *De Heresi*, AFP 19 (1949): 308. See also M. Angold, *Church and Society in Byzantium under the Comneni, 1081–1261* (Cambridge: Cambridge University Press, 1995), 490–495.

[44] The use of the *Vision of Isaiah* by southern French Cathars is attested by Durand of Huesca, *Liber contra Manicheos*, ed. C. Thouzellier, *Une Somme anti-cathare*, Spicilegium Sacrum Lovaniense. Études et documents, 32 (Louvain: Spicilegium sacrum Lovaniense Administration, 1964), 256–257, 287–288. The fact that the Inquisition of Carcassonne had a copy of the *Secret Book of St. John* implies, though it does not strictly prove, that it circulated among some of the Cathars of Languedoc who in theory were absolute dualists.

host and the Great Red Dragon with seven heads and ten horns and his supporting angels. The Dragon, they explained, was the evil God, who was co-eternal with the Good God; the Dragon had created the material world and the third part of the stars of Heaven which he drew to earth with his tail were angelic souls which he then imprisoned in earthly bodies. In the view of the absolute dualists the whole of human history was concerned with the fate of those imprisoned angels (Rev. 12, vv. 3–4, 7–9).

Catharism as revealed by Western sources was, in all its forms, an evolving faith, just as contemporary Catholicism was. It is therefore difficult to say categorically that the Cathars preserved the beliefs that they had received from the dualists of Byzantium and Bulgaria. All that can be said with certainty in the present state of our knowledge is that the two main schools of Catharism continued to work within the cosmological parameters which they had received from the Bogomils and to interpret the Christian revelation in the light of them. This was true even of the most radical Catholic theologians, John of Lugio and his school. John was the Elder Son (or coadjutor bishop) of the absolute dualist Albanenses in the second quarter of the thirteenth century. He and his followers were the only Cathars who were prepared to accept the historical books of the Old Testament as divinely inspired. Yet to judge from the report of his teaching given by Sacconi, John believed, just as all other absolute dualist Cathars did, that the account that the Old Testament gave of the creation of the world and of God's dealings with men related to the Evil God. Where he differed from other Cathars was in arguing that the Good God had inspired this account, presumably because it gave men knowledge of their true condition, which was a necessary preliminary to their being willing to accept the salvation which God offered in Christ.[45] The follower of John who wrote *The Book of the Two Principles* shared his views about biblical inspiration.[46]

Cathar theology tends to be treated by modern scholars (and I number myself among them) as though it were static. They agree that there were different schools, but make almost no attempt to trace developments within them. All the evidence about Cathar beliefs needs

---

[45] "Item iste Ioannes [de Lugio] recipit totam Bibliam sed putat eam fuisse scriptam in alio mundo." Sacconi, *AFP* 44 (1974), 56.

[46] *Livre de Deux Principes, Contra Garatenses, De omni creatione, De manifestatione fidelium*, ed., C. Thouzellier, Sources Chrétiennes, 198 (Paris Éditions du Cerf, 1973), 376–378.

to be classified by time and place, for only then will it be possible to give an adequate description of the way in which those beliefs evolved in the different Cathar schools. Until that has been done, it will not be possible to estimate in detail the extent of Cathar indebtedness in matters of faith to Bulgarian and Byzantine dualists.

The Dualist Counter-Church

Bob has recently called in question the validity of the term Cathar Church. What he presumably has in mind is the concept of a mono-lithic dualist counter-church that was envisaged by some Catholic writers in the thirteenth century. It is not clear when the papacy first became aware of the existence of Christian dualist communities in the Byzantine world.[47] Innocent III certainly became convinced that Bogomils were present in Bosnia, and by enlisting the help of the king of Hungary, who threatened military intervention, he caused the dissident leaders to agree to conform their practices to Catholic norms in the Accord of Belino Polje of 1203.[48] Then in 1204 the Bulgarian church acknowledged papal primacy, and Innocent sent a legate to crown the Tsar. Bulgaria was already popularly regarded in western Europe as the home of Christian dualism, and the ultimate source of Catharism, and Innocent must have become aware at that time that this opinion was well grounded. It was possibly because of papal pressure that in 1211 Tsar Boril convened a synod at Trnovo which legislated against the Bogomils.[49]

In 1223, Cardinal Conrad of Porto, Honorius III's legate in Languedoc, became alarmed by reports he heard there that a Balkan "antipope of the heretics" was seeking to reorganize the Cathar churches of southern France at a time when the Albigensian Crusade had just ended. In fact, he seems to have been misinterpreting news of a mission

---

[47] J. Hamilton, S. Hamilton, B. Hamilton, *Hugh Eteriano "Contra Patarenos"* (Leiden and Boston: Brill, 2004), 1–102.

[48] The Accord is translated in Hamilton and Hamilton, *Christian Dualist Heresies*, 257–259. I consider that this group had Bogomil characteristics, but other scholars argue that they were a reformist group who were wrongly labelled, notably. J.V. Fine, *The Bosnian Church: A New Interpretation. A Study of the Bosnian Church and it Place in State and Society from the 13th to the 15th Centuries* (New York and London: Columbia University Press, 1975), 126–134.

[49] *The Synodikon of Tsar Boril*, trans. Y. Stoyanov, in Hamilton and Hamilton, *Christian Dualist Heresies*, 260–262.

sent by the Bogomil bishop of Bosnia to reestablish moderate dualism in Languedoc. No doubt what confused Conrad was the use of the term *papa* to describe that bishop, since in the West this title was given only to the bishop of Rome.[50] But Conrad's report led the papacy to exaggerate the power of Balkan dualism, and Pope Gregory IX (1227–1241) even attempted to launch a crusade against the dualists of Bosnia and Bulgaria, although that was brought to an end by the Mongol invasion of eastern Europe in 1241–1242.[51] Strangely, the popes made no attempt to suppress Bogomilism in the Empire of Constantinople when it was under Latin rule from 1204 to 1261, and I can only suppose that they were unaware of its existence there.[52]

Perhaps as a result of this papal policy, Catholic writers in the thirteenth century treated the Cathar and Bogomil churches as though they were part of a single organization. Rainier Sacconi writes:

> There are sixteen churches of the Cathars altogether. But do not criticize me, you who read this, for calling them churches. Criticize them for doing so.[53]

No Catholic writer would pretend that this dualist church was united, because all apologists, Sacconi included, described in some detail the divisions that existed among the Cathars and that had originated in the Bogomil churches. Yet as Sacconi admitted, these divisions were less serious than they might at first sight have appeared:

> All the churches of the Cathars extend recognition to one another, although they hold different and opposing views, except for the Albanenses and the Cathars of Concorezzo who strongly condemn each other, as I have explained above.[54]

How far this goodwill extended to relations between the Cathar churches and the Bogomil churches of the thirteenth century is difficult to determine. The Cathars evidently maintained some contacts with the Balkan dualist communities, because Sacconi, presumably using information he had obtained while a Cathar minister, gives some statis-

---

[50] Text of Conrad's letter, Mansi, *Concilia*, 22, col. 1204; for my interpretation of it, Hamilton, "Cathar Council of Saint-Félix reconsidered," *AFP* 48 (1978): 44–49.

[51] Stoyanov, *The Other God*, 215–218.

[52] B. Hamilton, "Dualist Heresy in the Latin Empire of Constantinople," in C. Hawkesworth, M. Heppell, and H. Norris, eds., *Religious Quest and National Identity in the Balkans* (London: Palgrave, in association with School of Slavonic and East European Studies, University College, London, 2001), 69–77.

[53] Sacconi, *AFP* 44 (1974), 49.

[54] Sacconi, *AFP* 44 (1974), 59.

tics about Bogomil church membership, which are the only statistics about them that exist anywhere.[55] Nevertheless, evidence about contact between the Bogomils and Cathars in the century after 1230 is slight. Then in 1325 Pope John XXII complained to Prince Stephen Kotromanič of Bosnia that "a great crowd of heretics from many different regions has gathered together and migrated to Bosnia."[56] In his day "heretics" meant Cathars, and I am inclined to give some credence to this statement because it would explain why all traces of organized Catharism disappear from Western Europe before 1330. John Fine, even though he does not think that the Bogomil presence in fourteenth-century Bosnia was numerically significant, says of this letter: "Perhaps some heretics (probably a relatively small number), did flee from Italy towards the Balkans, and the Pope had reason to believe they might be headed for Bosnia or Dalmatia."[57] This may be an indication, therefore, albeit a slender one, that right to the end the Cathars preserved an awareness of their links with the Bogomils.

Yet although Catholic critics may have been mistaken to see the Cathars and Bogomils as members of a counter-church which, had it avoided schisms, would have been a powerful and diabolical mirror-image of the Catholic church, the Cathars did regard themselves and the Bogomils as forming a single church. It was inevitable that they should have done so because they based their teachings on the New Testament and claimed to be true followers of Christ, and therefore shared with Orthodox Byzantines and Latin Catholics the New Testament concept of *ecclesia*, the assembly of the faithful, which was, as St. Paul had taught, the mystical body of Christ. In that regard, the Bogomils and the Cathars undoubtedly shared a single faith. Euthymius Zigabenus reports:

> [The Bogomils] say that ours is the baptism of John, being accomplished in water, but theirs is the baptism of Christ, achieved, as they think, through the Spirit. So they rebaptize any one who converts to them ...[58]

The late Cathar treatise discovered by Venckeleer in Trinity College Library, Dublin, states:

[55] Sacconi, *AFP* 44 (1974), 50.
[56] *Pontificia Commissio ad redigendum Codex Iuris Canonici Orientalis: Fontes*, ser. 3, vol. 7(2), ed. A.L. Tautu (Vatican City, 1952), no. 78, p. 160.
[57] Fine, *Bosnian Church*, 178.
[58] *Against the Bogomils*, trans. Hamilton and Hamilton, *Christian Dualist Heresies*, 189.

> The Church performs a holy, spiritual baptism, which is the imposition
> of hands through which is given the Holy Spirit ... But the wicked
> Roman Church ... says that Christ referred to temporal water, which
> John the Baptist used before Christ preached ... Hence no man is saved
> who is not baptized with this [holy spiritual] baptism, just as all those
> who were outside the Ark were drowned in the Flood ...[59]

In that sense, I would argue, the Cathars and Bogomils were conscious
of being members of a single church; they alone were able to administer
the one, Christ-given sacrament of salvation. They seem to have been
prepared to tolerate a diversity of belief about important doctrines,
such as whether there was one God or two. What really divided both
the Cathars and the Bogomils was their conviction that some groups
within their movement had lost the capacity to perform valid baptisms
as a result of sin, but that meant that they became dead branches in the
vine of the church, it did not destroy the spiritual unity of the church.

So overall, I think Bob's skepticism about the existence of a dualist
church, as about much else, has been profitable to scholarship. I say
this not because I think he is right, but because he has made me
consider the evidence again and realize how much new work needs to
be done and, until it has been, how cautious I should be about making
generalizations.[60]

---

[59] Th. Venckeleer, "Un Recueil cathare: Le manuscrit A.6.10 de la Collection vau-
doise de Dublin. I. Une Apologie," *Revue belge de philologie et d'histoire* 38 (1960): 820–831.
I cite this Provençal text in the translation of Wakefield and Evans, *Heresies of the High
Middle Ages*, 604–606.

[60] Attention is drawn to M. Zerner, ed., *L'histoire du Catharisme en discussion. Le "concile"
de Saint-Félix (1167)*. Collection du centre d'étude médievales de Nice, I (Nice, 2001), and
particularly to J. Dalarun, A. Dufour, A. Grondeux, D. Muzerelle, F. Zinelli (I.R.H.T.),
"La charte de Niquinta, analyse formelle," pp. 135–201, who conclude: "L'impression
finale que l'on retire de ces observations est celle d'un document homogene, contem-
porain des événements relatés et dû à un même rédacteur." (p. 199). This work has
appeared since the present article was written.

NORTHERN CATHARISM

Malcolm Barber

Peter Maurel, who came from either Toulouse or Auriac, made his living as a *ductor* or *nuntius*, as the inquisitorial documents describe him, leading men and women from Languedoc into Lombardy, where they were able to meet the exiled leaders of the Cathar Church. Among the places he visited regularly was the small town of Sirmione, situated at the southern end of Lake Garda, where, in 1255, one of his clients, William Raffard from the village of Roquevidal in the hills north of Lavaur, met three Cathar "bishops," Bernard Oliba of the diocese of Toulouse, Henry of the diocese of Lombardy, and William Peter of Verona of the diocese of France.[1] In 1276 the community at Sirmione was broken up by Mastino della Scala, *capitano del popolo* of Verona, and in February, 1278, around 200 of them were burned to death. The fate of William Peter is unknown, but there is no documentary reference to any Cathar "bishop of France" after 1289.[2]

A century before the situation of the Cathar bishop of France had been very different. Sometime between 1174 and 1177 leading representatives of the Cathars assembled at the village of Saint-Félix-de-Caraman, located about 43 km. to the south-east of Toulouse, above the Lauragais plain. They had come to meet Nicetas, leader of the Bogomil Drugunthian Church in Constantinople, who had traveled there via Lombardy, accompanied on the last stage of his journey by northern Italian Cathars whom he had reconsecrated. The meaning and purpose of this council remain controversial but, at least for those historians who are willing to accept that the documents describing the meeting are genuine, there is agreement that one of the main aims was to reorganize the growing numbers of western dualists into a manageable regional structure. At this time there already seems to have been a broad division between "France," which is presumably to be interpreted in the manner of contemporaries to mean the lands north of the

---

[1] Bibliothèque Nationale, *Collection Doat*, 26, f. 15ʳ⁻ᵛ.

[2] See E. Dupré-Theseider, "Le Catharisme languedocien et l'Italie," in *Cahiers de Fanjeaux* 3 (1980), 303, and M.D. Lambert, *The Cathars* (Oxford: Blackwell, 1998), 87.

Loire, and "Albi," covering the southern territories of the Toulouse and Trencavel families, an area which, within a generation, would come to be known as Languedoc. Nicetas seems to have reconsecrated Mark, the leader of the Lombard Cathars, as bishop of that region, and to have done the same for Robert of Spernone, bishop of France, and Sicard Cellarier, bishop of Albi. In the course of the council, Nicetas consecrated three more bishops in Languedoc, those of Toulouse, Carcassonne, and Agen.[3] Given that a quasi-Catholic episcopal structure seems to have been acceptable to Bogomils and Cathars, the need was evident, for the four new bishoprics were already constituted as "churches," able to designate representatives to attend the council. Indeed, according to the copy of the proceedings made by Peter Pollan, "younger son" of the diocese of Carcassonne in 1223, "the Church of Toulouse" had actually been responsible for the invitation to Nicetas.

Although territorial boundaries between Toulouse and Carcassonne were established at Saint-Félix, no definition was given of Robert of Spernone's diocese. Its core, however, seems to have been within the Catholic ecclesiastical province of Reims. This encompassed an area which stretched from the Flemish coast on the North Sea and the Channel south-eastwards to the middle and upper reaches of the Marne beyond Châlons. The province contained eleven suffragan bishops, itself an indication of the number of important cities and towns in the region.[4] At the same time, most of the territories of the counts of Flanders and of Champagne, two of the greatest lords of northwest Europe, lay within the province. Both ecclesiastical and secular authorities had become alarmed about the spread of heresy well before the council of Saint-Félix. In October 1157, the first canon of the council of Reims, presided over by Archbishop Samson, was entitled *De Piphilis*, which, as the reference in the text to the "most impure sect of the Manichaeans" makes clear, was the current name for dualist heretics in the region. If, after warning, the heretics did not return to the Church, the leaders would be imprisoned for life and their followers branded on the face and banished from the territory. Any property would be con-

---

[3] See B. Hamilton, "The Cathar Council of Saint-Félix reconsidered," *Archivum Fratrum Praedicatorum* 18 (1978): 23–53.

[4] *Les Statuts Synodaux Français du XIIIe siècle*, vol. 4, *Les Statuts Synodaux de l'Ancienne Province de Reims*, ed. J. Avril. Collection de Documents inédits sur l'Histoire de France, vol. 23 (Paris: Bibliothèque nationale, 1995), 3. For a useful (although unannotated) summary of incidents between the eleventh and the thirteenth centuries, see M. Grisart, "Les Cathares dans le Nord de la France," *Revue du Nord* 49 (1967): 509–519.

fiscated. Those accused could only prove their innocence by means of the ordeal by fire.[5] In 1162, the French king, Louis VII, wrote to Pope Alexander III, describing how his brother, Henry, Samson's successor, the newly-elected archbishop, had recently traveled through Flanders, where he had found "depraved men, followers of the worst errors, [who] had fallen into the heresy of the Manichaeans, commonly called Publicans (*Populicani*)".[6] More specifically, at Arras, in 1172, Henry conducted a hearing in which Robert, a clerk accused of heresy, failed an ordeal by fire, was handed over to the secular arm and executed,[7] and sometime between 1176 and 1180, the next archbishop, William aux Blanches Mains, brother of Count Henry I of Champagne, presided over an archepiscopal court which examined two female members of "that most impious sect of Publicans" discovered in and around Reims itself, who refused to recant and were therefore handed over to the officials of the city to be burned to death.[8]

The secular lords were equally concerned. Although not always in harmony with each other, the houses of Champagne and Flanders consistently demonstrated their commitment to the faith through such extensive crusading activity that the province of Reims had become one of the key areas of support for the Holy Land. Henry I of Champagne had taken part in the Second Crusade in 1148–1149 and returned to Jerusalem on pilgrimage in 1179, while his successor, Henry II, actually died in the East in 1197, having participated in the Third Crusade in 1190–1192. The counts of Flanders had an even longer crusading pedigree which stretched back to Robert II on the First Crusade and encompassed Thierry of Alsace, who went on crusade four times between 1139 and 1164, and Philip I, who campaigned in Palestine and Syria in 1177–1178. According to the Cistercian Ralph of Coggeshall, Philip harassed the Publicans "pitilessly with righteous cruelty".[9] In 1183, at Arras, "a certain woman disclosed the deceits of many heresies in the count's land" to Archbishop William and

---

[5] *Corpus Documentorum Inquisitionis Hereticae Pravitatis Neerlandicae*, vol. 1, ed. P. Fredericq (Gent-J. Vuylstcke, 1889), no. 34, pp. 35–36.

[6] *Corpus*, vol. 1, no. 39, pp. 37–38.

[7] *Corpus*, vol. 1, no. 46, p. 45.

[8] Ralph of Coggeshall, *Chronicon Anglicanum*, ed. J. Stevenson. Rolls Series, 66 (London: Longman, 1875), pp.121–125, who recounts the story from information received from Gervais of Tilbury, who played a role in discovering these heretics. According to Ralph, one escaped by magic.

[9] Ralph of Coggeshall, *Chronicon Anglicanum*, p. 122.

Count Philip. They went under various names, including Manichaeans, Catafrigians, Arians and, in Pope Alexander III's lexicon, Patarines. William and Philip were presumably alert to the possibility since the previous year, Bishop Frumald had imprisoned four heretics in the city, reserving their cases for the archbishop, as he himself was too ill to deal with the matter. Their property was adjudged to be forfeit and they were condemned to death, although according to the anonymous monk who continued the chronicle of Sigibert of Gembloux, "many who were before guilty of heresy" escaped punishment through the grace of God which was demonstrated through their success in the ordeals of the hot iron and of water. In a parallel case in the city of Ypres, 65 km. to the north, another twelve accused also saved themselves by the ordeal of the hot iron.[10] Similar combined action was taken in 1204, this time 120 km. to the south, by Guido Paré, archbishop of Reims as well as papal legate, and Robert II, Count of Dreux, when, after a hearing lasting several days, a number of *infideles* were executed at Braine in the diocese of Soissons.[11]

Contiguous with the province of Reims were those of Cologne and Trier to the east and Sens (which included Paris) and Lyon to the south. In 1143 or 1144 Eberwin, Premonstratensian Prior of Steinfeld, near Cologne wrote to tell Bernard of Clairvaux of "new heretics" who had appeared in the vicinity, a matter brought to a head by a three-day debate between a man "who was said to be their bishop, and his companion," and members of the clergy. The existence of a hierarchy of auditors, believers and an "Elect," entrance to which was gained by a ceremony involving the imposition of hands, suggests that they were not only equipped to debate with the clergy, but also existed in sufficient numbers to form a structured organisation. Regrettably, as Eberwin saw it, they were "seized by the people, moved by excessive zeal, ...and put on a fire and burned."[12] Apparently almost contemporaneously, in 1145, in the same province, south-west of Cologne, the clergy of Liège wrote to Pope Lucius II describing heretics similarly divided into three classes of believers, auditors, and priests and other prelates, "just like us." These people had been saved from "a turbulent mob" only with difficulty. The occasion of the letter was to alert the pope to the

---

10 *Corpus*, vol. 1, nos. 48, 49, pp. 47–49.
11 *Ex Chronico Anonymi Laudunensis Canonici*, in *RHG*, vol. 18, p. 713.
12 Eberwin of Steinfeld, *Epistola ad S. Bernardum*, in *PL*, vol. 182, ep. 472, cols. 676–680.

arrival in Rome of one of these heretics—an auditor called Aimery—
who had promised to make pilgrimage to the shrines of the saints as
amends for his false belief. The Liège clergy also claimed, moreover,
that the heresy had spread from a place in France called Montwimers
or Mont-Aimé, which was a village situated on a small hill on the
Champenoise plain, about 30 km. south-west of Châlons-sur-Marne,
and thus from the extreme south of the province of Reims.[13] This would
be an extraordinary assertion to make about a community which must
have been tiny in the mid-twelfth century, as well as being 230 km. to
the south, had they not had some specific information upon which to
base their claim. In view of the later symbolism of this village in 1239,
when a mass execution of heretics took place there, it is reasonable
to assume that Mont-Aimé had a long history of heretical association
in the minds of the clergy, perhaps going back a century to the mid-
1140s.

The heresy persisted in the Cologne province for at least the next
twenty years. On 2 August, 1163, eleven *Cataphrygae* or *Cathari*, two
of whom were women, were captured in the city. According to the
Chronica brevis Coloniensis, their three leaders or "heresiarchs" were called
Arnold, Marsile, and Theoderic. Remaining stubborn in "their profane
sect," they were executed on a hill outside the city next to the Jewish
cemetery.[14] These were presumably the same executions described by
the *Annales Coloniensi maximi* as taking place on 5 August outside the city.
Having secretly entered the region from Flanders, these *Kathari* had
allegedly been detected because of their failure to attend church on
Sundays.[15] It is possible that their departure from Flanders was a result
of the sweep through the region by Archbishop Henry that year. They
were not always secret. In the same year, Eckbert, abbot of Schönau in
the neighboring province of Trier, wrote a long refutation of the beliefs
of the Cathars (the first of its kind) for the benefit of Rainald of Dassel,
Archbishop of Cologne. He was able to do this, he said, because when
he was a canon at Bonn, he and his friend Bertolph had had frequent
disputations with them.[16]

---

[13] *Corpus*, vol 1, no.30, pp. 31–32. The dating presents certain problems. See
W.L. Wakefield and A.P. Evans, *Heresies of the High Middle Ages* (New York: Columbia
University Press, 1969), 139–140, 684.

[14] *Corpus*, vol. 1, no. 40, p. 40.

[15] *Corpus*, no. 42, pp. 42–43.

[16] *Eckbert of Schönau's 'Sermones contra Kataros'*, ed. R.J. Harrison, vol. 1 (Ann Arbor,
MI: University of Michigan Press, 1990).

On the other side of the province of Reims lay that of Sens, extending beyond Nevers to the south, bounded on the west by the provinces of Rouen and Tours and on the east by Lyon. If, as Jean Duvernoy suggests, Spernone can be identified with Epernon, approximately 30 km. to the northwest of Chartres, then it is possible that Robert came from the western part of this province.[17] However, there are no reports of heresy in the Chartrain; it was along the eastern borders with the province of Lyon that heresy was detected. In 1167, Hugh of Poitiers, a monk at the abbey of Sainte-Madelaine at Vézelay in northern Burgundy, which lay just within the diocese of Lyon, reported the arrest of what he called *Deonarii* or *Poplicani* in the town. Questioned a number of times by Abbot William, at Easter they finally appeared in the presence of Guichard, archbishop of Lyon, Bernard of Saint-Saulve, Bishop of Nevers and Walter of Montagne, bishop of Laon. Two claimed repentance and volunteered for the ordeal by water. One of them was cleared, the other condemned, although saved from execution by the abbot, who substituted flogging. However, seven others were burned to death in the valley of the Ecouan.[18] On the other side of the ecclesiastical border, Robert of Auxerre, a Premonstratensian from St Marien in Auxerre, reported Publicans in Corbigny (70 km. to the south) in 1198, "among whom was the heresiarch Terricus, a great snare of the devil, who had hidden for a long time in a subterranean cave and had subverted many." He was captured and burned.[19] Two years later at Troyes, the Cistercian, Aubri of Trois-Fontaines, recorded the burning of eight *Popelicani*, five men and three women.[20]

These appear to have been relatively short-lived episodes; in contrast the pursuit of heretics at La Charité-sur-Loire was particularly prolonged, mainly because of the determination of Hugh of Noyers, Bishop of Auxerre, to root out what he saw as a hardened group of about a dozen local bourgeois. The bishop's initial visits to the town failed to produce a response to his citation and he therefore excommunicated them, probably at the beginning of 1198. He followed this by calling in Michael of Corbeil, archbishop of Sens, his metropolitan,

---

[17] J. Duvernoy, *Le Catharisme*, vol. 2, *L'Histoire des Cathares* (Toulouse: Privat, 1979), 147.

[18] Hugh of Poitiers, *Historia Vizeliacensis Monasterii*, in *RHG*, vol. 12, pp. 343–344.

[19] Robert of Auxerre, *Chronicon*, ed. O. Holder-Egger, *MGHSS*, vol. 26, p. 258.

[20] *Chronica Albrici Monachi Trium Fontium*, ed. P. Scheffer-Boichorst, *MGHSS*, vol. 23, p. 878.

who, in conjunction with Ansel, bishop of Meaux and Walter, bishop of Nevers, presided over an inquiry in the town in the course of the same year. These efforts threw up new accusations against two prominent local ecclesiastics—the dean of the chapter of Nevers and Rainaud, Abbot of Saint-Martin—which, in turn, set off a quite separate chain of events leading to appeals to Innocent III. Neither pope nor archbishop seems to have been convinced of the heresy charges, although they do seem aware of other irregularities. These two cases underline the problematical nature of the dispute between Hugh of Noyers and the bourgeois of La Charité, since it is not clear how far the accusation of heresy were fuelled by a genuine belief that these persons were inspired by Catharism, or by an underlying conflict over jurisdictional control. Between 1198 and 1206 there followed a complicated series of manoeuvres in which the accused used every device possible to avoid appearing before Hugh of Noyers: appeals to Peter of Capua, the papal legate, to the council of Dijon (December, 1199) and to Innocent III himself, as well as disappearances from the diocese of Auxerre whenever the pressure became too great. Hugh of Noyers claimed that his efforts lacked secular support and, indeed, his excommunication of Peter of Courtenay, Count of Auxerre and Nevers, and cousin of King Philip II, for violating church property, produced sufficient reaction for the bishop to find it prudent first to seek refuge in the monastery of Pontigny and then to leave the diocese altogether. In a letter to Philip II (who himself appears to have been a beneficiary of the bishop's absence) in 1203, Innocent III ordered the king to support the bishop "lest you seem to strive for the favor of heretics against whom the bishop of Auxerre has acted manfully and fought lawfully."[21]

Although the intensity of the conflict abated after the death of Hugh of Noyers at Rome in September 1206, the bishop nevertheless seems to have convinced an initially sceptical pope that heresy at La Charité really did exist and constituted a serious threat. After Hugh's death Innocent informed his successor, William of Seignelay, that not only had those who abjured heresy relapsed, but also they had secretly brought in "certain heresiarchs whom they call *consolatores*, who are killing your flocks with the poison of pestiferous doctrines," again sug-

---

[21] *Innocentii III Registrum sive Epistolarum*, in *PL*, vol. 215, cols.162–164. For a detailed account of these events, see E. Chénon, "L'Hérésie à La Charité-sur-Loire et les Débuts de l'Inquisition Monastique dans la France du Nord au XIIIe siècle," *Nouvelle Revue de Droit Français et Etranger* 40 (1917): 299–345.

gesting that he believed some sort of structured network existed.[22] According to Pope Honorius III, matters had not improved by 1217, since in April, he granted Gervais, archdeacon of Nevers, dispensation from living in the region on the grounds that the archdeaconate was "situated among faithless pagans" and, in an apparent reference to La Charité (30 km. downstream on the River Loire) and Corbigny (60 km to the northeast), "is contiguous with places suspected of heresy."[23] Honorius, perhaps reflecting his source, seems to have given himself licence to exaggerate, but nevertheless heresy had penetrated the chapter of Nevers in the past, for, in 1190, one of the canons, William of Châteauneuf, had been accused, and later had fled south to the more congenial environment of Narbonne. In 1201, his uncle, Everard, a knight, had been condemned by a council in Paris and executed at Nevers, and William was evidently frightened of a similar fate.[24] In the south he took the name of Theoderic and, according to the Cistercian chronicler of the Albigensian Crusade, Peter des Vaux-de-Cernay, was greatly esteemed by southern Cathars because he had come from France. By 1206 he was prominent enough to take part in an eight-day debate with Diego, Bishop of Osma, at the *castrum* of Servian, just to the northeast of Béziers.[25] In 1231, Gregory IX was claiming that new heretics had been discovered at La Charité, and two years later talking about "this detestable plague, which has lasted so long," making the town "like a deserted and impassable land."[26]

With the significant exception of the bourgeois of La Charité, the heretics themselves have no voice, but these references are too many and too varied to be dismissed as the posturings of the paranoid or the self-seeking; they must, at least in part, represent a genuine perception by the orthodox that dualist heretics existed in the second half of the twelfth century and that they were trying to spread their message. Nevertheless, they do not explain how the heresy came to be established in northern Europe in the first place. The Cathars saw themselves as the only true Christians and, as such, it was natural for them to proselytize,

---

[22] *Innocentii Registrum*, in *PL*, vol. 215, col. 1312–1313 (12 January, 1208).

[23] *Regesta Honorii Papae III*, vol. 1, ed. P. Pressutti (Rome: ex typographis Vaticana, 1888), no. 555, p. 97 (2 May, 1217).

[24] Robert of Auxerre, p. 260.

[25] Peter des Vaux-de-Cernay, *Hystoria Albigensis*, ed. P. Guébin and E. Lyon, vol. 1 (Paris: Champion, 1926), 25–26.

[26] *Les Registres de Grégoire IX*, vol. 1, ed. L. Auvray (Paris: A. Fontemoing, 1896), no. 637, p. 406 (6 May, 1231); no. 1145, pp. 649–650 (28 February, 1233).

although the need to do so with discretion, especially in the early stages, makes it difficult to trace the path of any missionary work they undertook. As such, it is not surprising that the origins of dualism in the West are the subject of intense historiographical debate. Some historians argue that dualism can be explained without recourse to outside influences; others believe the long-established Bogomil Church, evident in Bulgaria and Macedonia in the mid-tenth century, and in Constantinople a century later, was the inspiration for western Cathars.[27] However, the chronology and geography of the heresy in the north clearly support Bernard Hamilton's view that not only was there outside influence, but also that there were multiple entry points.[28] The reports of heresy in Flanders, Champagne, Burgundy, and Lotharingia all relate to areas with good communications with the wider world, communications which, in this period, were continually being improved under the pressure of commercial and ecclesiastical needs.

Italian commentators, looking back on these events from the perspective of the second half of the thirteenth century, believed that dualist heresy had originally spread in this way, reaching Languedoc and northern Italy from France and before this, that it had entered France from Constantinople. Federico Visconti, archbishop of Pisa, between 1254 and 1277, using the Cathar theme as the centerpiece of a sermon delivered on the Feast of St Dominic (5 August) sometime during his episcopate, seems to have derived his information from Pisan merchants who, like their Genoese counterparts, had probably traveled to Languedoc to meet Artesian merchants bringing Flemish cloth to the Mediterranean ports.[29] Anselm of Alessandria, papal inquisitor in Milan and Genoa, writing c. 1266–1267, attempted a historical sketch of the spread of Catharism in which he said that Frenchmen went to Constantinople where they met members of the Bogomil Church. This led them to set up their own Latin bishop in Constantinople and "afterwards, the French who had gone to Constantinople returned to their

---

[27] For a summary of these views, see M. Barber, *The Cathars. Dualist Heretics in Languedoc in the High Middle Ages* (London: Longman, 2000), 21–33.

[28] B. Hamilton, "Wisdom from the East," in *Heresy and Literacy, 1000–1530*, ed. P. Biller and A. Hudson (Cambridge: Cambridge University Press, 1994), 38–60.

[29] See A. Vauchez, "Les Origines de l'Hérésie cathare en Languedoc, d'aprés un sermon de l'Archevêque de Pise Federico Visconti († 1277)," in *Società, istituzioni, spiritualità: Studi in Onore di Cinzio Violante*, vol. 2 (Spoleto: Centro italiano di studi sull'alto Medioevo, 1994), pp.1023–1036. For trade links, see R.L. Reynolds, "Merchants of Arras and the Overland Trade with Genoa," *Revue Belge de Philologie et d'Histoire* 9 (1930): 495–533.

own land and preached and, having increased in number, established a bishop in France." A further consequence was that "the Provençals, whose territories adjoin those of France, hearing their preaching and seduced by the French, multiplied to such an extent that they created four bishops..." Similarly, heresy first entered Lombardy from France: "after a long time, a certain notary from France came into the *contado* of Milan, in the region of Concorezzo."[30] When internal disputes broke out among the north Italians, it was, according to an anonymous but authoritative Lombard source of the early thirteenth century, to "a certain bishop beyond the mountains" that they appealed for judgement.[31]

However, neither Federico Visconti nor Anselm of Alessandria provide a very precise chronology. André Vauchez thinks that Visconti was probably referring to the period between 1150 and 1170, although this is based on his knowledge of growing heretical activity at this time rather than upon any internal evidence from the sermon itself.[32] Anselm of Alessandria implies that the Frenchmen were crusaders, but he does not specify on which of the several occasions this might have been. Nevertheless, nobody places this later than 1204, while some historians would date these events much earlier either to the Second Crusade in the late 1140s or to the First Crusade in the late 1090s.[33] It is certainly possible that dualism entered the West before the 1140s. Heretics were discerned in Orléans in 1022 and Arras in 1025, but the earliest reference to "Manichaeans" north of the Loire occurs between 1043 and 1048 when Roger, Bishop of Châlons-sur-Marne, wrote to ask advice from Wazo, Bishop of Liège, on how to tackle what he saw as the enthusiastic interest of some of the rural population in "the perverse belief of the Manichaeans."[34] Nearly seventy years later, in c. 1114, Guibert, abbot of the small house of Nogent between Noyon and Laon, named two brothers from Bucy, near Soissons, who held orgies in cellars as a result of adhering to beliefs which resembled "none other than the inventions of the Manichaeans," as, he said, became evident to him

---

[30] Anselm of Alessandria, *Tractatus de haereticis*, in A. Dondaine, "La Hiérarchie cathare en Italie, II," *Archivum Fratrum Praedicatorum* 20 (1950): 308.

[31] *De heresi catharorum in Lombardia*, in A. Dondaine, "La Hiérarchie cathare en Italie, I," *Archivum Fratrum Praedicatorum* 19 (1949): 306.

[32] Vauchez, "Les Origines de l'Hérésie en Languedoc," 1027–1028.

[33] For views on this see the summary in Barber, *The Cathars*, 27–28.

[34] *Herigeri et Anslemi Gesta episcoporum Leodiensium*, ed. R. Koepke, *MGHSS*, vol. 7, p. 226.

when he re-read St Augustine's description.[35] Such isolated references have not generally been taken too seriously by historians; indeed, the view that educated men at this time, unfamiliar with heretics, would be likely to designate them Manichaeans whatever their beliefs has considerable validity, although, of course, these writers knew well that the word described dualist belief, even though Manichaeaism as such had died out in the Byzantine Empire by the end of the seventh century.

Whatever the ambiguities of the evidence for the initial penetration of Catharism in the north, once it was established adherents made efforts to spread their beliefs. In this context the case of Jonas, a clerk who contested the cure of the church of Neder-Heembeek, near Brussels, is intriguing. The matter was heard by Nicholas I, bishop of Cambrai, at some point between the end of 1164 and 1 July, 1167, but in the course of the hearing the bishop was informed of letters of Arnold of Weid, archbishop of Cologne (1151–1156), and Hillin of Falmagne, archbishop of Trier (1152–1169), as well Henry of Leez and Alexander of Oeren, successively bishops of Liège between 1145 and 1164 and 1164 and 1167 respectively, that Jonas had already been convicted of the heresy of the Cathars (de Cattorum) in their courts and was "damned by anathema."[36] This suggests that Jonas had at least two previous convictions for heresy (in the dioceses of Cologne and Trier) and possibly two more (in the diocese of Liège). Despite these he had remained free to continue what appears to have been an itinerant lifestyle, which, although it was an obvious impediment to his claim to the church at Neder-Heembeek, may nevertheless have enabled him to promote Cathar beliefs throughout the region. Paul Bonenfant makes the plausible suggestion that Jonas was a Cathar missionary; if so, then the lack of consistent action by the orthodox at this time must mean that others like him were able to spread heresy over this very wide area. That some at least moved from place to place across the region seems certain; at Liège in 1145 they were said to have come from Mont-Aimé, while the Cologne heretics burned in 1163 were from Flanders. If the case before Nicholas of Cambrai is any indication, Jonas was working his way in the opposite direction from the Rhine valley to the Meuse and thence into Flanders. Such a scenario is all the more likely in view

---

[35] Guibert de Nogent, *Autobiographie*, ed. and trans. E.-R. Labande. Les Classiques de l'Histoire de France au Moyen Age, 34 (Paris: Belles Lettres, 1981), 428–431.

[36] See P. Bonenfant, "Un clerc cathare en Lotharingia au milieu du XIIe siècle," *Le Moyen Age* 69 (1963): 271–280.

of the almost directly contemporary attempt to establish the heresy in England. According to the Austin canon, William of Newburgh, sometime between 1161 and 1166, a group of about thirty German men and women, led by a man called Gerard, came to England. These heretics, who had already spread their beliefs in France, Spain, Italy and Germany, "are generally called Publicans." They were prevented from doing so in England because their foreign origin drew attention to them. They were questioned by an episcopal synod at Oxford in 1166 and found to scorn the sacraments. Punished by branding and flogging, and turned out into the countryside in winter, they died of exposure. As William saw it, this "purged" England of heresy, of which it had previously been free since the time of Pelagius in the early fifth century.[37]

The perception of Catholic prelates and chroniclers that heretics were spreading their "poison," as William of Newburgh puts it, appears to be true, although some could not resist exaggerating the scale of it. Equally, however, the identification of the actual nature of this belief is dependent upon orthodox sources, unmoderated by Cathar literature such as that of Languedoc or Lombardy, limited though it is, or even by the testimonies of deponents filtered through the proceedings of the inquisitors. Although the level of detail varies considerably, there is no doubt that the orthodox believed that they were battling with adherents of some kind of dualist belief, organized into a three-tiered hierarchical system of auditors, believers and an elect, the last of which they interpreted as a kind of heretical priesthood. Progression from auditor to believer was by means of the ceremony of the laying-on of hands, or spiritual baptism, given only to adults, in contrast to the material baptism by water practised by the Catholic Church. It was presumably this structure over which Robert of Spernone and the council that accompanied him to Saint-Félix presided. In the sources these people are variously called Manichaeans, Publicans, Patarines, Piphiles, Textores, Bulgars, and, from the 1160s, Cathars. It seems safe to assume that writers using any of these terms meant some form of

---

[37] William of Newburgh, *Historia rerum anglicarum*, ed. R. Howlett, in *Chronicles of the Reigns of Stephen, Henry II, and Richard I*, vol. 1. Rolls Series, 82 (London: Longman, 1884), pp. 131–134. See *Councils and Synods with other documents relating to the English Church*, vol. 1, *871–1204*, ed. D. Whitelock, M. Brett and C.N.L. Brooke (Oxford: Clarendon Press, 1981), 920–925. On this, see P. Biller, "William of Newburgh and the Cathar Mission to England," in *Life and Thought in the Northern Church c. 1100–c. 1700*, ed. D. Wood (London: Boydell, 1999), 11–30.

dualistic belief, even though most did not always have the space or the knowledge to elaborate upon it.

However, between 1143–1144 when Eberwin of Steinfeld wrote to Bernard of Clairvaux and 1209 when the calling of the Albigensian Crusade changed the whole climate not only in Languedoc but in the north as well, there are, among others, five representative descriptions. Their value is enhanced by their geographical spread that, in covering Cologne, Reims, Lille and Arras, as well as apparently making reference to La Charité-sur-Loire, includes a large part of the area for which there are extant reports of heresy. Eberwin well understood that the heretics of Cologne regarded themselves as the only true Christians and, as such, they strove to follow what they interpreted to have been the apostolic life. For them, this meant not owning property, and avoiding milk and any food produced by coition, while accepting only adult baptism by the imposition of hands. He does not mention dualism as such, although he is describing Cathar characteristics. There were apparently two distinct groups in the city, in dispute with each other, as well as with the Catholic Church. However, twenty years later, Eckbert of Schönau, in writing his refutation in depth, while similarly describing their attempts to live an apostolic life by eschewing materialism and abstaining from the flesh, saw them explicitly as followers of Mani, whose death they celebrated in their own festival. Their view was that human souls were in fact apostate spirits, expelled from Heaven at the time of Creation and thereafter trapped in human bodies. Christ could not therefore have taken human form, nor been born of the Virgin Mary; logically he could not actually have been crucified. The Reims' description, dated between 1176 and 1180, is derived from an eye-witness, Gervais of Tilbury. His list of strictures coincides with the Cologne descriptions, particularly on marriage, baptism, intercession, and diet, but here the dualism is more explicit. God held no sway in the material world, since Luzabel, an apostate angel, had domain there. Souls were "infused" into these material bodies, which had been created by the devil. By implication the Old Testament represented that domain, since only the Gospels and canonical letters were acceptable to the heretics.

Two other accounts derive from clerics who emanate from the Flemish lands of the province of Reims. Alan of Lille was a theologian who taught in the Parisian schools. His quadripartite refutation of "heretics" (i.e. Cathars), Waldensians, Jews, and "pagans" (i.e. Muslims), entitled *De fide catholica*, was a comprehensive survey, set out in conventional academic form. It seems to date from sometime between 1185 and 1200, and follows an earlier treatise, *Quoniam homines*, written c. 1160. Given his origins the description of the Cathars might have arisen from personal experience, although as he taught at Montpellier as well as Paris he may have derived knowledge from southern as well as northern Catharism. In any case there is good reason to believe that he had encountered heretics directly and that his knowledge was not solely theoretical. God was the principle of Light, from which souls and angels and all things spiritual emanated, whereas Lucifer was the principle of Darkness, and therefore lord of the material world. As Eckbert and Gervais had also noted, when apostate angels fell from Heaven with Lucifer, they were caught up in human bodies; it might take eight transmigrations before they could be freed.[38]

The fifth account is an anonymous sermon, part of a collection, possibly by a canon of Saint-Pierre du Castel in Arras.[39] It seems to be broadly contemporary with Alan of Lille's *De fide catholica*. Bernard Delmaire suggests that it might be linked to the actions of William of Reims and Philip of Flanders in 1183, in which the continuator of Sigibert of Gembloux described an official hearing at which many of the heretics themselves spoke, although the chronicler did not record anything of what they said, contenting himself with the opinion that it was a filthy heresy. This link seems very likely, but in addition reference to the *Bulgari de Caritate* and all their accomplices, might well be interpreted to mean La Charité-sur-Loire, while the phrase "all the disciples of the evil Oton, who infect all the confines of the kingdom with their malignity" does suggest that he intended his views to apply to the Cathar community as whole. The canon's sermon is divided into two parts, although the second section, which was a refutation, has been lost. The heretics' fundamental belief is in the two principles, for they follow Mani and his accomplices. Thus, "God had nothing to do with anything that is transitory and seasonal." The Old Testament is to be shunned, since "the devil is he who gave the law of Moses." They therefore rejected the sacraments of the Church, believing baptism and confession to be worthless and the Eucharist to be the work of the devil;

---

[38] *Alani de Insulis De Fide catholica contra haereticos sui temporis*, in *PL*, vol. 210, cols. 306–378. For Alan of Lille's possible sources, see P. Biller, "Northern Cathars and Higher Learning", in *The Medieval Church: Universities, Heresy, and the Religious Life. Essays in honour of Gordon Leff*, ed. P. Biller and B. Dobson (Woodbridge: Boydell, 1999), 45–46.

[39] B. Delmaire, "Un Sermon Arrageois inédit sur les 'Bougres' du Nord de la France (vers 1200)," *Heresis* 17 (1991): 1–15, which includes text and commentary.

necessarily the clergy who administer such sacraments were equally useless since the Catholic Church was an institution created by men and not by God. Among them are those who call themselves *perfecti*, "who impose hands on others and tell them that they are thus given the Holy Spirit." These *perfecti* pray on bent knee in the presence of the believers, "murmuring I do not know what between their lips," and they recite the *Pater Noster*. They eat only vegetables, fruit, and fish, although they do drink "strong wine." The believers, however, "deliver themselves randomly to lust," since they despise the sacrament of marriage.

All five authors were undoubtedly educated men but, unlike the thirteenth-century Italian commentators, it is not completely clear whether they are talking about mitigated or absolute dualism. If it is accepted that Nicetas came to Saint-Félix not only to reorganize the Cathar Church, but also to establish uniformity of belief (an idea rejected by some historians), then it does appear that Robert of Spernone, previously an adherent of the mitigated version, which postulated a fall from Heaven by the devil and his co-conspirators against God, was converted to the absolute dualism of two co-eternal deities, which characterised the Drugunthian Church of which Nicetas was a member. This in turn suggests that the original missionaries to northern France came from Bulgaria or Bosnia, as Anselm of Alessandria says, where mitigated beliefs had been retained, despite the evolution of their Thracian neighbours. In fact, Nicetas's attempt to create unity did not endure, since it appears that the northern French Cathars soon returned to moderate dualism, probably around 1180.[40]

The calling of the Albigensian Crusade by Innocent III in March 1208, was a watershed in the history of Catharism, not because the crusades brought the heresy to an end, but because they mark a qualitative change in the attitude of the Church towards what it now perceived to be a major threat. The military might of the crusaders was concentrated in the Trencavel and Toulousan lands of Languedoc, but the preaching and recruitment took place in the north, in particular in those regions in which Catharism had apparently been present since at least the 1140s. All four of the major secular leaders in 1209—Odo III, Duke of Burgundy, Hervi of Donzy, Count of Nevers, Walter of Châtillon, Count of Saint-Pol (about 34 km. west of Arras), and Reginald of

---

[40] See Hamilton, "Cathar Council of Saint-Félix reconsidered," 31–33.

Dammartin, Count of Boulogne—were drawn from the provinces of Reims and Sens. They were accompanied by the archbishops, Aubri of Hautvillers, of Reims, and Peter of Corbeil, of Sens; only the third prelate, Robert Poulain, of Rouen, came from a province little affected by heresy. In Burgundy, the prominence of Arnold Amalric, the papal legate on the crusade, within the Cistercian Order, seems to have similarly encouraged a vigorous recruitment campaign by leading Cistercians from the heartland of their Order. Nor was this the enthusiasm of a single year, for the crusades needed replenishment on an annual basis, and they cannot be said to have really ended until the Treaty of Paris of April 1229. In this atmosphere it is not surprising that northern Cathars chose to maintain a low profile. In the twenty years of crusading there appears to have been only one reported incident (apart from the continuing saga of episcopal dissatisfaction with the bourgeois of La Charité), which was incorporated within the moralistic stories told by the Cistercian, Caesarius of Heisterbach, in his *Dialogus miraculorum*, produced for the education of novices. This took place in Cambrai in 1217, when the bishop, John of Béthune, ordered an unspecified number of suspects to undergo ordeal by fire. One man, apparently a noble, repented, but the others were executed.[41]

Crusading against heretics raised the stakes not only in Languedoc, but in Languedoïl as well. The failure to stamp out Catharism only made the Catholic prelates more determined than ever to eliminate it from society. From the 1220s onwards the policy was to hunt down heretics, individually if necessary, while simultaneously launching an intellectual attack upon their beliefs intended to expose the fallacies of dualism so thoroughly that nobody would ever entertain such thoughts again. While the crusades had been directed specifically at Languedoc, this new offensive was much wider in scope. Thus, although the most famous academic refutations have traditionally been seen as those of the Italians, especially those of the Dominicans, Moneta of Cremona and Rainier Sacconi, and the Franciscan, James Capelli, recently Peter Biller has demonstrated the extent of the intellectual effort devoted to this in the Parisian schools as well, much of which predates the work of the Italians, most importantly by William of Auxerre in his *Summa aurea*, written about 1220.[42]

---

[41] *Corpus*, vol. 1, no.69, p. 69.
[42] Biller, "Northern Cathars and Higher Learning," 25–53.

For the hunting of specific heretics, Pope Gregory IX created specialist inquisitors, which from the 1230s operated in both northern and southern France and in Germany. In France, in April 1233, the pope authorized a Dominican, Robert Lepetit, known as "the Bulgar" (a sobriquet apparently derived from his former heretical beliefs) to make inquiry into heresy in the ecclesiastical provinces of northern France. In the previous year he had worked in the Franche-Comté, but nothing is known of his activities there. Although mentioned only once he appears, at least initially, to have been accompanied by a Brother James.[43] He began in La Charité-sur-Loire, by now synonymous with heresy, where he spent nearly a year from the spring of 1233 onwards. Inquisitorial activity was then restricted in the provinces of Reims, Sens, and Bourges when the pope was persuaded by the local episcopacy that this new kind of juridical activity was an unjustified encroachment upon their diocesan rights, and it was not resumed until August, 1235. Thereafter, although his authority encompassed the provinces of Bourges, Reims, Rouen, Tours, and Sens, all of which the pope claimed had been invaded by "the ministers of Satan,"[44] Robert in fact concentrated his efforts in the central parts of the province of Reims, moving north from Châlons at the beginning of 1236 and reaching Lille about mid-March.

Over a period of nine to ten weeks he visited Péronne, Elincourt, Cambrai, and Douai. In all these places heretics were arrested, at least 60 of whom were executed by burning. The culmination of the campaign took place back in the south of the province at the small bourgade of Mont-Aimé in Champagne (about 5 km. south of present-day Vertus), where, on 13 May, 1239, between 180 and 187 heretics were burned to death. Given the past association of Mont-Aimé with Catharism, the symbolism of the choice was not to be missed, and great efforts were made to proclaim the unity of the orthodox by ensuring that the event was attended by all but one of the twelve prelates of the

---

[43] Robert the Bulgar's career has been extensively researched, although his activities remain controversial. See, among others, Chénon, "L'Hérésie à La Charité-sur-Loire et les Débuts de l'Inquisition," 322–345; C.H. Haskins, "Robert Le Bougre and the Beginnings of the Inquisition in Northern France," in *Studies in Mediaeval Culture* (Oxford: Clarendon Press, 1929), 193–244; Y. Dossat, "L'Hérésie en Champagne aux XIIe et XIIIe siècles," *Mémoires de la Société d'agriculture, commerce, sciences et arts du département de la Marne* 84 (1969), 66–73; G. Despy, "Les Débuts de l'Inquisition dans les anciens Pays-Bas au XIIIe siècle," *Problèmes d'Histoire du Christianisme* 9 (1980): 71–104.

[44] *Reg. de Grég. IX*, vol. 1, ed. Auvray, no.1253, pp.707–709 (19 April, 1233).

province (only the bishop of Amiens was not present), three of the eight bishops of the neighbouring province of Sens, as well as the bishops of Langres and Verdun. Notably, Thibaut IV, Count of Champagne, who was about to depart on crusade, was present as the chief secular lord of the region, and indeed was responsible for the actual execution of the unrepentant heretics handed over by the Church.[45] The mass burning brought together heretics from an area much wider than Mont-Aimé itself, for many had already been examined elsewhere by the bishops assembled there that day. Most of those executed appear to have been believers, given the *consolamentum* shortly before death by a man whom Aubri of Trois-Fontaines describes as the *archiepiscopus de Moranis*. This grand title may suggest that he was one of the successors of Robert of Spernone, but the reference to *Moranis*, which probably means the village of Morains, eleven km. to the south of Vertus, makes it more likely he was a local *perfectus*.[46]

The pyre at Mont-Aimé accomplished its aim. According to the Dominican inquisitor, Rainier Sacconi, himself an ex-Cathar with considerable inside knowledge, in 1250 there were fewer than 4,000 Cathars (i.e. *perfecti*) left in the entire world. Of this number, the Church of France, by this time domiciled in Verona and Lombardy, could contribute only 150.[47] In the province of Reims, the synodal statutes, first extant in the bishopric of Cambrai in 1238, have nothing to say about Catharism and, indeed, barely mention heresy at all.[48] Two short campaigns by Robert the Bulgar and his companion in 1233 and 1236, last-

---

[45] See M. Lower, "The Burning at Mont-Aimé: Thibaut of Champagne's Preparations for the Barons' Crusade of 1239," *Journal of Medieval History* 29 (2003): 95–108.

[46] *Chronica Albrici Monachi Trium Fontium*, pp. 944–945. See Dossat, "L'Hérésie en Champagne," 72.

[47] Rainierius Sacconi, *Summa de Catharis et Pauperis de Lugduno*, in A. Dondaine, *Un Traité néo-manichéen de XIIIe siècle: Le Liber du duobus principiis, suivi d'un fragment de rituel cathare* (Rome: Istituto storico domenicano, 1939), 70.

[48] *Les Statuts Synodaux de l'Ancienne Province de Reims*, for example p. 299, at Soissons at the end of the thirteenth century priests were ordered to prevent unqualified persons preaching within their parishes "on account of the dangers of heresy and errors which they might sow or could sow." For residual traces of heresy in the north, see L. Tanon, *Histoire des tribunaux de l'Inquisition en France* (Paris: L. Larose and Forcel, 1893), 117–118. According to the annals of the house of St Medard of Soissons, there were large numbers of Bulgars or Piphles in "various cities and *castella* throughout France, Flanders, Champagne, Burgundy and other provinces." Using the year 1236 as a focal point, the author says that Robert was active against them "for three successive years before and for five or more successive years after." *Corpus*, vol. 2 (Gent, 1896), no. 26, p. 47.

ing perhaps no more than fourteen months in total, together with the exemplary executions of 1239, had been sufficient to bring dualism to an end in the vast area encompassed by the ecclesiastical provinces of Reims and Sens. In Cologne and Trier it seems to have faded away even earlier. Although there is evidence of Cathars around Cologne, Bonn and Liège between the 1140s and the 1160s, by the beginning of the thirteenth century there appears to be little sign of any successors,[49] while half a century later Rainier Sacconi does not even mention Germany in his survey of surviving Cathar communities. The record in England is even less substantial: one attempt at proselytization in the 1160s, which ended in total failure, and a brief mention of executions in London in 1211.[50]

The relative ease of the destruction of northern Catharism inevitably raises the question of the extent of its strength in the first place. In 1145 the canons of Liège claimed that "all the cities of the kingdom of the Franks (*Gallici*) and of our own have to a great extent been infected"[51] and, indeed, reports of Cathars in the second half of the twelfth century come from a wide area stretching from Cologne and Bonn in the east to Ypres, Lille, and Arras in the west, and as far south as La Charité and Nevers. At Saint-Félix, thirty years after the letter of the troubled Liège clergy, Robert of Spernone was accepted as presiding over the Cathar bishopric of France. He appears to have been supported by at least a rudimentary organizational structure. Catholic accounts recognise that, in some localities, there existed a hierarchy of initiates, including a number of *perfecti* able to administer the *consolamentum*, while at the same time attempts at missionary work were evidently taking place. Although no literature survives, some Cathars were capable of debating with the orthodox, as Eberwin of Steinfeld observed at Cologne in the early 1140s where the arguments stretched over three days before the mob took matters into its own hands. Twenty years later Eckbert of Schönau and his friend Bertolph engaged directly with the heretics at Bonn. Occasionally, to the surprise of the chroniclers, arrested Cathars vigorously argued their case with the ecclesiastical opposition. The woman tried at Reims in the late 1170s, who had sup-

---

[49] See R. Kieckhefer, *Repression of Heresy in Medieval Germany* (Liverpool: Liverpool University Press, 1979), 12–13.

[50] *Cronica maiorum et vicecomitum Londoniarum*, ed. T. Stapleton. Camden Society, 34 (London: Sumptibus Societatis Camdenensis, 1846), 3; *Ex Radulphi Abbatis de Coggeshale Historia Anglicana*, ed. F. Liebermann and R. Pauli, *MGHSS*, vol. 27, p. 357.

[51] *Corpus*, vol. 1, no.30, p. 33.

posedly been mentor to the young girl targeted by the lascivious Gervais of Tilbury, countered the prelates who examined her "like someone
who had acquired knowledge of all the Scriptures and had always practised responses of this kind."[52] According to William of Newburgh, the
missionary group that came to England, while generally uneducated,
nevertheless had a leader called Gerard, whom William grudgingly
conceded had a "little learning."[53] The canon, William of Châteauneuf,
who fled from Nevers to Narbonne, was much respected for his learning among the southern Cathars and was a leading participant in the
public debate at Servian in 1206, perhaps not only on account of his
own merits, but also because he came from an area which had been
one of the first affected by the spread of dualistic belief from the Byzantine empire in the twelfth century. In these circumstances a number of
contemporary northern intellectuals including Alan of Lille, Everard of
Béthune, Alexander Nequam, and William of Auxerre thought that the
Cathars were important enough to merit elaborate refutations.[54]

   However, Catharism in the north did not in the long run fulfill this
apparent potential. Although Robert of Spernone's position was confirmed at Saint-Félix, it is clear that, even then, the Cathars themselves
thought that their supporters were far more numerous in Languedoc
than anywhere else, since they found it necessary to create three new
dioceses to add to the one which already existed at Albi. William of
Châteauneuf may have gained prestige among the Cathars because
of his northern connections, but by the beginning of the thirteenth
century he realized very well that he could live much more safely in
Narbonne than in Nevers, even though the former was not a notably
heretical city. By the 1230s and 1240s, when the inquisitors, the royal
officials, and the preaching friars began to make real inroads into the
Cathar organization in Languedoc, it was not to France that adherents
fled, but to Lombardy or Catalonia. Only one man, Peter of Bauville,
a participant in the murder of the inquisitors at Avignonet in 1242,
went to Champagne at this period, but he only did so under extreme
pressure and he did not remain there, moving on to Lombardy where
he lived in various cities and towns for more than thirty years.[55] This

---

[52] Ralph of Coggeshall, ed. Stevenson, p. 123.
[53] William of Newburgh, p. 132.
[54] Biller, "Cathars and Higher Learning," 25–53.
[55] See M. Barber, "Moving Cathars: the Italian Connection in the Thirteenth
Century," *Journal of Mediterranean Studies* 10 (2000): 5–19.

accords with papal perceptions. Although assailed by Louis VII and Henry of Reims with stories of "Manichaeans" in Champagne and Flanders, Alexander III remained cautious; at the Council of Tours in May, 1162 (which Archbishop Henry attended), the only action against heretics is to be found in canon four, which is aimed at the Albigensian heretics of Toulouse and Gascony.[56] Seventeen years later at the Third Lateran Council of March, 1179, the pope again referred specifically to Gascony, the Albigeois and the Toulousain, as places where those called "Cathars, Patarines or Publicans" had grown so strong they now manifested their errors in public.[57] This view had not changed by the time of Innocent III. For him the penetration of heresy among the upper classes in Languedoc and the lack of perceived secular co-operation in tackling the problem justified turning to the weapon of military intervention in the form of a crusade.

Northern Europe was, in fact, a much less friendly environment for Catharism than Languedoc. To succeed the Cathars needed the backing of influential people, an ineffectual and divided response from the established authorities, and a broad base of sympathy or at least toleration among the wider populace. None of these conditions existed in the north; symptomatic of the differences was that, in the second half of the twelfth century, while the southern clergy engaged in public debates with the Cathars, their northern counterparts handed them over to the secular arm and thus to execution. Once, in the notorious case of La Charité, the conflict between Hugh of Noyers, Bishop of Auxerre, and Count Peter of Courtenay seemed to offer an opportunity but, as the record of the main secular rulers shows, such disunity was relatively unusual in the crusading lands of Champagne and Flanders. In the north, with the exception of Everard of Châteauneuf, no identifiable member of the aristocracy adhered to the heresy in nearly a century, even though there are occasional references to unnamed nobles in the sources.[58] In contrast, in Languedoc, according to Federico Visconti, Cathar preachers targeted southern nobles "living in the mountains"

---

[56] *Corpus*, vol. 1, no.39, p. 39.

[57] *Decrees of the Ecumenical Councils*, vol. 1, *Nicaea to Lateran V*, ed. N. Tanner (London: Sheed and Ward, 1990), p. 224.

[58] For example, at Arras in 1183, *Corpus*, vol. 1, no.48, p. 48. In addition, there was the long-running, but ultimately undetermined case of William, canon of Langres, and his brother, Colin, *bailli* of the count of Nevers, begun by the bishop of Langres in 1211 but still unresolved in 1233. On this, see Duvernoy, *Le Catharisme*, vol. 2, *L'Histoire*, 143–144. This is probably, although not certainly, connected with suspicion of Catharism.

and succeeded in containing their inclination towards pillage and sexual licence within more acceptable social limits.[59] Prominent clerics are equally hard to find. Eberwin of Steinfeld understood that "many of our clergy and monks" were among their adherents, and three clerks, Jonas (Cambrai, 1164–1167), Robert (Arras, 1172) and Adam (Arras, 1183) are mentioned specifically, but without cognomina.[60] William of Châteauneuf is the only named ecclesiastic. Not surprisingly, given the precocious urban development of much of the region, *échevins* or other bourgeois do figure among the accused; in 1163, some of them were rich enough to offer Archbishop Henry a bribe of 600 marks.[61] However, it is noticeable that the only named members of this class—the dozen or so townspeople from La Charité—were capable of putting up prolonged resistance, even going as far to appeal to the pope. For this money was needed: Robert of Auxerre describes them as "very rich men."[62]

Most of the accused had neither the resources nor the social standing to resist. Weavers were associated often enough for *textores* to become one of the generic names for heretics,[63] although this appellation was not exclusive to northern Europe, while at Châlons in 1235, Robert the Bulgar picked up Arnolin, a *tonsor*. Higher in status, but still regarded as an artisan, was Nicholas, executed at Braine in 1204, described by the anonymous chronicler as "a painter (*pictor*) very famous throughout the whole of France."[64] Many were, as Ralph of Coggeshall saw it, "rustics and thus are not convinced by reason, corrected by authorities, or deflected by persuasion."[65] Elderly women feature in many cases, most notably in the burnings of 1239.[66] To adapt John Arnold's analogy, by the 1230s there was insufficient leaven in the lump,[67] despite the presence in their ranks of men and women who could argue a case. Ultimately, therefore, the leadership and the missionaries were unable to recruit on any scale. Georges Despy's analysis of the accused involved

---

[59] Vauchez, "Les Origines de l'Hérésie Cathar en Languedoc," 1026.

[60] Bonenfant, "Un clerc cathare en Lotharingia,", 271; *Corpus*, vol. 1, no.46, p. 45; *Corpus*, vol. 1, no.48, p. 48.

[61] *Corpus*, vol. 1, no. 37, p. 38.

[62] Robert of Auxerre, p. 258.

[63] For example, at the Council of Reims in 1157, *Corpus*, vol. 1, no. 34, p. 36.

[64] *Ex Chronici Anonymi Laudunensis Canonici*, p. 713.

[65] Ralph of Coggeshall, p. 124.

[66] *Chronica Albrici Monachi Trium Fontium*, p. 945.

[67] J.H. Arnold, *Inquisition and Power. Catharism and the Confessing Subject in Medieval Languedoc* (Philadelphia: University of Pennsylvania Press, 2001), 19–47.

in the campaigns of Robert the Bulgar, produces a total of about 60 executed (the number burned at Châlons in 1236 is nowhere stated), at least 20 imprisoned, three converted and one pardoned, and then, finally, at Mont-Aimé, up to 187 executed.[68] These are very small numbers, especially for such heavily populated areas.

The fact is that, compared with Languedoc, with its raging debates, brutal warfare and tireless inquisitions stretching from the 1150s to the 1320s, northern Catharism was but a whimper. It is not a lack of evidence that makes this picture difficult to reconstruct, as Jean Duvernoy and Peter Biller argue,[69] but a dearth of Cathars. Innocent III's crusades against Languedoc may not have turned out as he had hoped, but his perception of the location of the epicentre of Western dualism was entirely correct.

---

[68] Despy, "Les Débuts de l'Inquisition dans les anciens Pays-Bas au XIIIe siècle," 82.
[69] Duvernoy, *Le Catharisme*, vol. 2, *L'Histoire des Cathares*, 195; Biller, "Northern Cathars and Higher Learning," 42.

AUTHORITY AND THE CATHAR HERESY
IN THE NORTHERN LANGUEDOC

CLAIRE TAYLOR

I. *Introduction*

In *The Origins of European Dissent* R.I. Moore noted that the strongest
arena of the Albigensian heresy after the triangle formed by Toulouse,
Albi and Carcassonne was "in the area to the north and west, through
Cahors towards Périgueux and Bordeaux."[1] In other words, the medieval counties of Agen and Quercy. More recently M. Barber has
noted that the Cathar bishoprics established in the Languedoc in the
1170s, including one at Agen, must have been established "where their
main support lay," even though that of Agen was "probably marginal
even in the later twelfth century."[2] Something to the latter effect was
noted also in Rome in 1210.[3] On the other hand, one of the largest
executions in the history of the heresy took place near Agen, in 1249.[4]
It is the lack and nature of the sources in terms of both the history
of the heresy and the efforts of the Catholic church against it in the
Agenais that makes the number of its adherents to the heresy and
their significance in the intervening decades difficult to estimate. Even
with the notable exception of the work of Y. Dossat on the Agenais

---

[1] R.I. Moore, *The Origins of European Dissent*, 2nd edn. (Oxford, Basil Blackwell,
1985), 114. All citations of *Origins* refer to this edition unless otherwise stated. My thanks
to David Green for his comments on this paper. Issues and evidence discussed in this
paper are addressed in greater depth in Claire Taylor, *Heresy in Medieval France: Dualism
in Aquitaine and the Agenais, c. 1000–c. 1250* (London: Royal Historical Society, 2005).

[2] M. Barber, *The Cathars in Languedoc* (Harlow: Longman, 2000), 59 and 74.

[3] Peter des Vaux-de-Cernay, *Histoire Albigeoise*, eds. and trans. P. Guébin and
H. Maisonneuve (Paris: J. Vrin, 1951 [abbreviated hereafter as PVC *Histoire*]), 127 note 1.
This translation is used here primarily, although the Latin contains the best footnotes:
Hystoria Albigensis, ed. P. Guébin and E. Lyon, 2 vols. (Paris: Champion, 1926–1930),
abbreviated as PVC *Hystoria*. It has also been published in English: *The History of the
Albigensian Crusade*, eds. and trans. W.A. and M.D. Sibly (Woodbridge: Boydell Press,
1998).

[4] See below.

Cathar bishop Vigouroux de la Bacone and the inquisition, and the use of some of the inquisitorial evidence by other scholars, the secondary role usually accorded to the northern counties implies that there is less of interest to be learned from a region geographically at the fringes of the Occitan Cathar heartlands, and divided within itself over the issue, than from those in which Catharism was more firmly and popularly implanted.[5] But the region is worth study in period c. 1170 to c. 1249 as a distinct political and social sphere in which the heresy demonstrably took root, flourished, and was seriously persecuted.

In doing this various aspects of the subject on which R.I. Moore has passed comment in a more general sense will be addressed, and the ways in which his observations help us to understand the patterns of heresy and orthodoxy in the region will be discused. A central theme of *Origins* to be addressed is his understanding that heresy is best interpreted within specific social contexts.[6] The Cathar heresy did not establish itself in the Agenais and Quercy simply because of the nature of its message and the admiration inspired by its first missionaries and converts. Like its success elsewhere in the Languedoc, it occurred because some social groups were willing, because of their own particular circumstances, to reject Catholic authority, both secular

---

[5] For works addressing the northern Languedoc see esp. those collected in Y. Dossat, *Eglise et hérésie en France au XIIIe siècle* (London: Variorum Reprints, 1982); "Une figure d'inquisiteur, Bernart de Caux," 47–52, "L'inquisiteur Bernart de Caux et l'Agenais," 75–79, "Catharisme en Gascogne," 149–168, "Les restitutions de dîmes dans le diocèse d'Agen pendant l'épiscopat de Guillaume II (1247–1263)," 549–564 and "Un évêque Cathare originaire de l'Agenais: Vigouroux de la Bacone," 623–639. See also B. Guillemain, "Le duché d'Aquitaine hors du Catharisme," *Cahiers de Fanjeaux*, 20 (1985): 57–71; G. Passerat, "Cathares en Bas-Quercy: entre l'eglise de l'Agenais et celle de l'Albigeoise," *Europe et Occitainie: les Pays Cathares* (Carcassonne, 1992), 149–165; M. Capul, "Notes sur le Catharisme et La Croisade des Albigeois en Agenais," *Revue de l'Agenais* 90 (1964), 13–14 (this journal is abbreviated as *RA* hereafter). B. Hamilton has made important observations about the Agenais hierarchy in "The Cathar council of Saint Félix reconsidered," in *idem., Monastic Reform, Catharism and Crusades (900–1300)* (London: Variorum Reprints, 1979), 23–53. See also M. Roquebert, *L'épopée Cathare*, 4 vols. (Toulouse: Privat, 1970–1989), and *idem., Les Cathares de la chute de Montségur aux derniers bûchers, 1244–1329* (Paris: Perrin, 1998). For Quercy see also E. Albe, *L'hérésie Albigeoise et l'Inquisition en Quercy* (Paris: Revue d'histoire de l'eglise de France, 1910). Of the other general French accounts, J. Duvernoy pays most attention to the northern Languedoc, in *Le Catharisme*, I: *La religion des Cathares*, (Toulouse: Privat, 1976) and *Le Catharisme*, II: *L'histoire des Cathares* (Toulouse: Privat, 1979).

[6] For this case with special reference to Catharism in the Languedoc, see Moore, *Origins*, 233–237, esp. 237, 239–240, and 268.

and clerical. In this sense the role of the minor nobility will be shown to have been particularly important, as Moore himself noted, as the first and most influential adherents to the new belief.[7] It was also they who were amongst the first to fall victim first to the social and political transformation wrought by the Albigensian Crusade in the Agenais and Quercy: the imposition of rigid vertical ties of dependence largely alien to the region by the northern invaders, after 1215 imposed formally on the higher nobility also, and after 1229 under the ultimate control of the French crown. These changes and the resistance to them were, in turn, to impact on patterns of toleration of the heresy in the northern Languedoc.

Moore's observations on the persecution of heresy will also be addressed. One of his major contributions to our understanding of the subject is his view that persecution needs to be understood in the context of state-building. The rise of persecution from the early eleventh century, reaching its medieval climax in the thirteenth, corresponds to a re-emergence of statecraft. Both the identification of "otherness" and its destruction by authority is not, he reasons, a natural extension of any identification of difference within wider society. It is not the result of innate intolerance of diversity or, in the case of heresy, dissent, within human society. It is more as Weber described it, initiated by and imposed on society, and is in its very essence institutionalized as part of defining who is *within* and *beyond* society, that is to say *protected by* or *threatening to* Christian political order. In Moore's words, "persecution began as a weapon in the competition for political influence, and was turned by the victors into an instrument for consolidating their power over society at large."[8]

Sources and problems with sources

I have suggested that we lack certain sources for the northern Languedoc that might help us establish a clearer picture of the socio-political circumstances in which heretics both operated and failed to be successful. For the Agenais there is a comparative lack of sources relating to the laity when we contrast it with other parts of Aquitaine, by

---

[7] *Origins*, 237.

[8] The case is pursued throughout R.I. Moore, *The Formation of a Persecuting Society* (Oxford: Blackwell, 1987), quote at 146. See James Given, "Chasing Phantoms: Philip IV and the Fantastic," in this volume for further discussion.

whose dukes it was ruled until 1197. I suspect that this was in part because the region was not very closely governed, a point which will be discussed further. The secular lords of the region left only a few records and most of the information we have relates to their interaction with the powers at Bordeaux and Toulouse. The structure of internal authority is thus difficult to discern, but we can chart the influence of a few families, such as the Ferréol and de Rovinha. The departmental archives of Lot-et-Garonne do not contain many manuscripts from our period, but those documents that do exist are all published. They include some important charters relating to towns in the Agenais. French administrative documents contain much material concerning the property and descendants of convicted heretics. Sources for the secular clergy are unusually scarce, probably because the diocesan archive of Agen, a diocese that incorporated the Condomois until the early fourteenth century, was destroyed in the Revolution. However A. Ducom's rather dense account of the institutional history of Agen contains much of what remains as *pièces justificatives*.[9] When we come to Quercy the picture is rather different. Although we are again short of diplomatic material, various archives relating to important families survive in the archives at Cahors, as do documents for episcopal and monastic activity, and a good many have been published or form the basis of good secondary accounts, cited below. The major sources for the crusade in the two counties are three literary works; the *Chanson de la Croisade Albigeoise* of Guillaume de Tudela and his continuators, and the Latin chronicles of Peter des Vaux-de-Cernay and Guil-

---

[9] Sources are published in *Histoire Générale de Languedoc*, eds. C. de Vic and J. Vaissète, (revised by A. Molinier), 16 vols. (Toulouse: Privat, 1872–1904, abbreviated as *HGL*) (for the de Rovinha, see VIII 388, 1849 and 1878 and below as cited); *Archives municipales d'Agen, chartes première série (1189–1328)*, eds. A. Magen and G. Tholin (Villeneuve-sur-Lot: Impre. de X. Duteis, 1876 [abbreviated as *Agen … Chartes*]); *Enquêtes administratives d'Alphonse de Poitiers … 1249–1271*, eds. P.F. Fournier and P. Guébin (Paris: Imprimerie nationale, 1959 [abbreviated as *Enquêtes*]); *Catalogue des actes de Simon et Amaury de Montfort*, ed. A Molinier (Paris: Imprimerie nationale, 1874 [abbreviated as Molinier, *Actes*]); *Correspondance administrative d'Alphonse de Poitiers*, ed. A. Molinier, 2 vols. (Paris: Imprimerie nationale, 1894–1900 [abbreviated as Molinier, *Correspondance*]); A. Ducom, "Essai sur l'histoire et l'organisation de la commune d'Agen jusqu'au traité de Brétigny (1360)," *Recueil des travaux de la Société d'Agriculture, Sciences et Arts d'Agen* 2:11 (1889): 161–322 (abbreviated as Ducom, i) and 2:12 (1891–1893), 133–234 (as Ducom, ii). On the scarcity of sources see A. Richard, *Histoire des comtes de Poitou, 779–1204*, 2 vols. (Paris: A. Picard, 1903), I, 270–271; J. Boussard, *Le Gouvernement d'Henri II Plantagenet*, (Paris: Librarie d'Argences, 1956), 228; Y. Dossat, "Les resitutions des dîmes… d'Agen," 549 note 1.

laume de Puylaurens.[10] The most important sources for the "heretics" of the northern Languedoc are inquisitorial records transcribed from October 1669 onwards from the archives of the Dominican convent at Toulouse into BN mss Lat. Fonds Doat XXI–XXIV. These do not feature the Agenais very centrally, for although the inquisitors Bernart de Caux and Jean de Saint-Pierre spent eighteen months in the Agenais and Quercy during 1243–1245, not much of what survives even from the trials at Agen itself actually relates to that county. Pierre Seilha and Guillaume Arnaud held the first inquiry in Quercy from 1233 to 1239, aided by Guillaume Pelhisson, the major chronicler of this early period of the inquisition.[11] Much evidence for Quercy from this time onwards is from some of the same inquisitorial sessions from which we learn about the Agenais heretics. Most detailed is the evidence contained in Doat XXII, 1^r–69^v containing the testimony of key witnesses for Bas-Quercy including Pons Grimoard, seneschal for the county for the counts of Toulouse, Othon de Berètges, *bailli* for Moissac and Montcuq, and the knight Guiraud Guallard, trusted associate of many *perfecti* of the region. These witnesses were on very dangerous ground in the 1240s, having already been interviewed in the 1230s by Guillaume Arnaud but relapsed into the heretical life.

From Doat XXI, 185^r–312^v, reflecting Pierre Seilha's inquest of 1241–1242 in Quercy, we have evidence of seven hundred and twenty four sentences passed by a peripatetic court sitting at Gourdon, Montcuq, Sauveterre, Beaucaire, Montauban, Moissac, Montpezat, Almont and Castelnau-Montratier. This evidence reflects voluntary submissions made in the period of grace preceding detailed investigations, and as such is less detailed than the Bas-Quercy material and, like that for the Agenais, allows us more in the way of a fragmentary narrative of the social structure of the region than real insight. It has recently been observed of the inquisition that "(t)he first step was to drive a wedge into the façade of community solidarity so that the loyalties and fears

---

[10] William of Tudela *et al.*, *La Chanson de la Croisade Albigeoise*, 3 vols., ed. and French trans. E. Martin-Chabot (Paris: H. Champion, 1960-[abbreviated as *Chanson*]); William of Puylaurens, *Chronique*, 2nd edn., ed. J. Duvernoy (Toulouse: Le Pérégrinateur éditeur, 1996 [abbreviated as William of Puylaurens]). The chronicle of Peter des Vaux-de-Cernay is cited above.

[11] *Chronique de Guillaume Pelhisson (1229–1244), suivie du récit des troubles d'Albi (1234)*, ed. and trans. J. Duvernoy (Paris: CNRS Editions, 1994 [abbreviated as Guillaume Pelhisson]).

which held it together could be undermined."[12] This is an astute observation on the nature of peasant and early urban communities as well as
on the practices of the inquisitors, but unfortunately it is all but impossible to relate such very important discussions to the northern Languedoc. The subtle relationships governed by power, fear, love, and loyalty
do not really reveal themselves in the documentation, with the exception some evidence from Bas-Quercy, from which we learn far more of
the towns and family members involved and their inter-relationships,
far more than can be incorporated into this paper.

Other problems emerge from the sources, naturally. Clearly we cannot take at face value some of what is said. Many testimonies, perhaps in particular those made voluntarily, may implicate suspects in the
heresy unfairly. Except where we know a good deal about the communities in question independently of the testimony of accusers, for
example establishing who had designs on property which might fall to
them if confiscated, we cannot always tell where this is the case.[13] As far
as possible I have attempted to describe communities using primarily
accounts of heretical activity as it was admitted by those involved and
common currency in the circles in which they moved. In other cases I
have taken accusations as indication that that *kind of* activity took place,
but not assuming that those cited as involved were actually involved.
Notwithstanding the fact that the sources may mislead even so, in using
the Doat evidence I am attempting above all to establish the basis of
secular heretical networks originating among and between both peers
and families and in relationships of power and dependence. Several
detailed and interrelated genealogies may be re-constructed from the
Bas-Quercy evidence, and I am working under the assumption that in
most cases witnesses would both know who was related to who and
how, and that they would have few reasons to mislead or be misled in
this matter.

---

[12] Barber, *Cathars*, 148.
[13] Such problems are addressed elsewhere See for example L. Boyle, "Montaillou
revisited: *Mentalité* and methodologie," in ed. A.J. Raftis, *Pathways to Medieval Peasants*
(Toronto: Pontifical Institute of Mediaeval Studies, 1981), 119–140. Most recently see
J. Given, *Inquisition and Medieval Society: Power, Discipline and Resistance in Languedoc* (Ithaca,
NY: Cornell University Press, 1997); J. Arnold, *Inquisition and Power, Catharism and the
Confessing Subject in Medieval Languedoc* (Philadelphia: University of Pennsylvania Press,
2001); M.G. Pegg, *The Corruption of Angels: The Great Inquisition of 1245–1246* (Princeton:
Princeton University Press, 2001); C. Bruschi, and P. Biller (eds.), *Texts and the Repression
of Medieval Heresy* (York: York Medieval Press, 2003).

Very often I am drawing an impression of the scale of heretical activity in a town from the number of individuals cited as or admitting involvement, but this does not mean that everyone found guilty was guilty. On the other hand, an assertion of orthodoxy on behalf of a third party is not necessarily reliable either. In direct contradiction of the evidence of Guiraud Guallard, a horrifyingly well-informed turncoat, Guillaume Faber of Pechermer tells us that in spite of his own belief in the heresy his wife Bernarda had nothing to do with it. Of his sister Guillelma, he tells us likewise: Yes, she talked to heretics, but she did not believe what they said.[14] A similar tactic was employed by P. de Noye of Castelsarrasin in the case of his wife Raimunda.[15] Nonetheless, each woman tolerated heretics in her house and did little that we know of to distance herself from them. They were never Catholic in the new sense that the inquisitors had imposed on the region by the mid-1240s, by being a family or community traitor.

But this is not to say that the inquisitors had better allies in the few who revealed heretics in their communities to Catholic authority before the inquisition made this a strategy for personal survival. When questioned in 1243, Guiraud Guallard admitted having protected the de Bressols family when originally interviewed by Guillaume Arnaud in the 1230s, and likewise the heretic Vital Grimoard. This was because they had helped him so much in his own heretical faith.[16] Indeed, he had been something of an acolyte of Vital. Similarly, Pons Grimoard, the son of Vital had continued to aid and believe the heretics at the same time as carrying out the penance Guillaume Arnaud had given him.[17] In this way before the 1240s—and note, not simply before the Albigensian Crusade or the earliest wave of inquisition—it seems unlikely that many people of either faith considered anyone else to be doing anything especially wrong, or if they did they were not interested in doing anything about it.

Indeed, the distinction between a lay Catholic and a punishable heretical believer, a *credens* who was involved with and believed the teachings of the heretics but had not received the *consolamentum* and been initiated as a *perfectus* or *perfecta*, is probably misleading. Those who received the heretics in their homes and were related to them

---

[14] Doat XXII, 9ᵛ *cf. ibid.*, 17ʳ.
[15] Doat XXII, 28ᵛ.
[16] Doat XXII, 18ʳ.
[17] Doat XXII, 38ᵛ–40ʳ (in 1236) and 33ʳ–38ᵛ and 40ᵛ–42ʳ (in 1244).

and to other active *credentes* and found some value in what they taught probably constituted the majority of the population of the Languedoc. The heretics were part of everyday life, not absent even from abbeys and churches, and certainly not from the households and courts of those witnesses who regarded themselves as Catholics, and many people moved between the two faiths more than once. Those *credentes* given penances for heretical activity ranged between the fully fledged *credens* who would have been hereticated on their death-bed to the somewhat ambivalent Catholic who sometimes performed paid services for the heretical community. We will see that many local lords eventually tolerated heretics, but we would be foolish to believe everything the chroniclers of the crusade say about their actual beliefs.

We must apply the same caution to the humbler people whose guilt is implied only through the inquisitors' registers. We have most evidence for relatively important families, landowners and castellans in the countryside, and the lords and leading families of fortified towns. We have noted that Moore sees such people as primarily responsible for the influence of the heresy in the Languedoc generally and that this seems demonstrably to be the case in the less well-studied northern counties. On the other hand, we must keep in mind the extent to which this might appear to be so because it is precisely from this group that we have most records. Evidence in the Agenais is only of such people, relating as it does not to inquisitorial activity but to later claims on confiscated family property. In Bas-Quercy we have frequent references to servants, boatmen, and other humble people questioned about the services they provided to leading families and heretics, but little information about their own social circle or heretical initiative they took on their own account. Numerous accusations are made against people in Central and Haut-Quercy of whom we know nothing at all in terms of socio-economic status. Although it is commonly asserted, and with some justification, that the contrast between the Cathars and the distant, worldly clergy probably accounts for peasant adherence to the heresy, we must heed Moore's caveat that there is in fact "nothing which permits a sustained assessment of the impact of the heresies on the greatest part of the population."[18] This is nowhere truer than in the northern Languedoc, and I cannot make more than cautious speculations in that direction.

---

[18] *Origins*, 237.

II. *Heresy in Agenais society, to c. 1209*

The earliest heresy in the Agenais

B. Hamilton has argued that the first trace of Catharism in the west may perhaps be found as early as 1101.[19] Recently, M. Lambert rejected such an early date, although M. Barber is less certain that we can discount it.[20] The earliest account which Moore accepts as evidence of Bogomil influence in western heresy is the 1143 or 1144 letter of Eberwin of Steinfeld sent from the Cologne area. This appears to describe a native dualist movement, implying that the foreign heresy was already well established.[21]

The earliest date for which Moore has accepted evidence that Bogomil-influenced dualism was in the south of France specifically is the 1160s. This judgement was based upon two pieces of evidence; the "letter of Heribert" copied into the *Annales de Margam* in the year 1163, and the canons of the council of Tours of the same year.[22] Moore found the contents of the former to be "suggestive of Bogomilism" in various respects, and the declaration of the Tours canons that a "new" heresy was spreading from the Toulousain to other parts of the south to add weight to the evidence that the heresy first appeared in the region in this decade.[23] On the evidence available this judgement was sensible. But so was his desire for "better evidence" in this context.[24] In the 1990s an early-eleventh century version of the Heribert

---

[19] B. Hamilton, "Wisdom from the east: the reception by the Cathars of eastern dualist texts," in eds. P. Biller and A. Hudson, *Heresy and Literacy, 1000–1530* (Cambridge: Cambridge University Press, 1994), 38–60, at 43–45 and 59–60.

[20] M. Lambert, *The Cathars* (Oxford: Blackwell Publishing, 1998), 19–29 and 35–37; Barber, *Cathars*, 26–28.

[21] *Sancti Bernardi...epistolae* no. 472 in *Patrologia cursus completus, series Latina*, eds. J.P. Migne (and continuators), 217 vols. (Paris, 1852–1904 [abbreviated hereafter to *PL*]), CLXXXII, 676–680; Moore, *Origins*, 168–172. See also the chapters in this volume by B. Hamilton and D. Callahan for discussion of early Bogomil influence on western heresy.

[22] *Annales de Margam*, in ed. H.R. Luard *Annales monastici*, 5 vols. (London: Longman, Green, Longman, Roberts and Green, 1864–1869), I, 15; *Concilia*, ed. J.D. Mansi, introduction and 53 volumes (Graz, 1960–1961) (reprint of *idem.*, *Sacrorum conciliorum nova et amplissima collectio*, 53 vols. Florence: Expensis Antonii Zatta Veneti, 1759–1798 [abbreviated hereafter to Mansi]), XXI, 1177.

[23] Moore, *Origins*, 197–199, at 198.

[24] Moore, *Origins*, 199.

source was discovered.[25] The implications of its content for the still controversial nature of eleventh-century heresy are only partially relevant here.[26] What does matter is that the evidence Moore found explicitly for dualism in the 1160s came from Heribert, not from the canons of Tours, which are far less specific about the nature of what the heretics believed, as are the records of a similar assembly at Lombers in 1165.[27] As much as any historian of heresy, and more than most and before most, we have Moore to thank for arguing that just because something *seems* like dualism, because it resembles it or could be contextually related to it, does not make it *evidence* of dualism. In this he has challenged successfully established scholarship and encouraged us to look for evidence rather than simply perceiving patterns. This skepticism accounts for his dismissal of Bogomil influence in the eleventh century and the late date of the earliest evidence he accepts for western dualism in the twelfth. It may therefore be the case that Moore will now reject the 1160s as the earliest evidence of Bogomilism in the south of France and accept only the next earliest unmistakable evidence. This comes from the late 1170s, and is discussed below. On the other hand, the latter evidence relates explicitly to an already well-established heresy. Because we know that Cathars had been confronted as early as the 1140s in Germany, even by Moore's exacting standards the 1160s still seems a conservative date for the earliest Bogomil successes in the Languedoc. As he in any case noted, the Margam annalist would have copied the Heribert source into his narrative "where he thought it belonged."[28]

---

[25] G. Bounoure, "La lettre d'Heribert sur les hérétiques Périgourdins," *Bulletin de la Société Historique et Archéologique du Périgord*, 120 (1993), 61–72; G. Lobrichon, "The chiaroscuro of heresy: early eleventh-century Aquitaine as seen from Auxerre," trans. P. Buc, in eds. T. Head and R. Landes, *The Peace of God: Social Violence and Religious Response in France around the Year 1000* (Ithaca and London: Cornell University Press, 1992), 80–103.

[26] But see Moore, R.I., "Literacy and the making of heresy, c. 1000–1150," in Biller and Hudson, *Heresy and Literacy*, 19–37, esp.20–22, and Lobrichon as cited. *Cf.* M. Frassetto, "The sermons of Adémar of Chabannes and the letter of Heribert. New sources concerning the origins of medieval heresy," *Revue Bénédictine*, 109 (1999): 324–340 and C. Taylor, "The letter of Heribert of Périgord as a source for dualist heresy in the society of early-eleventh-century Aquitaine," *Journal of Medieval History*, 26 (2000): 313–349. For the most recent commentary on this debate see Lambert, *Medieval Heresy*, 3rd edn. (Oxford: Blackwwell Publishers, 2002), 36–37.

[27] Mansi XXII, 157–168; Moore, *Origins*, 203.

[28] Moore, *Origins*, 198.

Turning to the northern Languedoc specifically, the earliest account of heresy in any form recorded in the Agenais was in 1114 when Robert of Arbrissel preached at Agen against an otherwise unidentified sect.[29] This account is too early to be related to the heresies of Henry of Lausanne or Peter of Bruys, even though they both had supporters in Gascony and Henry's journey to Toulouse probably took him through the Agenais along the Garonne, which bisects the county. It may relate to one of the other "heresies" St. Bernard apparently encountered in the region while pursuing Henry.[30] Another connection between the county and doctrinal heresy was made sometime before 1150, when Abbot Hervé of Le Bourdieu at Déols called a sect who opposed marriage and the eating of meat not only "Manichaean" but also "Agenais."[31] In c. 1155 Agen's bishop Elie II de Castillon (1149–1182) made an appeal to Abbot Pierre II de Didonie of La Grand-Sauve for aid in restoring the lapsed faith of the people of Gontaud, on the river Canaule in the north of the county, and in c. 1160 the castle of Gavaudun, in a gorge carved by the Lède, was apparently so infested by "heresy" that it was attacked by the army of Bishop Jean d'Assida of Périgueux.[32] This is not the place to attempt to establish the nature of any of these Agenais incidents, although that Moore would accept none of them as evidence for Bogomil influence is certain. It is however important to note that by the second half of the twelfth century the Agenais already had a "heretical" history untypical of much of the Languedoc. Moore has suggested a connection between the success of Henry of Lausanne and the later successes of dualism in the central Languedoc.[33] These Agenais incidents may suggest that the ground had been likewise prepared in the northern counties.

In 1198 when Pope Innocent III was elected, one of his first actions was to write to the metropolitan of Auch instructing him to challenge the strength of Catharism in his archdiocese. The task was in turn entrusted to the bishops of Bazas, Comminges, Lodève, and Agen,[34]

---

[29] *Monumenta conventus tolosani ordinis fratrum praedicatorum*, ed. J.J. Percin (Toulouse: Joannem & Guillelmum Pech, 1693), II, 3.

[30] For Peter, Henry, and St. Bernard see *Origins*, 82–114.

[31] *PL* CLXXXI, 1426.

[32] *Gallia christiana in provincias ecclesiasticas distributa*, ed. D. Sainte-Marthe *et al.*, 16 vols. (Paris: V. Palme, 1744–1877 [abbreviated hereafter as *GC*]), II 911; l'abbé Cirot, *Histoire de l'abbaye et congrégation de Notre-Dame de la Grande-Sauve, ordre de Saint-Benoît, en Guienne* (Bordeaux: Th. Lafargue 1844), II, 90.

[33] *Origins*, 114.

[34] *PL* CCXIV, 71–72.

and was the result of the assertion by churchmen that heresy had been flourishing in Gascony in preceding decades.[35] However, no heretics were discovered within the sphere of Auch. The pope was rather missing the point, but the archbishop was not. In including Bishop Bertrand de Béceyras of Agen (c. 1183–1209) in his plans, in spite of the fact that the Agenais lay beyond his own authority in the archdiocese of Bordeaux, he was surely aware of the growth of Catharism in the Agenais by this date.

The earliest dating for it comes from the Dominican inquisitor Anselm of Alessandria, who reported in 1266/7 that the Balkan Bogomil heretics had inspired the establishment of French Cathar bishoprics, including one at Agen, between 1150 and 1200.[36] Moore now accepts B. Hamilton and A. Dondaine's evaluation of the still controversial evidence for a Cathar council held at Saint-Félix de Caraman, probably in 1174/1177, which supports Anselm's claim and gives us a more exact date for the establishment of the heretical see.[37] The source informs us that at this gathering the Bogomil Nicetas converted the southern French Cathars from the moderate dualist *ordo* of Bulgaria to the absolute dualist *ordo* of Drugunthia (the former taught that God had given rise to the evil principle which ruled the World, the latter that the two

---

[35] Mansi XXI, 718 and 1177, and XXII, 232; William of Newburgh in ed R. Howlett *Chronicles of the Reigns of Stephen, Henry II and Richard I*, 4 vols.(London: Longman, 1884–1889), I and II, at I, 329–330; Walter Map, *De Nugis Curialium*, ed. T. Wright (London: Camden Society, 1850), 62; Gervais of Canterbury, *The Historical Works of Gervase of Canterbury*, ed. W. Stubbs, 2 vols. (London: Longman and Company, 1879–1880), I, 285.

[36] *Tractatus de hereticis*, in ed. A. Dondaine, "La hiérarchie Cathare," in *Archivum Fratrum Praedicatorum* 20 (1950), 308–324, at 308.

[37] *Origins*, 205–207, esp.212–215 and note 19; A. Dondaine, "Les Actes du concile albigeoise de Saint-Félix de Caraman. Essai de critique d'authenticité d'un document médiéval," in *Miscellanea Giovanni Mercati* 5 (Rome, 1946), 324–355; F. Šanjek, "Le rassemblement hérétique de Saint-Félix de Caraman (1167) et les églises cathares au xiie siècle," *Revue d'histoire ecclésiastique*, 67 (1972), 767–799; B. Hamilton, "The Cathar council of Saint-Felix," appendix to the first edition of *Origins*, 1977, 285–287, and esp. his 1978 *AFP* article "The Cathar council of Saint-Félix reconsidered" reprinted in *idem., Monastic Reform, Catharism and Crusades, 900–1300* (London: Variorum Reprints, 1979), 23–53. *Cf.* R.I. Moore, "Nicétas, émissaire de Dragovitch, a-t-il traversé les Alpes?," *Annales du Midi*, 85 (1973), 85–90; and esp. Y. Dossat, "A propos du concile cathare de Saint-Félix: Les Milingues," *Cahiers de Fanjeaux* 3 (1968), 201–214, in which it is argued that the manuscript for the council as published by Guillaume Besse was forged (*Histoire des ducs, marquis et comtes de Narbonne*, Paris, 1660, 483–486). For a good overview of the debates surrounding the mission from the Balkans see Lambert, *Cathars*, 45–49. Lambert too notes that Hamilton's article "supersedes earlier work" except that like Barber he finds 1167 a more convincing date for the council (*Cathars*, 46–47 notes 4, for the quotation, and 7).

were eternally co-existent[38]). We hear that three new heretical bishops were elected and ordained into the new *ordo*, including Raymond de Casalis, appointed to lead the Cathars of Agen. The same council established boundaries for he heretical see, although those for Agen were not contained in the only portions of the surviving documentation to have come to light.[39] The new doctrine was quickly adopted by the southern French Cathars as a whole, according to Rainier Sacconi.[40]

How had this happened in the Agenais? Essential to Moore's understanding of religious dissent is a socio-political context for its origin and success. He provides us with this context in his account of the Languedoc in the second half of the twelfth century, in which he notes in contrast to northern France that "(p)ower ... was remarkably diffused. Lordship was divided between a multiplicity of claimants ... administration was rudimentary, and the church ... shared its fragmentation and feebleness." One cause of this was that land and castles were often held allodially, not in return for service, another result of which was the predominance of mercenaries in Occitan warfare. Bonds which were acknowledged were neither commonly regarded as implying hierarchy, nor were they especially binding or permanent. Anti-clericalism was rife. A somewhat worldly clergy had in fact lacked both the resources and secular support to gain an effective foothold since the Gregorian reforms and was regarded as an ill-educated laughing stock. It was in the families of the minor nobility in particular, weakened and impoverished by partible inheritance and resentful of the claims made by Catholic clergy on their genuinely meagre resources, that social factors combined to produce a culture open to the suggestions made by heretics.[41] With a few modifications, as noted below, this is a portrayal

---

[38] A good account of the nature and influence of the two varieties is given in Lambert, *Cathars*, 54–59. Some historians dispute that this doctrinal issue was the real focus of the council and see its significance for Catharism as essentially structural (Duvernoy, *Catharisme*, I, 105–107; A. Brenon, A., *Le Vrai visage du Catharisme*, 2nd. edn., (Portet-sur-Garonne: Editions Loubatières, 1995), 109, 122–128, *cf.* Lambert, *Cathars*, 46 note 6).

[39] The original Saint-Félix document is lost but the portions of the copy of it published by Besse are reproduced in Hamilton, "The Cathar council ... reconsidered," 51–53. Besse's version in fact refers not to *Ecclesia Agenensis* but to *Ecclesia Aranensis*, i.e. the Val d'Aran in the county of Comminges. Because of the supporting evidence it is now generally agreed that this was a scribal error in the manuscript.

[40] *Summa de Catharis et Pauberibus de Lugduno*, in ed. A. Dondaine, *Un Traité néo-manichéen du XIIIe siècle: Le Liber du duobus principiis, suivi d'un fragment de rituel cathare* (Rome: Istituto storico domenicano, 1939), 64–78, at 77.

[41] *Origins*, 233–237, quote at 233. See also Barber, *Cathars*, 68 and 69 on secular

and evaluation of the region that endures.[42] In the many cracks in orthodox power, Catharism implanted itself and flourished. These factors very much apply to the Agenais, and also to Bas-Quercy.

The Cathar diocese of Agen constituted the most westerly outpost of organized dualism.[43] In 1178 Robert of Torigny referred to those of the Languedoc as "heretics who are called Agenais" and at the end of the century Raoul Ardent described in some detail Cathar beliefs in the Agenais.[44] Guillaume de Tudela says that on the eve of the Albigensian Crusade their influence extended to Bordeaux.[45] But this was an exaggeration. By that date they were no longer an immediate problem for the Bordeaux officials of the dukes of Aquitaine for in 1196 they conceded control of the county to the count, of Toulouse as their vassals, after several centuries of dispute over its possession, and abandoned their claim to the county of Toulouse.[46]

Count Raymond VI continued the Plantagenet practice of governing the Agenais as a *senechaussé*, the seat of which was an impressive castle at Penne d'Agenais on the Lot, the first Toulousain seneschal being Hugues d'Alfaro, a Navarrese mercenary captain to whom Raymond gave his natural daughter Guillemette in marriage.[47] However, the influence of the counts was to be like that of the Plantagenets before them, distant and remote, for immediate power in fact lay elsewhere, a great deal of it accounted for by the possession of the *comitalia* by the bishops of Agen. Counts in all but name since the eleventh century, their power was diminished under the Plantagenets, but when

---

nobles and heresy. This society, in other words, had not yet experienced "The First European Revolution" as proposed in R.I. Moore, *The First European Revolution, c. 970–1215* (Oxford: Blackwell Publishers, 2000), esp.169.

[42] In the last decade or so see esp. L. Paterson, *The World of the Troubadours* (Cambridge: Cambridge University Press, 1993), 66–89; S. Bonde, *Fortress Churches of Languedoc; Architecture, Religion and Conflict in the High Middle Ages*, (Cambridge: Cambridge University Press, 1994), esp. 53–65; A. Vauchez, "Les origines de l'hérésie cathare en Languedoc, d'après un sermon de l'archevêque de Pise Federico Visconti (1277)," *Società, istituzioni, spiritualità: studi in onore di Cinzio Violante II* (Spoleto: Centro italiano di studi sull'alto Medioevo, 1994): 1023–1036; Barber, *Cathars*, 34–70; Lambert, *Cathars*, 41 and 64–69.

[43] *Cf.* Barber, *Cathars*, 73.

[44] Robert of Torigny in Howlett ed., *Chronicles ... Richard I*, IV, 279; *PL* CLV 2011.

[45] *Chanson* I 8–9 and 18–19.

[46] See Taylor, C., "Innocent III, King John and the Albigensian Crusade (1209–1216)", in ed. J.C. Moore, *Pope Innocent III and his World* New York 1997 (Aldershot: Ashgate, 1999), 205–228, at 206–208.

[47] Boussard, *Le Gouvernement*, 148–151; Ducom, i, 273, 82–88.

Richard conferred the *comitalia* on Bertrand de Béceyras it still entailed the exclusive right to mint *Arnaudines*, to administer justice and receive the revenues thereof, and to raise various other monies in a secular context.[48] But given the major political and religious events in the Agenais, not least his mission of 1198, and the resources available to him, the episcopate of Bertrand de Béceyras was unremarkable except for being plagued by corruption.[49] Thus in the period around the turn of the century, after heretics had already established themselves in the county, we find that its ecclesiastical and secular authorities were only as capable, or incapable, of challenging the subversion as those of the rest of the Languedoc. However, Moore sounded a warning against the generalization that Occitan bishops did nothing to counter heresy and describes their "rapid response" in the context of the conference against the heresy convened at Lombers in 1165.[50] In spite of the fact that this assembly was not attended by Bishop Elie of Agen, a less jaundiced view of clerical activity must indeed be taken in the case of Bishop Bertrand's successor, Arnaud II de Rovinha (1209–1228), as will be seen.

We should first examine other factors that contributed to the establishment of heresy in the twelfth-century Agenais, unique in this respect in Aquitaine. We might ask whether this was the result of a singular characteristic that the county had. Some historians indeed stress a particularly *Agenais* way of doing things. T.N. Bisson observes that "even in the twelfth century the men of the Agenais were understood to form a kind of regional community, with common rights and responsibilities," the clearest expression of which was the *Cour d'Agenais*, a semi-autonomous essentially secular body consisting of representatives of Agenais villages and its approximately twenty significant towns and one hundred and fifty nobles.[51] However his account of the *Cour* and its supposed twelfth-century origins is open to dispute, not least because it relies heavily on the assumption of a homogenous culture throughout the Agenais, which might in turn lead us to expect to find a unified

---

[48] AD Lot 2J54, 13, xviii; Ducom, i, 294–318.

[49] For which see William of Puylaurens, 48–49 and *PL* CCXV, 682–683.

[50] *Origins*, 200–201. Dossat agrees ("Le clergé méridional à la veille de la croisade albigeoise," *Revue historique et littéraire du Languedoc*, 1 (1994), 263–278). Barber also seeks to modify the view of the Languedoc as a religious backwater (Barber, *Cathars*, 61–63).

[51] T.N. Bisson, "The general court of Agenais in the thirteenth century," in *idem.*, *Medieval France and her Pyrenean Neighbours* (London/Ronceverte: Hambledon Press, 1989), 3–30, quotation at 4.

response to heresy within the region.[52] Neither of these appears to have been the case, and frequently the opposite is true.

In seeking to understand the religious preferences of the people of the Agenais, we should note that Gascon, Toulousain, and Poitevin-Aquitainian influences met here and produced a very diverse society.[53] A linguistic mapping of the region reveals the presence of a distinct Occitan subdialect extending from just south of the abbey of Blasimon in Entre-Deux-Mers into the Lot region and down towards Agen. It was a dialect close to that of Quercy and the Languedoc but containing elements of French. South of the river, however, the dialect was more obviously Gascon. But by the mid-twelfth century the region spanning the Garonne's broad fertile plain and extending up river into Bas-Quercy, to the Aveyron, Tarn and Garonne basin, formed a homogenous region of assarted agricultural land and commercial towns, the *Pays de la Moyenne Garonne*. The close identification between the regions is reflected in their treaties of mutual support after they began to gain self-government around the turn of the thirteenth century, notably the ports of Agen, Mas-d'Agenais, Marmande and Porte-Sainte-Marie in the Agenais, and Montauban, Moissac and Castelsarrasin in Bas-Quercy.[54]

---

[52] See J. Clémens, "Les origines de la cour générale de l'Agenais," *Actes du 110e congrès national des Soc. Sav.: Montpellier* (Paris: C.T.H.S., 1986), 69–80, esp. 69–72; T.N. Bisson, "The general court of the Agenais: a reconsideration", *Parliaments, Estates and Representation*, xx (2000), 23–30; C. Taylor, "The origins of the general court of the Agenais," *Nottingham Medieval Studies* 47 (2003): 148–167.

[53] Major scondary works describing the towns, lordships and religious life of the Agenais to c. 1249: Clémens, "Cour," esp. 69–73, idem., "L'espace coutumier d'Agen au Moyen Age," *RA* 109 (1982), 3–19, "La coutume d'Agen au XIVe siècle," *RA* 113 (1986), 303–311, and "Les Plantagenêts dans la diocèse d'Agen durant la seconde moitié du XIIe siècle," in ed. C. Desplat, *Terre et hommes du sud, hommage à Pierre Tucoo-Chala* (Pau: J & D éditions, 1992), 201–212; C. Higounet, *Le Développement urbain et le rôle de Marmande au Moyen-Age* (Agen, 1952), 1–5 and 14; A. Ricaud, *Marmande*, 2nd edn., (Marmande: Coussan-Marmande, 1975), 7, 35–36, 41–43; A. Lagarde, *Reserches historiques sur la ville de Tonneins* (Agen: P. Noubel, 1882), 6–9, 12 and 38–39; J.F. Samazeuilh, *Histoire de l'Agenais, du Condomois et du Bazadais*, 2 vols. (Auch: Foix, 1846–1847), I, 147–158, 186, 219–220, 259, 270 and 274–294; J.-B. Marquette, "Les Albret en Agenais (XIe siècle–1366)," *RA* 98 (1972): 301–311; G. Tholin, "Notes sur la féodalité en Agenais au milieu du XIIIe siècle," *RA* 23 (1896): 45–58 and 537–546 (cited as Tholin i); 25 (1898), 144–156, 171–178 and 257–265 (cited as Tholin iii); and 26 (1899), 62–78 (cited as Tholin iv), 77; P. Deffontaines, *Les hommes et leur travaux dans les pays de la moyenne Garonne* (Lille: S.I.L.I.C., Facultés catholiques, 1932), esp. 1–8 and 247–256.

[54] *Agen ... Chartes*, xiv–xix.

Agen itself contained a busy mercantile community that developed its own consular authorities, collected *péage*, and resisted secular interests. Its customs, conceded in 1196–1197 by Raymond VI, confirm existing exceptions to comital power. But the greatest economic power in the town remained the cathedral chapter of Saint-Caprais, and there is evidence of resentment by the townspeople manifesting itself in litigation by 1216.[55] Marmande had strategic importance for the control of the river and from 1196 lay on the border between Toulouse and Aquitaine. It too contained an active and ambitious moneyed class of merchants and nobles who had forced the concession of customs for the town arguably as early as 1182.[56] In stark contrast to the productive, tamed Garonne plain, the northern parts of the Agenais consisted of wooded hills and river gorges, dotted with tiny castles and settlements, dominated by those of the Lot. These were in most immediate communication with the Cahorsain and Haut-Quercy which, like the Agenais, were part of the Aquitainian sphere until the settlement of 1196. One of the most important families of the Agenais was that of Bishop Arnaud de Rovinha. By the late twelfth century they were lords of Tonneins-Dessus and Casseneuil. Casseneuil nestled low but securely fortified on a rocky outcrop where the Lot meets the Lède, at the junction of the Roman Périgueux-Agen road, and was held by 1209 by Hugues de Rovinha. Neighbouring Tonneins-Dessus was Tonneins-Dessous, controlled by another family, the Ferréols, which had influence at Gontaud also by the early thirteenth century.[57] Both of the distinct socio-economic spheres to the north of the Garonne appear typically Occitan, one of them rapidly becoming part of the mercantile economy and urban precociousness with which the Languedoc is often associated, the other dominated by autonomous minor castellans whose ties of loyalty to each other were fluid and voluntary, like those of the castellans we view typical of those tolerating heretics.

The portion of the Agenais to the south of the Garonne, in contrast, was culturally more Aquitainian. It is true that the most important commercial center was an essentially free port, Mas-d'Agenais,

---

[55] *Agen … Chartes*, i, ii, iv and v.

[56] P. Ourliac and M. Gilles, *Coutûmes de l'Agenais*, I: *Les coutumes du groupe Marmande: Marmande, Caumont, Gontaud, Tonneins-Dessous, La Sauvetat-du-Dropt* (Montpellier: Société d'histoire du droit et des institutions des anciens pays de droit écrit, 1976), 5.

[57] AD Lot F. 97 and 104; E. Albe, ed., *Inventaire des archives municipale de Cahors*, I: 1, Cahors, 36; *HGL* III, 308, 363–364, 411–412, 789, 810–811, and 846–847, VI, 174, and VII, 22–24.

which had won concessions and levied its own duties by 1200.[58] However it was untypical, for most towns felt the influence of powerful Gascon families. The viscounts of Lomagne were major land and property holders. The lords of Albret had influence in three Agenais centers; at Casteljaloux they shared power harmoniously with the bishops of Bazas, at Nérac their power derived from influence over its abbey, and at Meilhan they were co-lords by the end of the century, granting exemption from *péage* along the river to the monks of Grandselve in the Toulousain.[59] The largest and most important estate in the whole of the Agenais was the southern viscounty of Bruilhois. Like the Albret, its twelfth-century viscounts were families holding lands elsewhere in Aquitaine. Such families in fact had little to do with Agenais political life as represented by the *Cour* and their identity derived from a different culture entirely. For example, in general terms in the Agenais, as elsewhere in the Languedoc, nobility was defined most clearly by landholding and not lineage, conferred by property ownership in towns as well as in the countryside. Yet this would only seem to be true as a generalization north of the Garonne, for the estates and towns of the left bank held by nobles pertained to their wider family holdings or titles, and *noblesse* was apparently not acquired through urban activity.

Some major Agenais families worked in co-operation with the great abbeys in both Aquitaine and the Languedoc, most notably Benedictine La Réole and Le Grand-Sauve in Entre-Deux-Mers, and Cistercian Grandselve as noted in the case of the Albret already. But the Agenais as a whole had relatively few churches or religious foundations of its own by the mid-twelfth century, and the Garonne was a dividing line in terms of the scale of religious enthusiasm as expressed through foundations. The laity of the central and northern Agenais was not as well served spiritually as those in other parts of Aquitaine or even some other parts of the Languedoc. The Lot valley in particular was a wasteland in this respect, with the exception of Sainte-Livrade and a Benedictine house at Penne.

Similarly, the actively Catholic influence of lay lords in alliance with Gascon bishops and abbots south of the river was not matched to the north, where there existed only the veneer of an institutionally Catholic hegemony. The bishop was not without secular allies. The lords of Fumel, Madaillan, Clermont-Dessus, Boville, and Fossat held

---

[58] *Agen ... Chartes*, xiv, xvi, xviii.
[59] *HGL* VIII, 1795, 1816, 1849 and 1854.

major titles, lands, and revenues of him But although none of these appear as part of the Agenais resistance in the Albigensian wars, only one or two were actually to aid the northerners. In addition, there is little evidence for secular episcopal power south of the river and the essentially Gascon powers there were to have a range of responses to the crusade. Thus, although it is appealing to believe that in 1211 the army raised in the Agenais in support of the count of Toulouse consisted of "the whole Agenais; no one remained behind,"[60] the nobles of the county were actually very divided over the heretical issue once the Crusade demanded of them that they take sides.

It has been noted how difficult it is to establish exact boundaries of jurisdiction for the Catholic bishoprics of Agen and Cahors in the Middle Ages.[61] The task is even more difficult for the Cathar diocese of the Agenais. The Cathars of southern France followed the Bogomil and Italian dualist practice of naming their dioceses after orthodox bishoprics, but did not always limit themselves to their exact boundaries. Neither were the Cathar bishops based in the towns after which the Catholic diocese were named, being the seats of power of orthodox bishops.[62] Thus we cannot reconstruct the Cathar diocese of the Agenais as it was conceived in the Saint-Félix document by attempting to equate it closely with the boundary of the Catholic diocese. We should instead discuss the Cathars of the Agenais most usefully by establishing as far as possible where they were actually situated and in what geographical context we can show them to have operated.

Most importantly, we find no evidence for Cathars established in that portion of the Agenais on the left bank of the Garonne, proving very literally true Y. Dossat's observation that Catharism did not cross the river into Gascony.[63] Perhaps more surprisingly, we find no references by 1209 to heretical centers in the right bank Garonne towns themselves. We have some references, which we cannot date, to the leading of heretics from Bas-Quercy at Agen itself.[64] However, there is no evidence that the town actually contained an heretical community until the 1240s. This is the case for all the Garonne towns until we come to

---

[60] *Chanson* I, 208–209.

[61] Albe, *L'hérésie ... en Quercy*, 27.

[62] Hamilton, "The Cathar council ... reconsidered," 36–38, 40–42 and 52–53. A. Brenon proposes Agen as the seat of the Cathar bishop of the Agenais (*Le Vrai visage*, 119). I know of no evidence for this.

[63] Y. Dossat, "Catharisme en Gascogne".

[64] Doat XXI, 302^v–303^r and 303^v–304^r.

the junction with the Lot. Even then, we have no evidence of cathars in either Gontaud or Tonneins by the latter date in spite of "heretics" at Gontaud in the 1150s, Cathars at Tonneins by the 1220s, and attacks by the crusaders on both 1209.

Heretics were apparently found in the valley of the Lot alone, using the Garonne only for communication with the Cathars of Bas-Quercy. M. Capul notes that the Agenais Lot was important to them because the heavily forested cliffs and hillsides were full of caves.[65] As a vulnerable outpost of heresy in an essentially orthodox duchy it perhaps offered security not as easily provided by the towns on the Garonne, more closely under the scrutiny of secular and episcopal officials. The first heretics that we hear were encountered by the Albigensian Crusade were at Casseneuil. A failed siege of the town was the culmination of a sort of pre-crusade in 1209. This campaign will be discussed further below, but the attack perhaps indicates that it was not as arbitrary or fruitless as is sometimes assumed. Guillaume de Tudela tells us that after the attack a youth rushed to Villemur in the Toulousain and informed the townspeople that the crusaders were already striking camp.[66] But Villemur is one hundred kilometres from Casseneuil and far less easily accessible from the Agenais than Castelsarrasin, the most important seat of secular power in Bas-Quercy and *en route* also to Toulouse. The action of the messenger perhaps indicates that what was being accessed here was a heretical network, not one of secular authority, for Villemur was the nearest significant town in the organizational network of the Cathars, home of a Cathar deacon of the Toulousain. This and other evidence suggests that Casseneuil, a town with excellent natural and man-made defences, might have been the most important Cathar town north of Villemur, perhaps even the seat of the Cathar bishop of the Agenais. In 1214, when it was besieged again, Peter des Vaux-de-Cernay describes the town as one of the most important centers of the heresy and one of the oldest.[67]

Towns neighboring Casseneuil, most notably Castelmoron-sur-Lot, Villeneuve, and Pujols were to play an important role in the heresy and it seems possible that there may have been houses of Cathars in 1209, but there is no evidence for this. We do know of one heretic by c. 1209 at Saint-Livrade, Guillaume Amanieu. His goods were confis-

---

[65] Capul, "Notes," 10.
[66] *Chanson* I, 42–45.
[67] PVC *Histoire*, 198–199.

cated because of his belief before 1214 and on 13 April of that year were given to a relative, Pons Amanieu, who did homage for them at Penne d'Agenais to Simon de Montfort, the crusade's commander.[68] Guillaume appears untypical of the town however. Its abbey was apparently untouched by heresy and was to host the crusaders. There is possible evidence for Catharism north of the Lot by this time though. In the 1240s Gausbert de Clusel told the inquisitors at Moissac that he had taken heretics to Monflanquin. He does not attribute a date to this activity and it very possibly occurred later, but we do know of another heretically sympathetic family of the region, the de Balenx, *Balencs* itself being situated in the *bailliage* of Monflanquin. Its lords appear to have been dependants or otherwise closely associated with the lord of Casseneuil during the crusade, and they numbered among them an important female *credens*, Hartemanda, whose career spans the whole of the period under investigation.[69]

The Albigensian Crusade and Agenais heresy, to c. 1229

We should now attempt to assess the impact of the Albigensian Crusade on this pattern of heretical adherence in the Agenais.[70] Guillaume de Tudela is the only source to give us an account of the Agenais campaign of 1209. Its leaders and major recruiters were Count Guy II of Auvergne and Archbishop Guillaume of Bordeaux. Their army included four of the most important nobles with lands in the Cahorsain and Haut-Quercy; Bertrand II de Cardaillac, Bertrand de Gourdon, Ratier de Castelnau-Montratier, and viscount Raymond III of Turenne (of the Limousin, but with Quercinois estates and influence including at Castelnau-Montratier). Among the churchmen was Bishop Guillaume de Cardaillac of Cahors (1208–1234), the uncle of Bertrand de Cardaillac. All of these were vassals of Raymond VI and would be central to what would later occur in matters heretical in Quercy. Apparently absent, in spite of the fact that the crusade assembled at Agen in May, were the laity and most of the clergy of the Agenais itself with the exception of Bishop Arnaud. Indeed, it seems possible

---

[68] Molinier, *Actes*, 78.

[69] Doat XXI, 293^r–4^r; *Chanson* III, 341, and below.

[70] For further discussion of the nature of warfare during the Alibensian Crusade, see Laurence W. Marvin, "The Massacre at Béziers July 22, 1209: A Revisionist Look," in this volume.

that it was Arnaud who instigated the campaign. If so his motive was not just concern for orthodoxy: he was personally in dispute with Raymond VI over their respective rights in the county, a matter he had already referred to Rome.[71]

The army destroyed Gontaud and sacked Tonneins. It is not known whether the latter attack was on the de Rovinhas' Tonneins-Dessus or the Ferréols' Tonneins-Dessous, but it is far from unlikely that the bishop would attack members of his own family, for the most important activity of this campaign was aimed at his brother's town, Casseneuil, as we have seen, its well-equipped garrison commanded by Séguin de Balenx. Various aspects of the outcome of the siege raise questions. One that is relevant here is that numerous heretics were apparently captured from the unconquered town and burned. It was these events that caused a messenger to hurry to alert Villemur.

Matters in the next stage of the crusade to affect the Agenais are less obscure. In 1211, after Raymond of Toulouse was excommunicated again, the Agenais declared for him to the extent that he had enough support needed to force bishop Arnaud from his see and seize all comital resources.[72] In the following year the lands and communication routes surrounding Toulouse were captured, enabling the crusade now to target the Agenais, undoubtedly with the encouragement of the exiled bishop. The army approached along the Lot from Quercy via Montcuq, whose *bailli*, Guiraud de Montfabès, fled on 1 June ahead of the army and took refuge with Hughes d'Alfaro at Penne d'Agenais. Montcuq was given to crusader Baldwin of Toulouse, a northern-raised half-brother of Raymond VI.[73] The crusaders then amassed at Penne, on Sunday 3 June, and established two camps below the castle. Penne was almost impenetrable, well provisioned and reinforced by the *routier* chief Bausan and his army. Yet the mere presence of the crusaders sent shock waves through the Agenais. On 4 June, even before the siege was begun in earnest, de Montfort was received with honour at Agen and on 17 June presumptuously divided the *comitalia* between himself and the reinstated bishop.[74]

The besieging of Penne commenced properly on 6 June and continued throughout a hot month with neither side gaining the advantage.

---

[71] *Chanson* I, 38–45.
[72] *Chanson* I, 146–153; *PL* CCXVI, 836; Samazeuilh, *Histoire*, I, 237.
[73] PVC *Histoire*, 127.
[74] PVC *Histoire*, 127–133; *Chanson* I, 254–261.

De Montfort decided to begin the second phase of his conquest of the Agenais and sent Robert Mauvoisin to Marmande shortly after 17 July. The town surrendered after a mangonel bombardment and a northern garrison replaced the count's men.[75] The nobles of the Agenais began to declare for the crusade's commander, receiving their lands back as fiefs. Among those who defected that summer was possibly Hugues de Rovinha himself, for in 1214 he is described by Peter des Vaux-de-Cernay as breaking faith with de Montfort. On 25 July this mass defection, combined with a serious shortage of food and water at Penne and a lack of reinforcements, led d'Alfaro also to surrender. De Montfort put his own garrison in place and began to re-build this strategically important fortification.[76] Penne became his main base in the northern Languedoc, from which he would launch campaigns into Quercy. But because the Agenais had submitted almost without a fight, its inhabitants were not dispossessed in 1212. Unlike the landless *faidits* of the Lauragais, Albigeoise, and Trencavel lands, who had been conquered and their lands given to crusaders, and who were thus irrevocably opposed to the crusade, the loyalty of the Agenais lords was apparently taken for granted. The weakness of the Agenais resistance was not to be long lasting however. In truth, its lordships and towns were to change allegiance whenever it was necessary in order to avoid political subjection and the confiscation of their property or, indeed, whenever the dominant authority in their region looked like facing a reversal of fortune.

Thus it was that in 1214 confidence revived. Hugues de Rovinha appears to have recovered his nerve in February, openly defying the crusade by sheltering the murderers of the hated Baldwin of Toulouse.[77] In April, he received help from King John of England, duke of Aquitaine and Count Raymond's brother-in-law and lord for the Agenais, who took a detour via La Réole. De Montfort sensed the threat posed by Aquitainian involvement in the crusade and moved again to Penne on April 13. His fears were justified. Marmande surrendered to John who garrisoned it and placed in charge his seneschal for Gascony, Geoffrey Neville. Thus began a wave of defections in the Agenais with Aquitainian help. But events went the crusaders' way again when John left the region. The crusaders destroyed Montpezat and made for Mar-

---

[75] PVC *Histoire*, 130–132.
[76] PVC *Histoire*, 129–132 and 199.
[77] PVC *Histoire*, 199.

mande, whose citizens at first refused entry to the crusade but after
a short siege fled into Gascony. Neville and his garrison were granted
safe conduct and de Montfort installed his own men.[78] Now he could
turn his attention to the rebels and murderers at Casseneuil. On Monday 18th August it fell and its heretics and many other inhabitants were
massacred.[79]

This time the loyalty of the conquered region was not taken for
granted. De Montfort appointed Philip de Landreville, a knight of the
Île-de-France, as his seneschal for the Agenais and Pierre de Voisin as
his marshal. By late August the nobility of the Agenais had again done
homage to the crusade's commander, this time promising to demolish
their castles and recognising the authority of his officials. As part of
this process Hugues de Rovinha was apparently deprived of Casseneuil,
for de Landreville granted its revenues to Dominican Prouille.[80] De
Montfort returned briefly to the county later in the same year to ensure
that destruction of fortifications was actually taking place and also to
receive at Penne the homage of the Quercinois lord Raymond de
Montaut for lands he held in the Agenais.[81] In acting as its ruler he
was anticipating the ruling of the Fourth Lateran Council of 1215 that
he would be confirmed as count of Toulouse.

But de Montfort could not afford to wear this new title complacently
because The Toulousains soon began to organize again against him.
On 11 May 1216 the consuls of Agen were told to raise an army to
be commanded by Guillaume-Arnaud de Tantalon, Raymond's titular
seneschal in the county.[82] On 13 September 1217 the southern army
re-occupied Toulouse reinforced by, among many others, *faidits* from
the Agenais commanded by Hugues d'Alfaro and de Tantalon. Among
them were Guillaume Amanieu of Sainte-Livrade and Bertrand and
Guitard de Marmande.[83] The town held at bay the crusading army
until it disbanded following the death of de Montfort on 25 June 1218.

This naturally led to a revival throughout the entire region. However,
the Agenais was again divided in its reaction. Raymond and Amaury
de Montfort, the crusade's new leader, both arrived in the autumn to
win its co-operation. Many towns elected to declare for Raymond,

---

[78] PVC *Histoire*, 197–202; *HGL* VI, 446; Taylor, "Innocent III," 208–214.
[79] PVC *Histoire*, 198–202.
[80] *HGL* VI, 465.
[81] PVC *Histoire*, 204; Doat LXXV, 53[r]; *HGL* VI, 448.
[82] *Chartes ... Agen* vi.
[83] *Chanson* III, 302–303 and 308–313.

including Marmande, Aiguillon, and also Condom, who massacred their French garrisons in the process. Pons Amanieu of Sainte-Livrade now defected to the southern side. But at Agen itself the bishop's party had been in the ascendancy since his return in 1217 and remained for the crusade. Etienne Ferréol of Tonneins also entered the conflict on this side and was enfeoffed at Gontaud with Montastruc. The most famous event in this period was a protracted and terrible siege of the rebels at Marmande in 1219. The Catholic lords Vézian and Espan de Lomagne of the southern Agenais were among them, as was the recently dispossessed lord Gaston de Gontaud. Guillaume Amanieu was again present, as indeed was Pons. Coming clearly into focus here is the fact that heretical sympathy often had little to do with responses to the crusade, whatever the sources may have have said. When Prince Louis of France arrived at Marmande in June the terrified townspeople submitted. Its inhabitants—men, women and children, probably several thousand people—were massacred. Almost certainly among them were the lords of Lomagne and Gontaud and the tragically reconciled Amanieus, for the only known survivors were Gascon leaders Count Centulle of Astarac and Guillaume-Arnaud de Tantalon. The town remained in Gascon hands, however, those of the crusader Amanieu V d'Albret.[84]

After the defeat of Marmande furious arguments erupted within Agen. The largely Montfortist town almost admitted Amaury's soldiers but it was Raymond who won it over, promising amnesty for the crusaders' party, a large southern garrison, and further privileges.[85] By spring 1224 the Midi had been retaken by the Toulousains, by now under the young Raymond, his father having died in 1222. But Louis, king of France from 1225, persuaded Amaury to cede his inherited claims in the Languedoc. A royal crusade was declared and in June 1226 it marched down the Rhône. Some southern allies remained loyal and on 21 or 22 May of that year Raymond and the people of Agen made a further agreement, involving more communal concessions, that the two parties would make common cause against the crusade and the king.[86] However, Louis took Avignon after a three-month siege and,

---

[84] *Chanson* II, 298–299 note 3, III, 139 note 5, 164, 234–235, 252–261, 256–257 and 282–291; Molinier, *Actes* 168; Samazeuilh, *Histoire*, I, 158, 259–260 and 274; Marquette, "Les Albret," 308.

[85] *Agen ... Chartes*, xii and xiii.

[86] *Chartes ... Agen*, xvii.

rather than face invasion again, the desperately war-weary Languedoc submitted, with the exception only of Toulouse itself.

The death of Louis on the return journey to Paris raised southern hopes again briefly over the winter of 1226–1227. Etienne Ferréol defected to the south, although he was soon killed in fighting.[87] But the regency of Louis' queen, Blanche of Castille, was a strong one. Raymond had to sue for peace and, in Paris on 12 April 1229, in exchange for the lifting of his excommunication, he formally submitted in the Treaty of Paris. Raymond lost many lands in the Languedoc and was obliged to perform homage for the others.[88] In terms of the Agenais, in order to preclude any chance of further rebellion, the walls of castles and towns were to be destroyed including those of Casseneuil, Pujols, Agen, and Auvillars. Until his death in 1249, however, the diocese of Agen and Cahors were retained by Raymond VII, if not without Capetian and papal interference.

If we review the period to 1229 in an attempt to identify regional patterns of party allegiance or identity in the crusade, none except a desire for independence are easily discernible. The Agenais was not divided between Catholic and heretic any more than the rest of the Languedoc, for the more Catholic Agenais lords of Albret and Lomagne and the townspeople of non-heretical Agen, Sainte-Livrade, Mas and Condom found themselves on different sides. Nor did "heretical" towns of the Lot resist or suffer more than the "Catholics" of the Garonne: of the sieges of Marmande and Casseneuil and the assaults on Gontaud, Penne and Tonneins, only those on Casseneuil were declared by the crusade to have anything to do with heretical occupants. We find several Agenais lords acting as allies of the crusade, for example Anissant de Caumont, and some, like Hugues de Rovinha himself, forced to submit and to perform homage to de Montfort. Etienne Ferréol, on the other hand, embraced the crusader cause for a time and was one of that handful of trustworthy southerners placed in charge of the property of their dispossessed countrymen, but was also in a minority in rebelling against the French crown in 1226. Thus no simple model of loyalty or identity can be demonstrated in the period 1209–1229 and each town and lordship appears to have shifted for itself and judged its own chances of success by the fate of its neighbours. The lord of Albret

---

[87] William of Puylaurens, 132–133.
[88] The articles of the treaty are contained in *HGL* VIII, 878–894.

alone appears to have remained firmly northern in his allegiance, managing in 1219 to extend his territory to the right bank of the Garonne as a direct result.

When we relate the evidence for the location of heretical centers to c. 1229, we gain the impression that, in spite of military activity and the execution of heretics, the crisis no more thoroughly undermined heresy in the Agenais than it did elsewhere in the Languedoc. This process was to be the achievement of the inquisition. This does not go without saying even though it is well known to scholars. We have noted that heretics in the Agenais were few in the first place and I have hopefully established that the region received a good deal more attention from the crusade than is sometimes recognised. But little changed initially in terms of the location of heresy.

In spite of the fighting seen by the Garonne towns, almost no action was taken against heresy along the river, and this probably reflects the fact that it was very weak there. It is unlikely that the zealous Bishop Arnaud would have overlooked it, and whatever their feelings about him or the northern invasion the commercial centers of the region were essentially orthodox and the heretical presence limited to through-traffic.[89] Moore challenged the idea that the introduction of heresy into a region was especially related to mercantile interests such as those expressed in towns like these. The attacks on them thus follow a pattern identified by Barber, having little to do directly with the extirpation of heresy but being intended to undermine secular structures and render the Languedoc more easily conquerable and its heretics thus more vulnerable.[90] This pattern would also fit the assault on Penne in 1212, not heretical but crucial in terms of comital power, like Agen which submitted in the same year along with Marmande, and whilst the latter indeed containined heretics, no action was taken against them at that time. However, such a strategy depends upon the continued maintenance of a sense of fear in the region, which the crusaders did not yet achieve on a lasting basis in the Agenais. Thus we have evidence for families along the Lot who were still heretically sympathetic.

Inquisitorial sessions in Quercy reveal that on unspecified occasions at Casseneuil Hartemanda de Balenx had been the close associate of Cathars, listening to them preach, adoring them—by genuflecting, per-

---

[89] For example see Doat XXI, 239ᵛ.
[90] *Origins*, 172–174 and 265–266; Barber, *Cathars*, 66, 69, 133–135.

forming *melioramentum*, the customary way for *credentes* to acknowledge the status of *perfecti*—and believing them to be good men and to be saved. As directed by the formulaic questioning used by the inquisitors, she tells us that she gave them bread, wine, cider, fish, and cakes and had eaten with them and shared bread which they had blessed. On another occasion she sent blankets to them at a house where they were staying. Most importantly, she was frequently their *ductrix*, responsible for escorting them in their journeys through the Agenais, leading them from *Pradasol*, which she says lay near Casseneuil, and to a place she calls *Colorsach*.[91] It seems possible that her exodus from the Agenais was the result of the fall of Casseneuil in 1214, which, if not the seat of a Cathar bishop, was at least the Agenais' leading heretical center by this date. If anything its position was perhaps strengthened in 1212 by the likely submission of Hugues de Rovinha as a vassal of de Montfort, rendering him, his town and its Cathars free from outside intervention for another two years. Of Hugues, we hear little after 1214, although he lived at least until 1218.[92] The heretical life of the town seems to have ended with its fall, and the transferral of its revenues to Prouille implies the ongoing presence of Catholic authority.

From the 1220s Castelmoron emerges as the leading heretical town just as Vigouroux de la Bacone was the leading heretic. Several other townspeople had their property there confiscated by the inquisition before 1237 as Dossat has noted. We also have a reference to the heretic Giraud de Castelmoron who stayed at the home of Pierre de Noye at Castelsarrasin *en route* to Moissac, probably in the 1220s.[93] But Castelmoron apparently received no attention from the crusade and we may speculate that heretical operations from there were more covert and successful than they had been under the unfortunate Casseneuil.

Heretics are first in evidence at Tonneins in this period. Witnesses B. del Loc, Isarn Pontonier, and B. Nauta admitted that they had ferried them thence from their own town of Moissac.[94] Again it is unclear whether the evidence refers to Tonneins-Dessus or Tonneins-Dessous but it seems unlikely that they would have been tolerated by Etienne de Ferréol of Tonneins-Dessous for until late in the day he was a crusade partisan. Whereas many Catholic lords were southern

---

[91] Doat XXI, 216ʳ.
[92] *Agen ... Chartes*, ix.
[93] Arch. Nat. JJ 24B, 63ʳ⁻ᵛ, as cited in Dossat, "Un évêque," 624; Doat XXII, 27ᵛ–28ʳ.
[94] Doat XXI, 305ʳ and 293ʳ.

allies by 1229, few heretical sympathizers were crusaders. However, Raymond-Bernard de Rovinha of Tonneins-Dessus had confiscated property returned to him as part of the armistice of 1224, a restoration in part initiated by his kinsman Bishop Arnaud.[95] Perhaps, like Guillaume Amanieu, this had been seized for his belief or, like the majority of Agenais lords, for resistance.

The Agenais from 1229 to 1249: the increase of heresy along the Garonne

The region saw relative peace after 1229 for over a decade.[96] Then in 1241 Raymond VII rebelled again supported, among others, by many lords and nobles of the Agenais. But the southern alliance was short lived. Raymond was forced to besiege the count of Foix at Penne, the last conflict of the Albigensian wars in the Agenais, and to fight a battle against the royal army, which he lost. On 28 May 1242 the inquisitors Guillaume Arnaud and Etienne de Narbonne were murdered at Avignonet. Heavily implicated was the *bailli* of Castelsarrasin, Raymond d'Alfaro, son of Hugh d'Alfaro, seneschal for the Agenais and now governor of Avignonet. The count was thus forced into a truce.

If Raymond's fortunes were again in a downturn, those of some towns, notably Agen, were improving and had done so steadily throughout the first half of the century as a result of the concessions and amnesties it had won in exchange for its support. In March 1243 the town conformed to a general submission to the French Crown, but this time too was able to negotiate relative autonomy in terms of economic and judicial affairs. Other towns of the Garonne ensured their economic survival in the period with agreements to act in mutual accord and protection, also in conjunction with towns in Bas-Quercy. Even Marmande, decimated after the execution of its inhabitants in 1219, prospered and received an influx of commercially-minded immigrants as C. Higounet has shown.[97]

---

[95] *HGL* VIII, 779–780.

[96] Sources for the secular history of the Agenais from 1229 into the early 1250s: *HGL* VI, 502–503, 543, 586–808 and 753–755, and VIII, 893, 1087, 1113–1120, 1153–1157, 1261, 1854, 1856, 1952 and 1955; *Agen... chartes*, x–xviii; *Enquêtes*, 64–70; A. Teulet, et al, eds., *Layettes du trésor des chartes*, 5 vols. (Paris: H. Plon, 1863–1909 [abbreviated as *Layettes*]), II, 1777, 3045, 3048, 3166, 3169 and 3171; William of Puylaurens, 166–169; Doat XXIV, 155ᵛ and CXVII, 217ʳ–21ᵛ; *GC* II, 431–432; AD Lot-et-Garonne E. supplt. 2745 (II.1), 1–3). Major secondary works are those cited in note 54 above.

[97] Higounet, *Marmande*, 8–9.

The actively rebellious lords of the Agenais also saved themselves, as usual by pragmatism in the shifts of political power of the 1240s. In May 1242 a Raymond-Guillaume de Tonneins—probably of the Ferréol family from his first name, popular within this family—was involved in the insurrection following Avignonet. A Guillaume Ferréol of Tonneins-Dessous did homage to Raymond VII along with others including Amanieu d'Albret. However, as result of the southern weakness by 1243 those same lords did homage to the crown, as did Bernard de Balenx, Raimond de Pujols, Gaston and Vidal de Gontaud and also Bernard, Aimery, Hugues and Autinier de Rovinha (lords of Tonneins-Dessus, now also Auterive, and again of the de-fortified Casseneuil).

But as part of the process by which the towns gained concessions and the nobles regained lands and some autonomy, the clergy continued to lose secular power and resources, a process begun under the Plantagenets and continued by the St. Gilles and Montfortist counts of Toulouse in the 1220s. Their comital rights had been almost entirely eroded by the end of the 1240s, the consuls of the commune of Agen ceased to perform homage to them and they were excluded from either participating in or convening the *Cour d'Agenais*. Indeed the clergy as a whole was by now excluded from the *Cour* and would be until 1271. In addition, few records of donations or foundations exist for the period and those that took place again affected primarily the left bank of the Garonne. Thus we find the secular Agenais recovering after the wars, but the clergy, most notably the bishops, and the count somewhat alienated from the region in terms of political power.

This state of affairs perhaps helps in explaining changing patterns of heresy in the region after 1229 and the response of the authorities to it. In terms of the latter, something of an alliance between the count and bishops was to emerge. This was in spite of comital designs on the revenues of one of the few new foundations, a priory at Mas-d'Agenais established by 1224, in the 1230s. As part of understanding this *rapprochement* we must first of all emphasise two aspects of the comital agenda, strong orthodoxy and his determination to exercise control over what he held by right. These are stressed in all good studies of the inquisitorial period in the Languedoc, but nowhere better illustrated than by his relationship with the inquisition in the Agenais and Quercy.[98]

---

[98] A major source for the inquisition in the region is the *Chronique de Guillaume Pelhisson*, esp. 13–42. A recent concise overview of the inquisitorial period in the Langue-

From the outset Raymond VII was not happy to accept in his lands autonomous activity by the Dominicans. Othon de Berètges, his *bailli* in Quercy for Moissac, was tried in 1244 and revealed that in the 1230s he had been instructed by the count to obstruct them.[99] Raymond was supported in this by Bishop Arnaud IV de Galard of Agen (1235–1245), initially in the case of the inquisitor Bernart de Caux, himself a native of the Agenais. The papacy wanted an effective inquiry, not squabbles between Agenais Catholics, and the inquisition was removed from the control of the mendicants by Innocent IV in 1248 and put under that of Bishop Guillaume II of Agen.[100] This allowed the count to carry on the fight against heresy on his own terms, something he had already been doing. Arnaud de Tantalon was active on his behalf in 1237, for example, enacting the confiscations at Castelmoron. In 1243 the count and bishop had initiated an inquisition under comital control in the dioceses of Agen and Cahors, staffed by clergy of their own choosing.[101] Bishop Pierre de Reims (1245–1248) was instructed by Innocent IV to continue the episcopal-comital offensive at Agen.[102] Its culmination was the burning at *Béoulaygues* near Agen in 1249 of eighty people who had relapsed into the heresy, perhaps first found guilty by Raymond's inquest of 1243.[103]

This later period was more decisive than the crusade in changing the geography of Agenais heresy. Of course we would expect to find more references to the years immediately preceding the inquisition as they were uppermost in witnesses' minds. Nonetheless, the location as well as the scale of the heresy appears to have altered, having not only flourished along the Lot but implanted itself more strongly along the Garonne.

---

doc is given in Barber, *Cathars*, 169–175. Among the best modern works specifically devoted to the inquisition is B. Hamilton, *The Medieval Inquisition* (London: Holmes and Meier, 1981). For material specifically relevant to the northern Languedoc see *ibid.*, esp. 61–65; C. Douais, ed., *Documents pour servir à l'histoire de l'inquisition dans le Languedoc*, 2nd edn. (Paris: H. Champion, 1977 [hereafter abbreviated as Douais]), vi–xxii, cxliv–clxvi, ccx–ccxxiii; Y. Dossat, "Une figure d'inquisiteur," and "L'inquisiteur," Lea, *History*, II, esp. 16–41; Albe, E., *L'hérésie ... en Quercy*, Duvernoy, *La Catharisme*, II, 267–273, 281–286, and 353–355; Roquebert, *Les Cathares ... aux ... 1329* (Paris, 1998), 115–126, 169, 1828–1826, 196–197 and 205–207; Passerat, "Cathares," esp. 152–155.

[99] Doat XXII, 45ᵛ–46ʳ.

[100] *Spicilegium*, ed. L. d'Achery, 2 vols. (Paris, 1723), IV, 265; *HGL* VI, 57–58.

[101] Doat XXXI, 40ʳ⁻ᵛ; *HGL* VI, 737–738 and VIII, 1088–1089.

[102] *HGL* VIII, 1240–1241.

[103] William of Puylaurens, 184–185; *HGL* VIII, 1981.

Two of those burned in 1249 may have been Vital d'Artigues and
Giraude de Lamegia, for they were executed at some point at Agen
by order of Raymond VII.[104] Another was possibly Elie d'Aigrefeuille,
inhabitant of Agen in 1227 whose possessions were later granted to
Sicard d'Alaman.[105] Vital d'Artigues of Agen was also burned in his
hometown.[106] Heretics lived at Agen even after 1249. They included
Arnaud Pairol, Guillaume Baudès, and the brothers Elie and Gaucelm
de Clèves.[107] The properties of Elie Augue, Colombe Denovar, Guillaume Astorg, Guillaume Engas and Guillaume de Toulouse were confiscated at unknown locations in the Agenais.[108] There is evidence that
heretics were again at Gontaud in the period. In 1253 Guiraude, wife
of Stephen Dealas, recovered possessions confiscated earlier from her
heretical husband.[109] In 1289 Pierre Badouin of Gontaud regained his
own goods, earlier confiscated by Bernart de Caux.[110] Bernard Gasc
of Gontaud was in contact with heretics of the Languedoc who had
fled to Lombardy in fear of the inquisition.[111] In 1270 Marie d'Anduze,
countess of Périgord and viscountess of Lomagne, held property seized
earlier from heretics of Gontaud and nearby Hautefeuille and Fauil-
let.[112] Heresy even survived after 1219 at Marmande, for one Gaillarde
Marty had his possessions confiscated by Raymond VII.[113]

But the valley of the Lot, especially Castelmoron, was still the main
Agenais foyer for heresy. From the document by which Y. Dossat identifies Vigouroux de la Bacone with the town we know of ten other named
people whose property, confiscated by Raymond VII, was bought by a
Raimond Talon of Castelmoron in 1237.[114] The father of Bertrand and

---

[104] *Layettes*, IV 5600 and AD Lot F. 121 9ʳ (Vital); Arch. Nat., JJ 24B, 66ᵛ (Giraude) (as
cited in Dossat, "Catharisme," 161).

[105] *Un Cartulaire et divers actes des Alaman*, eds. E. Cabié and L. Mazens (Toulouse:
Imprimerie A. Chauvin et Fils, 1882), 18 (cited in Dossat, "L'inquisiteur," 77 and
"Catharisme," 163 and 166).

[106] Dossat, "Catharisme," 162–163.

[107] Arch. nat. JJ 24b, 64ʳ⁻ᵛ (cited in Dossat, "Catharisme," 166–167); Molinier, *Correspondance*, I, 455 and 93.

[108] BN ms. Lat. 9019, 35.

[109] *Agen … Chartes*, xlix.

[110] *Rôles Gascons*, 3 vols., ed. C. Bémont, Bordeaux, 1885–1906, II, 355–356.

[111] Doat XXVI, 2ᵛ.

[112] G. Tholin, "Documets relatifs à l'Agenais," *Archives historiques de la Gironde* 35 (1900):
12–14.

[113] Arch. nat. JJ 24b, 61ᵛ–62ʳ (cited in Dossat, "Catharisme," 162).

[114] Arch. Nat. JJ 24b, 63ʳ⁻ᵛ (cited in Dossat, "Catharisme," 164).

Savari de Castelmoron also had his goods confiscated in this period.[115] Among those identified by Dossat, the *credens* Hugues de Castelmoron held land not only in this town but at neighboring Casseneuil and Saint-Livrade. While the heretical community at Casseneuil had largely been decimated, we still find the Balenx family among the Agenais *credentes*. Raimond-Bernard de Balenx, who we have seen took an oath to King Louis in 1243 and witnessed a letter of Raymond VII in 1249, had his Casseneuil property confiscated because of his belief sometime in the same decade.[116] The heresy was still strong at Villeneuve-sur-Lot in the years leading up to the inquisition, encountered there by Adémar Einard as he told the inquisitors at Gourdon in 1241.[117] Although I have suggested that Pujols perhaps did not have a heretical community by 1223, this certainly changed for in 1270 the *consuls* of Villeneuve wanted to use stones from the homes of the condemned for new building works.[118] Even at Penne Raymond VII undertook confiscations, and we learn that members of the Nouaillac, Marty and Pelicier families were implicated in the heresy, the latter possibly members of the important family of the same name at Agen.[119] Another inhabitant of the region, Etienne Bouc, was condemned sometime before 1269.[120]

The Agenais Lot had sheltered Cathars for some decades before the 1240s, as we have seen. The continuation of this and its expansion within towns and families already embroiled in the heresy, people terrorised by the threat of military violence and the loss of property, is not difficult to understand. What was there in this period to make a return to Catholicism and respect for its clergy and soldiers appealing? Even fear of the inquisition did not return everyone into the fold, as we have seen. But the rising number of heretics identified by the 1240s along the Agenais Garonne and even after the Roman inquisition had left the region is harder to account for. The river towns, previously relatively orthodox, could not have been considered a safe-haven for heretics under the gaze of Raymond VII, Agen's bishops or the inquisitor Bernart de Caux. But the towns of the right bank, it would seem, had taken their new found autonomy from comital and episcopal

---

[115] Molinier, *Correspondance*, II, 1511.
[116] *HGL* VIII, 1119 and 1254; *Enquêtes* 245 and note 7.
[117] Doat XXI, 205ᵛ.
[118] *Enquêtes*, 312.
[119] Arch. nat. J 1031 A, 11 (cited in Dossat, "L'inquisiteur," 78 and see "Catharisme," 165–166).
[120] Molinier, *Correspondance*, II, 236.

power and begun also to flout to some extent the rigid and conservative religious values they shared with northerners who had murdered and pillaged their way along the river. They now tolerated a heretical presence.

III. *Heresy in Bas-Quercy, Haut-Quercy and the Cahorsain*

The Cathar hierarchy in Quercy

No Cathar diocese corresponded to the Catholic diocese of Cahors, the episcopal territory north of the Aveyron. This was perhaps a reflection of the uncertain political status of the region in the twelfth-century, for like the Agenais, it was fought over and occupied variously by Aquitaine and Toulouse. J. Duvernoy concludes that the Cathars of Quercy must have been considered under the authority of the Cathar bishop of Toulouse: the *perfecti* most active in Quercy in the 1220s were Guillaume de Caussade of south-eastern Quercy and Vigouroux de la Bacone, both under the ultimate authority of Guilhabert de Castres.[121] To an account of activity in Quercy by heretics of the Toulousain we should also add Bernard de Lamothe, a very important member of the Cathar hierarchy in the years of the crusade, and, before the crusade, Arnaud Arrufat, *perfectus* of Verfeil, and Raymond Aymeric, Cathar deacon of Villemur.

But their activities in the thirteenth century do not indicate to me a general Toulousain dominance of the Quercinois Cathars. It was through his exceptional talents during the crisis posed by the war that Guilhabert de Castres came to lead all the Cathars in the Languedoc. Thus we should not infer that influence over Quercy had been the prerogative of his predecessors. There is evidence of the heresy only in Bas-Quercy in the early decades of the thirteenth century. The fortified hill top towns of the Cahorsain, and also Cahors itself, were very alien territory to them. Thus the absence of a Cathar hierarchy in Quercy as a whole should not concern us and we only need to establish the orientation of the heretics of the Tarn-Aveyron-Garonne basin. This part of Quercy in fact pertained to the diocese of Toulouse at that time and was closely allied to the Toulousain politically, which

---

[121] Duvernoy, *Catharisme*, II, 230–234 esp. note 86, 257–266, esp. 264 and 284.

might strengthen Duvernoy's case. However the association of Bas-Quercy with the Catholic diocese of Toulouse was felt to be inappropriate and around a century later it was transformed into a new Catholic diocese, Montauban.[122] To me, the evidence does not point clearly to the dominance of any individual Cathar diocese over Bas-Quercy in the twelfth and early thirteenth century. If it was an extension of the Cathar diocese of Toulouse, it seems strange that Bernard de Lamothe appears there in preference to two Cathar deacons of the northern Toulousain, Pons Guilhabert and Arnaud de Cavelsaut. Both were based close to Bas-Quercy, at Verfeil and Villemur, but we find them in Bas-Quercy only very infrequently.[123] The presence of Bernard de Lamothe is surely largely explained by the fact that he was actually a native of the region and one who retained family contacts there. Guillaume de Caussade, who had very little to do with Bas-Quercy from the records we have, was most closely associated with the Cathar hierarchy of Albi who I find had little practical influence in Bas-Quercy.[124]

By far the most important heretic to be found in Bas-Quercy was Vigouroux de la Bacone, bishop of the Agenais. Y. Dossat, the authority on Vigouroux, notes the extent to which he was active in "cette region qui devait naturellement relever de lui". B. Guillemain has noted how easy communications were in the *Moyenne Garonne* for the heretics, and G. Passerat has noted what close associations the communities of Bas-Quercy had with the *perfecti* of the Agenais.[125] Just as there was a natural cultural association between Bas-Quercy and the Agenais, the same appears to have been true in heretical matters. The surviving inquisitorial documents concerning trials at Agen relate not to the Agenais heretics but mostly to those of Bas-Quercy. We have a good amount of evidence about the region at the start of the thirteenth century and there is little indication that it contained an independently organised Cathar hierarchy of its own. It was the heretics of the Agenais and Villemur who were to decide how the northern Languedoc in general should respond to the first campaign of the crusade in 1209, as indicated by the messenger sent from the former to the latter. It seems to

---

[122] Passerat, "Cathares en Bas-Quercy," 151.

[123] Doat XXII, 5ᵛ–6ʳ, 28ᵛ, 48ᵛ, 53ᵛ–54ʳ, 54ʳ, 54ʳ⁻ᵛ.

[124] *Cf.* Passerat, "Cathares," 149–165.

[125] Dossat, "Un évêque Cathare," 628; Guillemain, "Le duché," 60; Passerat, "Cathares," 149–165.

me that the Cathars of the Agenais had perhaps the strongest influence in Bas-Quercy. If this is so, then Vigouroux de la Bacone may have been considered their bishop also.

Heresy and society in Bas-Quercy to c. 1209

In contrast with the Agenais, before the crusade heresy in Bas-Quercy was an essentially urban phenomenon, its several large towns containing heretical communities.[126] They have been made famous in part by the deposition of the *perfecta* Arnauda de Lamothe whose family were from Montauban but who was moved with her sister Péronne to Villemur around the turn of the century by arrangement between Raymond Aymeric and Arnauda's kinsman, the *perfectus* Bernard de Lamothe. They were hereticated a couple of years before news of the attack on Casseneuil reached Villemur, when Arnauda tells us that Raymond Aymeric organized an evacuation into the Albigeoise. Arnauda's life as a hunted *perfecta* throughout the wars thereafter is well studied. Less well known is what she and other witnesses tell us about the social and heretical structures in her native region. The Lamothes were among the many minor nobles of Bas-Quercy. Since 1203 Guillaume de Lamothe and his son Raymond had been under the protection of Count Raymond himself. At Montauban Arnauda and her sister spent their early childhood with her mother Austorgue and brother Arnaud, frequently accepting Cathars into their home and adoring them.[127]

Further east, dominating the Garonne below its junction with the Tarn, lies Castelsarrasin, the administrative seat of Quercy for the counts of Toulouse. By 1209 it was already notorious for its support of the heresy and several of its leading families were implicated. Most important was the Grimoard family, of which Pons Grimoard, a *credens* himself from around 1204, was later the seneschal of Quercy. The elder generation of Pons' family dominated the heretical life of the town before the crusade. Pons' uncle Raymond Grimoard was the most

---

[126] Other than where specifically cited, for discussion of the towns and heretics of Bas-Quercy see esp. *L'épopée* I 96–100, 241–242, 477 and 527–528; E. Griffe, *Le Languedoc Cathare de 1190 à 1210* (Paris: Letouzey et Ané, 1971), esp. 89 and *idem.*, *Le Languedoc Cathare au Temps de la Croisade, 1209–1229* (Paris: Letouzey et Ané, 1973), esp. 117; Duvernoy, *Catharisme*, II, esp. 268; Albe, *L'hérésie ... en Quercy*, esp. 17.

[127] Doat XXIII, 2ᵛ–49ᵛ, at 2ᵛ–5ᵛ; *Layettes* I, 710; *Chanson* II, 299 note 5. Arnauda's testimony is extensively utilized most recently in Lambert, *Cathars*, 74–75, 77, 80, 132, 137–138, 144, 149, 150, 153 and 169–170.

important *credens* of Castelsarrasin and was later hereticated. Another uncle, Pierre Grimoard, was married to Na Berètges and fathered Raymond-Bernard Grimoard before also receiving the *consolamentum*. We have an account of a meeting in 1204 at their house at which many other heretics and *credentes* of the region were present. Several witnesses mention this event and so it seems unlikely that it was the regular monthly Cathar *apparallamentum* but possibly something more significant.[128] Pons Grimoard's cousin and the daughter of Raymond Grimoard, the *credens* Na Pros, was married into the de Cavelsaut family, also containing several credentes by c. 1200, including her husband Johannes.[129]

Other families of the town emerge more hazily in this early period. Nonetheless, we know that the Fabers of Pechermer, a suburb of Castelsarrasin situated on the Garonne road to Moissac, were already very important both socially and in terms of the heresy. Both of Guillaume Faber's parents died hereticated, as did many other family members, and the whole family had a good deal of contact with the Cathar hierarchy. Guillaume Faber married Bernarda de Ruptari, daughter of Guillaume-Arnaud de Ruptari, in the early decades of the thirteenth century.[130] Both the Fabers and de Ruptaris were also related to the Audebert family, active in the heresy into the late crusading period.[131]

To the north, at the confluence of the Tarn and Garonne, the abbey town of Moissac was far more subject to actively Catholic influences. Its protagonists in authority were the count of Toulouse and a series of dynamic and ambitious abbots. Both controlled secular rights in the town in a situation not dissimilar to that at Agen. The abbots were to prove active in promoting orthodoxy in the town and the abbey but were only partially successful. The important *perfectus* Raymond Imbert came from Moissac and had been hereticated before crusade and the Falquet de Saint-Paul family were influential *credentes*, many of whom were to aid the heretics throughout the wars.[132]

---

[128] Doat XXII, 34ᵛ, 38ʳ and 40ᵛ (Pons before the crusade); *ibid.* 4ʳ⁻ᵛ, 15ᵛ–16ʳ, 22ᵛ, 23ʳ, 23ᵛ–24ʳ, 34ʳ⁻ᵛ, 36ʳ, 37ᵛ (Raymond); *ibid.* 15ʳ and 21ʳ⁻ᵛ (Pierre); *ibid* 16ᵛ and 23ᵛ⁻ʳ (Raymond-Bernard). The *apparallamentum* is described in *Origins*, 221 and 222.

[129] Doat XXII, 7ᵛ, 9ᵛ–10ʳ, 15ᵛ, 15ᵛ–16ʳ, 17ʳ⁻ᵛ, 18ʳ, 19ᵛ–20ʳ, 20ʳ, 22ʳ, 23ʳ, 24ʳ, 28ᵛ, 34ʳ⁻ᵛ, 35ᵛ (Pros); *ibid.* 15ʳ⁻ᵛ, 16ᵛ, 19ᵛ–20ʳ, 22ʳ, 23ᵛ–24ʳ, 34ʳ⁻ᵛ, 36ʳ, 37ᵛ (Johannes).

[130] Doat XXII, 2ʳ⁻ᵛ, 4ʳ, 6ʳ, 9ᵛ–10ʳ, 11ʳ, 15ᵛ–16ʳ, 23ʳ⁻ᵛ, 26ʳ⁻ᵛ, 28ᵛ, 34ʳ⁻ᵛ, 34ᵛ–35ʳ, 35ʳ, 35ᵛ–36ʳ, 36ʳ, 36ᵛ, 37ʳ⁻ᵛ and 44ᵛ–45ᵛ.

[131] Doat XXII, 9ᵛ–10ʳ, 11ʳ⁻ᵛ, 13ᵛ–14ʳ, 20ᵛ–21ʳ, 24ʳ, 26ʳ⁻ᵛ, 34ʳ⁻ᵛ and 35ᵛ.

[132] Doat XXIII, 167ᵛ (Raymond Imbert); Doat XXI, 294ʳ⁻ᵛ and XXII, 6ʳ and 36ʳ⁻ᵛ (Falquet de Saint-Paul).

Finally, we should note the possibility that in this early period heretics found shelter in the rural Cistercian abbey of Belleperche, south of Castelsarrasin on the Garonne. We know that before the attention of the inquisition fell upon it B. d'Alegre de Borrel and Folquet entered the abbey as monks, and the latter lived there until the friars arrived in the region and he was forced to flee for Italy.[133] The river towns were probably also accustomed to heretics from the Agenais in the late twelfth century, because we know from more abundant evidence that they were in later years. How these heretical towns fared in the coming wars and inquisition will be addressed after an overview of the course of the crusade in the county of Cahors as a whole.

The course of the crusade in Quercy

After the second excommunication of Raymond of Toulouse his lands in Quercy were very vulnerable. Bishop Guillaume of Cahors, the crusader of 1209, was active in the army also from early February 1211 and transferred his homage for Cahors itself from the count to de Montfort on 20 June, and later in the year to King Philip of France. He was working in alliance with Abbot Raymond du Proët of Moissac who was in the camp in spring 1211. A good many other lords of central and upper Quercy transferred their homage that same summer too.[134] Never having received the heresy themselves, they saw no reason to lose their lands to the northerners by resisting the invasion. Thus, in the retinue of Baldwin of Toulouse we find the viscount of Monclar-de-Quercy and the Quercinois lord Hugues de Breil, and in August de Montfort received at Cahors the homages of the most important lords of Quercy, the crusaders of 1209; Bertrand de Cardaillac, Bertrand de Gourdon, Ratier de Castelnau-Montratier, and viscount Raymond of Turenne.[135]

In the following year de Montfort began rewarding his allies in the northern Languedoc and punishing those whom he considered traitors. When the siege of Penne-d'Agenais ended in late July 1212, he moved just across the Agenais border with Périgord to the castle of Martin

---

[133] *GC* XIII, 259; Doat XXII, 3ʳ; Douais, 95.

[134] *HGL* VIII, 160 and 611–612; Doat CXX, 3ʳ; Albe, *L'hérésie ... en Quercy*, 2. See also C.M. Dutton, "Aspects of the Institutional History of the Albigensian Crusade, 1198–1229," (Ph.D. thesis, University of London, 1993), 42. See above for more general accounts of the crusade.

[135] PVC *Histoire*, 101 and note 4; *Chanson* I, 176 and 202–203.

Algaïs at Biron. Algaïs was cruelly executed and his castle granted to the Quercinois Arnaud de Montaigu, a recent recruit by the crusade who had provided much needed reinforcements at Penne.[136] The crusaders returned via Montcuq to Bas-Quercy on 6 August. Its conquest was essential if they were to benefit from the easily won domination of the north by having access to it from the Toulousain. Its towns understood the special position they occupied both strategically, dominating the river system of the northern Languedoc, and psychologically, in support of the still resilient people of Toulouse. The first town to be attacked was Moissac. It was not as strategically important as Montauban or Castelsarrasin but it was more vulnerable and its fall would be a great blow to the other towns. In the disputes between Raymond VI and the monks, the people of Moissac typically sided with the count. The war made this tension more acute and earlier in 1212 they had expelled the abbot and he was imprisoned at Montauban. Now the town opted to resist the crusaders, who reached it on 14 August. The besieged had received a mercenary force from the count and initially had the upper hand. However, soldiers from Montauban unsuccessfully attacked a crusader party and were captured by Baldwin of Toulouse and his Quercinois allies Armand de Mondenard and Hugues de Breil. Other factors contributed to the demoralisation of Moissac and by early September it was clear that it could be overwhelmed.[137]

At this crucial point the garrison of Castelsarrasin deserted and the townspeople sent a delegation to the crusaders offering their surrender. This was accepted and the town was given to Guillaume de Contres. The people of Moissac now betrayed their garrison, which would be executed if captured, and opened the gates to de Montfort on 8 September. But Bas-Quercy was not quite lost. It was too late in the season to besiege Montauban, a better defended town, and so the success of the crusade in the Agenais and Quercy did not lead to the fall of Toulouse. Nonetheless, de Montfort had seriously reduced Toulousain influence along the Lot and the Garonne in Quercy and the Agenais by late summer 1212.

As for the many lords of central and upper Quercy who capitulated so readily, it has been noted that few are to be found at any point actually engaged in combat on behalf of the crusade.[138] The reality of

---

[136] *Chanson* I, 256–261; PVC *Histoire*, 113 and 132.
[137] *PL* CCXVI, 836; *Chanson* I, 261–277; PVC *Histoire*, 134–137.
[138] *L'épopée* I, 503.

northern domination was not only frightening but sickening to even the Catholics of the region, as we have seen in the Agenais, and many were to change sides. It was in this context of resentment that Baldwin of Toulouse was murdered. On 17 February 1214 he went to bed ·in the Quercinois castle of Lolmie, whose lords had done homage to him as lord of Montcuq. The treacherous castellans alerted two other Quercinois lords to his presence. One was Bertrand de Mondenard, a kinsman of Armand de Mondenard, the crusader of 1212 and vassal of de Montfort. The other was a Montfortist vassal in his own right, Ratier de Castelnau-Montratier. Both were now secretly southern partisans. During the night they and their men were let into the castle and seized the unsuspecting Baldwin from bed. After being starved for two days at Montcuq he gave the town back to its lords and was executed.[139]

· We have seen that as a direct result the confidence of the northern Languedoc revived, but this did not extend to Raymond VI who submitted to the papal legate Peter of Benevento. The Languedoc was placed under a peace until the anticipated arbitration in Rome of 1215. But during this peace the crusaders launched a campaign to punish Ratier de Castelnau-Montratier and the family of Mondenard. They were under the protection of Hugues de Rovinha at Casseneuil as we have seen, which would fall in late August, but their own castles were taken in the first two weeks of June. In this period de Montfort moved to Montpezat d'Agenais, pausing near-by Montcuq on 12 June to receive the submission of the Quercinois Déodat de Barasc, lord of Béduer and Lissac, who was forced to agree to destroy his own castles.[140]

Another illegal campaign then took place against the *routier* Bernard de Cazenac in southern Périgord and his castles were transferred to the crusader viscount Raymond of Turenne who, on around August at Casseneuil, had performed homage again to de Montfort and promised the service of ten knights and ten sergeants to be deployed in the dioceses of Agen, Cahors and Rodez. While it is beyond the scope of this paper to discuss the Dordogne campaign in great detail, not least because, in spite of Peter des Vaux-de-Cernay's somewhat hysterical

---

[139] PVC *Histoire*, 189–192; William of Puylaurens 92–93; *Chanson* II, 276.

[140] *Recueil des historiens des Gaules et de la France*, ed. M. Bouquet (revised L. Delisle), 24 vols. (Paris, 1738–1904 [hereafter *RHF*]), XIX 210; PVC *Histoire*, 197–198; Molinier *Actes* 8; *Chanson* III, 303 note 6.

protestations to the contrary, the castles did not and never would actually contain heretics, Turenne's gain certainly supports Moore's observation that nobles might be accused of heresy by "those who might have designs upon their land ...".[141] But in dispossessing de Cazenac the northerners were to involve one of the most capable leaders on the southern side in a war in which he had previously shown no interest. He famously went on to lead an army of embittered Catholic Quercinois, *faidits* like himself including Arnaud de Montaigu and the co-lords of Gourdon, to help relieve the 1217–1218 siege of Toulouse, and in 1228 he was rewarded with the governorship of Castelsarrasin when it was retaken by the south.[142]

But de Cazenac was not untypical in his hostility to the invasion. Support for the crusade by the new vassals of 1209–1212 sprang from pragmatism and also from religious allegiance, and in this they followed their bishop. He dominated Cahors, which thus features scarcely at all in our narrative, being largely beyond the heretical sphere and not attacked by the crusade. But in 1214 and most especially from 1217–1218 they began responding negatively to the humiliations inflicted on the Languedoc, a state of affairs to which they, by their early collaboration, had contributed. We have witnessed several of their defections and should add that the besieged in Toulouse in 1217–1218 included the Quercinois Bernard de Montaigu (probably a kinsman of Arnaud de Montaigu, the crusader of 1211, who was soon also to defect himself), Déodat de Barasc (another defector from the Montfortist party) and Araimfré de Montpezat. The latter was also among the defenders of Marmande in 1219.[143]

Thus far the lords of Haut Quercy resemble somewhat the towns of the Agenais: inherently Catholic and initially self-serving in their partisanship, but prepared actively to defy the crusade when the loss of lands and liberties was at stake. We shall later will see that the shifts in loyalty in the war years affected another change in central and Haut-Quercy as on the Agenais Garonne during the peace following 1229, one of confessional ambivalence and even allegiance to the heresy.

---

[141] PVC *Histoire*, 202–205 and *Hystoria* II, 228 note 5; AD Lot F.125; Doat LXXV, 51^r–52^r and 55^r–56^v; Molinier *Actes* 82, 88, 89a and 288; *HGL* VI, 448–451. The quotation is *Origins*, 236.

[142] *RHF* XIX, 648; *Chanson* III, 138–141; William of Puylaurens, 132–133; Doat XXII, 9^v.

[143] *Chanson* III, 139 note 5, 302–303 and 308–313.

Bas-Quercy and its heretics during the crusade

The lords north of the Aveyron contrast with the towns of Bas-Quercy, obvious targets for the crusaders from the start and both unable and unwilling to renounce their heretical partisanship. The survival of Catharism in Bas-Quercy throughout the wars is most impressive given the fall of Moissac and the submission of Castelsarrasin in 1212, not liberated until 1228, and the transferral of the remaining autonomous town, Montauban, to de Montfort by Pope Innocent III in 1215. At Castelsarrasin, as at Casseneuil, recognition of crusader authority in 1212 meant the avoidance of property confiscation by the northerners and thus the survival of the heresy in private homes. From the relative wealth of documentation for this period we can see that the heretics still had quite a high profile in the town in spite, presumably, of the presence of crusaders at points during these sixteen years and even of a northern garrison at times.[144] One explanation for this is that the crusaders failed to govern Quercy very closely, for neither side appears to have had a seneschal for the region in place for much of the 1220–1230 period.[145]

Whatever the reason, Castelsarrasin was the most important heretical community in Bas-Quercy, and Pons Grimoard and his wife Arnauda were its "first couple" in the crusade years. Pons was most important to the heretical community because as Raymond VII's seneschal he did nothing to hinder them and a good deal to aid them. Arnauda attended heretical gatherings until at least 1228. Raymond Grimoard, Pons' uncle, was an active supporter of the heretics for years and was himself hereticated in 1213 at Corbarieu, just south of Montauban, in the company of other *credentes* of Castelsarrasin. He met with Bernard de Lamothe in 1218, but was reconciled to the Catholic Church sometime after this. The *perfectus* Pierre Grimoard was still strong in his faith in around the same year, as was his son Raymond-Bernard, but we do not hear of either of them again and Na Berètges, wife of Pierre and Raymond-Bernard's mother, is mentioned after that date only without them.[146]

Pons Grimoard's cousin Na Pros, became one of the most active female *credentes* in the community, attending heretical meetings through-

---

[144] As suggested in Griffe, *Le Languedoc ... 1209–1229*, 175.
[145] From evidence in AD Lot F. 97, 98, 104 and 105.
[146] Doat XXII, 9ᵛ–10ʳ, 15ʳ–16ʳ, 21ᵛ, 22ᵛ, 23ʳ, 23ᵛ–24ʳ, 37ᵛ, and 43ʳ.

out the period of the crusade both at her father's house and very frequently at Guillaume Faber's. By c. 1218 she had female heretics and
believers at her house behind the market place at Castelsarrasin.[147] The
de Cavelsaut family into which Pros had married was a major Cathar
clan. Four members, Hugh, Guillaume, Pons, and Bernard were eventually hereticated. Bernard was still a *credens* by 1213 when he, Pros and
Bertranda, wife of Hugh, were at a large heretical meeting in Castelsarrasin, but Pons and Bernard, who seems to have been brothers, were
both hereticated by c. 1218, in which year Guiraud Guallard saw them
preaching to the rest of their family in an upper room at Johannes
de Cavelsaut's. The pair are mentioned almost always together up to
c. 1225 and were perhaps *socii*. Hugh was a *credens* in c. 1213 when he
and Johannes attended the heretication of Raymond Grimoard, and
was still so in c. 1225 when he was at the Fabers with Bernard de
Lamothe, but was hereticated by c. 1228 just before he died.[148] Another
family related to the Grimoards by marriage was that of Na Berètges,
wife of the heretic Pierre Grimoard. Featuring regularly in depositions
is Othon de Berètges, Na Berètges's brother and *bailli* of Raymond VII
for Moissac.[149]

During the crusade the Fabers of Pechermer were a mixture of
heretics, *credentes* and Catholics. Guillaume Faber was the head of the
family by 1222 at the latest and heretics, not least Vigouroux de la
Bacone and Bernard de Lamothe, were reported at the house by witnesses referring to the 1220s, and at his property at Moissac. Guillaume's sister Guillelma knew Bernard de Lamothe too, although as
noted above Guillaume tried to counter accusations of heresy on her
part and that of his wife Bernarda, insisting that even if they had had
contact with heretics they didn't believe what they said or adore them[150]

The de Bressols family of Castelsarrasin remained central to the
heretical life of Bas-Quercy too. Almost all the family members of
whom we know were *credentes* and were at Arnaud de Bressols' house in
c. 1224 and c. 1228 with Vigouroux de la Bacone. Much evidence again
comes from Guiraud Guallard. Arnaud appears to have been the head

---

[147] Doat XXII, 9ᵛ–10ʳ, 15ᵛ–16ʳ, 17ʳ⁻ᵛ, 19ᵛ–20ʳ, 20ʳ, 22ᵛ, 23ʳ, 23ᵛ, 24ᵛ, 28ʳ⁻ᵛ.

[148] Doat XXII, 11ʳ, 14ʳ, 15ʳ⁻ᵛ, 19ᵛ–20ʳ, 21ʳ⁻ᵛ, 21ᵛ, 28ᵛ, 34ʳ⁻ᵛ, 35ʳ, 37ʳ and 38ʳ (Hugh);
ibid., 4ʳ, 15ʳ⁻ᵛ, 22ᵛ, 37ʳ and 40ʳ (Guillaume); *ibid.*, 6ʳ, 17ʳ, 19ᵛ–20ʳ, 22ᵛ, 24ʳ, 24ᵛ and 35ᵛ
(Bernard); *ibid.*, 4ʳ⁻ᵛ, 15ʳ, 17ʳ, 19ᵛ–20ʳ, 22ᵛ, 24ʳ, 24ᵛ and 58ᵛ–59ʳ and Griffe, *Le Languedoc
... 1209–1229*, 177 (Pons).

[149] Doat XXII, 13ᵛ–14ʳ, 20ᵛ–21ʳ, 43ʳ and 45ʳ.

[150] Doat XXII, 9ᵛ–10ʳ and 17ʳ (Bernarda); *ibid.* 9ᵛ (Guillelma).

of the family, owning the house and a vineyard, and associated often with heads of other families, notably Guillaume Faber de Pechermer and Pons Grimoard in the 1220s.[151]

The inquisition at Moissac revealed heretical activity by a huge number of families in the town over the preceding decades, although almost all of it is very hard to date accurately. Most significant is that the seigneurial family entertained and adored Bernard de Lamothe in c. 1224. Implicated were the lady of Moissac and her daughter Na Ondrada, and Ondrada's two sons Bertrand and Arnaud-Guillaume.[152] We should note that Vital Grimoard, Guillaume Faber de Pechermer, and Othon de Berètges formed a connection between the communities at Castelsarrasin and Moissac, the former two owning property at Moissac used for lodging heretics and holding meetings, and the latter living at Castelsarrasin while being Raymond VI's *bailli* for Moissac.[153]

The most sizeable community of female heretics in Bas-Quercy was at Montauban. The *perfecta* Joanna d'Auvione was at the center of activity. Joanna and her fellow *perfectae* were received, fed, and adored at the homes of a Fabrissa and Guillelma de Sapiac, the latter of whom told the inquisition that she had been a *perfecta* of the town herself, had been reconciled by the bishop of Cahors, but had lapsed again to the status of *credens*. Another woman, Petronilla, had been hereticated twenty years prior to her deposition of 1241 and had lived as a *perfecta* for three years, but had escaped punishment because she had been reconciled by bishop Fulk of Toulouse.[154] Just as before 1209 the de Lamothe family at Montauban were heavily heretical. Hugues, as a *credens*, fought in the army of Raymond VI in 1217–1219 and the *perfectus* Géraud, possibly the brother of Bernard de Lamothe, spent time in Lombardy.[155]

Vigouroux de la Bacone, Cathar bishop of the Agenais, was a familiar face in all of these towns in Bas-Quercy. For example, at least twice in c. 1213 he was at Raymond Grimoard's house in Castelsarrasin, as testified by Pons Grimoard who was given the kiss of Peace by the heretic. Pons also met him and his *socius* at Moissac in that year at the Falquet de Saint-Paul house. Guillaume Faber de Pecher-

---

[151] Doat XXII, 2^{r-v}, 4^{v}–5^{r}, 8^{r}, 10^{r}, 11^{r}, 18^{r}, 19^{r-v}, 20^{r-v}, 31^{r-v} and 45^{r-v}.
[152] Doat XXIII, 266^{r}.
[153] Doat XXII, 16^{r-v} and 23b.
[154] Doat XXI, 240^{r}–42^{r}, 244^{v} and 268^{r-v}.
[155] *Chanson* II, 298–299 and III, 86–87, 92–93, 262–263 and 308–309 (Hugh); Toulouse ms 609, 43^{r} and 45^{r} (cited in *L'épopée* III, 364) (Géraud).

mer encountered Vigouroux at Castelsarrasin c. 1218 in the home of
the Campeiran family.[156] In the context of his authority as a *bailli* of
the county, Othon de Berètges, was accused of failing to apprehend
the heretic in spite of seeing him on at least three occasions at Castelsarrasin in c. 1224, twice at the house of Arnaud de Bressols with his
socius and also in the Pechermer home.[157] Guiraud Guallard stated in
1243 that he had seen him on three occasions in c. 1228; at Moissac
on the quayside, about to be led into a house of Guillaume Faber and
twice at the home of Arnaud de Bressols at Castelsarrasin, once with
Bernard de Lamothe. On each occasion he is in the company of the
most important families of heretical supporters in Bas-Quercy.[158]

   The life of the heretical church in the Languedoc revived significantly in the central 1220s under Guilhabert de Castres, and Bernard
de Lamothe was instrumental in his plans for Bas-Quercy. In c. 1223
and c. 1225 he was visiting and preaching at the Faber household
in Pechermer, at Na Pros de Cavelsaut's in c. 1223, and visited with
minor families of believers, most notably the Sanches, on occasions
between 1223 and 1228. Accounts also refer to meetings at Castelsarrasin between Bernard de Lamothe and Bernard de Cazenac hosted by
Pons Grimoard. Pons attests that they happened in c. 1225 but c. 1228
seems more likely, the year in which the town was recaptured and governed by de Cazenac, and in which at least one other meeting between
the heretic and the town's new lord took place, at the home of Arnaud
de Bressols. The last account of Bernard de Lamothe in Bas-Quercy is
in c. 1231, the year before his death, being entertained again in the de
Bressols home.[159]

   Because of the wealth of evidence for Bas-Quercy, in particular for
Castelsarrasin, only a fraction of which can be discussed here, we can
make a few assertions about the interplay between secular and heretical life by c. 1229. As elsewhere in the Languedoc it is difficult to make
a meaningful distinction between noble and non-noble. Aside from the
Grimoards, implicated in the political life of the south more widely
and constituting the heretical aristocracy of their town, the Faber family of Pechermer and the de Bressols, de Berètges and de Cavelsauts

---

[156] Doat XXII, 4^v, 36^{r-v} and 40^r–41^v.

[157] Doat XXII, 44^v–45^r.

[158] Doat XXII, 13^v–14^r, 14^{r-v}, 16^{r-v}, 20^{r-v} and 21^{r-v}.

[159] Doat XXII, 4^v–5^r, 9^v–10^r, 13^v–14^r, 14^v, 15^v–16^r, 19^v, 20^{r-v}, 20^v–21^r, 21^{r-v}, 21^v, 22^{r-v},
23^v–24^r, 35^r, 36^{r-v} and 45^{r-v}; Doat XXIII, 265^i.

emerge as the most important families because they were landowners.
It was on their property that heretics were most frequently protected
and in whose houses they most commonly preached. However a middle
range of related families, including the Targuiers, Audeberts, Mazelers,
Grans, Campeirans, and Sanches, do not appear to have operated in a
significantly different religious sphere. Not least, from the association of
the Sanches and Campeirans with Bernard de Lamothe and Vigouroux
de la Bacone it seems that hosting heretical meetings usually fell to the
more major families because they had larger and more suitable property rather than because they especially dominated religious practice.
The *perfecti* were in principle blind to social status, and in practice were
fed and accommodated by a cross-section of *credentes*. Having said this,
it is frequently the leading families who are to be found in conference—
rather than simply in religious practice or sharing meals—with leading
heretics. It would appear, predictably, that the politically and economically powerful and better connected families were most relied on in the
strategical plans of the heretics in their times of crisis and renewal. We
shall see this in practice throughout Quercy when we now turn to the
evidence for 1229 to c. 1249.

The heresy in Quercy after 1229

The terms of the Treaty of Paris involved destruction in all the major
towns of Bas-Quercy, and in this same stressful period the inquisitors
first entered the region. Pons Grimoard first admitted his heretical
activity and belief to the inquisitor Guillaume Arnaud on 29 March
1235. His case provides the earliest surviving inquisitorial document, a
letter of penitence dated the following year. Pons admitted being frequently in the company of important *perfecti* and was charged specifically with allowing the *perfectus* Guillaume de Caussade to escape from
his custody at *Loseler* (also known then as Beaucaire, now as Lauzerte).
He was sentenced to make four pilgrimages.[160] This penance had been
completed by 1244 when he and Othon de Berètges again gave statements to the inquisitors. Pons was dismissed, but Othon was convicted of letting Vigouroux de la Bacone escape from his custody in
the 1220s.[161] Another *credens* who continually ran risks on behalf of the
heretics in this difficult period was Guillaume Faber, harbouring the

---

[160] Doat XXII, 32ᵛ–44ʳ and 38ᵛ–40ʳ; *HGL* VIII, 1016.
[161] Doat XXII, 32–45.

perfectus Raimond Imbert of Moissac and receiving a one-hundred *livre* fine for allowing him to escape.[162] One of the most important trials associated with the town was in 1243, part of the investigation into the murders at Avignonet the previous year. Jean Vital told that shortly after the murders the heretic Stephen Mazeler arrived in Castelsarrasin where Guillaume Audebert had initiated a celebration, along with Guillaume Faber de Pechermer and Pons de Montmirat. Guillaume Audebert sang Stephen *sirventes* involving a grisly description of the death of the friars.[163]

The women of Castelsarrasin also continued in the heresy. Arnalda Grimoard was present in the town in 1244 when she was implicated by the testimony of Na Berètges.[164] Na Pros de Cavelsaut continued to defy the Catholic authorities to c. 1239. In addition to hosting various heretical meetings her house was still home to her heretic daughter Raimunda and used as a covert lodging for other named *perfectae* in whose protection and service she worked closely. One of the latest accounts of these women together is at the meeting with Vigouroux de la Bacone in 1228 or the early 1230s. Aurimunda was hereticated herself on the point of death in c. 1240, at which time she was still keeping the company of Petrona and Pros.[165]

At Montauban we find less detailed evidence, but still gain a picture of a strong heretical presence, and in the week before Ascension 1241 two hundred and fifty four people were convicted.[166] In 1244 Arnauda de Lamothe returned to her native town and made her famous deposition, and several other of the de Lamothes were still living there and were convicted as *credentes*.[167]

We have noted that heretics could infiltrate the abbey of Belleperche before the crusade. This was not the case in later decades however, for early in the 1240s Rostanh de Bressols led a condemned heretic, R. Stephani, to the abbey hoping for shelter. The pair were met by an angry and frightened brother, Otto, who later recounted the story to local *credentes*.[168] A heretical community did remain in the abbey town of Moissac. In 1234–1239 two hundred and ten people were burned

[162] Doat XXII, 8ʳ.
[163] Doat XXII, 11ʳ⁻ᵛ.
[164] Doat XXII, 42ᵛ–44ʳ.
[165] Doat XXII, 7ᵛ, 17ʳ⁻ᵛ, 17ᵛ, 19ʳ⁻ᵛ, 20ʳ, 24ᵛ, 25ʳ and 28ᵛ.
[166] Doat XXI, 229–282.
[167] Doat XXI, 233ʳ⁻ᵛ.
[168] Doat XXII, 12ʳ.

and in Ascension week 1241 the inquisition convicted ninety-nine.[169] Some escaped, however, and heretics of Moissac were among those who fled for Lombardy, including Raimond Imbert, who had narrowly escaped capture on the property of Guillaume Faber de Pechermer in 1239.[170]

Finally we turn to events that transformed the religious landscape between the Aveyron and Dordogne. Although Cahors itself was to remain beyond heretical influence, being most immediately influenced by its bishops, the essentially very orthodox religious attitudes of many lords dominating the towns of Haut-Quercy and the Cahorsain were apparently to change. Political events, as noted, bound them closer to the southern party. This was not the way that many powers in the Agenais behaved, "backing a winner" in order to secure their independence, but often when things were going against the south, apparently as a point of principle when the crusade was perceived to be going too far. However, there is little evidence that until this stage of disillusionment with the crusade was reached any of them were anything other than orthodox. Indeed, unlike in lands in which Catholics were regularly in contact with heretics and we cannot meaningfully distinguish between "Catholic" and "Cathar" families and towns, there is little evidence that the heretics attempted to gain a foothold in the Cahorsain or Haut-Quercy before the crusade. This was to change.

The infiltration began, it would appear, at Montcuq as part of that general relaxing of pressure and revival in heretical confidence that occurred in the 1220s, its "last age of comparative freedom." Indeed, Lambert observes astutely that while 1226 was a bad year for Raymond VII it was ironically one of reinvigoration for Occitan Catharism, in which the new heretical diocese of the Razès was founded.[171] Like the creation of the new diocese, the spread of the heresy to Montcuq cannot be a reflection of Cathar flight from the central Languedoc. Montcuq lies where the Agenais meets central Quercy, above the river valley of the Barguelonne. It is accessible from the Garonne at modern Lamagistere, but is more obviously part of the Agenais Lot and Haut- and Bas-Quercy spheres. A Cathar enclave of sorts was established there in this period. For example, the *credens* Bertrand de Rupe was well

---

[169] Doat XXI, 282ᵛ–306ʳ and AD Lot F. 106.
[170] Doat XXII, 8ʳ and XXV, 298ʳ.
[171] Lambert, *Cathars*, 135 (quotation) and 136.

acquainted with Vigouroux de la Bacone, sending *perfecti* to his home, perhaps at Castelmoron, and meeting him at Moissac to escort him through Quercy. Even a priest, François, escorted him and his *socius* in the Montcuq area, once from *La Costa* to *Prinhac*. He put his own property at the heretics' disposal and took them wine, bread, fruit, and oil on behalf of a *credens* Guillelmassa. He also held for a time a book and money, which he gave to Guillaume de Bausfan at the heretic's request, and hosted debates between Cathars and Waldensians.[172]

Important socio-political ties existed between Montcuq and the southern resistance. Jeanne de Lolmie, later convicted at Montauban, was probably of the Lolmie family of Montcuq implicated in the murder of Baldwin of Toulouse.[173] Othon de Berètges was *bailli* for Montcuq as well as Moissac in the 1220s and it seems likely that after Castelsarrasin was retaken in 1228 he and Pons Grimoard played an important supporting role in the revival of the heresy and its extension into central and upper Quercy.

In spite of the destruction of the walls of Montcuq, required by the Treaty of Paris, from the late 1220s a path was being paved for a more concerted effort to implant Catharism in the Montcuq region with the help also of lords of Haut-Quercy. Until their lands and those of their neighbours were terrorised by the crusade, the seigneurial family of Gourdon was among the most actively Catholic families of Quercy. Géraud de Gourdon was a member of the cathedral clergy at Cahors.[174] As we have seen, Bertrand de Gourdon crusaded in 1209 and made and renewed his homage to the de Montforts in 1211, 1217 and also in 1218. When the Languedoc surrendered to Louis in 1226 he did likewise. However, in 1218 he was also criticized by Rome for aiding the southern army.[175] In fact by the mid-1220s he was leading a double life as a vassal of the French crown and protector of notorious heretics. If not necessarily already a *credens* himself, he allowed Cathars to preach in Gourdon and even to establish a community there. He was visited by Vigouroux de la Bacone and Barthélemy de Carcassonne in 1223, although he apparently turned them away. By 1229 Gourdon contained the major heretical community in Haut-Quercy. However three days before the Peace of Paris was signed its *perfecti* left the town for safety,

---

[172] Doat XXI, 219ᵛ–20ʳ.
[173] AD Lot F.106.
[174] See Albe, *L'hérésie … en Quercy*, 19.
[175] Doat CLIII, 93ʳ⁻ᵛ and *Layettes* II, 1760 (for 1218); *HGL* VIII, 704–706 (for 1226).

having perhaps been forewarned of its outcome and implications.[176] If this was the case, it was surely because of the involvement of their well-connected patron in both parties.

Where did they go? Other *perfecti* became refugees as a result of the Peace, as we know again through the testimony of Arnauda de Lamothe. But in the case of the Gourdon heretics we might speculate that the exodus was more constructive. It might explain the sudden appearance of Cathars in Quercinois towns not previously accused of harbouring them. These were the towns of central Quercy. That the heretics would have been assured a welcome is likely for by c. 1229 we can establish seigneurial links between the family of Gourdon and those towns in the Cahorsain in which inquisitors were to later find Cathar enclaves. In 1241 at Sauveterre, lying between Castelnau-Montratier and Montcuq, a Guiraud de Gourdon admitted that he had previously received heretics on his property where he was blessed by them, adored them and listened to them preach.[177] This is perhaps the same Guiraud de Gourdon who in 1230 had ceded to Raymond VII property not only at Sauveterre but at three other locations—at Montcuq, at Mondenard twenty-seven kilometres to its south, and at *Montemaccistum*—and who also held land at Montaigu, ten kilometers west of Montcuq, which he had ceded to the count by 1248.[178] In 1241 a Fortanier de Gourdon was also associated with Mondenard.[179] Connections existed also between the lords of Gourdon and those of Castelnau-Montratier.[180] Thus by 1229 we find that the family had influence both in Gourdon and in and around Montcuq where Cathars had already been working to implant the heresy.

We also have evidence of close contacts between the Montcuq-Gourdon sphere and the heretics of Casseneuil in the Agenais. At Montcuq the *credens* P. de Casseneuil admitted being entrusted at Gourdon with a heretical book, which he had read, and Hartemanda de Balenx was given her sentence at Gourdon, the severity of which perhaps indicates the significance attached by the inquisitors to her activities. A Pierre de Penna associated extensively with Cathars and gives us

---

[176] Doat XXI, 189^r, 199^r and 201^v; Lambert, *Cathars*, 137.

[177] Doat XXI, 226^v–7^r. He is not to be confused with the *perfectus* of the same name whose title relates to the Gourdon estate at Caraman (see Duvernoy, *Le Catharisme*, II, 260 and Griffe, *Le Languedoc … 1209–1229*, 177 and note 13).

[178] *HGL* VIII, 1957 and 2004.

[179] AD Lot F. 126 and 428.

[180] AD Lot F. 365 and 366.

one of the fullest accounts of heretical theology to be found in the Quercy documentation. If, as I believe, the conversion of Montcuq took place through its connections with Gourdon, the Agenais, and Bas-Quercy, it seems not unreasonable to speculate that his name might refer to near-by Penne d'Agenais rather than Penne d'Albigeoise, to the east.[181] Gourdon itself was thus logically the first heretical center in the northern Languedoc to be targeted by the inquisition, during Advent week 1241 and again in the following year. Bertrand himself admitted having received heretics, although his son Fortanier appears to have been the most active Cathar sympathiser.[182] In spite of confessional differences within the family, the heretical community at Gourdon was refounded by the 1240s. That the extent of the heresy in the Gourdon area was again great is evident from the passing of two hundred and nineteen sentences against all sections of the urban and rural population, including a priest.[183]

There is also much evidence of the success in transmitting the heresy into the Cahorsain, although not successfully into Cahors itself. The inquisition in central Quercy took place in Lent 1242. The conversion of Montcuq had apparently been very successful for eighty-four people were convicted, the family of Saint-Genies featuring prominently.[184] At Sauveterre, between Montcuq and Castelnau-Montratier, Cathars and Waldensians had been preaching openly and the inquisition convicted five people, among them Guiraud de Gourdon.[185] Seven people were then convicted at Beaucaire. Most of them were part of a community established by Guillaume de Caussade under the protection of the castellan, probably in 1233, in which year Pons Grimoard saw him and his *socius* in the home of P. de Belfort.[186]

The inquisitors then convicted twenty-two people at Montpezat-de-Quercy. As we have seen the town had been a focus of support for the southern party during the crusade and, when captured and occupied by the crusaders, its *faidit* lord Aramfré de Montpezat continued to

---

[181] Doat XXI, 194ʳ and 202ᵛ–203ʳ (P.) and 216ʳ (Hartemanda) and 217ʳ⁻ᵛ (Pierre). See also Albe, *L'hérésie … en Quercy*, 14 and notes 11–13.

[182] Doat XXI, 186ʳ⁻ᵛ, 195ʳ⁻ᵛ, 197ʳ, 199ᵛ–200ʳ.

[183] Doat XXI, 185ʳ–213ᵛ.

[184] Doat XXII, 214ʳ, 222ʳ and 226ʳ⁻ᵛ.

[185] Doat XXII, 227ᵛ–8ʳ.

[186] Doat XXII, 37ʳ, 41ʳ, 219ʳ⁻ᵛ and 228ʳ⁻9ᵛ. For de Caussade see Duvernoy, *Le Catharisme*, II, 264 note 43 and 284–285 inc. note 35, and Albe, *L'hérésie … en Quercy*, 15–16.

organize against them from other bases. Etienne de Montpezat made a donation to the southern cause in 1224 of almost all his possessions. After the Peace of 1229 Bertrand de Montpezat and Geralda, wife of G.A. de Montpezat, protected heretics. Members of the Cabanolas family were also important *credentes*, providing Cathars with money.[187] Pierre Seilha then travelled to Montaut, whose lord had become vassal of de Montfort for Agenais lands in 1214 but in whose town Arnaud de Rupe had and read a heretical book and a landowner S. Sobressen was among those convicted.[188]

In spite of the important role played in the crusade by its castellan Ratier de Castelnau, the seigneurial family of Castelnau-Montratier, sometimes called Castelnau-Hélene, do not emerge as fervently Catholic in the period leading up to the inquisition, not apparently continuing a pattern of family donations to Beaulieu of earlier generations. The town under their governorship yielded eleven convictions.

M. Roquebert has explained this expansion of the heresy in central and upper Quercy in terms of evacuations of the Toulousain during the fighting.[189] I feel this is not the whole picture. Quercy, especially the area between Cahors and Bas-Quercy, was attacked and occupied many times and was no safe haven, and the evidence indicates that most southern partisans north of the Aveyron were not heretical supporters until after the wars. In fact heretics are not mentioned there in the period before 1229 except at Montcuq. Geographically and chronologically, it seems that the spread of the heresy into the region began with the strengthening of the community at Montcuq from Gourdon in the north, from the Agenais Lot, from Bas-Quercy and, in the case of Beaucaire, from Caussade. Lambert's observation that "(o)nce sympathy for Catharism was established within a *lignage* it could travel both horizontally through family connections and downwards through lines of dependency" is easily demonstrable throughout the whole of Quercy.[190]

---

[187] Doat XXI, 306ʳ–8ᵛ; *HGL* VI, 583–584.
[188] Doat XXI, 309–310.
[189] *L'épopée* I, 96–99.
[190] Lambert, *Cathars*, 68.

IV. Concluding observations

In c. 1250 Rainier Sacconi estimated that the Cathar church of Agen had been all but destroyed.[191] This was something of an exaggeration. From 1252 into the 1270s French officials were excommunicating and confiscating at Agen, Tonneins, and towns on the Lot.[192] The heresy continued at Montauban into the 1250s. However Guillaume de Pelhisson describes the heightened level of fear in the region in the 1240s. Catharism in Bas-Quercy was all but crushed by the scale of punitive activity in that decade and, crucially, the officials of Raymond VII lost the freedom to operate outside of his Catholic agenda. We hear of few further incidents after the mid-1240s. Even at Castelsarrasin leading families in the 1260s were making concessions to Grandselve.[193] In central Quercy, where it had arrived more recently, Catharism was apparently eliminated most easily, in spite of a handful of convictions in the 1270s.[194] There it faced the kind of activity that would ensure it never returned. It would never really take hold in Cahors. In 1226 its bishop had founded a Dominican convent in the town and was one of a network of houses that he and viscount Raymond of Turenne protected which were never tainted by the heresy.[195] That such action was necessary is illustrated by the infiltration of other religious houses in Quercy into the 1240s: Raymonda de Mazerac, prioress of Augustinian Lativia near Castelnau-Montratier, was discovered to have been a heretic for four or five years, and near to Gourdon the abbey of Linars contained a convent in which the heresy was protected by the de Goulème lords of Milhac.[196] Such enclaves could no longer survive in abbeys, and secular protectors such as the lords of Montaigu and Montpezat also lost the stomach to shelter heretics after being bound to the French crown by their submissions of 1243.[197]

---

[191] *Summa de Catharis*, 70.
[192] *HGL* VII, *ordonnance* 420; Molinier, *Correspondance*, I, 440 and 493, and II, 1513 and 2118; *Enquêtes*, 245 and 338.
[193] AD Haute-Garonne ms. Lat. 202, 106 (cited in H. Blaquière and Y. Dossat, "Confessions inédites de Catharisme Quercinois," *Cahiers de Fanjeaux* 3, 264–266); *Chronique de Guillaume Pelhisson*, 58–59; *HGL* VIII, 1869.
[194] See Albe, *L'hérésie ... en Quercy*, 23.
[195] *Ibid.*, 1–6.
[196] Doat XXI, 188^r-v, 193^v, 211^v and 307^r.
[197] See sources for 1243 submissions cited above.

But the way in which the heresy ended is not untypical of the Languedoc and not what makes the northern counties most interesting. These were the border lands of the Languedoc, the region where the heretical heartlands met Catholic Aquitaine and the archdioceses of Auch, Bordeaux, and Bourges, whose influence on the lords of the region in the late twelfth century was central to the varied responses to the heresy demonstrable by c. 1209. At the start of the crusade toleration of Catharism can be related to the patterns of orthodox lay religious enthusiasm in so far as where the latter was weakest— so far as we can measure it, for example from records of donations to and co-operation and association with abbeys and the establishment of new monastic houses—heretical success seems to have been greatest. Conversely, north of the Aveyron and south of the Garonne there is little or no trace of the heresy before the crusade. The influence of those key figures bishops Guillaume de Cardaillac and Arnaud de Rovinha and the Aquitainian viscounts of Turenne and lords of Albret, were the backbone of secular Catholicism, bolstered in the early period by orthodox activity by Quercinois lords such as those of Gourdon and Castelnau-Montratier and the Agenais abbey towns of Condom and Nérac.

However, the similarity between the "non-heretical" parts of the dioceses of Quercy and Agen cannot be taken too far. Arnaud de Rovinha, full of crusading zeal and anger at the protectors of heretics in the Agenais, lacked the vision of his colleague at Cahors and also his working relationship with the most powerful Catholic lords in his diocese. Only in the 1240s did the bishops of Agen collaborate with the count of Toulouse to establish a coherent organization for the detection and eradication of heresy. Even then they apparently did not rally their frail network of vassals in the county in this cause, just as Bishop Arnaud could not even mobilize them for the "pre-crusade" of 1209.

Neither should we over-simplify matters in assuming that the relative absence of religious houses and parish churches along the Agenais Lot accounts for heretical success there. The idea that clerical weakness was a direct cause of the rise of heresy was challenged by Moore, as we have seen. Bas-Quercy had thriving heretical communities and yet had successful abbeys at Moissac and Belleperche. While the latter was infiltrated by heretics, there is nothing to suggest that Moissac or Sainte-Livrade and Penne on the Lot were, anymore than were Condom, Meilhan, and Nérac. Nonetheless, as a generalization it was where Catholic activists were weaker or where, in the case of the diocese of Quercy and the Agenais Garonne, support for their alliance with the crusaders was to weaken, that Catharism was to grow most effectively.

In addition, although the heresy was eventually adopted by the mercantile Agenais towns as it had been by the urban communities of Bas-Quercy, a clear correlation between the two spheres may not be drawn. The families who dominated the latter were those demi-nobles so typical of the Languedoc, among them several whose power pertained to their association with the counts of Toulouse. The towns they dominated can be categorised among those "*castra* and fortified villages of powerful local nobles ... (t)heir families ... linked by marriage"[198] like those of the Lot, the Cahorsain, and Haut-Quercy. They were not like the mercantile notables who increasingly controlled the Agenais Garonne, in whose circles Moore found little to specifically account for the success of heresy.

More generally relating the above to Moore's observations that the persecution of "otherness," in this case heresy, is the product of a power trying to assert or consolidate its authority within a given society, and does not arise from human nature, some interesting points also emerge. To begin with, authority did not exist in the Languedoc in the sense that it was asserting itself in northern France, Aragon, or the Anglo-Plantagenet realm. Whatever the personal devotional sympathies of the count of Toulouse, he could do little to persecute a heresy protected by the wayward nobility of the region. The best he could do was to call on the powers on which he was in some way dependent, hence the appeal for help against the strengthening Cathar church by Raymond V of Toulouse in the 1170s, and the willing response of the kings of England and France and the papacy. Moore has noted that their power was used against vassals of Toulouse as recalcitrant politically as they were in religious affairs.[199] In this case as in 1209 and beyond those foreigners involving themselves against heresy in the Languedoc were also those who coveted power in the region. Raymond VI paid the price for this when, after Trencavel was dispossessed in 1209–1211, the northerners began taking over lands of which he himself had control, including in

---

[198] Barber, *Cathars*, 68.
[199] Moore, *Persecuting Society*, 145 and *Origins*, 215, 255 and 257. By 1173 the count was a vassal for Toulouse of the king of England as duke of Aquitaine (Taylor, "Innocent III," 206).

the Agenais and Quercy. The attempts of Raymond VII to reverse this process by initiating repression of his own came too late to stop the victory of the Capetian house. Until 1249 the persecution of heretical "otherness" had been a path by which foreign powers could assert and legitimate control in the south, which was why he resisted an inquisition run by anyone other than himself.

But the result in the northern Languedoc by the end of the crusade, and in particular after the Peace of Paris, was not only political rebellion against the invasion, but ideological rebellion also in the form of tolerance of heresy if not actual belief. In this the lords of Haut-Quercy in particular flew in the face of their traditional lords, the counts of Toulouse as well as of the French and the clergy, and the towns of the Agenais Garonne began to distance themselves from the religious influence of the co-comital powers of Agen as they had been doing in any case as communes. Heresy was no more "natural" to them than was its persecution but, ironically given fundamental dualist indifference to political struggle, Catharism became allied with the defence of southern-French autonomy. As Moore has noted in general terms of the response to Occitan Catharism, its repression was much greater than the threat it posed actually warranted.[200] In the over-reaction to heresy that justified the violence in Agenais and Quercy, the crusade made havens for heresy in some of the most Catholic castles and towns of the Languedoc.

---

[200] *Persecuting Society*, 151.

THE MASSACRE AT BÉZIERS
JULY 22, 1209: A REVISIONIST LOOK

LAURENCE W. MARVIN

On July 22, 1209, one of the most notorious massacres of the Middle Ages took place in the Languedoc town of Béziers. What happened there has been recounted many times, beginning with a letter from the papal legates who witnessed it, to the many chroniclers, historians, and writers who have written about it since the thirteenth century. Though the news of the sack and massacre no doubt brought joy to most conventional Christians outside Languedoc, history has not been kind to the men who participated in it. Since the nineteenth century, no credible historians who write even a few words about the Albigensian Crusade and Béziers in particular have applauded what happened in 1209 as a Christian triumph. J.C.L. Sismondi's English translator and editor, for example, saw the entire crusade arising out of terrible religious fanaticism.[1] The editors and authors of the *Histoire générale de Languedoc* said what happened at Béziers was "font un carnage horrible."[2] While Guizot's *A Popular History of France* does not mention what happened at Béziers directly, the Albigensian Crusade made sure that, "… nearly all the towns and strong castles … were taken, lost, retaken, given over to pillage, sack, and massacre, and burnt by the crusaders with all the cruelty of fanatics, and all the greed of conquerors."[3]

The twentieth century has generally followed that tone. Many, though certainly not all scholars and popular writers since 1945, like E.F. Jacobs, Zoé Oldenbourg, Michel Roquebert, Joseph Strayer, Walter Wakefield, Jonathan Sumption, Bernard Hamilton, and Stephen

---

[1] J.C.L. Simonde de Sismondi, *History of the Crusades against the Albigenses in the Thirteenth Century with an introductory essay by the translator*; translator unknown (London: Wightman and Cramp, 1826), v–xxiv, xxxvii–xl.

[2] C. Devic and J. Vaissete, *Histoire générale de Languedoc avec des notes et pièces justificatives* ed. A. Molinier et al (Toulouse: E. Privat, 1879): 8: LVII, 288.

[3] M. Guizot, *A Popular History of France, From the Earliest Times.* 5 vols. trans. Robert Black. (Boston: D. Estes and C.E. Lauriat, 1872), 2: 97.

O'Shea have tended to view the storming of Béziers as a particularly violent act if not an atrocity.[4] This continues to be reflected in both current scholarship on the Albigensian crusade or in works that only tangentially mention it.[5] Some scholars have forgotten the context, not questioning but assuming that the massacre at Béziers was uniquely horrible. The massacre at Béziers, however, deserves to be reexamined and reevaluated in a spirit devoid of condemnation or passion and discussed not only in comparison with the typical violence of the age but also within the limits of the possible. By doing so we come up with new interpretations that get us closer to a true understanding of events

---

[4] E.F. Jacobs. "Innocent III," *The Cambridge Medieval History* vol. 6 ed. Bury, Tanner et. al. (Cambridge: Cambridge University Press, 1957), 25; Zoé Oldenbourg, *Massacre at Montségur. A History of the Albigensian Crusade*, trans. Peter Green (New York: Pantheon Books, 1961), 119–120; Joseph R. Strayer, *The Albigensian Crusades*, 1971 (Ann Arbor:, MI: University of Michigan Press, 1992), 62–64; Michel Roquebert, *L'Épopée Cathare I, 1198–1212: L'invasion* (Toulouse: Privat, 1970), 261–264; Walter M. Wakefield, *Heresy, Crusade and Inquisition in Southern France 1100–1250* (Berkeley and Los Angeles: University of California Press, 1974), 100, 102; Jonathan Sumption, *The Albigensian Crusade* (London: Faber, 1978), 92–94; Stephen O'Shea, *The Perfect Heresy. The Revolutionary Life and Death of the Medieval Cathars* (New York: Walker and Co, 2000), 84–89; Bernard Hamilton, *The Albigensian Crusade* (London: Historical Association, 1974), 18–19, and "The Albigensian Crusade and Heresy," *The New Cambridge Medieval History* vol. 5 c. 1198–c. 1300 (Cambridge: Cambridge University Press, 1999), 167. In both places Hamilton states that the entire population of Béziers was killed in the sack.

For examples of those who do not view the sack in such a horrible light, see Hoffman Nickerson, *The Inquisition. A Political and Military Study of its Establishment.* 2nd edition 1932. reprint (Port Washington NY: Kennikat Press, 1968), 118–120; Pierre Belperron, *La Croisade contre Les Albigeois et L'Union du Languedoc a la France (1209–1249)* (Paris: Plon, 1942), 1967, 186–194; Monique Zerner-Chardavoine, *La Croisade Albigeoise* (Paris: Julliard, 1979), 103–104; Michael Costen, *The Cathars and the Albigensian Crusade* (Manchester: Manchester University Press, 125); Malcolm Barber, *The Cathars. Dualist Heretics in Languedoc in the High Middle Ages* (Harlow, England: Longman, 2000), 121–122.

[5] Malcolm Barber, "The Albigensian Crusades: Wars like Any Other?" *Dei gesta per Francos. Crusade Studies in Honour of Jean Richard*, eds. Michel Balard, Benjamin Z. Kedar, and Jonathan Riley-Smith (Aldershot: Variorum, 2001), 45–55. Barber says on p. 53, "Viewed within this context, it can be seen that the Albigensian crusades went far beyond the normal conventions of early thirteenth-century warfare, in the scale of the slaughter, in the execution of high-status opponents, male and female, in the mutilation of prisoners, in the humiliation and shaming of the defeated, and in the quite overt use of terror as a method of achieving one's goal." He was not talking of Béziers solely here obviously but as one of a string of atrocities done by both sides during the crusade. To his credit, he presents one of the most balanced viewpoints on the subject. Recent tangential mentions include Jane Sayers, *Innocent III. Leader of Europe 1198–1216* (London: Longman, 1994), 160, "The sack of Béziers was carried out with untold and mindless ferocity."

and their impact. Therefore aspects like the size of the crusading army and the preparedness of the city, and an analysis of the sack, fires and massacre form the heart of this paper.

Recruitment

By the summer of 1209, a considerable army had gathered to wage the crusade. No scholar has ever attempted to analyze carefully the numbers involved for the summer of 1209, partially because figuring out the kind of people attracted to it is impossible to ascertain with precision. There are no extant crusade sermons for this phase of the Albigensian Crusade, even though there was extensive preaching of it, and papal letters were sent to the prelates and nobles of France.[6] How the troops were recruited and how many mustered for the campaign of 1209 cannot be known. Some of the army may have been raised within traditional feudal ties, drawing a large number of nobles with their knightly retainers.[7] Indeed, the Cistercian chronicler Peter des Vaux-de-Cernay mentioned an extensive list of participants including four bishops, five nobles, and other lords by name and too many others to name, while the southern cleric William of Tudela mentioned a similar list as well as two additional nobles and other lords by name.[8] Other chroniclers compiled their lists as well.[9] Presumably these nobles and prelates brought their retinues or *familia* and other armed men.

While undoubtedly some of the manpower for this campaign came from this traditional source, listing nobles and bishops cannot account

---

[6] Peter des Vaux-de-Cernay, *Hystoria Albigensis*, 3 vols. eds. Pascal Guébin and Ernest Lyon (Paris: Champion, 1926–1939), 1: 69–74, hereafter abbreviated as PVC; English trans. *The History of the Albigensian Crusade* by W.A. and M.D. Sibly (Woodbridge: Boydell Press, 1998), 40–42, hereafter abbreviated as S&S.

[7] Rachel Louise Noah, "Military Aspects of the Albigensian crusade" (M.Phil thesis, University of Glasgow, 1999), 33.

[8] PVC, 81–84; S&S, 47; William of Tudela, *La Chanson de la Croisade Albigeoise*. ed. Eugène Martin-Chabot (Paris: H. Champion, 1931), 24–25, 34–37, hereafter abbreviated as WTud; English trans. *The Song of the Cathar Wars. A History of the Albigensian Crusade* by Janet Shirley (Vermont: Ashgate Publishing Co., 1996), 14, 16–17, hereafter abbreviated as Shirley.

[9] Robert of Auxerre, *Chronicon*. ed. O. Holder-Egger, *Monumenta Germaniae Historica: Scriptores* 26 (hereafter abbreviated as MGH SS) Hanover, 1882, 273; Albert of the Three Fountains, *Chronica*, MGH SS 23 ed. P. Scheffer-Bolchorst (Hanover, 1863), 889; William the Breton, *Gesta Philippi Augusti. Oeuvres de Rigord et de Guillaume le Breton*, ed. François Delaborde (Paris: Librairie Renouard, H. Loones, successeur, 1882), 258–259.

for the vast majority of pilgrims who had no feudal ties to anyone.[10]
No apparatus existed to recruit the rank and file, and in the absence
of evidence, it appears that the commoners who were recruited or
showed up were not much different than the types who did duty in
the earlier crusades to the Middle East. In that sense the common
crusaders represented a cross section of the European population and
served without a clear sense of term or obligations of service to a leader.
As will be discussed below, it was not a well organized, disciplined, or
supplied army.

Besides the obvious social and geographical origins of men like the
papal legates Arnaud-Amaury and Milo, and nobles like Simon de
Montfort, the sources occasionally reveal the geographical if not the
social origins of the men who participated. William of Tudela's account
is especially good for this, occasionally reading like a travelogue of
armed visitors to his part of the world. For the army of 1209, he mentions crusader contingents from Auvergne, Burgundy, the Ile-de-France,
Limousin, Gascony, Rouergue, Saintonge, and Germans from all the
regions of Germany.[11] His contemporary, Robert of Auxerre, adds Normans to the list.[12] The cosmopolitan nature of the army came with
a price: its "international" nature undoubtedly contributed to tensions
within the ranks, as there was bound to be linguistic confusion and
other misunderstandings that lessened the overall military effectiveness
of the army, as had happened to earlier crusading armies in the Middle
East.[13]

The manifest incentive for enlisting was to gain the papal indulgence. How crusaders would earn it was uncharted territory because
the goal of the Albigensian Crusade, to eliminate heresy from a Christian land, was unique. The first mention of the forty-day period of
service emerges from William of Tudela's recounting of the siege of
Béziers.[14] Even though William composed his account prior to 1213, it
is hard to tell whether or not the forty-day period was a recognized

---

[10] Claire Dutton, "Aspects of the Institutional History of the Albigensian Crusades,
1198–1229," (Ph.D diss. University of London, 1993), 215. She also points out other
possibilities.

[11] WTud, 38–39; Shirley, 17.

[12] Robert of Auxerre, 273.

[13] John France, *Victory in the East. A Military History of the First Crusade* (Cambridge:
Cambridge University Press, 1994), 18–21; Simon Lloyd, "The Crusading Movement,
1096–1274," in *The Oxford History of the Crusades* ed. Jonathan Riley-Smith (Oxford:
Oxford University Press, 1999), 51–52.

[14] WTud, 52–53; Shirley, 20.

institution on the campaign of 1209. The requirement for earning the indulgence by performing a forty-day period in Languedoc definitely emerged in 1210, but even then it was not a policy instituted by the pope but by the legates in Languedoc.[15] The forty days service might account for the supposed feudal nature of the army, but there may be other reasons for this term of service that will never come to light.[16]

At least one characteristic of this army does make the campaign of 1209 stand out from other military operations of the period, or in fact those waged in Languedoc subsequently. All the medieval and modern scholars agree that the crusading army of 1209 was an extremely large one and would be the largest raised for the crusade between 1209 and 1218. The numbers of any army during the Middle Ages are difficult to figure out with any accuracy, and this is no less true for the Albigensian Crusade.[17] The eyewitness account of the two legates who accompanied the army, Arnaud-Amaury and Milo, does not mention any numbers, and the best they could tell Innocent III was that the army was the largest Christian army ever gathered.[18] William of Tudela was the closest source to the events who hazards a guess in figures, but leaves us no better off for having done so. According to his account, there were 20,000 knights (*vint melia cavaliers*) as well as 200,000 commoners (*e plus de docent melia*) of varying stripes present in the army.[19]

---

[15] Dutton, "Institutional Aspects," 211, 213. Laurence W. Marvin, "Thirty-Nine Days and a Wake-Up: The Impact of the Indulgence and Forty Days Service on the Albigensian Crusade, 1209–1218," *The Historian* 65 no. 1 (2002): 75–94.

[16] One might be Christ's sojourn in the wilderness, or perhaps imitating the forty days of Lent as a period of austerity and sacrifice.

[17] Hans Delbrück, *Numbers in History* (London: University of London Press, 1913); Bernard S. Bachrach, "Early Medieval Military Demography: Some Observations on the Methods of Hans Delbrück," *The Circle of War in the Middle Ages. Essays on Medieval Military and Naval History*, ed. Donald J. Kagay and L.J. Andrew Villalon (Woodbridge: Boydell Press, 1999), 3–20, and "The Siege of Antioch: A Study in Military Demography," *War in History* 6 (1999): 127–146. Bachrach has begun to reexamine our attitudes towards numbers in medieval armies and endorses larger numbers than previous scholars have currently argued for. Unfortunately, what the chroniclers report often has no basis in reality.

[18] *Innocent III Romani Pontificis Opera Omnia, Patrologia Latina* (hereafter abbreviated as PL) 216, 1855, columns 138–139, "... cum tanta multitudine signatorum quanta inter Christianos non creditur aliquando convenisse ..."; Austin P. Evans, "The Albigensian Crusade," *A History of the Crusades*, Kenneth Setton et al, and ed. (Madison: University of Wisconsin Press, 1969), 287; Costen, 121.

[19] WTud, 36–37; Shirley, 17; PVC, 98; S&S, 53. Peter des Vaux-de-Cernay mentions that 500,000 were in the crusading army at Carcassonne. This could reflect ever greater numbers flocking to the crusade between the siege and sack of Béziers but likely just means "a lot".

Other chroniclers suggest a sizeable army, as does Robert of Auxerre, whose lord participated in this initial campaign. He mentions no numbers but said in addition to the nobles, other lords, and prelates, that *vulgarium numerus infinitus* made up the army.[20] Modern scholars have agreed that the army was unusual in size, though most have wisely not attempted to come up with actual numbers.[21] A scale can be suggested however, by considering other contemporary armies, especially the Fourth Crusade, organized, preached, and conducted in the decade before the Albigensian Crusade. The treaty signed between the crusaders and Venetians listed very specific numbers. Of course the Fourth Crusade turned into a relative disaster partially because the parties who sealed the deal proved unable to estimate the eventual numbers of participants correctly. This was not the chroniclers' fault who reported the numbers as specified in the treaty but reflects the basic human inability to predict demand. Even in the postmodern age of electronic ticket sales, airlines, and events promoters frequently incorrectly assess how many people will actually take a flight or attend a concert. Geoffrey of Villehardouin reported that the treaty called for the Venetians to transport and care for an army of 33,500, composed of 4,500 knights (*chevaliers*), 9,000 squires (*esquiers*) and 20,000 infantry (*serjanz a pié*).[22] Far fewer actually showed up, perhaps about 14,000.[23] The time, distance, and most of all the expense kept the crusade from gaining its expected manpower. For another near-contemporary army size scholars have come up with some reasonable numbers for Philip Augustus's army at Bouvines in 1214. This army consisted of perhaps as many as

---

[20] Robert of Auxerre, 273; see also William the Breton, *Gesta*, 258.

[21] Strayer, 52, 53, says "many thousands," Sumption, 86, says about 20,000, of which half were non-combatants, but he never explains how he came up with his number; Philippe Wolff, *Histoire du Languedoc* (Toulouse: Privat, 1967), 200, estimates 5–6,000 knights or more, but does not give a concrete number for the other members of the army.

[22] Geoffroy Villehardouin, *La Conquête De Constantinople*, ed. and trans. Edmond Faral (Paris: Société d'édition "Les Belles lettres," 1938), 1:22–25; Donald E. Queller and Thomas F. Madden, *The Fourth Crusade. The Conquest of Constantinople*, 2nd ed. (Philadelphia: University of Pennsylvania Press, 1997): 10–11, 17, 215–216 endnote 19. What Villehardouin actually meant by "*escuiers*" is still an unanswered question.

[23] Villehardouin, *La Conquête* 1:58. Villehardouin maintained that the number of ships mustered by the Venetians could have accommodated three times the number of crusaders who showed up, suggesting the actual numbers were at only about one third of the 33,500. Queller and Madden, *Fourth Crusade*, 48, and 232 endnote 60, propose that about 14,000 men arrived at Venice to take part in the crusade.

7,600 men broken down into 1,300 knights, 300 horse sergeants and between five and six thousand infantry.[24]

These two examples give us a scale of the possible size of an early thirteenth century army, from which we can estimate the size of the crusader army of 1209. There are some caveats in doing so. One, the Albigensian Crusade follows neither of the above examples too closely. The Fourth Crusaders had to contend with massive logistical require-ments for a journey by sea that would necessarily restrict army size, and Philip Augustus' army in 1214 was limited by his financial ability to pay for mercenaries, his personal standing with his vassals, and his royal influence over the civic militias of towns and cities which owed military obligations to him. The crusading army destined for service in Languedoc in 1209 had none of these restraints. The expenses for a march south could not compare to those incurred on a sea journey of much greater distance.[25] The crusaders could march overland in geo-graphically and climatically favorable conditions. The "overhead" for this crusade would be necessarily light, because even though Innocent had decreed taxes be raised to support it, this was done on a limited basis and did not include areas outside what is now modern France. As well, if the forty day period of service was in place (but we should not subscribe too closely to this for 1209) to win the indulgence, the financial outlay for the church, nobles, and individuals was light, and in fact, for nobles not much more than they might incur in a regular campaign season of forty days. The campaign of 1209 thus represented the best of all possible worlds: It was a cheap crusade with relatively few logistical or geographical difficulties, and it did not depend on the egos of secular rulers for leadership. Most certainly the Albigensian Crusade

---

[24] Laurence W. Marvin, "Warfare and the Composition of Armies in France, 1100–1218: An Emphasis on the Common Soldier," (Ph.D diss. University of Illinois Urbana-Champaign, 1997), 158 and footnote 109 for a summary of scholarship. See also J.F. Verbruggen, *The Art of Warfare in Western Europe during the Middle Ages from the Eighth Century to 1340*, 2nd ed. trans. Sumner Willard and R.W. Southern (Woodbridge: Boydell Press, 1954, 1997), 242–247; "Le Problème des Effectifs et de la Tactique a la Bataille de Bouvines (1214)," *Revue du Nord* XXI no. 124 (Oct–Dec 1949): 181–193; Ferdinand Lot, *L'Art Militaire et les Armées au Moyen Age en Europe et dans le Proche Orient*, 2 vols. (Paris: Payot, 1946), 1:224–230.

It must be emphasized that coming up for accurate numbers for the French forces of Bouvines is much less cut and dry than that for the Fourth Crusade.

[25] Dutton, "Administrative Aspects," Richard Kay, "The Albigensian twentieth of 1221–1223: an early chapter in the history of papal taxation," *The Journal of Medieval History* 6 (1980): 307–315, esp. 307.

drew poor pilgrims of a type that would not or could not participate
in the Fourth Crusade because of the distance, mode of transportation,
and expense.[26] Since the army of 1209 had few inherent disabilities that
would have limited its size, the possible numbers of crusaders in the
campaign of 1209 might have been quite high. If 33,500 was an overly
optimistic and ultimately unsustainable number for a crusade overseas,
and 7,500 was the best a king could do given the limited resources of
any one kingdom, then a range of 10–30 thousand is a realistic figure
for the number of people who participated in this first campaign of the
Albigensian Crusade. If we split the difference, or average it out, then
20–25,000 is a fair number.

If the above analysis fails to convince, the qualitative nature of the
sources supports the estimate of a large army. William of Tudela said
that the crusading army stretched along for "a league" and swamped
the existing road system on its march south.[27] It was so large that much
of its baggage including armor, food, and other supplies was shipped
by river.[28] This suggests an army of considerable size or a lack of
discipline that made it straggle along such a great length. This large
crusader force had gathered from its various locales in Lyon around 24
June, though a smaller army unconnected with the main army had
already moved in from the west from Agen and had besieged and
taken a few towns.[29] The main crusader army left Lyon, regrouped at
Montpellier, and left that city on 20 July, occupied the town of Servian
as its inhabitants surrendered it, then marched to Béziers and made it
to the western banks of the Orb river on the evening of 21 July.[30]

---

[26] Queller and Madden. *The Fourth Crusade*, 1–6. The 1199 tax levied on the clergy
was to be used to pay transportation costs in Outremer, a situation not present for the
Albigensian campaign of 1209. Even though for the Albigensian Crusade the money
collected was to go directly to crusaders, poor, ill-trained pilgrims were not the most
effective soldiers, and they were therefore less likely to share in the tax money. So the
tax acted as a disincentive for those who did not have ready fighting skills.

[27] WTud, 50–51; Shirley, 19.

[28] WTud, 39; Shirley, 17.

[29] WTud, 38–45; Shirley, 17–18. Claire Taylor, "Dualist heresy in Aquitaine and the
Agenais c. 1000–c. 1249," (Ph.D diss. University of Nottingham, 1999), 166–168. This
branch of the crusade dispersed after it failed to take Casseneuil. See also Claire Taylor,
"Authority and the Cathar heresy in the northern Languedoc," in this volume.

[30] PL 216, col. 139. PVC, 80, fn 2; Roquebert, 1: 247–248. As the editors of the Latin
text point out, the army did not necessarily move as a unit from Lyon to Montpellier,
and though units began leaving Lyon for Montpellier around 24 June other bands were
still moving through in the first few days of July. By 20 July though, the army had
reassembled because it appears to have moved *en masse* towards Béziers.

Preparedness of the City

The army's formation and progress was not a surprise to the people or leaders of Béziers. According to William of Tudela, after hearing the army had left Montpellier, Raymond-Roger Trencavel, viscount of Béziers, hastened to the city and arrived there the morning of 21 July. At a gathering of citizens that day Raymond-Roger exhorted the people to defend themselves against the crusaders and promised them eventual support. After delivering his pep talk he rode on to Carcassonne to prepare the defenses there.[31] The two main chroniclers interpreted Raymond-Roger's quick exit from Béziers differently. William of Tudela suggested the viscount's leadership and presence was necessary at Carcassonne, and this certainly sounds plausible. Evidently Raymond-Roger believed, as did everyone on either side, that the citizens of Béziers did not need his actual presence in order to resist the crusade. Peter des Vaux-de-Cernay takes a cheap shot at the young viscount, believing him to have fled his duties out of fear of the approaching army. Based on Raymond-Roger's solid conduct later that summer defending Carcassonne, William of Tudela's account holds more weight.[32] The viscount's warning was sufficient in advance of the army to allow those who wished to flee the city to do so, because the Jews of Bèziers left with their viscount and presumably went on to Carcassonne.[33] The Jews apparently believed that they would be especially vulnerable to the depredations of the crusade, a tradition that by now had a long history dating back at least to the First Crusade.

By the time the crusader army reached Béziers on the evening of 21 July, few residents had opted to flee. Renaud de Montpellier, bishop of Béziers, had accompanied the army on part of its journey and now took a last opportunity to convince his flock to give up before blood would be spilled.[34] At a large public gathering, probably in the

---

[31] WTud, 46–49; Shirley; PVC, 89–90; S&S, 49–50.

[32] For a modern interpretation of Raymond-Roger's behavior see Fernand Niel, "Béziers pendant la Croisade contre les Albigeois," *Cahier d'Etudes Cathares* 4 no. 15 (1953): 139–157, especially 141–144. Niel suggests that because the Trencavels had had serious problems with the people of Béziers, including the assassination of Raymond-Roger's grandfather in 1167, that the young viscount was more willing to allow the city to see its own defense without his direct support.

[33] WTud, 48–49; Shirley, 19. In this same passage William mentions that the citizens grew apprehensive after their viscount talked to them, but there seems to be little anxiety based on their subsequent thoughts and actions.

[34] Henri Vidal. *Episcopatus et pouvoir épiscopal à Béziers à la veille de la Croisade Albigeoise*

cathedral church of St. Nazaire, the bishop strongly urged the citizens
of Béziers to make their peace with the crusade, even if it meant
some despoliation of their goods.[35] He urged them to hand over to the
crusade any heretics, and even had a list of Cathars to help facilitate
their removal. Failing that, he encouraged the loyal Catholics to flee
the city in order to avoid being lumped in with the heretics.[36] His words
did not meet with a favorable reception. Well aware of the army's size,
since the townspeople could see it before them now, and fully warned
by their own bishop, the townspeople knew what they were risking.

There were several factors for why the people of Béziers chose not to
comply with the demands of the crusade. First, there was the obvious
reluctance to hand neighbors, friends, and relatives over to a crusading
army that would certainly not treat them well. Second, there was
the common though unexpressed belief that the odds were with them
because it was hard for an army to take a city quickly. The Bitterois had
had time to strengthen the city's defensive works, as Peter des Vaux-
de-Cernay relates in an anecdote.[37] The citizens believed they would
still be holding out after a month of sieging.[38] Third, the townspeople
were sure that the huge size of the crusading army would actually be
its downfall, believing it could last no more than two weeks.[39] Though
William of Tudela does not express their reasons for thinking this way,
any large military force would outstrip its food supply, and this, along
with the indiscipline inherent in any army of this polyglot composition
and size, meant it would dissolve as quickly as it had formed.

Finally, there were the tactical and geographical difficulties inherent in besieging a city. William of Tudela's account and the legates'
letter report how strong and well defended Béziers was.[40] The army

---

(Montpellier: [s.n.], 1951), 43. In theory the bishop had considerable power in the city,
but here he encouraged rather than ordered.

[35] WTud, 48; Shirley, 19. "probably" is used as a qualifier in the previous sentence
because William of Tudela does not specify what church it was, but most scholars agree
on the cathedral as the meeting place.

[36] PVC, 90–91; S&S, 50.

[37] PVC, 88–89; S&S, 49. In this anecdote a mysterious old man tells the workers
that strengthening the fortifications of the city would protect it against humans but not
from God. What the anecdote reveals is that the defenders had had time to strengthen
some of the defenses at least. How Peter des Vaux-de-Cernay would have heard this
story cannot be determined.

[38] WTud, 50–51; Shirley, 19–20.

[39] WTud, 50–51; Shirley, 19.

[40] PL, 216, col 139; WTud, 50–51; Shirley, 19.

encamped on the left side of the Orb river, at least 220 meters from the walls. From the heights where the cathedral church stood, the crusader camp, deceptively far away across the river lulled the people of Béziers into a false sense of security. Both by personal observation and the fact that none of the sources mentions it, the Orb cannot be forded anywhere close by, so the crusaders had to cross a bridge that should have been under close observation and would narrow the point of attack. To get into the town required climbing a steep hill, on top of which perched the Cathedral church.[41] So geographically and defensively the advantage lay with the defenders. Based on the above analysis it seems obvious both sides had prepared themselves for the possibility of a lengthy siege, anticipating hard and drawn out fighting.

The Population and Defenders of the City

Like the number of crusaders in the army, the population of Béziers cannot be assessed definitively. Just as some have overestimated the crusading army, both medievals and moderns have tended to either under or overestimate the population of the city, from a low of 8,000–9,000 to a high of 100,000.[42] The best discussion of the evidence, but perhaps not the most recent, has been compiled by J.C. Russell.[43] His data for Béziers is based on hearth tax records for 1342, on the eve of the Black Death. Russell gives a theoretical population for the city of approximately 14,500. This is a reasonable number though several things have to be kept in mind. One, in theory the population could have been larger prior to this era.[44] Two, and more likely, the

---

[41] Partially based on personal observation in June 2000 at Béziers.

[42] Sismondi, (15,000), 36; Belperron, 190–192, summarizes several numbers ranging between 8,000 and 25,000; Evans, (8–9000), 289, fn 14; Philippe Wolff, "Une discussion de témoignages: le massacre de Béziers en 1209," in Documents de L'Histoire du Languedoc ed. Philippe Wolff (Toulouse: Privat, 1969), 114 (no more than 10,000); Strayer, (8–10,000), 61; William the Breton, 258–259, suggested at least 60,000; Caesarius of Heisterbach, Dialogus Miraculorum, ed. Joseph Strange (Cologne: Confluentia, Hergt, 1851), 1:302, and Dialogue on Miracles, trans. H. von E. Scott and C.C. Swinton Bland with an introduction by G.G. Coulton. 2 vols. (London: G. Routledge & Sons, 1929), 1:346 has the highest medieval estimate at over 100,000.

[43] Josiah Cox Russell. Medieval Regions and their Cities (Bloomington, IN: Indiana University Press, 1972), 161–162.

[44] William Chester Jordan, The Great Famine. Northern Europe in the Early Fourteenth

population was smaller than 14,500 in 1209. Even if we accept either one of the above possibilities, Béziers may have had a larger population than normal on the day of the storming because of refugees fleeing into the city ahead of the crusade. Unfortunately the main sources are silent as to whether this was the case, and there appears to be few if any refugees actually in the city except possibly some from Servian, a small village about eight miles northeast of Béziers, which had been occupied by the crusade on the march to Béziers.[45] Béziers was the first city of size to be hit by the forces of the main crusade, and the crusaders did not sack and destroy many towns prior to getting there. As well, since Béziers provided the object lesson to show the people of Languedoc what the crusade was capable of, with the possible exception of what happened to Servian, the people of the region did not flee their areas for Béziers, as they would *after* the storming.[46] There is one other number worth mentioning, though it does not help us determine the overall population of the city. This is the list of Cathars in the possession of the bishop of Béziers.[47] This list contained some 222 names of known Cathars, but is so problematic as to be almost valueless for determining the overall population of the city other than the fact that we know there must have been at least 222 Cathars in Béziers at the time of the massacre. Whether this list along with unnamed sons, fathers, and wives represent all the Cathars is not at all clear. If the list contained the names of all the open heretics of the city, this was a remarkably small number for a town perhaps as large as 14,500 in a region supposed to be infected with heresy. The list may only record known perfects, which would mean that Cathar *credentes* were much higher in number and Cathar sympathizers even more numerous. Still it does not help us with the overall population.

Century (Princeton: Princeton University Press, 1996), 8. Though Jordan confines the area of the "great famine" as north of the Loire River of France, it is possible that this affected population farther south.

[45] PL 216, col. 139; Devic and Vaissette, *Histoire générale*, 8: 286–287; Roquebert, 1: 246–247; Shirley, 18 and fn 16. None of the three main chronicle sources of the crusade—Peter des Vaux-de-Cernay, William of Tudela, or William de Puylaurens—mention the occupation of Servian. It had, however, acted as a strong center of heresy prior to 1209 and would have drawn the ire of the crusade.

[46] Sismondi, 36 says the city was full of refugees, but none of the sources supports this view.

[47] See L. Domairon ed., "Role des Hérétiqués de la ville de Béziers a l'Époque du désastre de 1209," *Le Cabinet Historique* 9.1 (1863): 95–103 for a printed list and comment; Malcolm Barber. *The Cathars*, 65–66 for an explanation of their social origins.

We are left with two choices, neither of them completely satisfactory. If we believe the chronicler's and legates' reports of casualties, the population of Béziers had to have been far higher than 14,500. Otherwise we must accept Russell's numbers in lieu of new evidence or analysis of the population.[48] This means that since the crusaders outnumbered the defenders, the former's ability to devastate the population once in the city was great.

The Siege and Sack

The actual coverage of the siege and sack of Béziers is not as thorough as one might like, which is why there are so many problems associated with interpreting the incident. The only eyewitnesses who left an account were the papal legates Milo and Arnaud-Amaury. In addition Peter des Vaux-de-Cernay and William of Tudela discuss what happened, but neither of these works is satisfactorily detailed in the telling of events.[49] On the positive side, there is not wide disagreement as to the sequence of events. The citizens of Béziers, confident behind their high walls and strong defenses, badgered the crusader army camped outside its walls across the Orb river with jeers, sorties, and arrow fire. In a scuffle on the bridge over the Orb, a crusader was hacked to death and thrown over the bridge.[50]

The main brunt of the citizens' harassment fell on the thousands of pilgrims and camp followers of both sexes who had encamped closest to the walls. The sources consistently use the same type of words to describe these camp followers: *ribaldi, arlotz, vulgi,* and *gartz.*[51] Figuring out what they meant by these terms has been an interesting journey into creative interpretation. Peter des Vaux-de-Cernay said they were, "... sergeants (*servientes*) of the army, who in the popular language were called 'ribalds' ..."[52] Clearly this refers to the less affluent crusader infantry but Peter Vaux-de-Cernay usually used *pelegrini* or

---

[48] Barber, 66. The latest scholar in English to consider the numbers, Barber seems to support Russell.

[49] See also S&S, Appendix B for an analysis of the attack.

[50] WTud, 55; Shirley, 20.

[51] PVC, 91, WTud, 53–55; PL, 216, col. 139; William of Puylaurens, *Chronique 1203–1275.* ed. and trans. Jean Duvernoy (Paris: Centre National de la Recherche Scientifique, 1976), 60–61 (hereafter referred to as WPL).

[52] PVC, 91. "... servientes exercitus, qui publica lingua dicuntur 'ribaldi'..."

crucesignati to describe poor pilgrim/crusaders. Several modern historians have taken the sources' use of the word *servientes* to imply that Peter des Vaux-de-Cernay meant these men were the hangers-on or servants of other soldiers, knights, nobles, or prelates.[53] Zoé Oldenbourg and Michel Roquebert have suggested that these *ribalds* were *routiers* or mercenaries, an interesting theory that has some merit.[54] It seems unlikely, however, that thousands of soldiers in the first campaign of the crusade were *routiers* because mercenaries would serve no real purpose in this particular crusading army, nor would they have much incentive to serve. A *routier's* chances of gaining land was always very slight, and since this was a crusade done on the cheap there was not much money changing hands. The nobles who participated appear to have had all the followers they wanted, and of course there were plenty of pilgrims anxious to gain the indulgence. There simply does not seem to be a lot to draw mercenaries for this campaign. If anything, using *routiers* was a *southern* tradition, not a northern one. In the course of the crusade Simon de Montfort increasingly used mercenaries to hold onto his possessions, but this practice emerged only in the months after the storming of Béziers. Since most of our main sources liberally use some word meaning *routiers* or mercenaries, it seems inexplicable as to why they would not use it for these kind of men if they were at Béziers. *Routiers* would have been a convenient scapegoat to blame the subsequent massacre on and if that were the case, the crusaders would bear

---

[53] Sumption, 92–93; Belperron, 189–190; Evans, 288; Strayer, 62–63. Janet Shirley's translation of William of Tudela's account also suggests these were servants. See Linda M. Paterson, *The World of the Troubadors. Medieval Occitan Society, c. 1100–c. 1300* (Cambridge: Cambridge University Press, 1993), 56–61 for a better definition of the Provençal words and others that specifically refer to mercenaries.

[54] Oldenbourg, 105–106; Roquebert I: 254–258. *Routiers* have had a long and checkered past in the Middle Ages. A quick definition would be they were mercenaries who fought in recognized units for money. The reason it was unlikely that there were many at this incident is that the crusading fervor for this campaign seemed to make paying someone to go on crusade superfluous. For a general discussion of *routiers*, see H. Géraud, "Les Routiers au Douzième Siècle," *Bibliothèque de L'Ecole des Chartes* 3 (1841–1842): 125–147 and "Mercadier. Les Routiers au Treizième Siècle," *Bibliothèque de L'Ecole des Chartes* 3 (1841–1842): 417–433; Herbert Grundmann, "Rotten un Brabanzonen: Söldner-heere im 12 Jahrhundert," *Deutsches Archiv für Erforschung des Mittelalters.* (1942): 419–492.

Without a doubt mercenaries played a vital role in the Albigensian Crusade after 1209. See Steven Isaac, "Down Upon the Fold: Mercenaries in the Twelfth Century" (Ph.D dissertation Louisiana State University, 1998), 302–315 for the *routiers'* presence in the Albigensian Crusade.

less responsibility for what happened. The middle ground between the interpretations simply means viewing these *ribalds* as the rank and file pilgrims who constituted the bulk of the army.

A group of *ribalds* grew incensed under the goading fire and harassment from the city, crossed the bridge and river, and attacked the walls and gates of Béziers.[55] William of Tudela said they had a "king" or leader who mobilized them to attack, and the existence of a leader of some kind partially accounts for why Roquebert thought these may have been *routiers*. But the troubadour goes on to say that they grabbed clubs because they had nothing else, and this suggests they were pilgrims or poorer crusaders, not organized mercenaries. This attack was swift and largely spontaneous.[56] The *ribalds* moved so quickly that before the militia of Béziers could respond, the *ribalds* were across the bridge and well on their way to battering in the gates. The nobility and knights of the crusading army held back or were unaware of what was going on until the attack was well underway. According to the legates' letter, at the time of the *ribalds'* attack, the leaders of the crusade were discussing how to get the loyal Catholics out of the city, presumably before a proper siege began.[57] By the time the better-equipped crusaders realized what was happening and had armed themselves, the *ribalds* had entered the town. The citizens began to abandon their positions and flee to protect their families, collecting in the churches as the most defensible buildings. During the frenetic capture of the town the crusade leadership could not control events, and many knights scrambled to join in to get their share of booty.[58]

With the town firmly in crusader hands but not under any coherent leadership, division of the spoils led to further loss of life. As part of restoring order, the barons of the crusade began to collect the booty and kick the "*garz*" out of the houses they had seized. Incensed, the *ribalds* began to set the town on fire in retaliation for the loss of their too-easily won possessions and to ensure that if they did not get to keep what they had seized, no one would.[59] Though one should

---

[55] Evans, 288, suggests the *ribalds* simply forced the bridge during the melee in which the crusader was thrown off it.

[56] PL, 216, col. 139; PVC, 91; S&S, 50; WTud, 54–55; Shirley, 20.

[57] PL, 216, col. 139; S&S, 289.

[58] PVC, 90–93; WTud, 53–59; PL 216 col. 139; WPL, 60–61. The legate's letter and Peter des Vaux-de-Cernay specifically mention that this was done without consulting the leadership of the crusade.

[59] WTud, 61; Robert of Auxerre, 273.

not excuse their behavior it is understandable given that they had captured the town and by right of storm the plunder belonged to them.[60]

Analysis and Commentary

Even though the sack of Béziers may very well be the most infamous episode of the entire crusade, there is not much to report from a military standpoint. The chroniclers and legates discussed no tactics or strategy because there was none. From a moral standpoint even the legates seemed struck by the swiftness of the attack and the starkness of the death and destruction.

The events of Béziers have always had a particularly unsavory twist because of the words reported by one German chronicler, Caesarius of Heisterbach, who was not present at the sack and wrote long after the events. This author has done more to take an uncommon event and place it in the pantheon of horror than any medieval chronicler or modern commentator. In his vast compendium of stories and anecdotes, the *Dialogus Miraculorum*, or *Dialogue of Miracles*, Caesarius briefly described the siege and sack of Béziers. According to his account, after the *ribalds* placed ladders against the walls and swiftly entered the town, the papal legate, Arnaud-Amaury, was asked how the crusaders would separate the good Christians from the heretics.[61] He is reported to have replied with a bit of scripture and an important addition: "Kill them. God knows who are his."[62] This phrase is often taken to best sum up the war against Catharism in Languedoc. Whether the legate actually said those words is a topic at which most scholars have taken a crack. As a Cistercian monk, it is highly possible that Caesarius had access to

---

[60] See below, p. 220 and footnotes 90–92.

[61] For biographical information on Arnaud-Amaury, see Marie-Humbert Vicaire, "Les Clercs de la Croisade," in *Paix de Dieu et guerre sainte en Languedoc au XIIIe siècle. Cahiers de Fanjeux* 4 (1969): 265–268; Dutton, "Administrative History," 80–82; and Beverly Mayne Kienzle, *Cistercians, Heresy and Crusade in Occitania, 1145–1229* (Woodbridge: York Medieval, 2001), 138–161.

[62] *Dialogus Miraculorum*, 1: 302; *Dialogue of Miracles*, 346. The second part of this is the Scripture; according the New Revised Standard version, Timothy 2:19, "The Lord knows those who are his." English translators have different versions of the Latin, "Caedite eos. Novit enim Dominus qui sunt eius", usually with exclamation points added.

eyewitness testimony from Cistercians who had accompanied the crusading army that summer, so his account may have some limited value.
His compendium however, was written a decade or more after the sack,
sometime between 1219 and 1250. He never went to Languedoc, hence
his work is far removed from both time and place.[63] Jacques Berlioz,
who made the most thorough investigation into the context and veracity of the infamous saying, has come up with the same idea everyone
else has: we do not know whether Arnaud-Amaury spoke the words
but based on what we know of the legate's character, he *might* have said
them.[64] Where the sources are less politically charged about outcomes,
as for example, the siege of Minerve in 1210, they portray Arnaud-
Amaury as a rigid, unwielding man, who left very little compromise
open for Cathars who refused to come back to the faith. Still, when he
had similar opportunities to kill large numbers of unarmed people, as
he did at Minerve, Arnaud-Amaury gave the Cathars who surrendered
a fair chance to abjure their heresy and avoid being killed.[65] Even if
Arnaud-Amaury did say these words, the attack on Béziers was a spontaneous one with little preparation and little direction from the desig-
nated leadership of the crusade. Could or would the *ribalds* have heard
the papal legate, who himself may not have been exactly sure what was
going on? What happened at Béziers cannot be laid at the feet of one
man.

No one would deny that some sort of mass killing took place and
that the city was at least partially destroyed, but, in spite of the following contrary evidence, it should be emphasized how little real planning
had gone into it. According to William of Tudela, Raymond-Roger had
apparently warned the citizens of Béziers that if they did not surrender
they would be given no quarter, as a means of subduing other areas.[66]
William suggests this was a policy decided on beforehand by the cru-

---

[63] Coulton, introduction, *Dialogue of Miracles*, xv–xvi; Jacques Berlioz, *"Tuez-les Tous,
Dieu Reconnaîra les siens." Le Massacre de Béziers (22 juillet 1209) et la croisade contre les Albigeois
vus par Césaire de Heisterbach* (Portet-sur-Garonne: Loubatières, 1994), 6, states it was
composed between 1219 and 1223.

[64] Berlioz, 99–100. See also Kienzle, *Cistercians, Heresy and Crusade*, 161, who summarizes the negative consensus of Arnaud-Amaury's character and adds, "I can only agree
with those assessments and extend them to say that Arnaud Amaury demonstrated the
worst of Cîteaux, an appalling contradiction of monastic spirituality and its ideals of
humility, prayer and contemplation."

[65] PVC, 157–161; S&S, 83–85. This portrayal of him as rigid and unyielding even
comes from Peter des Vaux-de-Cernay, a member of the same monastic order.

[66] WTud, 56–56; Shirley, 21.

sade leadership, even though he mentions it only halfway through his account of the sack. Whether the policy was formulated before or after the massacre occurred is uncertain. In other words, since the sack of Béziers had the desired result of terrifying the people of Languedoc, it is easy to assume that this policy may have been decided on before hand even if it actually was decided on after the storming of Béziers. We must also question whether this policy was in fact adopted at all. The legates did not say anything in their letter that can be unequivocally interpreted as an official adoption of a "no surrender, no quarter" attack on Béziers.[67] Peter des Vaux-de-Cernay does not mention it, and if the policy existed it failed at the very next siege, at Carcassonne. Not only was this city surrendered after negotiations rather than stormed and sacked, the negotiated settlement was done specifically to avoid the very problems the sack and burning of Béziers caused. In addition, Arnaud-Amaury himself threatened to excommunicate anyone who sacked Carcassonne after its surrender for the very practical reason that doing so would prevent the city from being used as a base for a new lord loyal to the crusade.[68] Beyond this, the crusade leadership consisted of pragmatic men who knew that the anomalous success of Béziers could not be replicated and that to abide by or adopt a policy of no quarter for resisting the crusade would surely backfire when the geographical and tactical advantage lay so heavily with the defenders.[69]

As the citizens left the walls and gathered their families, they sought refuge in the city's churches. The scale of the massacre resulting from this panic has not been and perhaps cannot ever be accurately assessed. In one church alone, La Madeleine, Peter des Vaux-de-Cernay estimated 7,000 people were killed on the day of the sack.[70] The structure of La Madeleine in 1209, still largely extant, is simply not big enough to accommodate that many people, even terror-stricken people packed in

---

[67] PL, 216, col. 140; S&S, appendix B, 289–290. The English translators believe a later passage in the letter concerning the surrender of Carcassonne suggests the army had adopted this harsh policy prior to the siege of Beziers, but the letter was written in hindsight, after Carcassonne capitulated.

[68] PVC, 99; S&S, 54 and appendix B, 289–290; WTud, 74–83; Shirley, 24–26; PL, 216, col. 140.

[69] Evans, 289, Strayer, 66–67. Strayer believed the massacre at Béziers to be deliberate, because the siege of Carcassonne was so controlled. Contrary to strengthening an explicit policy this supports the idea that Béziers was a fluke and that the leaders of the crusade had not intended the destruction that happened there.

[70] PVC, 92; S&S, 51.

like cordwood.[71] Perhaps they packed in *around* the church and church-yard, seeking sanctuary in the vicinity. That certainly makes a lot more sense and is more plausible, but still does not address the problem of the 7,000 figure. Murdering 7,000 people is not an easy thing to do by hand and seems highly unlikely in the short space of an afternoon. If we concede for a moment that 7,000 people were killed in or near the church, even in a short period of non-stop butchery, that means there would have to be 291 killed an hour; or about five every minute, or one every 12 seconds, *for 24 straight hours.* If we assume the entire army of 20–25,000 crusaders *all* participated, they would have to each dispatch less than one person a piece, certainly within the realm of possibility. This strains credulity however, to assume that every member of the army personally killed someone, since only a tiny army could place every person in the front ranks of the killing zone. This also assumes that everyone wanted to participate in cold blooded murder in the first place. Many humans will not kill in cold blood even when highly encouraged to do so.[72] Since few men will kill an enemy face-to-face, let alone an unarmed one, the quota to produce the body count would have to be correspondingly higher for those who would, making it harder to believe the size of the massacre in the short amount of time in which it took place.

---

[71] S&S, 49, and Appendix B, 289–293. From personal observation in June 2000, even allowing for the very human limitations of estimating numbers, there appears no possible way to cram 7,000 people in this church. Sibly and Sibly suggest that Peter des Vaux-de-Cernay may have gotten his churches mixed up and that the 7,000 number may refer to the cathedral church of St. Nazaire located closer to the gates and walls. Even this cathedral could not accommodate that many people. Besides, Peter des Vaux-de-Cernay was very explicit as to what church it was, earlier referring to the assassination of the viscount of Toulouse in La Madeleine in the twelfth century.

[72] This even includes taking into account societies whose ideology was just as extreme as the passions that elicited the Albigensian Crusade. In Christopher Browning's *Ordinary Men. Reserve Police Battalion 101 and the Final Solution in Poland* (New York: HarperCollins, 1992), 60–70, many of the policemen who had a quota of Jews to kill in Józefów, Poland in 1942 when actually facing their victims were unable to kill them.

Juxtaposed with this are modern massacres like those of the Cheyennes at Sand Creek, Colorado in 1864, the My Lai massacre in Vietnam in 1969 and Rwanda in 1994. Joanna Bourke has suggested in, *An Intimate History of Killing. Face to Face Killing in Twentieth-Century Warfare* (London: Granta Books, 1999), that many soldiers will overcome any initial revulsion to actually enjoy killing up close, even men from societies who traditionally find such violence abhorrent, such as the twentieth century United States, Great Britain, and Australia.

This sort of debate could go on indefinitely and suffice to say both sides have too many sources to definitively demonstrate the validity of their respective positions.

The papal legates' letter to Innocent III optimistically claimed 20,000 people died at Béziers.[73] Pessimistically, based on the numbers arrived at earlier in this paper, that is more people than lived in the town. Even if we assume that Béziers was swollen with refugees fleeing ahead of the army—again, improbable—it is unlikely that the city had 20,000 in it in 1209. It is possible that the numbers of 7,000 or 20,000 are based on a massacre lasting longer than one day. William of Tudela states the crusade encamped in the meadows outside Béziers for three days, though this appears to have been a resting period rather than a continued butchery.[74] Even if the massacre lasted more than one day its scale of 7,000 or 20,000 is no more plausible. Allowing for a duration of three days that the crusade tarried in the vicinity, we must be willing to accept that the killing did not go on 24 hours a day. This assumes of course, that 7,000 or more people stood around and allowed themselves to be killed *en masse*, which would have been harder the longer the killing lasted. If the crusading army surrounded the entire town, which they did not initially because they had to cross the Orb river, then unless all 14,500 townspeople were captured, some got away.

While no age of humankind has been exempt from mass killings, it is only in the twentieth century that humans possessed the technology to kill on a large scale with minimal impact (beyond the psychological) to the perpetrators. The most infamous twentieth century mass killings familiar to Western audiences tend to be those in which technology played a part.[75] Still, the twentieth century is cursed with plenty of examples of low-tech killings. Much low-tech mass killing has taken the form of mass starvation, such as what happened to the Armenian population of Turkey from 1915–1919, and China in the 1960s. As a means of brief comparison with what happened at Béziers, the closest modern example of low-tech mass killing to it occurred in Rwanda in 1994. In a tragic sense Rwanda represents a kind of standard or limits of the possible that we might use to gauge pre-modern massacres across time and place, including of course what happened in Béziers. Like what happened in Béziers, the number of people who died violent deaths in Rwanda during 1994 is not known with any precision, even

---

[73] PL, 216 col. 139.
[74] WTud, 62–63; Shirley, 22.
[75] The fact that populations could be concentrated in camps as in Russia, China, Germany and elsewhere bespeaks of a control the thirteenth century world did not possess. The most infamous mass killing of all of course, the Holocaust, involved the highest technological solution.

though in theory we should be better able to measure the before and after population of a twentieth century national state than for a thirteenth century city. The consensus view is that between 500,000 and one million people were killed in about three months in the spring and summer of 1994.[76] Some 10–50,000 of that number were Hutus who lost their lives because they were sympathetic towards or mistaken for Tutsis, not unlike what happened to Christians in Languedoc.[77]

One of the most important factors that makes the killings in Béziers and Rwanda a useful comparison is that, although human beings have become increasingly subtle and ingenious in how they dispatch members of their own species, Rwanda stands out as a particularly low-tech genocide. With the exceptions of vehicles, walkie-talkies, cell phones, and the occasional firearm, the actual manner of killing in Rwanda between late April and August 1994 was often no more sophisticated than what happened at Béziers in 1209. The vast majority of the victims in Rwanda were caught and killed in remarkably old-fashioned ways, namely by sharp edged objects, such as machetes, spears, and farm implements like scythes or blunt instruments like hammers, clubs with or without spikes, or metal bars.[78] Both in Béziers and in Rwanda, the victims often fled into churches, perhaps for many of the same reasons. Churches ostensibly gave them some strength in numbers, physical protection, and the remote possibility that a house of God might protect them. In both cases, however, it also made it easier for the murderers to cordon off the victims to kill them.[79] Some of the larger churches in Rwanda harbored several thousand refugees, presumably crammed in very tightly, which would lend credence to Peter des Vaux-

---

[76] Gérard Prunier, *The Rwanda Crisis. History of a Genocide* (New York: Columbia University Press, 1995), 261–265; Human Rights Watch et. al., *Leave None to Tell the Story. Genocide in Rwanda* (London and New York: Human Rights Watch, 1999), 1, 15–16; Mahmood Mamdani, *When Victims become Killers. Colonialism, Nativism, and the Genocide in Rwanda* (Princeton: Princeton University Press, 2001), 5, 283, endnote 1. Prunier arrives at a number of 800,000, and further suggests that about 80% of this total was dead in one six week period from the second week of April to the third week of May, though killings occurred sporadically for the next two months. Mamdani explains that deciding on a number is at best a loose consensus and is not very exact.

[77] Human Rights Watch, 212; Mamdani, 5; Christopher C. Taylor, *Sacrifice as Terror. The Rwandan Genocide of 1994* (Oxford: Berg, 1999), 6.

[78] Human Rights Watch, 25, 127–128; Paul Magnarella. *Justice in Africa. Rwanda's Genocide, Its Courts, and the UN Criminal Tribunal* (Aldershot and Brookfield: Ashgate, 2000), 19–21; Mamdani, 4–5.

[79] Prudier, 253–254; Human Rights Watch, 9–10, 210, 334, 340–341, 390–391, 393, 450, 452, 486; Mamdani, 225–228.

de-Cernay's statements that 7,000 people died in La Madeleine. As the Tutsis of Rwanda clustered in their churches or other sizeable public buildings, their assailants were confronted with densely packed places where it was hard to get at the majority of the people in them. Faced with such situations the perpetrators in Rwanda invoked partial high-tech solutions, using mortar fire or hand grenades to flush people out of buildings. If the crusaders were determined to slaughter the population of Béziers, they were faced with a similar problem of how to get at their victims. It would seem that the only way to force people out of their churches was to set the structures on fire. This may account for why the fires in Béziers were set, though the chroniclers do not say so. The mass murderers of Rwanda encountered a dilemma once they had their prey at hand which we can consider for Béziers as well: The assailants physically could not kill more than a few hundred people a day with non-gunpowder weapons.[80] Assuming that the physical capabilities of twentieth century Rwandans are not substantially different from thirteenth century Europeans, what this suggests is that in Béziers, where the massacre clearly did not last as long, the physical ability of the crusaders who participated was not high enough to kill as many people as the legates or chroniclers have stated. We cannot assume religious zeal gave the crusaders any more physical strength than Rwandans had, because Rwandans had historically deep-rooted ethnic and cultural animosities on the same scale as that which might produce religious fervor.[81] It seems obvious that perpetuating a massacre of local scale like Béziers or a national one like Rwanda required a fairly high physical and energy state anyway.

One additional possibility to account for the high death rate reported by legates and chroniclers would be fire, which destroyed at least part of the city. A large fire could theoretically incinerate or suffocate thousands in a relatively short time. Conflagrations in early modern London, nineteenth century Chicago, and fire bombings by allied planes in World War II of Hamburg, Dresden, Tokyo, and other cities had the potential to kill thousands. The people of Béziers crammed themselves into the large public buildings of the city, perhaps accounting for much

---

[80] Prudier, 254; Human Rights Watch, 212; Mamdani, 5–6. The Human Rights Watch reports that assailants spaced the killings over several days by resting at night and maintaining a proper diet. Mamdani specifically mentions how physically demanding it is to kill someone with a machete.

[81] Taylor, *Sacrifice as Terror*, chapters two, three and four. The reasons range from colonialism to race mixing.

of the population. Beyond William of Tudela's remarks that *ribalds* set the fires in retaliation for having their spoils taken away by the crusade leadership, the setting of the fires may have been to flush out the people from their churches and other buildings. While this reason is hardly less sinister than simply lighting the fires to cause the death of the people in the churches, the former seems more likely if the crusaders wanted to separate Christian from Cathar or even to extort valuables from their prey.

Still, casualties from the fires might not have been as high as we think. In 1203–1204, Constantinople suffered three different fires set by members of the Fourth Crusade, and while in the first and third fires the inhabitants of the city knew in advance what was happening and fled from the affected areas, the second fire of 19 and 20 August 1203 in which there was little warning killed something less than 150 people.[82] This total is even more startling even if we go with the most conservative estimate of the population of Constantinople in 1203–1204: 200,000.[83] As T.F. Madden points out, the fact that, even without ample warning, fire in a crowded pre-modern city more than ten times the size of Béziers killed no more 200 people must make us rethink our ideas about other fires. This surprisingly low casualty rate also occurred in other notorious premodern fires.[84] In the 1666 London fire, which happened in a city of 500–600,000, perhaps 100 lost their lives.[85] In the 1871 Chicago fire less than 300 people died in a city of

---

[82] Thomas F. Madden, "The Fires of the Fourth Crusade in Constantinople. 1203–1204: A Damage Assessment," *Byzantinische Zeitschrift* 84/85 (1991–1992): 72–93, esp. 74, 85–89. Madden estimates the entire loss of life between the three fires to be around 200 lives. See also Queller and Madden, *Fourth Crusade*, 146–147.

[83] Josiah Cox Russell, *Late Ancient and Medieval Population. Transactions of the American Philosophical Society* n.s. vol. 48.3, (Philadelphia: American Philosophical Society, 1958), 99; Madden, "Fires of the Fourth Crusade," 85–86 summarizes the scholarship that has estimated the population of Constantinople ca. 1204, and believes the city had about 400,000 at the time of the fires.

[84] Premodern here must by necessity refer to the era before building codes, regulations on building materials, ordinances on fire safety equipment, and, most of all of course, modern fire departments equipped with both electrical and internal combustion equipment.

I have specifically not discussed two other famous fires, in Lisbon in 1759, and San Francisco in 1906 because obviously these were the sites of natural disasters, rather than human-caused blazes.

[85] Madden, "Fires of Fourth Crusade," 86; Walter George Bell, *The Great Fire of London in 1666* (London and New York: John Lane Company, 1920), 176–177; Jill John Bedford, *London's Burning* (London, 1966), 186–187. According to some contemporary accounts like the *London Gazette*, no one had died, and other low totals seem equally

300,000.[86] It is true that the chroniclers of the Fourth Crusade and other infamous fires prior to the twentieth century seem to be more concerned with the loss of buildings and other habitations than they were with recording the loss of life, and there might have been higher totals had the situation been reversed.[87] Even when using the fires of Constantinople as an analogy for what happened at Béziers, we must bear in mind that because the latter city was smaller and surrounded by a large army more people may have been trapped in the fires and a higher percentage may have died than in fires at Constantinople of 1203–1204, London of 1666, or Chicago of 1871. Still, consider this: if 7,000 or more people died at Béziers of a human engineered fire, the scale of the massacre puts it in a high place in the pantheon of human disasters. In other words, poor, backward medieval humans were capable, with nothing more than swords and torches, of causing a disaster of modern proportions.

Beyond the possibilities of whole scale destruction and slaughter was the fact that the crusade was about financial gain as well. While no doubt there was a healthy percentage of those who simply wanted to eliminate Cathars and their sympathizers by burning their towns, it remains hard to believe that there were 20,000 zealots in the army who would willingly burn up whatever booty those thousands still carried on their persons, unless the fire broke out spontaneously in several parts of the city. Fire cannot be easily controlled even with the best of modern methods, so the crusaders were almost as vulnerable as the people of the town. The crusading army could only ensure maximum loss of life by remaining close enough to stand in great danger themselves. Since none of the chroniclers report that anyone of the crusading army lost their lives due to the fires, we must assume that either crusaders were not very close to it, or the extent of the fires was exaggerated by the chroniclers and papal legates. Even the destruction of property

---

inexplicable, but the consensus would be that surprisingly few lost their lives directly to the fire.

[86] Bessie Louise Pierce, *A History of Chicago vol. 3: The Rise of a Modern City 1871–1893* (New York, 1957), 3–19; Karen Sawislak, *Smoldering City. Chicagoans and the Great Fire, 1871–1874* (Chicago, 2). Approximately 100,000 were made homeless. Pierce offers many statistics as to losses in businesses and real estate but lists no numbers of the human deaths in the fire.

[87] Madden, "Fires of the Fourth Crusade," 85, fn 90, 87–89. What the chroniclers of the Fourth Crusade and even modern commentators have discussed in greater detail is the destruction of buildings. At Constantinople, perhaps one third of the population were left homeless by the fires.

may not have been as disastrous as one might think. We can base this assumption on several factors. One, if the city had been devastated both in population and in property, it is difficult to believe it would still function as a major town in the area, as it continued to do so after the sack. Two, less than a month after the sack, the new viscount of Béziers, Simon de Montfort, gave the Cistercians a house (*domus*) which had belonged to a Cathar, suggesting at least some private residences escaped destruction.[88] Three, while the cathedral of St. Nazaire was destroyed in the fires, La Madeleine still has much of its Romanesque exterior.[89] If hundreds or thousands died in the latter church, this would suggest a selective fire, one that had to kill many but not be hot enough to damage the structure beyond repair, unless of course most died by smoke inhalation.

In the last analysis it will forever remain impossible to say how many people of Béziers died in the sack and fires of 1209. Since the chroniclers and legates seemed to have greatly exaggerated their numbers, we can downsize those numbers and come up with more realistic figures than they did. Perhaps 700 instead of 7,000 people died in La Madeleine, which is closer to its actual capacity. The body count reported by the legates may have been more like 2,000 instead of 20,000, still a large percentage of the population but not more than actually lived there in 1209. On the one hand, it is entirely fair to doubt the inflated numbers and suggest lower, if equally unprovable, figures. On the other hand, the people who may have died from exposure from loss of their living spaces, or starved to death because they had no possessions or livelihood in the weeks and months after the attack is beyond speculation.

---

[88] Vaissette, 8 #145, col. 572; "Catalogue des Actes de Simon et D'Amauri de Montfort," ed. Auguste Molinier, *Bibliothèque de l'École des Hautes Études*, 34, 1873: 452–453 # 29; Domairon, "Role des Hérétiquès"; Belperron, 193; Robert J. Kovarik, "Simon de Montfort (1165–1218) His Life and Work: A Critical Study and Evaluation based on the Sources," Ph.D. diss, St. Louis University, 1963, 138. Interestingly enough, the house's owner, Amela de Rieussec, does not appear on the list of the named heretics in Béziers, unless it refers to Amelius Bertrandus of the burgh of Saint Jacques as claimed by Belperron, or B. Amelius Sutor of the burgh of Saint-Aphrodise. The burgh of Saint Jacques is contained within the walls on the south side of the Béziers of 1209. The Saint-Aphrodise burgh was farther north than the town and outside the main circuit of town walls, which might have allowed it to escape severe destruction.

Bourain, "Le massacre de 1209," in *Histoire de Béziers*, 106, also suggests the fires were not as destructive as some believed.

[89] This is clearly visible from the outside. St. Nazaire on the other hand is a Gothic structure built after 1209.

According to common military practice, any city that did not surrender and fell by assault was liable for sack and widespread murder of
its inhabitants.[90] This concept was far older than the Middle Ages and
dates back to the beginnings of humankind.[91] The standard formula for
dealing with a captured city in the ancient world was the slaying of the
adult males and the enslavement of women and children.[92] Medieval
warfare was far more complicated, in that slaughtering those who had
surrendered or had no visible means of defense was against Christian
ethics, and of course no Christian could be enslaved.[93] War in Languedoc was even more problematic because, though Occitan culture, language, and traditions were different than northern France, there were
far fewer differences than say, war on the Spanish or Baltic frontiers
or in the Latin East at the same time period. In a war against heretics
and their protectors, however, those who would not surrender could
expect no mercy, and, if we take William of Tudela at his word (I do
not), that the crusade had already stated its intention to grant no quarter to garrisons that refused to surrender upon approach, the people
of Béziers took a large gamble. Therefore, what happened at Béziers
did not stand out as beyond the pale for proper behavior in war in the
Middle Ages.

Mass killings that took place in the Middle Ages do share a common factor: they tended to occur between somewhat disparate groups,
such as in frontier areas and between other types of borders, including
religious ones.[94] If we look at the Southern French, with their different historical development and heresy, then the Albigensian Crusade
and what happened at Béziers fits into the common factor mentioned
above. *But no worse.* Matthew Strickland's excellent book shows that,
in contemporary warfare of the twelfth and early thirteenth centuries
in both the Anglo-Norman world and the Celtic fringe, war without

---

[90] Frederick H. Russell, *The Just War in the Middle Ages* (Cambridge: Cambridge
University Press, 1979), 209, 256.

[91] Paul Bentley Kern, *Ancient Siege Warfare* (Bloomington, Indiana: Indiana University
Press, 1999), 22–25.

[92] Kern, *Ancient Siege Warfare*, 135–162, 227–236, 323–355. Even if Greek and Roman
authors spoke of their own horror about what happened after a successful storming,
murder, rape, fire, and torture continued to be a fixture of ancient siege warfare.

[93] *Decrees of the Ecumenical Councils vol. I. Nicaea—Lateran V* ed. and trans. Norman
P. Tanner et. al. (Washington D.C., 1990), 224, Canon 27. According to the Third
Lateran Council, anyone who defended or supported Cathars would be anathematized
which implies they could be dealt with in a severe manner.

[94] Barber, "Albigensian Crusades: Wars Like Any Other?", 51–54.

quarter happened all the time.[95] In the crusading world of the Middle East, again, both Christians and Muslims slaughtered innocents, non-combatants, and surrendered opponents. We have only to look at what happened to the population of Jerusalem in 1099 at the hands of the people of the First Crusade, or the slaughter of the Latin field army by Saladin's forces after it surrendered at Hattin in 1187 to demonstrate that no one was immune from suffering from, or participating in, mass killing.[96] The fact that the majority of the townspeople in Béziers were Christian seems to make what happened worse, but one should not hold thirteenth century people to twenty-first century ethical standards. For the men of the day, the townspeople had harbored heretics and had therefore explicitly forfeited their right to be treated like Christians in war.

The men of Béziers were well aware of what they stood to lose, and the fact that they lost should not draw our attention any more than the losing sides have done in thousands of human conflicts since the beginning of time. Though of course we have no numbers, it would be a given that most of the able-bodied men of the town served in the communal militia. This makes them on that day combatants who willingly faced the possibility of losing their lives to protect themselves, their families, possessions, and the Cathars they knew or to whom they were related. The townspeople stood behind good walls where the geography favored the defense.[97] They had interior lines of supply, movement and defended familiar territory. Presumably they were armed and equipped similarly to the crusaders, and in fact as a militia of burghers they might very well have been better furnished than the bulk of the crusader army. The defenders of Béziers had shown their willingness to kill to defend

---

[95] Matthew Strickland, *War and Chivalry. The Conduct and Perception of War in England and Normandy, 1066–1217* (Cambridge, 1996), 222–224, and chapter 11, 291–329.

[96] Raymond d'Aguilers, *Le "Liber" de Raymond d'Aguilers* ed. J.H. Hill and Laurita L. Hill (Paris, 1969), 150–151; *Gesta Francorum et Aliorum Hierosolimitanorum.* ed. and trans. Rosalind Hill. (London: Thomas Nelson and Sons Ltd., 1962), 90–92; for Hattin see Ibn al-Athir in *Arab Historians of the Crusades.* trans. Francesco Gabrieli (London, 1969), 123–125. The *Gesta* and Raymond's account confirm a bloodbath in the taking of Jerusalem, especially around the temple. In the *Gesta* the crusaders supposedly walked ankle-deep in blood; in Raymond's account the blood was up to the knees and bridles of the crusaders' horses. In Ibn al-Athir's account the Templars and Hospitallers are killed after their surrender at Hattin to make sure they can never fight against Islam again.

[97] WTud, 50–51; Shirley 19; Robert of Auxerre, 273; Berlioz, *Tuez-les Tous*, 60–61; Monique Bourain, "Le Massacre de 1209," in *Histoire de Béziers* ed. Jean Sagnes. (Toulouse: Privat, 1986), 103–105, which contains a discussion of the fortification of the city.

themselves, as the incident on the bridge over the Orb shows. Moreover, it was the aggressiveness of the militiamen defending Béziers that,
of course, caused the *ribalds* of the crusading army to charge in the first
place. If the assault came as a surprise it was one equally surprising
to the leadership of the crusade. The militia of Béziers failed to keep
a watchful eye, suffered from overconfidence, and at least a segment
of them felt bold enough behind their walls to sortie against this huge
army. On the one hand to their credit and bravery they were heavily
outnumbered. On the other hand, the vast majority of the army facing them consisted of pilgrims who had marched from different parts of
Western Europe with little more than the shirts on their backs. By the
time the army made it to Béziers, they had been away from their homes
for at least a month since they had left Lyon in June. They were hungry,
tired, operating far from home, and poorly armed. William of Tudela
confirms it when he says "... there were more than 15,000 of them,
with not a pair of shoes between them. In their shirts and trousers they
began to go round the town taking the walls apart stone by stone, they
jumped down into the ditches and set to work with picks, and others
went to batter and smash down the gates."[98] One must conclude that
the siege of Béziers was a fair fight, even if in this case the besieging
army was larger than the defending army.

The massacre of unarmed men, women, and children has much less
defense, but we cannot hold what happened at Béziers to a different standard than what commonly took place in other parts of Western Europe. There are many good if less notorious examples elsewhere in Europe to show where unarmed civilians were treated with
harshness bordering on atrocity. The Peace and Truce of God movements began with the purpose of protecting peasants, women, and children against depredations.[99] The Peace and Truce, of course, began
in the south of France, so war against civilians there was not a novelty. The area of Languedoc was long one in which law and order
was hard to enforce and innocent people suffered because of it.[100] In
the decrees of the third Lateran Council in 1179 various mercenaries

---

[98] WTud, 54–55; Shirley, 20. The translation in the text is Shirley's.

[99] Thomas Head and Richard Landes, "Introduction," *The Peace of God. Social Violence
and Religious Response in France around the Year 1000* (Ithaca, NY: Cornell University, 1992),
3–9; Hans-Werner Goetz, "Protection of the Church, Defense of the Law, and Reform:
On the Purposes and Character of the Peace of God, 989–1038," idem, 264–270.

[100] Isaac, "Down Upon the Fold", 300; Costen, 24, 34, 39. I refrain from the many
instances that Peter des Vaux-de-Cernay mentions depredations against noncombat-

including Aragonese and Navarese *routiers* were condemned for their violence against churches, monasteries, and non-combatants.[101] *Routiers* especially plagued the south, partly because feudal ties were so weak that lords were forced to hire mercenaries to protect their lands. *Routiers* and much of the knightly class had few loyalties or scruples about killing and looting unarmed men, women, and children.[102] Examples from the north and the rest of Europe are rife. During the reign of Louis VI several notorious vassals like Thomas of Marle and Hugh le Puiset regularly plundered villages and towns.[103] In 1124 for example, Count Waleran of Meulan, while plundering territories in north France belonging to Henry I of England, seized peasants working in the woods and cut off their feet.[104] For a closer contemporary example, at the siege of Château Gaillard in 1204, Philip Augustus refused to allow civilians who had fled from the town of Les Andelys into Château Gaillard and had then been expelled by its garrison to go through his lines to safety. Philip forced several hundred of them to spend three cold months exposed to the elements between the castle walls and his blockading army.[105] He relented only after many had died and reports of cannibalism began to surface, no doubt because it was beginning to ruin his reputation as a Christian king.

The events of 1209 had had a long gestation of half a century and did not have to culminate in a crusade. Bear in mind that it took considerable effort to preach and attract enough people to draw military action to Languedoc. Clerics like Bernard of Clairvaux had been preaching against heresy in Languedoc since 1145, and even this

---

ants since he uses the examples as propaganda to show the evilness of the native nobility like Raymond VI and the Count of Foix.

[101] *Decrees of the Ecumenical Councils*, Lateran III, canon 27, pp. 224–225; Barber, *The Cathars*, 57.

[102] Barber, *The Cathars*, 57–58, 68.

[103] Suger, *Vie de Louis VI le Gros*. ed. and trans. Henri Waquet. (Paris: Les Belles Lettres, 1964), 130–131; 173–175. Suger painted these men in the darkest colors he could of course.

[104] Orderic Vitalis, *The Ecclesiastical History of Orderic Vitalis* vol. vi. ed. and trans. Marjorie Chibnall (Oxford, 1978), 348–349. Admittedly the mutilation of the peasants seems extreme even for Orderic but the chronicler mentions the plundering and burning of lands so much it appears to be quite commonplace.

For more discussion on the plundering and looting of noncombatants see Strickland, 176–181 and Richard W. Kaeuper, *Chivalry and Violence in Medieval Europe* (Oxford, 1999), 176–185.

[105] William the Breton, *Gesta*, 217 and *Philippide* ed. François Delaborde (Paris, 1885), 197–200.

greatest of Christian monks had nominal success stopping the spread of heresy.[106] Though Innocent III had offered an indulgence for military campaigning in the south as early as 1208, a papal legate had to be murdered to gain any takers. Crusaders were lured south only by the promise of earning an easy indulgence compared to campaigning in the Latin east and the possibility of gaining land. Coaxing the French king Philip II to lead a crusade south proved impossible, even with the promise of an indulgence and possible land acquisition. Admittedly the King of France had serious political problems to deal with until after the battle of Bouvines in 1214, but even though his son took the cross in 1213, Louis only became an active crusader in 1215, before Montfort's star had fallen very far from its constellation.[107] Had there been a serious reverse at Béziers, the crusade might have ended before it began.

The swift victory of Béziers seemed like God's judgment for the crusaders, even though its success was never duplicated. The only other comparable-sized town to Béziers that fell in Languedoc that year as a direct outcome of military action was Carcassonne, but that resulted from negotiation, not a clear case of divine favor like Béziers. Béziers always provided the beginning exclamation point for any subsequent action of the crusade. The people of Languedoc were introduced in July 1209 to the high stakes they faced: possible near-extinction for recalcitrant Cathars, change in religious practices for those afraid to die for their beliefs, and political domination from the outside even for those who had always remained faithful to the church. It raised fear among the inhabitants that the northerners were better fighters than they were, or at least suggested they would be more brutal. This formidable military reputation, greatly fostered by what happened at Béziers helped sustain much smaller crusading armies through many troubles, until the loss of Beaucaire in 1216 shattered Simon de Montfort's aura of

---

[106] Beverly M. Kienzle, "Tending the Lord's Vineyard: Cistercians, Rhetoric and Heresy 1143–1229. Part I. Bernard of Clairvaux, the 1143 Sermons and the 1145 Preaching Mission," *Heresis* 25 (1995): 29–61; Costen, 55; Malcolm Lambert, *The Cathars* (Oxford: Blackwell, 1998), 40. Lambert believes St. Bernard enjoyed considerable short-term success in Languedoc but he certainly did not halt the spread of heresy.

[107] PVC, 73; S&S, 41–42, and Appendix F, 305–306. Peter des Vaux-de-Cernay reports that Philip II said he was "…beset on his flanks by two great and dangerous lions…" meaning John King of England and Otto of Brunswick, usurper emperor of the Romans. Because of this the King of France's response would have to be limited at best.

invincibility. Since Béziers gave the northerners false hope that perhaps God *was* on their side after all, it ensured that crusaders would continue to make the trip south decades after. The swift and brutal events of July 22, 1209 were the worst of all possible situations for preventing the time of troubles that was to come. Therein lays the tragedy of Béziers, and what sets it apart from other mass killings in the Middle Ages.

HERESY, GOOD MEN, AND NOMENCLATURE

Mark Pegg

"I didn't strongly believe the heretics to be 'good men' [*boni homines*]," confessed na Flors dels Mas before the inquisition into heretical depravity of the Dominicans Bernart de Caux and Joan de Sant-Peire on Saturday, 8 July 1245, in the cloister of Saint-Sernin in Toulouse, "quite the contrary, I thought them good as frequently as I didn't."[1] "I never believed that the heretics were 'good men' [*boni homines*]," testified Peire de Garmassia to the same inquisition almost a year later on Thursday, 17 May 1246, "nevertheless, I believed that their works were good, even if their faith was bad."[2] Almost six thousand other women and men from the Lauragais (a fertile plain between the Ariège and Agout rivers) were interrogated in the verandas of Saint-Sernin between these two testimonies and, although not all of them were as explicit in their reflections on naming and morality, each person used the term "good man" with a depth and nuance that, somewhat surprisingly, most modern scholars have missed.[3] That is, of course, with the notable exception

---

[1] Toulouse, Bibliothèque municipal, MS 609, fol. 22ʳ, "...dixit quod non credidit firmiter hereticos esse bonos homines, sed quotiens credebat ipsos esse bonos et quotiens discredebat."

[2] MS 609, fol. 157ᵛ: "Item, credidit quod heretici nunquam fuerunt boni homines, opera tamen eorum credebat esse bona et fidem malam."

[3] The original parchment leaves of Bernart de Caux and Joan de Sant-Peire's inquisition are lost. Two other Dominican inquisitors, Guilhem Bernart de Dax and Renaud de Chartres, had the Lauragais testimonies copied onto paper sometime after October 1258, though no later than August 1263. This copy has been in the Bibliothèque municipal of Toulouse since 1790 and is now catalogued as MS 609. It consists of two hundred and sixty folios, though only two hundred and fifty-four are paginated, with each leaf measuring 291 millimeters high and 236 millimeters wide. A startling fact about MS 609, and one that can never be forgotten, is that it is only two books, five and four, arranged in that order, out of an estimated ten that Bernart de Caux and Joan de Sant-Piere originally compiled. There is much debate about how many testimonies MS 609 actually contains. This vagueness is due to witnesses being referred to by different names in different places throughout the manuscript. Consequently, Y. Dossat, *Les crises de l'Inquisition Toulousaine au XIIIe siècle (1233–1273)* (Bordeaux: Impr. Brière, 1959), 232, gives the figure of 5,471; C. Douais, *Documents pour servir à l'histoire de l'Inquisition dans le Languedoc*, 2 vols. (Paris: Renouard, H. Laurens, succ., 1900), 1, p. cliii, has 5,600; C. Molinier, *L'Inquisition dans le Midi de la France au XIIIe et au XIVe siecle: étude sur les*

of Robert Moore who, in one of those sharp insights we have come
to expect from him, thought that the very label "good man" for a
thirteenth-century male heretic in the Toulousain and the Lauragais,
along with "good woman" for a female heretic, must reveal something
fundamental about the role and place of heresy in these rural communities.[4] It is in thinking about this relationship of nomenclature and
heresy, particularly for the thousands questioned by the great inquisition of Bernart de Caux and Joan de Sant-Peire, that some implications, at once specific and general, will be suggested about the study of
dissent and persecution in the Middle Ages.

No one at Saint-Sernin, it should be stated at the outset, ever used
Cathari to describe heretics in the Lauragais and Toulousain. Admittedly, the Tuscan pope Alexander III used the term at the Third Lateran Council in 1179 when he proclaimed a crusade against the heretics
and mercenaries infecting the Toulousain and the Albigeois.[5] As did the
Dominican inquisitor (and former "heresiarch" at Piacenza) Rainier
Sacconi in his *Summa de Catharis et Pauperibus de Lugduno* of 1250 where,
towards the end of a detailed analysis concerning the *Cathari* of Lombardy, he added a small section about the "Cathars of the Toulousain
church, and those of Albi and Carcassonne" that simply noted that
these *langue d'oc* heretics were obviously connected to the *langue de si*
dualists.[6] Yet, in eight decades of Cistercian preaching against heresy

---

sources de son histoire (Paris: Sandoz et Fishbacher, 1880), 190, argued for somewhere
between 8,000 and 10,000; R. Abels and E. Harrison, "The Participation of Women
in Languedocian Catharism," *Medieval Studies* 61 (1979): 220, counted 5,604; W. Wakefield, "Inquisitor's Assistants: Witnesses to Confessions in Manuscript 609," *Heresis* 20
(1993): 57, opts for 5,600; J.B. Given, *Inquisition and Medieval Society: Power, Discipline, and
Resistance in Languedoc* (Ithaca, NY: Cornell University Press, 1997), 39, decided on 5,518;
and M.G. Pegg, *The Corruption of Angels: The Great Inquisition of 1245–1246* (Princeton:
Princeton University Press, 2001), 169 n. 52 accepts Dossat's figure. More detailed pale-
ographic discussions of MS 609 are in Dossat, *Les crises de l'Inquisition Toulousaine au XIIIe
siècle*, 56–86, and Pegg, *The Corruption of Angels*, 20–27, 151–160.

[4] R.I. Moore, "Synthèse," in *Heresis: Actes de la 6e session d'Histoire Médiévale organisée
par le Centre d'Etudes Cathares/ René Nelli 1er-4 Septembre 1993* (Arques: Centre d'Etudes
Cathares, 1996), 295–304, esp. p. 299.

[5] Canon 27 (*De hæreticis*), *Sacrorum Conciliorum*, 22, col. 231.

[6] Rainerius Sacconi, *Summa de Catharis et Pauperibus de Lugduno*, is in the preface
of Antoine Dondaine's *Un traité néo-manichéen: le Liber de duobus principiis, suivi d'un
fragment de rituel cathare* (Rome: Istituto storico domenicano, 1939), 77 [trans. Walter
Wakefield and Austin Evans in their *Heresies of the High Middle Ages: Selected Sources
Translated and Annotated* (New York: Columbia University Press, 1991), 345]. Now, see
C. Thouzellier, *Catharisme et Valdéisme en Languedoc à la fin du XIIe et au début du XIIIe siècle.
Politique pontificale—Controverses* (Paris: Presses Universitaires de France, 1966). 19–26, and

in the Toulousain and Lauragais, starting with Bernard of Clairvaux in 1145 and ending with Hélinand of Froidmont in 1229, the only heretics denounced were a grab-bag of "Manicheans," "Arians," "Publicani," "Paterini," "Albigenses," and good men.[7] The noun "Cathar" (apparently first used in the middle of the twelfth century by a group of heretics from Cologne, or so Eckbert of Schönau wrote in his *Sermones contra Catharos* of 1163)[8] is, and always has been, used with such an appalling lack of discrimination by modern historians that, for all intents and purposes, it is an epithet of confusion rather than clarity. It gets thrown about like Cathar-confetti, artfully adorning all sorts of individuals and groups accused of heresy in the Rhineland, England, northern France, northern Italy, Catalonia, and Languedoc, from the eleventh to the sixteenth centuries, whose connections with one another, though worth reflection, are at best problematic.[9]

"It should be understood," sneered Peter des Vaux-de-Cernay at the start of his history of the Albigensian crusade, "that some of the heretics were called 'perfected' heretics or 'good men,' others 'believers of the heretics.'"[10] The use of *perfecti* and *perfecte*, like *Cathari*, is taken

---

the more general discussion of Italian heresy (and one which assumes a strong, and obvious, connection to the heretics of Languedoc) in Carol Lansing, *Power and Purity: Cathar Heresy in Medieval Italy* (New York-Oxford: Oxford University Press, 1998), esp. 4–5, 15–16, 37–39, 188–190.

[7] On this preaching, see B.M. Kienzle, *Cistercians, Heresy and Crusade in Occitania, 1145–1229* (York-Woodbridge: York Medieval Press/Boydell Press, 2001). It should be noted that Kienzle adopts the classic historiographic narrative of Catharism as the omitted "truth" distorted in the sermons and, because she starts with this unwarranted preconception, actually misses the remarkable vision of heresy within Cistercian preaching.

[8] Eckbert of Schönau, *Sermones contra Catharos*, PL 195, col. 31: "Catharos, id est mundos." Now, see R.I. Moore, *The Origins of European Dissent* (London: Allen Lane, 1977), 176–182.

[9] For example, M. Camille, *The Gothic Idol: Ideology and Image-making in Medieval Art* (Cambridge: Cambridge University Press, 1989), 211, glossing the *Chronicon Universale Anonymi Laudunensis (1154–1219)*, ed. A. Cartellieri (Leipzig: Dyksche Buchhandlung, 1909), 62–63, labeled, with no evidence at all, a certain "Nicholas, the most famous painter in all of France" a Cathar simply because he was examined and burnt with a group of *infideles* in 1204. Or A. Del Col, *Domenico Scandella detto Mennocchio: I processi dell'Inquisizione (1583–1599)* (Pordenone: Biblioteca dell'Immagine, 1990), liii–lxxvi, where the ideas of that sixteenth-century miller from Friuli, Mennocchio—the same Mennocchio made famous by C. Ginzburg in *Il formaggio e i vermi: Il cosmo di un mugnaio del '500* (Turin: G. Einaudi, 1976)—were clearly derived from Catharism because, and this is Del Col's only evidence, they were so similar.

[10] Peter des Vaux-de-Cernay, *Historia Albigensis*, ed. P. Guébin and E. Lyon, (Paris: Champion, 1926), I, §13, pp. 13–14 and §§14–15, pp. 15–16.

for granted by modern scholarship and yet not once were these words
uttered at Saint-Sernin.[11] Indeed, no good men were ever called Albigenses during the inquisition of Bernart de Caux or Joan de Sant-Peire,
despite this being the term of choice amongst Catholic chroniclers and
Capetian bureaucrats for the heretics of Languedoc.[12] Instead, what did
echo through the verandas of Saint-Sernin, in the ebb and flow of Occitan being translated into Latin, was *boni homines, probi homines, bons omes,
prozomes, prodomes,* for the good men, and *bone femine, bone domine, bonas
mulieres, bonas femnas, bonas domnas, bonas molhers,* for the good women.
Persons who admitted to (or were accused of) believing in the heretics
were known, rather straightforwardly, as *credentes, crezedors,* or *crezens.*[13]
The *bon omes* and *bonas femnas* themselves, just to add one more sobriquet to the list, usually referred to each other as the "friends of God,"
amici Dei, amicx de Dieu, or so hundreds of testimonies recalled.

Significantly, "good man" was a title adopted by all Lauragais and
Toulousain men in situations circumscribed by courtesy. Nobles,
knights, artisans, tradesmen, merchants, even simple peasant farmers,
were described in charters, wills, oaths, communal decisions, court
appearances, in everything and anything, as *boni homines* and *probi homines.*[14] Such general usage, especially for *bonus homo,* appeared as early the

---

[11] For example, D. Müller, *Frauen vor der Inquisition: Lebensform, Glaubenszeugnis und
Arburteilung der Deutschen un Französischen Katharerinnen* (Mainz: Philipp von Zabern, 1996)
is a nuanced study marred by a tension (largely between footnotes and text) between
using terminology like "perfect," with all that this implies, and the evidence (frequently
the great Saint-Sernin inquisition) that does not warrant such usage.

[12] See, for example, *Historia Albigensis,* 1, pp. 3–4 and n. 3. Now, see the discussions
in HGL, 7, pp. 33–37; A. Borst. *Die Katharer, Schriften der Monumenta Germaniae Historica*
(Stuttgart: Hiersemann, 1953), p. 249, n. 5; L. de Lacger, "L'Albigeois pendant la crise
de l'albigéisme," *Revue d'histoire ecclésiastique,* 29 (1933): 276–283; M. Lambert, *The Cathars*
(Oxford: Blackwell, 1998), 69; and Wakefield and Evans, *Heresies of the High Middle Ages,*
p. 720 n. 1. On the meaning of *Albigenses,* see C. Thouzellier, *Hérésie et Hérétiques: Vaudois,
Cathares, Patarins, Albigeois* (Rome: Edizioni Di Storia e Letteratura, 1969), 223–262 and
J-L. Biget, "'Les Albigeois': remarques sur une dénomination," in *Inventer L'Hérésie?:
Discours Polémiques et Pouvoirs avant L'Inquisition,* ed. M. Zerner (Nice: Centre d'études
médiévales, Faculté des lettres, arts et sciences humaines, Université de Nice Sophia-
Antipolis, 1998), 219–256.

[13] J. Duvernoy, "L'acception: 'haereticus' (*iretge*) = 'parfait cathare' en Languedoc au
XIIIe siècle," in *The Concept of Heresy in the Middle Ages (11th–13th C.): Proceedings of the
International Conference, Louvain May 13–16, 1973,* ed. W. Lourdaux and D. Verhelst (The
Hague, 1976), 198–210. See, for example, MS 609, fol. 110^v, where Peire Pausa from
Gardouch noted: "De Poncio Guilabert credit quod sit credens hereticorum."

[14] On this, see esp. J.H. Mundy, *Society and Government at Toulouse in the Age of the Cathars*
(Toronto, 1997), 60–66. Also see the comments of F.L. Cheyette, *Ermengard of Narbonne
and the world of the troubadours* (Ithaca, NY, 2001), 167; J.H. Arnold, *Inquisition and power:*

eleventh century.[15] In the singular it was often applied to fathers with sons (signifying *senior* over *junior*) and uncles whose nephews had the same Christian and last names. *Dominus*, frequently a courteous name for any man, was only applied to the lords of villages by the scribes at Saint-Sernin. In the Toulousain and Lauragais "good man" also does not seem to have ever been explicitly applied to Catholic prelates or monks, rather *dompnus* or *dominus* was used instead.[16] Nevertheless, in this play of *cortesia* and cognomens, even an heretical good man was, like a priest, sometimes called *domini*.[17]

The Lauragais was (as it still is) an exceedingly fertile region, with all the land under cultivation, roughly ninety per cent in the thirteenth century and largely devoted to cereals (as it still is), fragmented into thousands of little parcels of soil, wood, marshland, garden, and mountain slope.[18] According to the *Liber Reddituum Serenissimi Domini Regis Francie*, compiled in 1272 or 1273, that is, after the county of Toulouse had been absorbed into the kingdom of France, the hamlet of Mas-Saintes-Puelles in the Lauragais, for instance, was surrounded by a parquet-pattern of two hundred and ninety-three miniscule plots of land, fifty-two vineyards, six gardens, and two meadows.[19] Although it is difficult to calculate the actual size of all these pieces of terrain, since the scribes of the *Liber Reddituum* never precisely state the measurements they used, one can still imagine the smallness going on here by recalling that for Mas-Saintes-Puellles these petty holdings would have extended no further than five to seven hundred meters from the village walls.[20] The importance of all this fragmentation, and the fact that

---

Catharism and the Confessing Subject in Medieval Languedoc (Philadelphia, 2001), 143–144; and P. Biller, "Cathar Peacemaking," in *Christianity and Community in the West: Essays for John Bossy*, edited by S. Ditchfield (Aldershot, 2001), 1–23, esp. p 1 n. 1.

[15] For example, HGL 8, n. 46, col. 208, where "boni homines, tam nobiles quam rustici" occur in the Carcassès in 1037.

[16] Mundy, *Society and Government at Toulouse in the Age of the Cathars*, 66.

[17] Esteve Rozenge, for example, MS 609, fol. 4ᵛ, remembered reciting before some good men in 1227: "Lords, pray God for this sinner, that it might make me a good Christian and may lead me to a good end."

[18] J-P Cazes, "Structures agraires et domaine comtal dans la bailie de Castelnaudary en 1272," *Annales du Midi*, 99 (1987): 453–477.

[19] Paris, Archives nationales: JJ 25, *Liber Reddituum Serenissimi Domini Regis Francie* [550 folios], fol. 197, for Mas-Saintes Puelles, and Cazes, "Structure agraires et domaine comtal dans la bailie de Castelnaudary en 1272," 457.

[20] Cazes, "Structures agraires et domaine comtal dans la bailie de Castelnaudary en 1272," 458–461, and A. Durand, *Les paysages medievaux du Languedoc: Xe–XIIe siecles* (Toulouse, 1998), 130–133.

almost every person in a village possessed one or two of these holdings, often without any service owed to someone above them, meant that all men, no matter their status, were often quite impoverished.[21] This impoverishment and fracturing of rights was, in part, caused by the custom of the Toulousain and the Lauragais, written down and formalized in 1286, where all the male children of a married couple were the equal heirs of any property. It was for this reason that so many villages had so many co-seigneurs, so many related nobles of varying degrees of wealth, so many ordinary men sharing small houses and little vineyards with brothers, in short, so many men deserving, and expecting, the honor and courtesy that went with being a *bon ome* or *prodome*.[22]

That "good man" was an inescapably common form of address must have made the interrogations at Saint-Sernin even more tense and confusing for many people (the transcribing and translating scribes included) who thought nothing of saying *bon ome* in the customary etiquette of the Lauragais. It should be pointed out that *boni homines* was unquestionably the most frequent term used by the thousands confessing at Saint-Sernin rather than *probi homines*, yet in all the times that the later title occurred in a testimony, or at least was chosen by the scribe recording the testimony, *prodome*s was nothing more than another way of referring to the *bons omes* of a village, whether they were heretics or not. Michel Verger, when recalling for Bernart de Caux why he was so courteous to some Waldensian men twenty-five years earlier in 1221, added another example of the mundane, but no less

---

[21] G. Jorré, *Le Terrefort Toulousain et Lauragais: Histoire et Géographie agraire* (Toulouse, 1971), esp. 69–105; P. Portet, "Permanences et mutations dans un terroir du Lauragais de l'après-croisade: Fanjeaux, vers 1250-vers 1340," *Annales du Midi*, 99 (1987): 479–493; M. Bompaire, "Circulation et vie monétaire dans le Tarn médiéval (XIᵉ–XIVᵉ siècles)," *Bulletin de la Société des Sciences, Arts et Belles-Lettres du Tarn*, new series 45–46 (1991 et 1992): 479–491; V. Allegre, "Caractères généraux des vieilles églises du Lauragais," *Mémoires de la Société Archeologique du Midi de la France*, 31 (1965): 75–94; and J-R de Fortanier, *Recueil de Documents relatifs à l'Histoire du Droit Municipal en France des origines a la Révolution: Chartes de Frânchises du Lauragais* (Paris, 1939), esp. his introductions to each set of village charters. On heresy and the Lauragais economy, see G. Semkov, "Le contexte socio-économique du catharisme au Mas Sainte Puelles dans la première moitré du XIIIᵉ siècle," *Heresis*, 2 (1984): 34–55. Cf. the difference in monastic holdings, in that they were grouped together, as shown by M. Bourin-Derruau in her "Un exemple d'agriculture monastique en Lauragais: Les domaines de Prouille en 1340," in *Le Lauragais: Histoire et Archéologie, Actes du LIVᵉ Congrès de la Fédération historique du Languedoc méditerranéen et du Rousillon et du XXXVIᵉ Congrès de la Fédération des Sociétés académiques et savantes de Languedoc-Pyrénées-Gascogne* (Castelnaudary, 13–14 juin 1981), ed. J. Sablou and P. Wolff (Castelnaudary, 13–14 juin 1981) (Montpellier, 1983), 115–125.

[22] Mundy, *Society and Government at Toulouse in the Age of the Cathars*, 130–133.

powerful, ubiquitity of this terminology when, in trying to explain his past behavior, he simply stated, "I believed them to be 'good men'."[23]

Indeed, how men and women confessed at Saint-Sernin, and how these spoken testimonies frequently differed from what was recorded on parchment, is seen in the way that, though the "heretics" were almost always the *bons omes* and *bonas femnas* to those confessing, the scribes of the inquisition would occasionally translate these references to the "good men" and "good women" as simply *heretici*. (This was unlike the situation with the Waldensians who were always called, and transcribed as, the *Valdenses*.) Sometimes a person testifying at Saint-Sernin inten-tionally damned the good men and good women as heretics, rather like the worried mother of the knight Gardoz Vidal who, when her boy lay gravely wounded in a house at Toulouse, gently questioned him, "Son, it's been said to me that you gave yourself to the good men [*boni homines*], that is, the heretics."[24] Then there were men like Artau d'En Artigad who, with Bernart de Caux listening, self-consciously described the *bons omes* as "the good men who are called heretics," *boni homines qui vocantur heretici*.[25] So, even without scribal editing, a man like Artau d'En Artigad knew what he had to say at Saint-Sernin, knew, whether he believed it or not, that particular good men were *heretici* for the inquisition—or rather that the common honorific *bon ome* was now so connected to heresy that it could no longer be said without some qual-ification. How all this self-correction, this conscious relabelling a *bon ome* as a heretic, or hearing one's confession read back and recogniz-ing that references to the good men and good women were sometimes rewritten as *eretges*, actually affected an individual once he or she left Saint-Sernin's cloister is open to speculation. However, there can be no doubt that such a process emphasized, for those still unsure, what constituted the two friar-inquisitors' lexigraphic vision of the world.

"Bless us, good men [*probi homines*], pray God for us," were the words, as recalled by the peasant Bernart Cogota, that initiated the ritual greeting identified as heretical "adoration," *adoratio*, by the friar-inquisitors and sometimes known as the *melioramentum* amongst the good men and good women themselves.[26] As a man or a woman said this to

---

[23] MS 609, fol. 136ʳ.

[24] MS 609, fol. 45ᵛ, "'Fili, dictum est mihi quod tu es datus bonis hominibus, id est, hereticis.'"

[25] MS 609, fol. 135ʳ, "... dixit ipsi testi quod ibi erant boni homines qui vocantur heretici ..."

[26] MS 609, fol. 2ʳ, "Benedicite, probi homines, orate Deum pro nobis". Pons de

the *bons omes* or the *bonas femnas*, the head was lowered and, bending at the knees, he or she genuflected three times.[27] Occasionally, a person only said *benedicte, benezion*, "bless us," as they bowed, with the good men replying "God bless you."[28] Every person questioned at Saint-Sernin either recounted, acknowledged, or denied, these courtesies. The friar-inquisitors accumulated all acts of adoration, as they objectified these rather commonplace civilities, because such evidence allowed them to reconstruct the *cortesia* that went into, and helped shape, the habitual relations in a village. In the same way that the title *bon ome* for a heretic drew upon a familiar word of respect, it seems fair to say that what the friar-inquisitors catalogued as adoration, and a number of testimonies suggest this, also emulated a routine village greeting. It was this use of everyday words and nods that leads us straight into the way in which villages in the Lauragais and Toulousain understood holiness and the good men. The holy was to be understood and embraced as something decidedly ordinary, in which routinely polite words and actions, when said and done at particular times and places, instantly transformed the tiny cosmos of a village.

Remarkably, the *dominus* Jordan de Sais, confessed to Bernart de Caux on Monday, 11 December 1245, that he had adored two of his *homines proprii*, Peire Gausbert and Arnaut Faure, in 1220.[29] This noble, through simple behavior, through simple words, briefly evoked a sensation of otherworldliness, in a relationship where it might be least expected, that of a lord honoring his servile peasants. Jordan de Sais never forgot that Peire Gausbert and Arnaut Faure were his men, just as they never forgot that he was their lord, the world of Cambiac was not turned upside-down, indeed, it was entrenched and reinforced through such acts. Similarily, the noble Raimon de Rocovila, one of the

---

Rozenge, for example, recalled on fol. 3ᵛ, "Benedicite, boni homines, orate Deum pro nobis."; whereas Pelegrina de Mont Seruer's recitation for the good women on fol. 2ᵛ was, "Benedicite, bone muleres, orate Deum pro nobis."

[27] For example, MS 609, fol. 5ʳ, where Guillelme Companha phrased it "... et alii adoraverunt ibi dictos hereticos, ter flexis genibus, dicendo: 'Benedicite, boni homines, orate Deum pro nobis.'"

[28] For example, MS 609, fol. 231ʳ, where Arnaut Hugon said "... ipse testis et dictus Ramundum [Fabri] adoraverunt ibi dictos hereticos, flexis genibus, dicendo: 'Benedicite.' Et ipsi heretici respondebant: 'Deus vos benedicat.' Et audivit ibi predicationem eorum."

[29] MS 609, fol. 238ᵛ: "Dixit etiam quod vidit Petrum Gausbert et Arnaldus Faure, hereticos, homines suos, in domibus ipsorum hereticorum apud Cambiac, et ipse testis, flexis genibus ter, dicendo, benedicite, adoravit ipsos hereticos ..."

lords of les Cassés, admitted adoring the *bon ome* Raimon Sirvens, "my *rusticus*," his serf, in 1229.[30] The holiness of Peire Gausbert and Arnaut Faure only existed because they were intimately part of Cambiac, as men accepting that they were caught within the familiar local rhythms of a village and yet outside of them, as accessible doorways to God momentarily opened through a holy greeting, as good men whose very mundane existence was always suggesting and proving that there was a transcendent reality beyond these visible constraints. It was this sense of the ubiquity of holiness, of something extraordinary passively dwelling in the ordinary, that allowed a few *bons omes* to be small boys and, much more frequently, innumerable *bonas femnas* to be little girls.[31]

What has been said so far about "good man" cannot quite be said for the designation "good woman." In the Toulousain and Lauragais all older or married women, no matter who they were, received the blanket title of *domine* in notarial documents, whereas at Saint-Sernin only noblewomen were called *domina, domna, na,* "lady."[32] This specificity by the inquisitorial scribes lets us see and hear when noblewomen who wished their nobility to be known, and transcribed, were testifying. This confessional and scribal precision also allows us see and hear, particularly in acts of adoration remembered by women, when the *bonas domnas*, "good ladies," themselves chose to stress their own nobility. The importance of noble good women emphasizing their nobility, a phenomenon that never seems to be necessary for the good men, and that this quality was a distinct part of their specific holiness, has been greatly underestimated. It certainly motivated the good woman Berengaira da Seguerville when the castellan Arnaut de Auriac seized her in a wood in 1233 because, so her son testified, she was instantly released due to the fact that she was noble.[33] The use of "good woman," *bona femna, bona molher*, to mean a holy woman, rather than the socially revealing use of *bona domna*, was a deliberate, if not always successful, exercise at imitating commonplace masculine notions of respect and holiness.

---

[30] MS 609, fol. 216[r]. Now, see Cheyette, *Ermengard of Narbonne*, pp. 149–167, for a very good discussion on the complexities of serfdom in Languedoc (although, it should be noted, he does accept the standard account of Catharism throughout his narrative).

[31] Pegg, *The Corruption of Angels*, esp. 100–101, 118–119. Cf. B. Hamilton. "The Cathars and Christian Perfection," in *The Medieval Church: Universities, Heresy, and the Religious Life. Essays in Honour of Gordon Leff*, ed. by P. Biller and B. Dobson (Woodbridge, 1999), 12, mistakenly comments that "the Cathar Church was confined to adults."

[32] Pegg, *The Corruption of Angels*, 95–96.

[33] MS 609, fols. 67[r]–67[v], "… quia erat de nobili genere."

Na Aimersent Viguier's last day as a *crezen* happened in 1223 when she was very young and very pregnant. An aunt, na Geralda de Cabuer, took her to hear two noble "good ladies," *bonas domnas*, preach in the house of a knight. Aimersent Viguier, following instructions, genuflected three times and politely repeated, "Bless us, good ladies [*bone domine*], pray God for these sinners." The *bonas domnas* then preached a long sermon to large group of noble men and women. Once this homily was over, *cortesia* was again performed through adoration but, as Aimersent Viguier painfully recalled for Bernart de Caux, the "good ladies" then rudely pointed to her swollen adolescent body and, in front of everyone, declared "that I was carrying a demon in my belly." The *bonas domnas* and their noble believers all laughed at Aimersent Viguier's embarrassment.[34] In the days that followed this incident, Aimersent Viguier was constantly bullied by her husband that she had to love these "good ladies," just like everyone else did, but "I didn't want to love them," she stressed to the inquisition, "after they'd told me that I was pregnant with a devil."[35] It was an acute sense of embarrassment in a small world obsessed with formalized politeness, where divinity resonated in such ritualized naming and greeting, that made the young girl feel a deep emotional agony touching on the cosmological.

Bons omes, even with scribal pecularities like *bononios* or *bonozios*, was also never a synonym for "Bosnians," as some modern scholars have naively assumed the Occitan to mean.[36] No one at Saint-Sernin, whether speaking in the vernacular or writing in Latin, remembered or recorded any Balkan acquaintances.[37] On this point about familiar

---

[34] MS 609, fol. 239ᵛ, "Et dicte heretice dixerunt ipsi testi, coram omnibus, quia erat adolescentula pregnans, quod demonium portabat in ventre. Et alii ceperunt ridere inde."

[35] MS 609, "Sed ipsa testis noluit diligere, postquam dixerunt sibi heretice quod pregnans erat de demonio." On this particular recollection of Aimersent Viguier, see P. Biller, "Cathars and Material Women," in *Medieval Theology and the Natural Body*, ed. by P. Biller and A.J. Minnis (Woodbridge, 1997), 61–63.

[36] For example, Lambert, *The Cathars*, 62, misreads *bonomios sive bonosios* in Guilhem de Puylaurens' *Chronica*, p. 32, as referring to the "'*Bonosii*', that is Bosnians," and so the Cathars.

[37] G. Rottenwöhrer, *Der Katherismus: Die Herkunft der Katharer nach Theologie und Geschichte* (Bad Honnef: Bock and Herchen, 1990), vol. 3, 74–114, 570–571; H. Fichtenau, *Ketzer und Professoren: Häresie un Vernunftglaube im Hochmittelalter* (Munich, 1992), pp. 70–119; B. Hamilton, "Wisdom from the East: the reception by the Cathars of Eastern dualist texts," in *Heresy and Literacy, 1000–1530*, ed. P. Biller and A. Hudson (Cambridge, 1994), 38–60, which, it should be pointed out, opens by stating that "[n]o reputable scholar now doubts that Catharism was an offshoot of medieval eastern dualism…";

terminology being adopted, and adapted, by the good men and their believers, far too much has been of the fact that some *bons omes* were

---

Lambert, *The Cathars*, 29–59; M. Barber, *The Cathars: Dualist Heretics in Languedoc in the High Middle Ages* (Harlow, 2000), 6–33; and P. Biller, "Through a Glass Darkly: Seeing Medieval Heresy," in *The Medieval World*, ed. by P. Linehan and J.L. Nelson (London, 2001), 308–326, are all good, as well as nuanced, recent summaries of the evidence (and scholarship) for missionary and doctrinal connections between the Cathars and the Bogomils. J. and B. Hamilton, *Christian Dualist Heresies in the Byzantine World c. 650–c. 1450* (Manchester, 1998) is an exceptional collection of translated sources on dualism and has a useful "Historical Introduction," 1–55. The visit by the supposed Bogomil bishop of Constantinople, papa Nicetas, to Saint-Félix-de-Caraman in the Lauragais happened in 1167. The document that records Nicetas' journey is lost and only exists as an appendix to Guillaume Besse's *Histoire des ducs, marquis et comtes de Narbonne, autrement appellez Princes des Goths, Ducs de Septimanie, et Marquis de Gothie. Dedié à Monseigneur l'Archevesque Duc de Narbonne* (Paris, 1660), pp. 483–486. This document, given to Besse by "M. Caseneuue, Prebendier au Chapitre de l'Eglisle de Sainct Estienne de Tolose, en l'an 1652," p. 483, is more than likely either a mid-thirteenth-century forgery by some good men or their followers (rather than a seventeenth-century forgery) or a late thirteenth-century collation of a number of disparate documents by a friar-inquisitor in Toulouse. Also, if it really existed, it probably was preserved until the seventeenth century in the Dominican inquisitorial archives at Toulouse or Carcassonne, where a number of other apocryphal documents supposedly demonstrating eastern links were filed away by inquisitors in the late thirteenth century. B. Hamilton, "The Cathar Council of S. Félix Reconsidered," *Archivum Fratrum Praedicatorum*, 48 (1978): 23–53, is generally assumed to have proven the historical validity of Besse's appendix. Now, because so much about this document has a Borges-like quality, and because one needs to already believe in connections between Cathars and Bogomils to see the evidence within the text (even though the text itself is the foundational proof underlying this belief about Catharism and Bogomilism), it is far more prudent, for the present, to remain unconvinced about its historical veracity. In support of Hamilton, see, for example, Pilar Jimenez, "Relire la Charte de Niquinta – 1) Origine et problématique de la Charte," *Heresis*, 22 (1994): 1–26, and her, "Relire la Charte de Niquinta – 2) Sens et portée de la charte," *Heresis*, 23 (1994): 1–28; P. Biller, "Popular Religion in the Central and Middle Ages," in *Companion to Historiography*, ed. M. Bentley (London, 1997), 239–240; Lambert, *The Cathars*, 45–59; and Barber, *The Cathars*, 21–22, 71–73. A further point that is never addressed when considering this supposed document is that, when not studied in some idealist vacuum, it bares no resemblance to the historical and cultural realities of the good men and good women in the Lauragais of the late twelfth and early thirteenth centuries. Cf. Yves Dossat, "A propos du concile cathare de Saint-Félix: les Milingues," *Cahiers de Fanjeaux: Cathares en Languedoc*, 3 (1968): 201–214, where it is argued that Besse's document was a seventeenth century forgery (and probably forged by Besse). It has also been argued that Bogomil dualism was secretly carried back by crusaders returning from twelfth-century Outremer. On such heretical transmissions from the Levant, see C. Thouzellier "Hérésie et croisade au XIIᵉ siècle," *Revue d'histoire ecclésiastique*, 49 (1954): 855–872, was the first to strongly suggest the importation of dualist beliefs by returning crusaders. Along similar lines to Thouzellier, Karl Heisig in "Ein gnostische Sekte im abendlandischen Mittelalter," *Zeitschrift für Religions und Geistesgeschichte*, 16 (1964): 271–274, suggested that crusaders brought ancient Gnostic practices back from the East to the Rhineland. For recent arguments for Eastern

named deacons, like Izarn de Castres, or bishops, like Bernart Marti.[38]
These titles do reveal a sense of hierarchy on the part of certain good
men, and their believers, but it is a long way from elaborate ecclesiastical structures, heretical dioceses, systematic protocols, in short, a
"Church" out of words that, if anything, were simply used to help dif-
ferentiate a person deserving even more respect than that accorded the
day-to-day *probi homines* of any village, whether the intimate "friends
of God" or not. Indeed, and this can never be emphasized enough,
no "Cathar Church" was discovered by Bernart de Caux and Joan
de Sant-Peire and no such entity will ever be unearthed by modern
historians—unless, of course, hundreds of references to *heretici* and *boni
homines* keep being persistently, and rather unashamedly, translated as
"Cathars" and "perfects."[39]

Yet, in making the Cathars such coherent and concrete figures, in
classifying certain individuals and their thoughts as similar to each
other, in joining dissenting dots until we get a pervasive heretical
"Church," we lose the specificity of what heresy and *bon ome* meant
at particular times and places in a kind of cultural determinism; in that
if there were no Cathars, no widespread organized *ordo* of dissent, then
something intrinsic to the Middle Ages must have produced them, no
matter the evidence to the contrary. This social fatalism, implicit in so
much research on heresy and medieval alterity, where particular words,
thoughts, and actions, get lost in the grand scheme of things, effectively
predestines the Middle Ages to be full of dissent, obsessed with the
marginal and, as a consequence, gripped with an immutable need to
persecute.

No one is denying that the great inquisition of Bernart de Caux and
Joan de Sant-Peire was a frightening innovation or that ordinary men
and women consciously chose different paths, albeit through familiar
words, to the holy than those authorized by the Church. Nevertheless,
it must be stressed that the hindsight applied to the medieval heretic,
shaped by an historiography that has barely changed in two hundred
years, has so predetermined the Middle Ages to be what they suppos-

---

influence on Western heresy see Daniel Callahan, "Ademar of Chabannes and the
Bogomils," and Bernard Hamilton, "Bogomil Influences on Western Heresy," in this
volume.

[38] For example, MS 609, fol. 186ᵛ.

[39] For example, Lambert, *The Cathars*; Barber, *The Cathars*; and Hamilton, "The
Cathars and Christian Perfection," stress the existence of a "Cathar Church."

edly became, that the vital importance of why men and women thought or did things at specific times and places simply vanishes into generalizations that are either trivially true (the Church feared heterodoxy) or obviously false (there was a "Cathar Church"). Notions of alterity or marginality have actually caused us to mistakenly narrow our avenues of research into heterodoxy, to end where we should begin our interpretations of dissent in the Middle Ages, to ignore the implications inherent in a name. It is not at the margins that we should look in comprehending heretics like the good men but, as has been briefly suggested here, in the very familiar, distinctly mundane, rhythms of medieval existence.

CATHARS, CONFRATERNITIES, AND CIVIC RELIGION: THE BLURRY BORDER BETWEEN HERESY AND ORTHODOXY

SUSAN TAYLOR SNYDER

Historians commonly argue that heretics were people on the margins, placed there by church propaganda but kept there by their refusal to participate in mainstream orthodox ritual. Particularly after a conviction for heresy before the inquisition, the line that the church imposed between heresy and orthodoxy marginalized Cathars not only in religious terms but also in social ones. From Henry Charles Lea to R.I. Moore to James Given, medievalists have cited cases in which heretics had trouble finding work or participating in civic corporations because their religious affiliations and legal convictions set them apart from the orthodox faithful.[1] The lesser sentences given out by the inquisitors often involved public penance or marking the convicted with some sort of sign, usually by ordering him or her to wear large yellow crosses sewn onto the front and back of the outer garment. The public nature of the penance was supposed to mark the heretic as dangerous, and these historians have argued that, even after the penance was done or the crosses legally put aside, the public memory of them would still make people avoid and exclude the heretic.[2]

In Bologna around the year 1300, however, this was not always the case, and people involved in the Cathar movement, from those who had received multiple convictions for heresy to those who had never appeared before an inquisitor, participated willingly in orthodox religious and civic ritual.[3] Some took an active role in their local parishes and even joined or had strong connections to confraternities that had

---

[1] H.C. Lea, *A History of the Inquisition of the Middle Ages* (New York: Macmillan, 1906), 1:232, 236 and 366; R.I. Moore, *The Formation of a Persecuting Society* (Oxford: Blackwell, 1987), 86; and James Given, *Inquisition and Medieval Society: Power, Discipline and Resistance in the Languedoc* (Ithaca, NY: Cornell University Press, 1997), 38.

[2] Given, *Inquisition and Medieval Society*, 66.

[3] For further consideration of religious life in Bologna, see the article by Carol Lansing in this volume.

actually been founded to counter Cathar belief. Yet they themselves saw no contradiction between their orthodox and heretical religious affiliations, even when the religious messages of the perfects and the confraternities were supposedly in direct opposition to each other. Instead, they believed that the Cathar perfects, the local parish clergy, and the activities of the confraternities all had positive religious and sometimes social value.

In May of 1299, Diotesalvi Ricupri, the rector of Bologna's famed *societas devotorum*, was called before the inquisitor Guido da Vicenza to give evidence against one of his associates, Avanzo da Funi. Diotesalvi said that after the inquisition had convicted Avanzo for heresy and made him wear the crosses, he had met Avanzo in the house of the society several times and heard him say many religiously suspect things and question the power of the inquisition. Avanzo had told Diotesalvi that the mundane powers, meaning the inquisition and the church, could arrest the feet of the body and not the feet of the soul, by which he meant that they had no real spiritual power. Diotesalvi admonished Avanzo to no avail but continued to associate with him, and Avanzo remained a member of the *societas*.[4] What was the problem with this? The *societas devotorum*, the society of the devout, was the famous Bolognese flagellant confraternity, founded in 1260, whose statutes and rituals

---

[4] *Acta S. Officii Bononieab anno 1291 usque ad annum 1310*, eds. Lorenzo Paolini and Raniero Orioli (Rome: Istituto storico italiano per il Medio Evo, 1982), 39–40. "Dominus Deotesalvi, quondam domini Recupri, capelle Sancti Stephani de Bononia,… Interrogatus si cognoscit vel cognovit aliquem hereticum vel hereticam, credentem, fautorem, deffensorem et receptatorem hereticorum aut infamatum vel suspectum de heresi vel male loquentem de fide catholica, respondit quod quidam, qui dicitur frater Avancius, qui fuit de Funi districtus Bononie, fuit socius et amicus dicti testis, quia dictus testis credebat quod esset bonus homo. Tamen advertit quod dictus Avancius dicebat verba inordinata et contra fidem Romane Ecclesie et fuit punitus per fratrem Aldrevandinum et cruce signatus, sicut patet per sententiam latam contra eum per dictum fratrem Aldrovandinum. Post autem predicta, dictus testis dicit quod dictus Avancius dixit ipsi testi: 'Tu vocaris Deotesalvi, quia invenio quod per te debet salvari totus mundus, sive tota humana generatio.' Interrogatus de loco, tempore et presentibus, respondit quod possunt esse quatuor anni vel circa, in civitate Bononie, in capella Sancti Mathey de Acharixiis, in domo devotorum, de presentibus non recordatur. Item dixit quod audivit dictum Avancium dicentem, postquam abiuravit heresim et fuit cruce signatus per fratrem Aldrevandinum quod potencia mundana abstulerat sibi pedes corporis, set non poterat aufferre pedes anime. Nam dictus testis congaudens ipsi Avancio, quia videbatur reversus esse ad viam veritatis, unde visitavit eum et dicebat ei: 'Frater Avancii, ego multum gaudeo, quod vos estis reversus ad viam veritatis, et fidei catholice.'"

served as a model for other flagellant confraternities throughout northern Italy and perhaps even across the Alps.[5]

Flagellation was a form of bodily penance meant to make up for the sins of the flagellant as well as the sins of others, but part of its purpose was also to reaffirm the body's place in salvation and underscore the orthodox belief in bodily reincarnation at the end of days.[6] It served as a reminder that the body was as much a part of the individual believer as the soul and, thus, could serve, through discipline, as a vehicle for salvation through penance. Flagellation also allowed the believer to share Christ's Passion and suffering during the crucificixion. After all, the Roman soldiers whipped Christ before placing him on the cross.[7] In fact, the statutes of the *societas devotorum* stress this connection between the flagellant and Christ; they claim that when the confraternity's members beat themselves, they did so "in honor of the sweet Christ, who wanted to be beaten and to die for the redemption of sins."[8] Thus, the act of voluntary flagellation also reaffirmed the physical incarnation of Christ by insisting on and providing an example of Christ's voluntary suffering.

All of this was completely antithetical to Cathar teachings. The Cathars believed that the spiritual world had been created by God and that the material world had been created by Satan. The few remaining Cathar texts discuss this in detail. The *Interrogatio Iohannis*, also called

---

[5] This confraternity, despite its contemporary fame, has received very little attention from modern scholars. For its history and influence, see Mario Fanti, "Gli inizi del movimento dei disciplinati a Bologna e la confraternità di Santa Maria della Vita," *Bollettino della Deputazione di storia patria per l'Umbria* 66 (1969): 181–232; Giancarlo Angelozzi, *Le confraternite laicali: un'esperienza cristiana tra Medioevo e età moderna* (Brescia: Queriniana, 1979), 20–28; G.G. Meersseman, *Ordo fraternitas: Confraternite e pietà dei laici nel medioevo* (Rome: Herder editrice e liberia, 1977), 469; G.G. Meersseman, "Disciplinati e penitenti nel Duecento," *Il movimento dei disciplinati nel settimo centenario dal suo inizio* (Spoleto: Arti grafiche Panetto & Petrelli, 1962), 62–66; John Henderson, "The Flagellant Movement in Central Italy, 1200–1400," *Religious Motivation: Biographical and Sociological Problems for the Church Historian*, ed. Derek Baker (Oxford: B. Blackwell, 1978), 156; Nicholas Terpstra, *Lay Confraternities and Civic Religion in Renaissance Bologna* (Cambridge: Cambridge University Press, 1995), 3–5, 12.

[6] Henderson, "The Flagellant Movement," 151.

[7] John 19:1. On flagellation as a way to imitate Christ, see John Henderson, *Piety and Charity in Late Medieval Florence*, 113–114; Giles Constable, "Attitudes toward Self-Inflicted Suffering in the Middle Ages," *Culture and Spirituality in Medieval Europe* (Brookfield: Variorum, 1996), 10–11.

[8] *Statuti delle società del popolo di Bologna*, ed. A. Gaudenzi (Rome: Tip. del Senato, 1896), 2:424. "...se verberando in honorem dulcis Christi, qui in redemptionem peccatorum voluit verberari et mori..."

The Secret Supper, depicts St. John the Divine asking Christ questions about the creation and salvation after the resurrection. In it Christ relates the story of how Satan made human bodies out of earth and entrapped angelic souls into them so that they could serve Satan.[9] For the Cathars human bodies were not essential parts of humans but only prisons designed for us by Satan. They also believed that the final resurrection would be a purely spiritual one and that nothing that people did to their bodies could effect salvation. Thus, for Cathars flagellation, along with all other forms of bodily penance, was useless and ran counter to good doctrine.

Most Cathars also rejected the incarnation of Christ but believed instead that Christ had only taken on the appearance of becoming human while in actuality retaining his angelic form. In the *Interrogatio Iohannis*, Christ says that, when God sent him into this world, he first sent the angel Mary to receive Christ, and that, instead of being born from Mary's body, Christ entered and exited her through the ear.[10] Because Christ never had an actual human body, he did not really suffer during the passion, not while the Roman soldiers beat him, nor on the cross itself. Also, when John asked Christ what he meant by his body and his blood, Christ answered by stressing the importance of repeating the Lord's Prayer.[11] For the Cathars Christ was literally the *logos*, the word, in the form of prayer. The ritual of the *consolamentum*, the Cathar sacrament that offered the only assurance of salvation, also stressed the connection between the body of Christ and the Lord's Prayer as a way of performing a "spiritual baptism."[12] Christ was not sent to humanity to suffer and die on the cross but, instead, to reconnect the angels trapped in human bodies with the divine through prayer so that they could escape their bodies and gain salvation. Therefore, the Cathars did not believe that the imitation of Christ should include physical suffering, including flagellation.

For the orthodox, however, flagellation was one way of not just downplaying the Cathar message but of proving it wrong. Flagellant confraternities like the *societas devotorum*, in fact, have often been portrayed as anti-Cathar from their inception, both by medieval polemi-

---

[9] *Le Livre secret des cathares: Interrogatio Iohannis*, ed. Edina Bozóky (Paris: Beauchesne, 1980), 58.

[10] *Interrogatio Iohannis*, 68.

[11] *Interrogatio Iohannis*, 72.

[12] "De acceptione consolamenti," *Un traité néo-maichéen du XIIIe siècle: Le Liber de duobus principiis*, ed. Antoine Dondaine (Rome: Istituto storico dominicano, 1939), 158.

cists and modern scholars.[13] Giles Constable has shown that Dominic himself stressed the use of flagellation among the laity as a way of avoiding sin and heresy.[14] Giancarlo Angelozzi also found very convincing evidence that the *societas devotorum*, in particular, had strong ties to the Militia of the Virgin, another Bolognese confraternity. The Militia had been founded by a relative of Dominic's great patroness Diana d'Andalo, as part of a movement originated by the inquisitor Peter of Verona, later St. Peter Martyr, to create associations of laypeople to aid the inquisition in its work. This confraternity's members pressured the communal government to cooperate with the inquisition and acted as lay officers for the inquisition, as well as sought out heretical activity in the town.[15] These connections to the Dominican order and, more specifically, to its inquisition show that the society of the devout was at least supposed to participate in the prosecution of heretics.

But what about Diotesalvi? As the rector of the *societas devotorum*, he was its highest officer, but by his own admission, he was fraternizing with a known, convicted and unrepentant Cathar believer but did almost nothing about it. Diotesalvi told the inquisitor that his conversations with Avanzo had begun about four years before Diotesalvi's appearance before the inquisition in 1299, but the rector did not inform on Avanzo until he was formally cited and coerced by the inquisitor.

But Diotesalvi's brush with the inquisition did not seem to change his ways. Two years later, a group of Florentine merchants who had immigrated to Bologna accused Cursio di Nerli Bonelle, also a Florentine immigrant, of heresy. They told the inquisitor that, while they had been negotiating a business deal with Cursio in 1298 and were having the final act written out by a notary, Cursio had complained about the inquisition imposing the crosses upon his sister and said that the Dominicans and the Franciscans and the Roman curia were only interested in money. He also said that even if the body of Christ had been as

---

[13] Salimbene de Adam, *Chronica*; Meerssemann, *Ordo fraternitas*, 469 and 771; John Henderson, "The Flagellant Movement and Flagellant Confraternities in Central Italy, 1260–1400," *Studies in Church History* 15 (1978): 147–160; Gary Dickson, "The Flagellants of 1260 and the Crusades," *Journal of Medieval History* 15 (1989): 246–248.

[14] Constable, "Attitudes," 16.

[15] Angelozzi, *Le confraternite laicali*, 85. For the Militia of the Virgin see Meerssemann, *Ordo fraternitas*, 771–772; Christine Caldwell, "Peter Martyr: The Inquisitor as Heretic," *Comitatus* 31 (2000): 171–172; and N.J. Housley, "Politics and Heresy: Anti-heretical Crusades, Orders, Confraternities, 1200–1500," *Journal of Ecclesiastical History* 33 (1982): 196–206.

large as a mountain, it would all have already been consumed.[16] This last statement openly rejected the place of Christ's body in salvation. It was a very common statement among Cathar believers and shows up over and over again in inquisitorial registers. The notarial act produced during this meeting was recorded in the *Libri memoriali* of the Bolognese commune, the urban government's register of notarial protocols used to validate transfers of real and moveable property. The extant document shows that the meeting took place in the house of the *societas devotorum*, and it lists Diotesalvi Ricupri as a witness, but neither of those pieces of information appears in the inquisitorial register.[17]

Cursio di Nerli Bonelle was undoubtedly very closely connected to the Cathar movement. His family was part of a minor branch of the Florentine Nerli family, which Carol Lansing studied in her book *The Florentine Magnates*, in which she argues that in the 1240s the Nerli were one of the most prominent Cathar families in Florence and had even founded a house for the perfected women in their family.[18] By the time of Cursio's trial in 1301, his family had been Cathar for at least four or five generations, and Cursio himself had undoubtedly been raised in the heretical faith; his mother, his brother and his sister had all been

---

[16] *Acta S. Officii*, 125–126. "Brunettus de Ferro ...suo sacramento dixit quod modo possunt esse tres anni vel circa, quod ipse testis erat Bononie, in domo Buvalelli de Buvalellis, iuxta curiam Sancti Ambroxii, cum ser Manetto Munsili de Florentia et ser Lapo Bochamatta et cum ser Cursio quondam Neri Bonelle, qui habitabat in dicta domo Bononie, tunc pro quodam negocio et tunc dictus Cursius Bonelle, cum essent in verbis et ratiocinarentur simul, dixit, audiente dicto teste et presente, quod qui habet de bonis istius mundi non expedit sibi aliud nec alia gratia Dei in hoc mundo; et quod ista curia Romana et isti fratres predicatores et minores illud quod faciunt hodie et dicunt, faciunt tantum pro una achataria et ad achatariam habendam et pro alia re. Item dixit quod audivit tunc a dicto Cursio dicente quod corpus Christi quod levatur cotidie in ecclesiis, si esset ita magnum sicud est maior mons de mundo, modo esset consumptum. Item dixit quod audivit tunc dictum Cursium dicentem quod fratres sibi fecerant magnam iniuriam et iniustitiam, quando cruce signaverunt sororem suam. Item dixit quod iam audivit a pluribus personis et maxime a suprascripto ser Manetto quod mater dicti Cursii fuit cruce signata Florentie per inquisitorem hereticorum dicte terre, eo quod fuit credens hereticorum."

[17] ASB, Comune, Libri memoriali, 95:359ʳ. The protocols actually record two transactions, dated July 21, 1298, a loan of ninety livre that Cursio made to Lapo di Castellini Bochamatta on behalf of Cursio's nephew Bracino and the payment for a piece of land that Cursio sold to Lapo. Both transations took place in "bononia in domo deuotorum presentibus Guidoto condam Lupi de Florentia, domino Iohannes d. Iacobini, domino Deotesalui spadario condam Recupri et Montanario condam Pergolani feratoris testibus."

[18] Carol Lansing, *The Florentine Magnates* (Princeton: Princeton University Press, 1992), 122–124.

convicted by the inquisition, either in Florence or in Bologna. But an examination of his business dealings in Bologna as recorded in the *Libri memoriali* shows that he often did business in the house of the *societas devotorum*, a fact that indicates that he was most likely a member of the confraternity.[19]

Why would people raised as Cathars join a flagellant confraternity? After all, flagellation was antithetical to the Cathar message, and this confraternity in particular was supposed to take an active role in combating Catharism. A traditional answer to this question would be to say that they were using it to hide from the inquisition. Medieval inquisitorial handbooks, like that of Bernard Gui, warned inquisitors that heretics would try to seem pious and even take part in orthodox sacraments and lie about their beliefs in order to hide their true religious affiliations.[20] In the late nineteenth century, H.C. Lea, in his massive history of the inquisition, claimed that Gui was right, and in the twentieth century many historians have read the movements of Cathar believers back and forth across the line between heresy and orthodoxy in the same way.[21] But there was something more than that going on in these cases. When Avanzo and Cursio were in the house of the society, they did not try to hide their religious beliefs but, instead, engaged the other members of the confraternity in conversations about religion and made statements that were both blatantly Cathar and blatantly anti-inquisitorial and anti-mendicant.

In yet another case, a member of the confraternity, Matteo di Giovanni, stated that he and two other members, a carpenter named Martinello and a certain Giacobo, often met under the portico in front of Martinello's house, and Martinello would tell the others that God had not caused plants to be born, just as it was not God who caused men and women to be born, but other men and women.[22] This statement rejects the divine origins of the human body and, again, is a very com-

---

[19] Transactions involving Cursio appear in ASB, Comune, Libri memoriali, 94:644ʳ; 95:359ʳ; 101:113ʳ, 134ᵛ, and 290ʳ; 102:68ᵛ; 103:75ᵛ–76ʳ, 89ᵛ, and 345ᵛ; and 104:15ʳ–ᵛ.

[20] Bernard Gui, *Manuel de l'inquisiteur*, ed. and tr. G. Mollat (Paris: Société d'édition les belles lettres, 1964), 1:48.

[21] Lea, *History of the Inquisition*, 1:94.

[22] *Acta S. Officii*, 241–242. "Item dixit dictus testis quod audivit magistrum Martinellum, magistrum de lignamine, capelle Sancti Egidii, pluries dicentem quod Deus non faciebat nasci frumentum, sed humor terre, et quod si quis proiceret frumentum sub porticu non nasceretur. Item audivit dictum magistrum Martinellum dicentem quod Deus non faciebat nasci homines neque mulieres, sed alii homines et mulieres."

mon Cathar statement, that people's bodies are not created by God but simply born from other people, their parents, through sexual generation, just as plants come from other plants. Bodies, therefore, had no place in salvation. Martinello was not trying to hide his nonorthodox beliefs from the, perhaps, more orthodox members of the confraternity; instead, he was actively and repeatedly trying to engage them in discussions about religion.

A similar statement can be made about Brunetta, the former maid of Cursio di Nerli Bonelle's mother, who, after the death of her employer, retired to live in the *ospedale* of the *societas devotorum*, another indication that Cursio was most probably a member of the confraternity. In the *ospedale* Brunetta engaged others in discussions and disputes about religion. She told others who lived in the *ospedale* with her that capital punishment was against God's commands and that eventually everyone would go to heaven, both statements of Cathar belief.[23] In fact, her choice of topics is interesting because her assertion that all people would eventually go to heaven actually has its basis in the Cathar belief that human bodies are just prisons created by Satan. The Cathars taught that if a person died without receiving the *consolamentum*, he or she would simply be reborn into another body, another earthly prison, and would continue to be reincarnated over and over again in this way until receiving the *consolamentum*. The visible world would only come to an end once all the angelic souls trapped by Satan had been released through the *consolamentum*, once all people had entered heaven.[24] Brunetta, therefore, although living on the charity of the flagellant confraternity, still openly discussed Cathar doctrine.

---

[23] *Acta S. Officii*, 41. "Cum enim quidam homo duceretur ad decapitaionem, dicta mulier dixit dicto testi: 'Magister, iste sunt fortune,' et cum dictus testis diceret et peteret ab ea, si dictus homo qui ducebatur ad decapitationem potuerat cessare quim conmisistet maleficia et homicidium quod perpetravit, ita quod non decapitaretur, respondit dicta mulier quod non potuit facere dictus homo ne conmitteret dicta peccata, quia sic ordinatum fuit sibi a Deo in punto nativitatis sue... Item dixit quod audivit eam dicentem, quod omnes homines, boni et mali, debebant salvari in die iudicii, et omnes ire cum Christo in Paradisum, quia Christus hoc promiserat beato Iohanni de dono speciali, et hoc frequenter audivit ab ea in dicta domo et in anno proxime preterito, multis vicibus."

[24] *Interrogatio Iohannis*, 64. On Cathar views of reincarnation and the *consolamentum*, see Anne Brenon, *Le vrai visage du catharisme* (Portet-sur Garonne: Editions Loubatières, 1988), 66–68; *idem.*, "Les fonctions sacramentelles du consolament," *Heresis* 20 (1993): 33–55; Jean Pierre Bonnerot, "Consolamentum, réincarnation et évolution spirituelle dans le catharisme et le christianisme original," *Cahiers d'études cathares* 98 (1983): 3–58; and Malcolm Lambert, *The Cathars* (Oxford: Blackwell, 1998), 161.

She expressed a sincere interest in religion and may even have been attempting to proselytize.

The discussions are the key to understanding this situation. These people had a great interest in religion and in ritual and were not afraid to discuss theology with their friends, neighbors, and business associates. They also did not see a contradiction between their religious statements and the religious rituals that they would participate in as members of a flagellant confraternity. The Cathars believed that self-flagellation could not effect salvation, but they also believed that it did no spiritual harm. In fact, the Cathar believers whom we find in the *societas devotorum* used the confraternity to make contact with other people interested in religion. Their willingness to discuss their Cathar beliefs or leaning clearly show that they expected the other members of the confraternity to take an interest in religious discussions. In some ways they seem to have separated the ritual and the appearance of holiness from the theology behind the actions.

The Cathars in Bologna praised the Cathar perfects for their asceticism and holy demeanor while condemning the Franciscans and Dominicans for avarice and unholy actions. But at the same time many Cathar believers also had strong ties with the local Carmelites of San Martino dell'Aposa. The Carmelite parish had the highest number of identifiable Cathar believers of all the parishes in Bologna, and it was the center of what Lorenzo Paolini identified as the Cathar zone.[25] Bompietro di Giovanni, who was burnt as an obdurate heretic in May of 1299, had attended mass often at the Carmelite church and donated wine to the Carmelites for the sacrament. Five months before his conviction, Bompietro's mother-in-law had written her will on her deathbed in Bompietro's house, and instead of the usual crowd of prominent neighbors and clergy, the witnesses were almost entirely Carmelite friars.[26] Many Cathar believers also belonged to the society of the Vai, a part of the city militia that was centered upon the Carmelite church. The Vai held their meetings there, gathered there when the city called up the militia, and based the divisions of its jurisdiction upon the direction and distance of its members' homes from San Martino.[27] Unlike the Dominicans and the Franciscans, the

---

[25] Lorenzo Paolini, "Domus e zona degli eretici: L'esempio di Bologna nel XIII secolo," *Rivista di storia della Chiesa in Italia* 35 (1981): 371–387.

[26] ASB, Libri memoriali, 94 (1298): 293ᵛ.

[27] *Statuti delle Società del Popolo di Bologna*, 1:351–358, contains the statutes of the Vai,

Carmelites in Bologna seemed holy to the Cathar believers and were very much a part of their daily lives and religious actions.

What was important to the Cathar believers in Bologna was the appearance of asceticism and proper religious ritual. After receiving the *consolmentum*, a Cathar believer became perfected and entered into a state in which he or she avoided all sexual contact and products of coitus. The perfects were strict vegetarians, and because many believers told stories of carrying wine, vegetables and fish to them, this aspect of asceticism was obviously a very important marker of sanctity. Fasting also served as part of the preparations for flagellation in the *societas devotorum*, and ascetic practices among the laity were very much a part of religious activity and ritual in the confraternity. Many of the Cathar believers in Bologna also took part in processions of the Vai or of the society of the devout or other confraternities on holy days as part of larger rituals and as part of the urban lifestyle. They processed not only on the feast of St. Martin, the patron of the Vai, but also on the feasts of Peter Martyr, the patron of the Militia of the Virgin, and Dominic, one of the patrons of the city, who were both also the patrons of the inquisition.

The Cathar perfects did not fast or perform other ascetic acts for the same reasons that the members of the *societas devotorum* did. The flagellants used their bodies as a means of receiving God's grace and salvation by denying or inflicting pain upon their bodies as penance for their own and the world's sins. The perfects, on the other hand, believed that not only physical bodies but also sex and procreation were creations of Satan and tainted with sin. They avoided eating meat, eggs, milk, cheese, and other products of coitus for the same reason that they abstained from sexual contact or even from casual contact with members of the opposite sex. This was why a pregnant woman and Cathar believer named Fabrissa from Toulouse prayed to God to deliver her from the demon in her belly.[28] Giving in to the procreative

---

which specify that the society consisted of three groups of members, those who lived "a sero Apose," those who lived "a mane Apose," and those who lived "extra seralium." The Aposa creek flowed directly behind San Martino, which was just inside the *seralium*, the ditch that marked where the Bologna's eleventh-century walls had stood. Thus, the members of the Vai chose physical markers that met at San Martino to define their membership.

[28] Paris, Bibliotheque Nationale, Collection Doat, 25:40^r, cited in Peter Biller, "The Common Woman in the Western Church in the Thirteenth and Early Fourteenth Centuries," *Studies in Church History* 27 (1990): 154.

act or any of its products meant giving in to Satan and producing more bodies in which the devil could trap more angelic souls. Ascetic practices did not ensure salvation for a Cathar perfect but, instead, showed that the perfect was just that, perfected and outside of the cycle of procreation and reincarnation created by Satan.

This does not mean that the average Cathar believer, or at least believers like Avanzo da Funi, Cursio di Nerli Bonelle, Martinello and Brunetta did not understand Cathar and Catholic forms of asceticism. The statements that they made rejecting the salvific power of the Eucharist and the idea that God had created the entire world, including human bodies, show that they did have at least a basic understanding of Cathar doctrine concerning the body and its lack of a role in salvation. Instead of expecting the *societas devotorum* to ensure their salvation or bring them closer to Christ through his suffering, these people used the confraternity to create contacts with others interested in religion. It provided them with an opportunity for religious discussion—and perhaps even with the hope of persuading their fellow flagellants of the truths of Catharism.

For these people, the line imposed between heresy and orthodoxy by orthodox polemicists was not as important as proper religious action and reverence of those who were holy in action and not only in name. The Cathar perfects, the Carmelites, and the flagellants of the *societas devotorum* displayed acceptable ascetic and religious actions while the Dominicans and the Franciscans did not. Although the Cathar believers in Bologna were more than willing to engage in religious conversation and debate, the line that they placed between heresy and orthodoxy was based not upon theology or doctrine but upon practice and aspect.

IDOLATRY AND FRAUD: THE CASE OF
RIPERANDO AND THE HOLY MANAGLIA

CAROL LANSING

In May of 1300, the Bolognese civic court condemned Riperando Abri-
ari for idolatry and magic. He was sentenced to die by fire, and executed the same day. Riperando in fact had confessed not to idolatry
but to a clever religious fraud, and his tale would have the amusing
charm of a contemporary novella were it not for his horrific execution.
Riperando told the court that while lodging in an inn in the Bolognese countryside he and a partner ran a sting operation that successfully duped the innkeeper Berta and her mother-in-law Thomasina.
Riperando spun them a yarn about the divine origins, supernatural
power and immediate history of a wooden image he called sancta managlia. The next day, a man who was secretly his partner turned up at
the inn with the image and after a show of reluctance sold it to the
women for a large sum.

Riperando's fascinating and problematic story sits at the intersection of heresy, popular religion, magic, and fraud. Why include it in a
volume devoted to medieval heresy? Over the last decade or so, historians have rethought our understandings of heresy. Following the lead
of R.I. Moore, they have explored some of the ways in which heresy
was an invented category. Moore argued in a path breaking 1987 study
that the twelfth and thirteenth centuries saw the rise of persecution
of groups defined as deviant, including not only heretics but lepers,
homosexuals, and Jews. The details of that argument have sparked
lively debate but the overall point is an important one. One of Moore's
achievements was to break out of the narrow confines of the internal
history of heresy. More recently, historians have pressed this further by
dismantling some of our assumptions about popular heresy before the
thirteenth century. Early heresy, they have shown, is in part the result of
the imposition of categories derived from the thirteenth-century Inquisitions and inquisitorial manuals back on earlier religious groups.[1] The

---

[1] See *Inventer l'hérésie? Discours polémiques et pouvoirs avant l'Inquisition*, ed. Monique

effect of this research is to explore ways in which medieval heresy as scholars have understood it is the invention of later centuries.

Riperando's sentence allows us a rare glimpse of religious practices and attitudes outside of the usual institutional contexts. His confession evidently was not shaped by the categories and questions of the Dominican inquisitors in Bologna. It is fascinating precisely because it is not easily categorized. Some of the material in Riperando's confession closely resembles contemporary accounts of people who were considered heretical. How did he differ from them, and is he best understood as a simply con artist and not a heretic?

Riperando's tale appears in a legal sentence from a register of the actions of the court of the Bolognese podestà, a text that includes his confession.[2] Around April 21, 1300, a man named Francesco Sammarini who believed that Riperando had defrauded his wife and mother captured him in the countryside and turned him over to the civic court, lodged in the old palace of the podestà in the Piazza Maggiore in Bologna. An inquest was held. To my knowledge, the record of the inquest does not survive, but Francesco Sammarini and other local witnesses would have given depositions.[3] Riperando then was questioned and confessed. It is possible that he confessed under torture.[4] The court gave him the required formal opportunity to produce a defense, and then on May 14 finally condemned, sentenced and executed him. It is that sentence which survives. It incorporates the text of his confession, as recorded in Latin by the court's notaries.

Zerner, Collection du Centre d'Études Médiévales de Nice, vol. 3 (Nice: Faculté des Lettres, Arts et Sciences Humaines Université de Nice Sophia-Antipolis, 1998).

[2] Archivio di Stato di Bologna (hereafter ASB) Comune, Curia del Podestà, Accusationes 22b, register 21, 2 recto.

[3] On medieval Bolognese court procedure, see Massimo Vallerani, "L'amministrazione della giustizia a Bologna in età podestarile," *Atti e memorie delle Deputazione di storia patria per le provincie di Romagna*, n.s. 43 (1993), 291–316, and his "I processi accusatori a Bologna fra Due e Trecento," *Società e storia* 78 (1997): 741–788.

[4] For a recent discussion of medieval judicial torture see Edward Peters, "Destruction of the flesh—salvation of the spirit: the paradoxes of torture in medieval Christian society," *The Devil, Heresy and Witchcraft in the Middle Ages*, ed. Alberto Ferreiro (Leiden: Brill, 1998), 131–148. See also Mario Sbriccoli, "'Tormentum idest torquere mentem.' Processo inquisitorio e interrogatorio per tortura nell'Italia comunale," *La Parola all'accusato*, ed. Jean-Claude Maire Vigueur and Agostino Paravicini Bagliani (Palermo: Sallerio, 1991), 17–32.

The sting operation

Riperando confessed that he was staying in the inn of Francesco Sammarini in the countryside when he spun a yarn to Berta and Thomasina with the intent of deceiving them and extorting money. His source, he told the two women, was a Good Friday sermon preached by the archbishop of Milan. His story was long and parts are a bit garbled in the formal version of his confession included in his sentence. A wealthy merchant from the other side of the mountains named Raymond Bonifatii was on a journey to Rome when he stopped on a bridge near Milan, sent away his associates, and went to a certain fountain near the road. He then sent his nephew off to buy what they needed to celebrate Easter in Milan. Then, Raymond set a *tubarrum* of scarlet on the ground and on it placed an image made like a person, which he called santa managlia ("quamdam ymaginem formatam ad modum hominis quam vocabat sanctam mannagliam"). He began to pray to the thing to send peace from heaven to earth and to give him the grace to go to Rome and use his wealth to take ship across the sea, presumably to go on Crusade. Then, he wrapped the thing in a red cloth and, thinking that he tucked it between his tunic and his underclothing, in fact put it between his tunic and his robe, so that when he got back on his horse, he dropped the santa managlia.

When he came to Milan, he asked his nephew whether he had lost any of his things. The nephew replied, "Your money and horse are here, but when you mounted your horse back by the fountain, you tucked something in your bosom and I don't know whether you still have it." The merchant searched himself and could not find the santa managlia. He immediately stripped all the clothes from his back and began to go back, searching for the image. He failed to find it.

Raymond then encountered the archbishop of Milan, who asked him about what he had lost. Raymond responded, "I have lost something that gave me glory in this world and in the end would give me Paradise." The archbishop led him to Milan, and called together all the Milanese people because he wanted to preach about the things he had heard from Raymond. However, he did not know what to say. One of his chaplains advised him to send for a certain saintly hermit who could tell him all the things he needed. When the hermit came to him, he advised the archbishop to consult a sacred text: "If you have something of the *libro pocolactis* which Saint John made when he slept on the chest on the left side of our Lord Jesus Christ, I will say to you what you should preach." The archbishop responded that he had portions of the book, two notebooks, and three paper rolls.

The ensuing account of the origins of the santa managlia is thus attributed to a holy hermit's interpretation of Saint John's sacred text. It is somewhat jumbled in the court notary's version. The hermit told the archbishop, "Find there [that is, in the book] how this thing that Raymond lost was a thing that was born when God was wounded, when blood fell breaking open a rock in the hour of Adam. It was from a certain plant. The thing began to weep. Then God said to it that it should not grieve, and brought it back to life, and on the third day came into the light. When he baptized it in the river Jordan, Saint John said, 'What do you baptize?' God responded, 'This thing is such that whoever has it will always have glory in the world and paradise afterwards, and it can be someone who seeks paradise for himself and for many others. Whoever takes it from another by force will go raving upon the earth for nine days and nine nights, but whoever buys it will be glorified by it, and the greater the price paid, the greater the glory.' He spoke of this managlia on the newest (first) day."

Then, Riperando turned from this explanation of the thing's origins to its recent past, and recounted the adventures of the man who happened to find the figure after the merchant dropped it. How Riperando explained why he knew all this is not clear, since it could not have been in the archbishop's sermon. Riperando was evidently letting his listeners know that those who revealed the secret location of the Managlia would suffer supernatural sanctions. So, he explained, the man who had found the figure was staying at an inn in Piacenza and went along with the innkeeper to the archbishop's sermon. She asked him to sell her the image for fifty imperial pounds, a chest and an iron collaretto, since he wanted to take up arms and go on Crusade. When she visited a neighboring moneylender to raise the one hundred imperial soldi she lacked, the moneylender's godfather asked her what she planned to do with the money. She responded, "I will tell you, in good faith that you will not divulge this to anyone. I am buying from one of my lodgers the santa managlia that the archbishop of Milan preached about on Good Friday, for the price of forty imperial pounds and a chest and an iron collaretto, and all that I lack is 100 imperial soldi." Immediately after she said this, the woman became mad and raving and died in her madness.

When the man who had found the image heard the rumor that she was dead, he began to flee with the thing. The moneylender chased after him with a great quantity of money, hoping to buy the santa managlia from him. When the moneylender pursued the man outside the gates of Piacenza, he met a servant girl and asked her whether she had encountered the man. The servant responded, "I did meet someone who quickly fled." Immediately upon saying this, her arm withered. Then the moneylender turned back, saying, "I see that God does not want me to have the santa managlia." It is said, Riperando told the two women, that the servant girl with the withered arm is kept in a church as a miracle.

After Riperando told this yarn, his secret partner showed up at the inn. The next morning, Riperando left and his partner remained and divulged a great secret to the women. He was the man who had found the thing: "I would like you to pledge me good faith so that I can say something to you." The two women promised not to reveal what he told. He said, "I have a most sacred thing which I would like to give to a holy hermit for safekeeping if there is one in the area. If you were good Christians and holy persons I would give it to you, but otherwise not, since this is a thing which must be kept safe. It must be near a person who will ask it to send down peace from heaven to earth." With some reluctance, he entrusted it to Berta and Thomasina for the hefty sum of 36 pounds, along with some armor to enable him to go on Crusade. Berta's husband found out about the deal, captured the fleeing Riperando and handed him over to the podestà's court. The partner, who had actually sold the thing, got away with the money.

Riperando confessed to some details about the image. The santa managlia sold to Berta and Thomasina was one of many. His partner carved these things and then Riperando painted them. One of them was found on his person. "It was formed like a man, short of stature with a big head, long hair and beard and the other members short, and was red." He also talked about how they marketed the images. He was taking this one to Ferrara to the wife of Nascimbene the spice dealer, because she had asked him for a mandragora. A mandragora, or mandrake root, was a plant formed somewhat like a human being and used in a variety of magical concoctions, notably aphrodisiacs, as in Machiavelli's *La Mandragola*. Riperando planned to sell it to her as a mandragora for twenty soldi, a paltry sum in comparison to the price paid by Berta and Thomasina. If she did not accept it, he would sell it to someone else, either as a mandragora or as a santa managlia, in whichever way he could get a higher price. He had done this before: about two years ago he sold another figured image of a man as a

mandragora to a woman of Monferici, near Padua for thirteen soldi.
He had sold five or more of these images to men and women, getting
ten soldi from one, eleven from another, and fifteen from another, the
more he was able to deceive the buyers.

Riperando also sold other forms of magic. He and his associate
had worked together for about a month, making and selling powerful
brevia, written spells. They sold them to many women along the banks
of the Po and in other places, selling it to one for six pennies and
another twelve, as much as they could get. He said they made a
spell for removing fevers, illnesses of the eyes and of the womb, which
he believed to be genuinely effective. He also confessed that he was
accustomed to write words on wax and then say that it was a spell that
created hate and love. In the past three years, he had sold as many of
these as he could, more than twenty, in many places.

The text and the court

Before analyzing this narrative, it is important to consider how it was
constructed. It is not a simple transcript of events or even of Riperando's statements. Instead, it is an abbreviated version of a Latin record
of the formal representation of these persons and events in the court.
The judge held an inquest and probably collected depositions from witnesses. To my knowledge the record of the inquest and that testimony
does not survive. It is also important to note that Riperando probably spoke in Milanese vernacular. The notary who recorded the sentence and probably the inquest as well was Vermiglio, a member of the
entourage of the Florentine nobleman serving as Bolognese podestà in
1300, Pino di Stoldo dei Rossi.[5] This means that Vermiglio may not
always have fully understood Riperando as he translated his statements
into the formulaic Latin of the law. Riperando spoke in response to the
court's questions and may have suffered torture. In effect, the confession we have was very much shaped by the court's legal categories and
process.

---

[5] See Massimo Vallerani, "Ufficiali forestieri a Bologna (1200–1326)," 289–310, esp.
p. 306, and, on Pino dei Rossi, Sergio Raveggi, "I rettori fiorentini," 595–644, esp. 625,
640, in *I Podestà dell'Italia Comunale*, Part I, ed. Jean-Claude Maire Vigueur, Collection
de l'École Française de Rome, 268 (Rome: Istituto storico italiano per il Medio Evo,
2000).

At the same time, the content also surely reflects Riperando's desperate calculations about what he should or should not say. How much did he know? The Bolognese, or at least those who show up in the extant records, had seen judges at work and had some sense of how the court operated. They were aware of the idea of public reputation, *pubblica fama*, and even of the local statutes on infamy, which were systematically read to them by the podestà's notaries. Riperando was an outsider and presumably unfamiliar with the sophisticated Bolognese court. He surely hoped to represent himself as a simple fraud rather than an idolator and caster of spells, or a heretic. This may be why he did not confess to selling other figures as managlias rather than mandragora. He may not have known that once he admitted to things like magic spells and counterfeiting, he was a *persona infamata*, infamous in law, which left him little legal protection.[6] He was condemned as an enchanter, idolator, fortuneteller, fraud, and counterfeiter (*incantator, ydolator, divinator, deceptor, coniator*) who used lies to trick the two women.

The case was heard in the podestà's criminal court. This was probably a strategic choice on the part of the aggrieved innkeeper, Francesco Sammarini. There was an energetic and ambitious Dominican Inquisition in Bologna in these decades, and Francesco could have handed Riperando over to them. However, people distrusted and hated the Inquisitors. In May 1299, a year before the death of Riperando, when two living men and one dead woman were burned for Cathar heresy, hundreds of townsfolk rioted in protest.[7] Even before the riot, the Inquisitor's entourage was attacked as they passed through the countryside. It may be that the reason Riperando was not questioned by the Inquisitors is that Francesco Sammarini chose to take him to the

---

[6] On infamy see the summary article by Edward Peters, "Wounded names: the medieval doctrine of infamy," *Law in Medieval Life and Thought*, ed. Edward King and Susan Ridyard, Sewanee Medieval Studies, 5 (Sewanee, TN: University of the South Press, 1990), 43–89, esp. 80–86, and Francesco Migliorino, *Fama e infamia. Problemi della società medievale nel pensiero giuridico nei secoli XII e XIII* (Catania: Editrice Gianotta, 1985).

[7] The registers are edited in Lorenzo Paolini and Raniero Orioli, *Acta S. Officii Bononie ab anno 1291 usque ad anno 1310*, Fonti per la storia d'Italia, vol. 106 (Rome, Istituto storico Italiano per il medio evo, 1982). See Lorenzo Paolini, *L'eresia catara alla fine del duecento*, in *L'eresia a Bologna fra XIII e XIV secolo*, (Rome: Istituto storico italiano per il medio evo, 1975), 93–96. On the riot, see Susan Snyder, "Woman as Heretic: Gender and Lay Religion in Late Medieval Bologna," (Ph.D. Dissertation, University of California, Santa Barbara, 2002), and her "Orthodox Fears: Anti-Inquisitorial Violence and Defining Heresy," *Fear and its Representations in the Middle Ages and Renaissance*, Arizona Studies in the Middle Ages and Renaissance, vol. 6, ed. Cynthia Kosso and Anne Scott (Brepols: Turnhout, 2002).

podestà's court. An attempt to get justice from the Dominican Inquisitors would have been highly risky. They might well have levied a huge fine, as they did against others accused of aiding heretics, or confiscated their property. Francesco's wife and mother after all had actually purchased the managlia: judging from Riperando's confession, if anyone was actually guilty of idolatry, it was the two women. Further, the inquisitors had a reputation not for fairness but for greed, corruption, and injustice, as Susan Snyder and others have shown.

The podestà's court was comparatively reliable. Bolognese, even countryfolk, were very accustomed to using the court to get justice or at least to pressure people to resolve disputes. The worst result for Francesco would be a modest twenty soldi fine for a false accusation. Further, my guess is that the podestà's judges had a reputation for carrying out the law with reasonable fairness, in the contado as in town. It is incontrovertible that the court process could be cruel, relying in some cases on torture. We have heartbreaking testimony from a 1289 inquest in which witnesses, most of them judges, describe a Bolognese man's reaction when the court tortured and effectively killed his son. He walked into the palace of the commune, took the responsible judge by the shoulders and shook him as he poured out his grief and rage.[8] Nevertheless, judges clearly did their best actually to carry out the law. Dozens of homicide inquests from the contado reveal judges and their officers diligently investigating, and occasionally they must have succeeded in uncovering the people responsible. It is not surprising that Francesco marched his prisoner to the podestà's judges.

The sales pitch

What shall we make of Riperando's confession? At first glance, it seems yet more confirmation of my Uncle Sidney's longstanding career advice: the real money is in religion. Why sell a mandragora for a few soldi when you can get ten times that amount if you call it a santa managlia? The answer also is clear: the thirteenth-century court paid little attention to magic accusations or love potions, but Riperando was burned alive. How did he make his yarn convincing enough actually to sell the managlia? He made clever use of the traditional claims of Catholic Christianity. He used the authority of the archbishop of Milan

---

[8] ASB, Comune, Curia del Podestà, Libri Inquisitionum et testium 7, 11, 9 recto-12 recto.

to gain credence for his tale. His pitch implies that he thought popular preaching had a real impact: people learned about marvels from the archbishop's Good Friday sermon. The tale of a pious merchant from across the mountains on his way to Rome was particularly credible because it was the Jubilee year. The roads were in fact full of pilgrims on their way to Rome, some of them as the court records show pitifully easy prey. Riperando also connected his story to Crusading zeal. The men who sold the managlia did so for this laudable purpose, not personal gain. A donation to send someone on Crusade was an act of piety worth an indulgence; perhaps contributing weapons and funds to a Crusader in exchange for the managlia had the same effect. Riperando also assumed that his prospective buyers placed faith in the piety and authority of holy hermits, even unnamed, generic ones. Hermits both male and female were common in the period, though they are now somewhat overlooked, since no religious orders celebrated their history.[9] The hermits in the story are just people with authority and secret knowledge from their ascetic life.

Riperando further invoked the authority of sacred texts to support his story: it is all written in the Book of John. As in the popular religious movements described by Brian Stock and R.I. Moore, religious authority was reliant on texts but not textual.[10] Apparently, Riperando could write, since he confessed that he wrote *brevia*, spells. The account of the provenance of the managlia reveals some familiarity with central moments in the Bible, but collapses biblical history: the Creation and the Crucifixion are conflated in the tale of divine blood dripping on a plant, and its baptism in the River Jordan. The yarn has the fantastic quality of the tales told by Cathar preachers and by Joachites. Both groups were active in the region during these decades. People heard all sorts of stories, from all sorts of preachers. Some of the miracle stories in the Golden Legend were hardly more plausible than Riperando's story about the managlia. Its truth after all was vindicated by a miracle, the servant girl whose arm withered when she betrayed the managlia's location, who was kept in a church as evidence.

---

[9] See André Vauchez, *La sainteté en Occident aux derniers siècles du Moyen Age: d'après les procès de canonisation et les documents hagiographiques* (Rome: Ecole française de Rome, 1988).

[10] Brian Stock, *The Implications of Literacy: Written Language and Models of Interpretation in the Eleventh and Twelfth Centuries* (Princeton: Princeton University Press, 1983), and the essays collected in *Heresy and literacy, 1000–1530*, ed. Peter Biller and Anne Hudson, (Cambridge and New York: Cambridge University Press, 1994).

Idols, demons and magic

Riperando's story sits at the intersection of popular religion and heresy with magic and fraud. The holy managlia is an odd hybrid, a baptized plant with supernatural effects. Animated by divine blood, it was originally able to grieve, but is apparently not sentient in the contemporary world. In the Latin text it is termed a *res*, suggesting that Riperando called it not a person but a thing, not Saint Managlia but the holy managlia. The court took the view that it was an idol. What did idolatry mean in the thirteenth century? It was perceived as a continuing problem, often cast in terms of inappropriate veneration of images of the saints. In the 1230s William of Auvergne bishop of Paris made reference to "pagan idols still cherished by old women," but considered worship of saints' images a greater problem.[11] Thomas Aquinas gave a standard formulation of the difference between orthodox reverence and worship of an idol, *latria* and *idolatria*. The mind moves towards an image as a certain thing, or towards an image insofar as it is the image of something else. "...we must say that no reverence is shown to Christ's image as a thing—for instance, carved or painted wood, because reverence is not due save to a rational creature. It follows therefore that reverence should be shown to it insofar only as it is an image."[12] On these grounds, the managlia was surely an idol. It was not an image of something else, but as a thing of carved and painted wood, to be reverenced in itself. Richard Trexler in a discussion of miracle-working images in late medieval Florence argued that the difference in practice between an icon like the Madonna of Impruneta and an idol was whether it worked. If an image had no spiritual power, it was an idol, "pure object, without spirit, without efficacy."[13] The problem with this view is that it does not allow for the role of demons. An idol in fact could be efficacious because it was demonic.

Idolatry charges were not unknown in these decades.[14] The most notorious examples are the trials of the Templars and the postmortem

---

[11] *De Legibus Opera* I, fol. 33, col. 3, quoted by G.G. Coulton, *The Fate of Medieval Art in the Renaissance and Reformation* (Oxford: B. Blackwell, 1928), 375. See Michael Camille, *The Gothic Idol* (Cambridge: Cambridge University Press, 1989), esp, pp 207–208 and p. 380n.

[12] *Summa Theologica* 3, q. 25, a. 3.

[13] Richard Trexler, *Public Life in Renaissance Florence* (New York: Academic Press, 1980), 70–72.

[14] See for further examples William R. Jones, "Political Uses of Sorcery in Medieval

trial of Boniface VIII for among other things idolatry and heresy, both trials engineered by the French crown. As testimony from Boniface's trial suggests, idols were inhabited by demons and idolatry meant the worship of demons. The most detailed accusation of idol worship against Boniface came from a Franciscan tertiary deposed in 1310, who also said that he saw Boniface sacrifice a chicken inside a magic circle. The witness reported that he saw Boniface remove a piece of gold fabric to uncover a window in his bedchamber in the papal palace and then worship something there. He asked the pope's chamberlain whether there was a picture in the window and why the pope worshipped it. "It is not a picture but an evil Maestà," the chamberlain replied.[15] The witness opened the window and saw an idol there. The chamberlain frantically stopped him and explained, "In that window is a certain idol with a diabolic spirit enclosed in it. Master Thaddeus of Bologna gave it to him, and the pope adores the idol and keeps it for his God and acts and believes according to the doctrine of the spirit in it."[16] Master Thaddeus has been identified with Taddeo Alderotti, a Florentine physician teaching in Bologna. Boniface's idol and its demon were thus said to come from a member of the medical faculty at the Bolognese Studio![17]

Riperando may have been aware of the risk that the managlia could be considered demonic, and went to some lengths to suggest that he sold it as a force for good, not evil. There is no suggestion in Riperando's sentence that the court was concerned that the managlia was genuinely diabolic. This is characteristic: the hard-nosed thirteenth-century civic judges paid little attention to accusations of magic and even the employment of demons.[18] Accusations of the use of magic and spells were fairly common, typically tacked onto other

---

Europe," *Witchcraft, Magic and Demonology*, ed. Brian P. Levack (New York and London: Garland, 1992), 196–213.

[15] This phrase is awkward to understand. Norman Cohn read it as "the majesty of evil." As the editor, Jean Coste, suggested, a Maestà meant an icon, typically the Virgin in Majesty.

[16] *Boniface VIII en Procès: Articles d'accusation et dépositions des témoins (1303–1311)*, ed. Jean Coste (Rome: L'Erma di Bretschneider: Fondazione Camillo Caetani, 1995), 525–526.

[17] Robert Davidsohn identified Master Thaddeus with Taddeo Alderotti, a Florentine physician. See Nancy Siraisi, *Taddeo Alderotti and his Pupils* (Princeton: Princeton University Press, 1981).

[18] See for another example Archivio di Stato di Bologna, Comune, Curia del Podestà, Libri Inquisitionum et Testium 14, 1, 3 recto.

charges.[19] The usual targets were women considered sexually suspect, generally prostitutes or pimps. A woman denounced to the court as a female sodomite was also accused of love magic. In August 1297 someone notified the court that Agnesia, who was the concubine of an innkeeper, "was a receiver of pimps for sodomites and also of heretics and other infamous persons, especially Monna Necha." Necha, the notification continued, was a Sienese woman living in Bologna "who cast spells on men and women and is a diviner and a woman who makes experiments and who can teach how to make transfigurations of people to extort money, and who daily says to people conversing with her 'I can make the person you want love you at your will, I am the greatest woman in the world and could bring up tempests and hailstorms so that no one could escape death if I wished to do so,' and she deceives men and women throughout the city, and says that she can summon demons to do her wishes."[20] The court summoned Agnesia– who actually showed up with guarantors, and was prepared to provide a defense and witnesses–and then did not proceed. According to the marginalia, this was because she lived in an inn, not in one of the parishes listed in the statute. This probably meant the statute on prostitution, which was specific to a list of parishes.[21] I found no evidence that the court took any interest in the lurid doings of Monna Necha. The unnamed person who notified the court implied that she was a heretic, since Agnesia was denounced as a receiver of heretics as well as pimps for sodomites.

Magic accusations involving human images did occasionally surface. Usually made of wax, an image could be used to harm and kill a person or to make someone fall in or out of love.[22] So for example a husband accused his wife of repeated attempts on his life, using poison and also

---

[19] For magic and sorcery cases from Tuscan towns in the fourteenth and fifteenth centuries, see Gene Brucker, "Sorcery in Renaissance Florence," *Studies in the Renaissance* 10 (1963), 7–24, reprinted in *Witchcraft, Magic and Demonology*, pp. 117–134, and Christine Meek, "Men, Women and Magic: Some Cases from Late Medieval Lucca," *Women in Renaissance and Early Modern Europe*, ed. Christine Meek (Dublin: Four Courts, 2000), which cites further studies.

[20] ASB, Curia del Podestà, Libri inquisitionum et testium 42, register 1, 1 verso-2 verso.

[21] The marginalia reads "non potest procedi quia in hospite factum et quia non est de capellis prohybitis per statutum."

[22] See Richard Kieckhefer, "Erotic magic in medieval Europe," *Sex in the Middle Ages: A Book of Essays*, ed. Joyce E. Salisbury (New York and London: Garland Publishing, 1991), 30–55, esp 38–42.

magic. She made a human image, stuck spines in the chest, kidneys, ribs, head and breast, then broke it in the middle, hoping to kill him.[23] Destructive sexual passion could be explained in terms of this kind of magic: witnesses testifying in an inquest into the fama or reputation of a woman named Guilelma stated that she was not only a prostitute but an affaturatrix, an enchantress. A former customer explained that he knew she was a magician because she kept at the head of her bed an image made like a human figure that had spines stuck in it. Other witnesses recounted how she had so enchanted Ghino the son of Ser Pace that he left his father and had followed her for the past two years. He had abandoned all good works and would do whatever she wanted.[24]

Men could be accused of erotic magic as well. In 1286, a physician from Arezzo was said by witnesses to use a variety of forms of magic and science, including astrology and an astrolabe. Jacobina, the unhappy wife of a goldsmith, tried to run away with him, and gave him some of her husband's money and valuables. After the goldsmith recovered Jacobina, he went to court to lodge an accusation against the physician in order to recover the property as well. The charge was seduction through magic. The doctor had given Jacobina evil potions to eat and drink, and "also made another concoction of wax, a similitude of a god, in the image of a woman. He stuck a needle in the heart of this image or concoction of wax, and buried it under the ground next to the door of the house where Jacobina lives. Because of these concoctions and evil things, Jacobina lost her right mind and good sense. Because she is out of her mind, she continually longs to be with [the doctor], and remains near the door of her house, where the wax image was buried."[25] Was this magic charge disingenuous? Witnesses did testify that a wax image was found buried near the doorsill, though it was not clear that the doctor had placed it there. Perhaps the magic charge saved face, since Jacobina could and did testify that her passion for the doctor was outside her control. After most of the property was returned, her husband dropped the charges. Apparently, the magic charge was a way to pressure the doctor to return the goods.

---

[23] ASB, Curia del Podestà, Accusationes 5a, register 7, 17 recto.

[24] ASB, Libri Inquisitionum et testium 14, register 12, 3 recto-7 verso.

[25] ASB, Accusationes 5a, register 1, 55 verso-56 verso; Jacobina's prior deposition is *Libri Inquisitionum et testium* 7, register 9, 7 recto. Further records of this case remain and Armando Antonelli is preparing a study.

Fraud and sincerity

What do we make of Riperando? He seems a character from a Mark Twain story, dropped like the Connecticut Yankee into the Middle Ages. His tale raises questions about how we read reports of heretical preaching: a second-hand report about Riperando could easily make him look like an itinerant holy man rather than a huckster. Further, the Inquisitors in Bologna did question and sentence people who clearly were not involved in religious movements and were not so different from Riperando. Fra Giacomo Flamenghi, questioned in 1299, was a Vallambrosan monk who refused to attend religious services, participate in the sacraments or honor fasts. He denied that Boniface had any legal right to the papacy, since he had arranged the death of Pope Celestine, "the best man in the world." And he admitted that he had faked miracles for the money in Barletta, using *acqua vite* and the veil of the Virgin.[26]

And yet, the one interpretation that historians rarely accept in cases of religious dissent is fraud. Medieval accounts of heretics often accuse them of fraud for personal gain. The accounts of Tanchelm and Henry of Lausanne translated by R.I. Moore are twelfth-century examples.[27] Thirteenth-century Italian sources are full of tales of religious frauds, orthodox and heretical. Salimbene de Adam, the gossipy Franciscan chronicler, loved discreditable tales of religious fraud. He wrote at length of a wine carrier in Cremona named Albert, who after his death in 1279 was venerated as a saint. Many miracles were reported in the towns of the region. Popular processions moved through the streets to the Church of Saint Peter, where Albert's relics were preserved and other wine carriers gathered, and people gave them purple cloth, samite, canopies and money. Parish priests saw this and were quick to have images of Albert painted in their churches so that they would share in the donations. Some men, Salimbene reports, told the mendicants "You think nobody can work miracles but your own saints, but you are clearly deceived as has been made clear through Albert." When a man came to Parma from Cremona with a relic of Saint Albert, the little toe of the right foot, people gathered and carried the relic in pro-

---

[26] See *Acta Sancti Officii Bononie*, nos. 44, 46, 49–52, pp. 73, 76–77, 81–84. For the fourteenth century, see Grado Merlo, *Eretici e Inquisitori nella società piemontese del trecento* (Turin: Claudiana, 1977).

[27] R.I. Moore, *The Birth of Popular Heresy* (London: St. Martin's Press, 1975), 28–38.

cession to the cathedral and placed it on the high altar. Then a canon came forward, kissed it and discovered it to be a clove of garlic.[28] Salimbene put Armanno Punzilupo in the same category. Armanno was a holy man in Ferrara considered by the Dominican Inquisition to be a Cathar perfect. After his death and burial in the cathedral, he came to be venerated by the local population and the cathedral canons as a miracle-working Catholic saint.[29] Salimbene also was quick to class the followers of Fra Dolcino not as religious dissenters but as self-serving frauds.

Boccaccio's fictional frauds and phony miracles were not so different. The amiable and eloquent Fra Cipolla, Brother Onion, promises to show a gullible crowd a feather dropped by the angel Gabriel in the Virgin's bedchamber at the time of the Annunciation. When the friar opened the box to reveal the feather to his listeners, he discovered that some jokers had substituted lumps of coal. Undeterred, Fra Cipolla explained them—after a long preamble about his travels to Jerusalem— as some of the coals used to martyr Saint Lawrence on the grill.

Could Riperando's confession have been considered evidence for popular heresy? It is worth remembering that the working definition of heresy in the thirteenth century was flexible, based on practice and not belief. The inquisitors in Bologna heard cases like the renegade monk; Salimbene did not distinguish between the followers of Albert and Fra Dolcino. Riperando by his confession was teaching people to pray to a carved statue. And yet, when medieval heretics are accused of fraud or corruption, historians tend to dismiss that charge as part of stereotypical attacks on people being constructed as deviant. Heretics have to be sincere believers, seeking religious answers, not sex, power or wealth. Why? The question recalls a point in the debate between the anthropologists Marshall Sahlins and Ganath Obeyesekere over the death of Captain Cook at the hands of the ancient Hawaiians.[30] Sahlins

---

[28] *The Chronicle of Salimbene de Adam*, trans. Joseph L. Baird, Giuseppe Baglivi, and John Robert Kane, Medieval and Renaissance Texts and Studies vol. 40 (Binghamton, New York: Medieval and Renaissance Texts and Studies, 1986), 734–735, pp. 512–523.

[29] See Gabriele Zanella, *Itinerari ereticali: Patari e catari tra Rimini e Verona*, Istituto storico italiano per il medio evo, Studi storici 153 (Rome: Istituto storico italiano per il medio evo 1986), appendix 1.

[30] See Ganath Obeyesekere, *The Apotheosis of Captain Cook: European Mythmaking in the Pacific* (Princeton: 1992), Marshall Sahlins, *Islands of History* (Chicago: University of Chicago Press, 1985) and *How "Natives" Think: About Captain Cook, for example* (Chicago: University of Chicago Press, 1995), and the lucid review by Clifford Geertz, "Culture war," *The New York Review of Books* 42: 19 (30 November 1995), 4–6.

argued that the Hawaiians because of the timing and circumstances of Cook's arrival on the island perceived him as the god Lono, and then sacrificed him when he returned at a ritually inappropriate moment. Obeyesekere in response argued that the ancient Hawaiians were not so trapped in their mental categories that they were unable to recognize Cook's humanity. But for Europeans, they always have to be natives, "the other."

Why then do medieval heretics have to be sincerely religious? The idea of a "medieval mind" has a long history, including most recently the notion that medieval people were incapable of atheism.[31] Ironically, the notion that authentic religion is a matter not of ritual practice but of sincere belief largely derives from the sixteenth century.[32] Some Protestant reformers considered medieval heretics their spiritual ancestors, members of the true church who stood in opposition to the corrupt institution.[33] While most historians no longer hold that view, they tend like Westerners more generally to view religion through the lens of Protestant notions of conversion and inner transformation. For religion to be authentic, it must be sincere.[34]

From this perspective, perhaps the most intriguing and baffling characters in Riperando's confession are those glimpsed on the margins: the buyers. Presumably, they were sincere. Riperando confessed that he had sold more than five of these things "to men and women." All of the actual buyers he mentioned were women: Berta and Thomasina, the wife of Nascimbene the spicedealer in Ferrara, and the woman of Padua who bought a mandragora for thirteen soldi. This list recalls the medieval trope of women's gullibility: foolishness was coded as a female attribute. But why would people, male or female, pay large sums for a managlia? The answer perhaps is that it was efficacious. It required no priest and its effects were automatic, like magic, *ex opere operato*. Surely in the late thirteenth century this approach to spiritual aid was some-

---

[31] See Susan Reynolds, "Social Mentalities and the Case of Medieval Skepticism," *Transactions of the Royal Historical Society* 6th series: I (1991), 21–41.

[32] See John Martin, "Inventing Sincerity, Refashioning Prudence: The Discovery of the Individual in Renaissance Europe," *American Historical Review* 102 (1997): 1326–1333.

[33] See the discussion in Abraham Friesen, "Medieval Heretics or Forerunners of the Reformation: the Protestant Rewriting of the History of Medieval Heresy," *The Devil, Heresy and witchcraft in the Middle Ages*, ed. Alberto Ferreiro (Leiden: Brill, 1998), 165–190.

[34] See Webb Keane, "From Fetishism to Sincerity: On Agency, the Speaking Subject, and their Historicity in the Context of Religious Conversion," *Comparative Studies in Society and History*, 39 (1997): 674–693, and his "Sincerity, 'modernity,' and the Protestants," *Cultural Anthropology*, 17 (2002): 65–93.

thing of a relief: it was a consolation to have this automatic blessing, the more you pay the more you get. After all, the idea was not such an anomaly: the Catholic clergy in some ways also offered intercession for a price. More importantly, Catholic preachers and confessors advocated inner intention as true measures of sin and contrition, an approach that could open the door to agonizing self-doubt and fear. Perhaps the notion that daily prayer to a high-priced exotic religious artifact could have a similar effect was consoling. Riperando's success in marketing his holy managlias thus speaks to anxieties produced by thirteenth-century pastoral care.

CHASING PHANTOMS:
PHILIP IV AND THE FANTASTIC

JAMES GIVEN

One of the seminal works of late twentieth-century scholarship on medieval Europe is R.I. Moore's *Formation of a Persecuting Society*.[1] In this work Moore questioned the common assumption that the twelfth- and thirteenth- century persecutions of various "out-groups"—heretics, lepers, sodomites, Jews, etc.—were directly related to the objective challenges to Christian society posed by these groups. As Moore phrased it, "Some years ago I asked in an examination paper for school-leavers, 'Why were heretics persecuted in the thirteenth century?' The question was very popular and the answer, with great confidence and near unanimity, 'because there were so many of them.' The existence of people whose religious convictions differed from those approved by the church was in itself the cause of persecution... I have no doubt that if I had asked the reasons for the rapidly increasing severity of action to segregate lepers at this time I should have received precisely the same answer—'because there were so many of them'—or that the persecution of the Jews which was also being greatly intensified would have been accounted for by the increase not of their numbers but of their wealth and economic influence."[2]

Thanks to Moore, and others, we now realize that, although there were indeed heretics, lepers, sodomites, and Jews in medieval Europe, their persecution originated not so much in any objective characteristics that these groups possessed as in the needs, desires, and practices of those who ruled, or aspired to rule, society.[3] Persecution tells us much more about the persecutors than it does about the persecuted. And in many cases those whom the rulers of society persecuted were phantoms of their own imagining rather than the real enemies of Christendom.

---

[1] R.I. Moore, *The Formation of A Persecuting Society: Power and Deviance in Western Europe, 950–1250* (Oxford: Basil Blackwell, 1987).

[2] Moore, *Formation*, p. 1.

[3] A point also made by Gavin I. Langmuir in *Toward a Definition of Antisemitism* (Los Angeles and Berkeley: University of California Press, 1990). See also John Boswell,

In this essay I will apply this insight to the emergence in the early fourteenth century of charges of fantastic evil-doing—demonolatry, magic, and sexual perversion—as a staple of the discourse of political conflict at the highest levels of European society.[4] Why were fantasy, fear, and power so closely linked in the early fourteenth century?[5] Part of the answer, I will suggest, lies in the glaring contradiction between the vaunting aspirations of early fourteenth-century rulers and the limited means at their disposal for realizing those aspirations.

European kings had long presented themselves as sacral rulers. In the thirteenth and fourteenth centuries they were engaged in the painful and conflict-ridden process of transforming these claims into real political mastery of their kingdoms.[6] Yet, even as their power grew, the contradictions between their aspirations and their achievements were often glaring. A Philip the Fair of France presented himself as the "champion of the faith and defender of the church,"[7] but his government could find the most elementary tasks of government exceedingly difficult.

In an environment where real men and women remained stubbornly resistant to efforts to rule them, combating and defeating fantastic enemies had its advantages. By leveling accusations of demonology, witchcraft, and heresy, a king took on enemies that were at once terrifying but defenseless, since they were mere chimeras of the medieval imagination. In the shadow realm of the fantastic and the imaginary, a king could symbolically and dramatically act out his crucial role in Christian society.

Let us begin the examination of this process with two stories, both from the reign of King Philip the Fair of France. In one, where the king's government confronts real subjects, it appears beleaguered and

---

Christianity, Social Tolerance, and Homosexuality: Gay People in Western Europe from the Beginning of the Christian Era to the Fourteenth Century (Chicago: University of Chicago Press, 1980).

[4] See the essays of William R. Jones, "Political Uses of Sorcery in Medieval Europe," *The Historian* 34 (1972): 670–687, and Malcolm Barber, "Lepers, Jews and Moslems: The Plot to Overthrow Christendom in 1321," *History* 66 (1981): 1–17.

[5] For some interesting speculations, see Jacques Chiffoleau, "Dire l'indicible: remarques sur la catégorie du *nefandum* du XIIe au XVe siècle," *Annales: Economies, Sociétés, Civilisations* 45 (1990): 289–324.

[6] Joseph R. Strayer, *On the Medieval Origins of the Modern State* (Princeton: Princeton University Press, 1970).

[7] Joseph R. Strayer, "France: The Holy Land, the Chosen People, and the Most Christian King," in *Medieval Statecraft and the Perspectives of History* (Princeton: Princeton University Press 1971), 307.

ineffective. In the other, where it deals with imaginary enemies, it appears a formidable juggernaut.

The first story: In 1300 Philip IV imposed a tax to fund his military expenses in the county of Flanders.[8] Pierre de Bogis, a royal *viguier* in the *sénéchaussée* of Carcassonne was given the task of collecting the levy in the county of Foix. Accordingly, Pierre made his way into the foothills of the Pyrenees. When he arrived at Foix, he found the town appareled as if for war, with the gates shut and chains stretched across the bridge spanning the Ariège river. To the mob assembled to greet him Pierre read his letters of commission, an oration to which the crowd turned a deaf ear. Frustrated at Foix, Pierre made his way down the Ariège to Varilhes; there he managed to collect some money. With seven mules loaded with coin he set off for Carcassonne. His journey was interrupted by the *bayle* of Foix and a group of his henchmen who relieved Bogis of his mules and his money. Pierre appealed to the count of Foix's castellan at Varilhes for aid, but was ignored.

Once back in Carcassonne, the *viguier* had the Fuxéens cited to appear before the king's justices to answer for their contempt of royal authority. Two sergeants were dispatched to deliver the summons. They had no better luck than Bogis. At Foix they too confronted a closed town and a threatening mob. At Tarascon they also found the town gates barred. And in the village of La Barguillère they were set upon and nearly killed by an enraged mob. The counts of Foix, Roger Bernard III and his son Gaston I, refused all royal requests to turn over for trial those responsible for these acts. Faced with this steadfast contumacy, the king's courts in 1305 sentenced the people of Foix, Tarascon, and four other localities to heavy fines. In 1308, however, these were drastically reduced. Thereafter the crown apparently decided that raising direct taxes in the county of Foix was more trouble than it was worth.[9]

The second story, far better known than the first, presents a radically different image of royal power. On October 12, 1307, Jacques de Molay, grand master of the old and venerable order of the Knights of the

---

[8] Joseph R. Strayer, "Consent to Taxation under Philip the Fair," in *Studies in Early French Taxation*, by Joseph R. Strayer and Charles H. Taylor (Cambridge, Mass: Harvard University Press, 1939), 53–55.

[9] Gabriel de Llobet, *Foix médiéval: recherches d'histoire urbaine* (Foix, n.d.) and Paris, Bibliothèque Nationale, Collection Doat, vol. 26, fols. 40ʳ–56ᵛ.

Temple attended the funeral of Catherine of Valois, Philip the Fair's sister-in-law.[10] The next day, October 13, Molay, along with the rest of the Templars throughout the kingdom of France, was arrested by the king's agents and charged with heinous crimes against the faith. Four and a half years later Pope Clement V abolished the order. And two years after that Molay went to the stake, condemned as a heretic but insisting on his innocence and that of the order as a whole.

These two incidents paint a contradictory picture of French royal power at the beginning of the fourteenth century. On the one hand, Philip IV was able to bring about the destruction of an ancient military order founded in the aftermath of the First Crusade, an order that had accumulated property throughout western Europe and which for over two hundred years had been the hard core of the defense of the kingdom of Jerusalem. Many of its members had died as martyrs at Hittin, Mansurah, and Acre. On the other hand, his agents were harried, beaten and robbed by outraged taxpayers.

The destruction of the Templars is the most striking example of how allegations of fantastic wrong doing figured in the high politics of early fourteenth-century France. But the Templars were not the first to have had such charges levied against them. This honor went to Bernard Saisset, bishop of Pamiers.[11] Bernard had been abbot of the monastery of Saint-Antonin in the city of Pamiers. When the diocese of Pamiers was carved out of that of Toulouse in 1295, he became its first bishop. Determined and belligerent, Saisset by 1300 had behind him a long history of quarrels with his neighbors. On the one hand, he was at odds with the bishop of Toulouse over the delimitation of the borders of his new diocese. On the other, he was engaged in a protracted dispute with the counts of Foix over their rights in Pamiers. To block the counts' aspirations, Saisset had in 1269, while still abbot of Saint-Antonin, prevailed on Louis IX to assume co-dominion with him over the city. But the counts did not abandon their claims. When in 1295 the royal garrison withdrew from Pamiers there ensued a confused period of raids,

    [10] H. Géraud, ed., *Chronique latine de Guillaume de Nangis de 1113 à 1300 avec les continuations de cette chronique de 1300 à 1368*, 2 vols. (Paris: J. Renouard et cie, 1843), 1: 360; Malcolm Barber, *The Trial of the Templars* (Cambridge: Cambridge University Press, 1978), 47.

    [11] J.-M. Vidal, "Bernard Saisset, évêque de Pamiers (1232–1311)," *Revue des Sciences Religieuses* 5 (1925): 416–438, 565–590; 6 (1926): 50–77, 177–198, 371–393 and Georges Digard, *Philippe le Bel et le Saint-Siège de 1285 à 1304*, 2 vols. (Paris: Librairie du Recueil Sirey, société anonyme, 1936), 2:51–79, 82–92.

sieges, murder, and arson as Count Roger Bernard III tried to enforce his claims in the city. Through all of this Philip IV did little to assist Saisset. A compromise between the bishop and the count was finally arranged through the arbitration, not of the king, but of the lord of Mirepoix.

Saisset thus had little reason to feel much gratitude to Philip. His opinion of the king seems to have become distinctly sour. At least by 1301 Philip was receiving reports that Saisset was a traitor. According to these, the bishop had tried to persuade a number of the leading aristocrats of Languedoc to rebel against the king. One of these was Roger Bernard, the count of Foix, to whom Bernard held out the possibility of being the avenger of the people of the south, oppressed by the French.[12] Saisset's approach to the count, however, proved costly. The count informed the bishop of Toulouse; the bishop in turn informed the king. In May 1301 two royal *enquêteurs*, Richard le Neveu, archdeacon of Auge, and Jean de Picquigny, *vidame* of Amiens, were sent south to investigate. Picquigny, after having collected more testimony, went to Pamiers. There during the night of August 11–12 he rousted the bishop out of bed to summon him to appear before a royal court the following day. All of the bishop's temporal goods were seized, and his residence ransacked in search of incriminating evidence.[13] The bishop's chamberlain, treasurer, and *viguier* were arrested and carted off to Toulouse. There they were joined in prison by the *damoiseau* Raimond de Benauges. If one can believe Saisset's protestations, Picquigny had them brutally tortured; Raimond de Benauges' arms were broken and his life was despaired of. All but Raimond were persuaded to give evidence against their master.[14]

The bishop was escorted north under humiliating conditions to answer to the king. On 24 October 1301 he appeared before Philip at Senlis. The meeting, held in the presence of numerous nobles and ecclesiastics, was tumultuous, full of threats of physical violence against the bishop. Saisset was accused of treason, sedition, and other crimes. It was also alleged that he was a manifest heretic. Among other things, he had spoken against the sacrament of penance and maintained that

---

[12] Pierre Dupuy, *Histoire du différend d'entre le pape Boniface VIII et Philippe le Bel roy de France* (1655; reprint ed., Tucson: Audax Press, 1963), 633–634.

[13] Dupuy, *Histoire*, p. 652. Dupuy's transcriptions are often defective; see Digard, *Philippe le Bel*, 2: 59 n. 3.

[14] Dupuy, *Histoire*, 652 and Digard, *Philippe le Bel*, 2:59.

fornication committed by people in holy orders was not a sin. He had also asserted that Pope Boniface had acted against truth and justice in canonizing Louis IX, who was residing in hell. Moreover, King Louis had prophesied that in the time of his grandson his descendants would lose the kingdom, which would be ruled by a different dynasty.[15] Saisset had also asserted that the king, who issued false coin, was a counterfeiter.[16] Ironically, in light of what was to come, he was denounced for having called Pope Boniface VIII a "devil incarnate."[17]

Thus began a protracted affair which pitted the papacy against the French crown, and which finally issued in the infamous assault on Boniface VIII at Anagni. As this greater quarrel developed, Philip lost interest in Saisset. By 1302 the bishop had been released from captivity and had made his way to Rome. By late 1305 he had returned to his diocese.

Although some accusations against Saisset, especially those involving heresy, smack of the fantastic, such charges played a relatively minor role in the campaign against him. But with the affair of another bishop, Guichard of Troyes, we enter deeply into the realm of the chimerical.[18] Guichard was the son of a peasant, who had risen to become abbot of Montier-la-Celle, a member of the Parlement of Paris, and finally, in 1298, bishop of Troyes. He was also a confidant of Blanche de Champagne, widow of Theobald III, count of Champagne, and of her daughter Jeanne, the king's wife.

In 1300 his lucky streak ran out. In that year Jean de Calais, a canon of the cathedral of Troyes, and a former treasurer of the count of Champagne and administrator of Queen Blanche's dower lands, came under suspicion for various crimes while in office. The queen had him arrested and entrusted to the bishop's custody. Jean escaped and fled to

---

[15] Dupuy, *Histoire*, 635, 638.

[16] Dupuy, *Histoire*, 633. One of the witnesses against Saisset, Iacobus de Molino of Pamiers, claimed to have been present when 4,000 *livres* of Tours were paid over by the count of Foix to the bishop as part of their peace agreement. He said that he had heard the bishop say of the king's money: "Audi, dixit idem Episcopus, Comes credit quod ego multum curem de ista pecunia, quam mihi soluit, quam facit Rex, sed ego in tota illa pecunia non darem stercus, quia praua et falsa est, et sine lege, et falsum qui eam faciet fieri, nec in Curia romana daret homo vnum stercus in ista pecunia."

[17] Dupuy, *Histoire*, 628–630.

[18] Abel Rigault, *Le Procès de Guichard, évêque de Troyes (1308–1313)* (Paris: A. Picard et fils, 1896), pp. 300–313; Jean Favier, *Philippe le Bel* (Paris: Fayard, 1978), 456–461.

Italy. Guichard was accused of accepting a bribe to let him escape, a charge that the fugitive himself confirmed from exile.[19]

When Queen Blanche died in 1302, Guichard was accused of having poisoned her. Fortunately for Guichard, despite the best efforts of his enemies, the investigation of these charges petered out. But in 1308 more crimes were laid at his door. He was accused of consorting with a witch. More important, he was said to have used magic to bring about the death of Queen Jeanne in 1305. He had had a waxen image of the queen made. This he baptized; then he stuck a pin into its head, broke the image into pieces, and cast them into a fire.[20] He was also said to have personally prepared a poison compounded of toads, scorpions, and spiders with which to kill various princes of the realm.[21]

Guichard was arrested and several members of his entourage were questioned. Vigorous application of torture produced the desired confessions.[22] The image of the bishop that emerged from these coerced confessions was as monstrous as it was fantastic. He was the son of an incubus that had impregnated his mother.[23] He was a murderer and a thief, a simoniac, a sodomite, usurer, forger, and counterfeiter.[24] Despite his predilection for sodomy he had nevertheless had a son by a nun, whom he had subsequently had murdered. He had conjured up the devil, who had appeared in the form of a flying monk with horns on the front of his head.[25] He was a heretic; he spat on the cross. But, as in the case of Bishop Saisset, the royal government eventually lost interest in him. After repeated protests from Pope Clement V, Guichard was handed over to the pope for safekeeping in Avignon. Ultimately, he was transferred from the see of Troyes to the see of Diakovar in Bosnia, a post he probably never occupied, and which he resigned soon after the election of Pope John XXII. He died in January 1317.

Philip and his advisors pursued not only French bishops, but the pope himself. The arrest of Bishop Saisset eventually brought Philip and Boniface VIII into conflict. In this struggle with the head of the church, the king and his ministers made use once again of fantastic

---

[19] Jean de Calais was later reported to have stated on his deathbed that Guichard played no role in his escape.

[20] Rigault, *Guichard*, 75–81.

[21] Rigault, *Guichard*, 81–89, 277.

[22] Rigault, *Guichard*, 92–94.

[23] Rigault, *Guichard*, 283–284.

[24] Rigault, *Guichard*, 284–287.

[25] Rigault, *Guichard*, 74–75.

allegations, but this time on a much grander scale. In January 1302 Philip received from Boniface the toughly worded bull, *Ausculta Fili*. In it the pope set out a lengthy list of grievances against the king and announced that he was summoning the prelates of the French church to Rome. The king's ministers promptly burned this letter. Free of the inconvenience of the actual text, they circulated a forgery, *Deum Time*. In this Boniface was made to say unambiguously that the king of France was subject to the pope in both spiritualities and temporalities.[26]

A host of accusations was leveled against the pope by the king's advisors. To quote T.S.R. Boase's eloquent summation of the charges, the pope is "an open materialist, having no belief in the immortality of the soul, and holding that all happiness was found in this world; he does not believe in transubstantiation and never pays honour to the host during mass; he neglects all fasts; he refuses confession to prisoners, and forces clerks to reveal the secrets of the confessional; he has approved a book by Arnold of Vilanova, condemned as heretical by the University of Paris; he condones all sexual sins, and commits most of them; he keeps a private demon and consults sorcerers; he has clerks executed in his presence urging on the executioners; he murdered Celestine [his predecessor as pope] and imprisoned all who questioned his abdication; he makes money of everything and declares that the pope cannot be a simonist; he has caused the loss of the Holy Land through using the funds for other purposes: he breaks legal marriages and has made a married nephew a cardinal; he has set up silver images of himself in the churches, so that people should worship him; he treats all Frenchmen as Patarines; he has often repeated that he would gladly lose the church to ruin France, that he will make martyrs of all Frenchmen, and that he would rather be a dog or an ass than belong to that country."[27]

Armed with these allegations, the king and his government took steps to rally public opinion. At a general assembly of the realm in April 1302, Pierre Flotte, the king's minister, denounced the pope. The laity at the council, refusing to recognize Boniface as a legitimate pope, wrote to the cardinals in Rome demanding that they depose him.[28] In the following months public opinion was further massaged. On 24 June at an assembly in the gardens of the Louvre the bishop of Orléans

---

[26] Thomas S.R. Boase, *Boniface VIII* (London: Constable, 1933), 301–303.
[27] This is Boase's summary of Guillaume de Plaisians' speech on April 14, 1303, Boase, *Boniface*, 333–334.
[28] Boase, *Boniface*, 334.

and some mendicants spoke against the pope, and a citizen of Paris announced that the estates of the kingdom and of the city of Paris had endorsed the charges against him.

In reply Boniface VIII drew up a bull, to be published on September 8, excommunicating the king and releasing his subjects from their allegiance to him. On September 7, however, one of Philip's agents, Guillaume de Nogaret, together with Italian enemies of the pope, seized Boniface in the town of Anagni. After three days of fighting, rioting, looting, and debates between Nogaret, who wanted to take Boniface to France to stand trial for his alleged misdeeds, and Sciarra Colonna, a member of a family with a virulent enmity to Boniface, who wanted to kill him, the townspeople rescued the pope and drove his attackers out.[29] A few weeks later, on October 12, the pope was dead.

Philip pursued him even in death. In 1310, at the king's demand, Pope Clement V began an investigation into the charges against Boniface. However, by this time the king had become more interested in his effort to destroy the Templars. In February 1311 Philip informed Clement V that he would leave the pope to resolve the investigation as he saw fit. Ultimately, the pope declared that the king of France had acted from good motives.[30]

And so we have come back to the Templars. A month before the arrest of Molay and his colleagues, Philip IV on September 14, 1307, sent a secret letter to all his *baillis* and *sénéchaux*. In it he announced that he had learned from men "worthy of faith" that the members of the Order of the Temple were crucifying Christ anew: "A bitter thing, a lamentable thing, a thing which is horrible to contemplate, terrible to hear of, a detestable crime, an execrable evil, an abominable work, a detestable disgrace, a thing almost inhuman, indeed set apart from all humanity."[31]

According to the accusations, the Templars, when received into the order, denied Christ three times and spat upon his image. They were

---

[29] Boase, *Boniface VIII*, 341–351. A more recent discussion of these events is in Agostino Paravicini Bagliani, *Boniface VIII: un pape hérétique?* (Paris: Payot, 2003), 299–391.

[30] The whole dreary investigation can be followed in Jean Coste, ed., *Boniface VIII en procès: articles d'accusation et dépositions des témoins (1303–1311)* (Rome: L'Erma di Bretschneider: Fondazione Camillo Caetani, 1995). See also Boase, *Boniface VIII*, 297–379.

[31] From the order for the Templars' arrest, issued 14 September 1307; Georges Lizerand, ed. and trans., *Le Dossier de l'affaire des Templiers* (Paris: Société d'edition "Les Belles Lettres," 1964), 16. Translation from Barber, *Trial*, p. 45.

then stripped naked and kissed by the Templar in charge of the reception on the lower spine, the navel, and finally on the mouth, "in shame of human dignity." They were also instructed to engage in sexual relations with other members of the order whenever required to do so. And finally they had turned to the worship of idols.[32]

On 24 October Molay appeared before the inquisitor of France, Guillaume de Paris, who also happened to be the king's confessor. He admitted that during his reception into the order he had denied Christ and spat, not on an image of Christ on the cross, but on the ground next to it.[33] The Grand Master's act of self-incrimination was the beginning of seven years of captivity. During this period the French monarchy rolled out an impressive campaign to demonstrate that the Templars, both as individuals and as an order, were guilty of the monstrous crimes of which they had been accused.

Coercive imprisonment and torture on a grand scale were employed to extract confessions. Templars were kept chained up, shackled to their prison walls, and fed only on bread and water.[34] One Templar claimed to have been interrogated while weights were hung on his genitals.[35] Another asserted to papal commissioners that his feet had been held to a fire so long that the flesh of his heels had burned away and bones had fallen out, a fact he demonstrated by producing a pair of small bones for the commissioners' inspection.[36]

While the Templars were persuaded to confess, efforts were made to sway public opinion. In the days immediately following the Templars' arrest the king's servants held meetings with various ecclesiastics and inhabitants of the city of Paris. Jacques de Molay repeated his confession in the presence of masters of the University of Paris.[37] In May 1308 at a great assembly of the realm held at Tours the assembled delegates declared that the Templars deserved death for their crimes.[38]

The king's allies did not shrink from judicial murder. In November 1309 commissioners charged by Pope Clement V with investigating the corporate guilt of the order began holding hearings in the

---

[32] Lizerand, *Dossier*, 16–29; Barber, *Trial*, 45.
[33] Lizerand, *Dossier*, 32–37.
[34] K. Schotmüller, *Der Untergang des Templer-Ordens*, 2 vols. (Berlin: Ernst Siegfried Mittler & Sohn, 1887), 2:67, 69.
[35] Jules Michelet, ed., *Procès des Templiers*, 2 vols. (Paris: Impr. royale, 1841–1851), 1:218.
[36] Michelet, *Procès des Templiers*, 1: 5.
[37] Barber, *Trial*, 63–64.
[38] Barber, *Trial*, 84–88.

hall of the bishop of Paris' residence. Hoping for a relatively unbiased hearing, Templars by the hundreds offered to present a defense of the order.[39] This movement was crushed by the archbishop of Senlis, Philippe de Marigny.[40] In May 1310 he convened a council in Paris to judge those Templars resident in his province. Fifty-four brothers who had offered to defend the order were condemned as relapsed heretics. The papal commissioners tried to prevent their execution but failed. On May 11 the Templars were burned outside the walls of Paris. As a contemporary chronicler noted, "all of them, with no exception, finally acknowledged none of the crimes imputed to them, but constantly persisted in the general denial, saying always that they were being put to death without cause and unjustly; which indeed many of the people were able to observe by no means without great admiration and surprise."[41] In the next few days more executions followed. The defense of the order collapsed. Ultimately in 1312 Pope Clement V, under pressure from Philip IV, declared the order abolished.

But Jacques de Molay had one more role to play. On 18 March 1314, before the doors of the cathedral of Notre Dame and in the presence of a commission of three cardinals, Molay and three other Templars were sentenced to perpetual imprisonment for their crimes. However, Molay and Geoffroi de Charney, the preceptor of the order of the Temple in Normandy, repudiated their confessions. The cardinals turned the two over to the provost of Paris until they could discuss what to do. When Philip IV learned of what had happened, however, he ordered the immediate execution of Molay and Charney. They were taken to a small island in the Seine and burned. A contemporary chronicler noted, "They were seen to be so prepared to sustain the fire with easy mind and will that they brought from all those who saw them much admiration and surprise for the constancy of their death and final denial…"[42]

Many historians have noticed the recurrent pattern of allegations of sodomy, heresy, and demon worship that Philip used against his enemies. Indeed, this pattern of what often seems a cynical manipulation

---

[39] Barber, *Trial*, 130–133.
[40] The archbishop was the brother of the king's chief minister, Enguerrand de Marigny, and owed his position to the king's favor.
[41] Géraud, *Chronique latine*, 1:377–378. Translation from Barber, *Trial*, 157.
[42] Géraud, *Chronique latine*, 1:402–404. Translation from Barber, *Trial*, 241.

of fantasies and dreams has been a troubling subject for the king's historians.[43] At times it is difficult to regard Philip as anything other than an opportunistic thug, ready to use whatever means were at hand to attain his ends. Yet, for E.A.R. Brown, who has delved deeply into the question of Philip's character, Philip was a much more complex figure. As she puts it, Philip was a "captious, sternly moralistic, literalistically scrupulous, humorless, stubborn, aggressive, and vindictive individual, who feared the eternal consequences of his temporal deeds."[44]

I will not speculate on the psychology of a man dead for almost 700 years. Instead, I want to step back and look at what we might call the "style" of Philip's rule. Reflection on this aspect of his regime helps throw some light on the contrasting images of the king's government as simultaneously strong and weak. I will argue that in dealing with at least some of his political opponents, Philip engaged in a type of government by terror. This may seem a startling conclusion about a man who has been labeled by one eminent historian a "constitutional king."[45] But thinking about Philip's rule as involving an element of terror helps us understand the conflicting images of royal power in early fourteenth-century France.

My argument relies heavily on the work of E.V. Walter. Walter has explored the phenomenon of rule by terror through a study of the expansionist nineteenth-century Zulu kingdom. For Walter, terrorism or organized terror is not a single entity. Instead it is a process, involving the act of violence itself, the emotional reactions to that act, and its social consequences.[46] Walter also makes a key distinction between "systems of terror" and "zones of terror." A "*system of terror* may be broadly defined to include certain states of war as well as certain political communities, as long as the term refers to a sphere of relationships controlled by the terror process. To designate such a sphere as a 'system of terror,' however, implies that all the individuals within it are involved, in one role or another, actually or potentially in the ter-

---

[43] See, for example, the tangles into which his two principal biographers get themselves: Joseph R. Strayer, *The Reign of Philip the Fair* (Princeton: Princeton University Press, 1980), 287–292, and Favier, *Philippe le Bel*, 443–449.

[44] Elizabeth A.R. Brown, "The Prince is Father of the King: The Character and Childhood of Philip the Fair of France," *Mediaeval Studies* 49 (1987): 315.

[45] Joseph R. Strayer, "Philip the Fair—A 'Constitutional' King," in *Medieval Statecraft and the Perspectives of History* (Princeton: Princeton University Press, 1971), 195–212.

[46] E.V. Walter, *Terror and Resistance: A Study of Political Violence, with Case Studies of Some Primitive African Communities* (Oxford: Oxford University Press, 1969), 5.

ror process." In the case of societies where terror is applied only to a specific category of people, such as criminals, slaves, particular ethnic groups, etc., it is more appropriate to speak of a "zone of terror." Outside this zone, "power relations follow the rules of an ordinary system of authority."[47] Yet at times, "instead of relying entirely on authority, conventional rules, and legitimate techniques, the men in power ... choose to initiate the process of terror. The form may be called a *regime of terror* ..."[48]

Walter's typology cannot be applied mechanically to early fourteenth-century France. Philip the Fair certainly did not preside over a "system of terror." To say that he created a "zone of terror" may also be an overstatement. Yet it is clear that at times Philip and his advisors carved out a zone where the normal rules of politics did not apply, where fear and force, even if garbed in a cloak of legitimacy, prevailed.

The overwhelming majority of Philip's interactions with his subjects fell within "conventional rules" and "legitimate techniques." At most times Philip was, as Joseph R. Strayer has put it, a sort of "constitutional" king: "Philip tried to conform to the traditions of the French monarchy and the practices of the French government. As far as possible, he governed the realm through a well-established system of courts and administrative officials. He always asked the advice of responsible men; he was influenced by that advice in working out the details of his general policy. He tried to stay at least within the letter of the law; he tried to observe the customs of the kingdom. When he had to go beyond established custom he always sought to justify his action and to obtain the consent of those who were affected."[49]

Philip was serious about his role as a sacral king. He portrayed himself as embodying the loftiest ideas of Christian kingship. As E.A.R. Brown has put it, "One of the most striking aspects of the declarations that emanated from Philip's court was the unprecedented insistence on the connection between the king's causes and those of God and Jesus Christ."[50] Philip himself declared that no other kingdom abounded in "such peace, such regard for justice, such prosperity, such happiness" as did France. This prosperity derived from "a highly developed regard for

---

[47] Walter, *Terror*, 6.
[48] Walter, *Terror*, 7.
[49] Strayer, "Constitutional King," 209.
[50] Brown, "The Prince is Father," 288.

justice, from which in turn, by the grace of God, has come the fullness
of our peace."[51]

So, how to account for this strange mixture of terror, "constitu-
tionalism," and deep regard for the norms of Christian kingship? In
answering this question, we should remember that being a king in the
early fourteenth century was no easy task. Throughout much of western Europe kings had made themselves the effective leaders of political
society. Much was now expected of them, but the tools they had with
which to fulfill those expectations were limited. Philip's reign came at
the end of a long period of institutional development of the French
monarchy.[52] His government had more capacity to effect its will than
those of his predecessors, but it was nevertheless constrained by many
factors.

To borrow some social science terminology, we can say that Philip's
government had a low degree of what is known as autonomy from its
social formation.[53] When a state has a high degree of autonomy from
other institutions in society, it can become a social actor in its own right,
endowed with its own interests apart from those of any particular social
class, prepared to and capable of acting contrary to the wishes of those
classes that are socially and economically dominant.[54]

One could argue that medieval royal governments had a relatively
high degree of autonomy. Royal governments were in important respects the personal responsibilities of kings. Royal servants were the
king's personal agents, freely chosen by him and answerable only to
him. They thus may have had an unusually high capacity to act contrary to the interests of the politically and economically dominant
classes.

---

[51] Joseph R. Strayer, "France: The Holy Land, the Chosen People, and the Most
Christian King," in *Medieval Statecraft and the Perspectives of History* (Princeton: Princeton
University Press, 1971), 310–311.

[52] A staple of textbook generalizations: see Elizabeth A. Hallam, *Capetian France, 987–
1328* (London: Longman, 1980), 156–161, 239–247, 291–297. See also Strayer, *Reign*, 100–
236.

[53] Theda Skocpol, *States and Social Revolutions: A Comparative Analysis of France, Russia,
and China* (Cambridge: Cambridge University Press, 1979), 24–33.

[54] Stephen D. Krasner, "Approaches to the State: Alternative Conceptions and
Historical Dynamics," *Comparative Politics* 16 (1984): 230–240; Martin Carnoy, *The State
and Political Theory* (Princeton: Princeton University Press, 1984), pp. 54–55, 108–109,
200–202; Nicos Poulantzas, *Political Power and Social Classes*, trans. Timothy O'Hagan
(London: Sheed and Ward, 1973), 255–321.

On the other hand, the autonomy of the medieval state seems to have been relatively limited. Kings were definitely members of a particular social class, the land-owning aristocracy. Like other aristocrats, their economic well-being depended to a large degree on their capacity to extract surplus from the peasants living on their estates. The techniques they used to do this did not differ qualitatively from those of other aristocrats. Kings thus shared the interests of the dominant class in a direct and personal fashion. Moreover, kings were bound to other members of the aristocracy by many personal ties, including those of vassalage and marriage. They participated in an aristocratic culture that was largely closed to members of other classes. Finally, their governments were staffed primarily by members of the aristocracy.

Ironically, the very success that the Capetians had enjoyed by 1300 in systematizing and institutionalizing their political authority also constrained their zone of political maneuver. The development of a more defined and far-reaching legal system paradoxically restrained royal options in the field of justice. The king had the duty to do justice, but that duty was more and more circumscribed by precedent, ordinances, and the theorizing of a self-conscious legal profession with a high regard for itself. If a king wanted to appear to rule "justly," there were bounds to what actions he could take. In short, the growth in the size of the kingdom and the sophistication of its government inevitably created a dense "web of resistance" to royal desires and goals.[55] Philip thus found the space in which he could maneuver relatively narrow, and he had a lot of problems with which to deal.

It would be an exaggeration to say that Philip and his dynasty faced a crisis of legitimization, the favored breeding ground for systems of terror,[56] but he and his policies were disliked by many of his subjects. Perhaps nothing annoyed them so much as his constant chase after

---

[55] Walter, *Terror*, p. 17: "An established power system is a web of resistances as well as a circuit of control, and innovators aflame with the *libido dominandi* often take drastic measures to cut through the web." On the complex and shifting nature of the role of kings' will in shaping justice, see J.C. Holt, *Magna Carta* (Cambridge: Cambridge University Press, 1965) and J.E.A. Jolliffe, *Angevin Kingship* (New York: Barnes and Noble, 1955).

[56] Several years ago Edward Peters observed that the digesting of new ideas about political society in the fourteenth and fifteenth centuries "witnessed a crisis of rulership during which the question of who would profit most from the new theories, the king or the commonwealth, seems to have been in considerable doubt." Edward Peters, *The Shadow King: Rex Inutilis in Medieval Law and Literature, 751–1327* (New Haven, Conn: Yale University Press, 1970), 214.

cash. The expedients devised to bring in money for the king's military projects alienated many, and troubled the king's own conscience.[57] The tactics sometimes used by royal commissioners more resembled brigandage than the orderly execution of a state duty.[58] In 1306 Philip's manipulation of the kingdom's coinage touched off riots in Châlons, Laon, and Paris. In Paris rioters forced the king to take refuge in the Temple.[59] In 1314, despite a last-minute agreement with the Flemings, Philip's failure to stop collection of a tax granted for a prospective war with Flanders led to widespread unrest in the period immediately after his death.[60]

Some questioned Philip's fitness to rule. Bishop Saisset was reported to have said that Philip was the handsomest man in the world, but did nothing except stare at men.[61] Bernard Délicieux, a Franciscan friar who led a major anti-inquisitorial movement in the first years of the fourteenth century, claimed that Philip was of no use to his subjects, being more like a pig who wanted nothing else than always to be with his wife than a king. Moreover, the king was more interested in money than justice.[62] Even within the ranks of dedicated supporters of the Capetian dynasty there were dark thoughts about Philip. Jean de Joinville, companion and biographer of Louis IX, at the time of Louis's canonization in 1297 made the pointed comment that the sainted king's acts promised "great honor to those of his line who were like him in doing well, and equal dishonor to those descendants who did not choose to follow him in performing good works; great dishonor, indeed, to those of his line pursuing the paths of evil, since people would point to them and say that the sainted king from whom they were

---

[57] Elizabeth A.R. Brown, "Taxation and Morality in the Thirteenth and Fourteenth Centuries: Conscience and Political Power and the Kings of France," *French Historical Studies* 8 (1973): 17.

[58] Charles-Victor Langlois, "Les doléances des communautés du Toulousain contre Pierre de Latilli et Raoul de Breuilli (1297–1298)," *Revue Historique* 95 (1907): 23–53.

[59] Favier, *Philippe*, 164–166, 201–202.

[60] Brown, "Taxation and Morality," 19.

[61] Dupuy, *Histoire, Preuves*, 653. This statement should be treated with some caution, coming from the proceedings against Bishop Saisset, which, as we have seen, contain a good deal of the fantastic in them.

[62] Alan Friedlander, ed., *Processus Bernardi Delitiosi: The Trial of Fr. Bernard Délicieux, 3 September–8 December 1319* (Transactions of the American Philosophical Society, 86, pt. 1) (Philadelphia: American Philosophical Society, 1996), fols. 71^r–71^v (pp. 116–117). See Friedlander's biography of Délicieux, which replaces all previous work: *The Hammer of the Inquisitors: Brother Bernard Délicieux and the Struggle against the Inquisition in Fourteenth-Century France* (Leiden: Brill, 1999).

sprung would never have committed such evil."[63] It is hard to imagine that Joinville was speaking of anyone other than Louis's grandson, Philip IV. To us, at a distance of seven centuries, Philip may appear a "constitutional" king and a major architect of the French monarchy's governing structure, but to many of his subjects he, or at least his agents, appeared more like reiving brigands than the agents of a "most Christian king."[64]

To summarize, to be a king in the late thirteenth and early four-teenth centuries was no easy task. Aspirations and expectations were grand, but the kingdom was an immense patchwork of individuals and institutions that hampered the king and his agents at practically every turn. Philip knew many successes, but he also knew failure. His reign was a balancing act amidst a host of other power actors: great lords, churchmen, town governments, village communities, and his own nascent bureaucracy. The actual business of governing was messy and carried on in the face of obstructionism, foot-dragging, and endless, petty, and sometimes not so petty, challenges.[65]

Under these circumstances it becomes easier to understand why Philip and his ministers may have created a zone of terror, with its fan-tastic allegations of chimerical crimes. Whether Philip and his agents actually believed the charges they leveled against their victims is, of course, at the distance of seven hundred years, impossible to ascer-tain. Perhaps they did; perhaps they didn't. But the charges of heresy, sodomy, idolatry, and trafficking with demons were by their very nature difficult to refute. Paradoxically, to prove that one is innocent, not only of an act that one has not committed, but that no one has ever com-mitted, is not an easy task.[66] To the politically active part of the king-dom's population, the very outlandishness of the accusations may have

---

[63] Brown, "The Prince is Father," 320.

[64] Langlois, "Doléances," 23–53. Cf. the remarks on the contemporary English royal government and its dealings with its subjects in J.R. Maddicott, *The English Peasantry and the Demands of the Crown, 1294–1341* (Oxford: Past and Present Society, 1975).

[65] See, for example, the events surrounding the anti-inquisitorial campaign in the south of France; Friedlander, *Processus*, fols. 226^r–226^v, 233^r–233^v (pp. 246–247, 252).

[66] On this phenomenon with regards to charges that Jews committed ritual murder, see Gavin I. Langmuir, "Thomas of Monmouth: Detector of Ritual Murder," in *Toward a Definition of Antisemitism* (Los Angeles and Berkeley: University of California Press, 1990), 209–236 and, in the same volume, Gavin I. Langmuir, "The Knight's Tale of Young Hugh of Lincoln," 237–262. That medieval Europe had no monopoly on such thinking, see Lawrence Wright's *Remembering Satan* (New York: Knopf, 1994) for a discussion of events in late twentieth-century America.

made them more believable. For who would believe that the *rex chris-tianissimus* would invent such allegations?[67] Charges of fantastic wrong doing were particularly useful against ecclesiastics, members of a trans-national institution and the carriers of the ideas that legitimized royal rule.

More importantly, the campaigns against these fantastic enemies also helped portray the monarchy as competent and effective. Some of Philip's real enemies—the Flemings, the English, angry tax-payers, etc.—were not so easy to deal with. Contending with them was a frus-trating, protracted process, one in which it was difficult for a man to make himself appear a capable monarch. But once the king and his ministers escaped the trammels of reality and entered the world of fan-tasy, they fought on a terrain where victory was relatively easy.[68] When one fights with phantom enemies guilty of non-existent crimes, there is no conceivable objective standard for measuring whether they have actually been defeated or not. The temptation to accept authority's claims of success against non-existent, but terrifying, enemies can be very strong.

Philip was fortunate in that he did not simply have to proclaim the guilt of his opponents. Legal developments in the thirteenth century had given him and other rulers a tool that allowed them to extract a confession from almost anyone. This was the procedure by inquisition, with its frequent recourse to torture. Moreover, in the case of the Templars there could be invoked the inquisition of heretical depravity, where many of the normal procedures of canon law were ignored.[69] The ability of a judge to proceed with an investigation without a formal accusation being lodged against the suspect and to use torture enabled the king and his ministers to procure whatever admissions of guilt were needed. The trappings of legality could be maintained while the accused were deprived of any effective means of demonstrating their

---

[67] Many contemporaries, like Giovanni Villani, doubted the truth of the charges against the Templars, and believed that it had been greed and rancor that had led to the attack on the order. R.E. Selfe and P.H. Wicksteed, *Selections from the First Nine Books of the Croniche Fiorentine of Giovanni Villani*, trans. by R.E. Selfe and P.H. Wicksteed (London: Archibald Constable and Co., 1896), 378; cited in Barber, *Trial*, 230. But what mattered was public opinion in France, which largely supported the king.

[68] Christina Larner, *Enemies of God: The Witch-hunt in Scotland* (London: Chatto and Windus, 1981), 195, makes a similar observation, remarking that the persecution of witches helped solidify the legitimacy of early modern states.

[69] James Given, "The Inquisitors of Languedoc and the Medieval Technology of Power," *American Historical Review* 94 (1989), 336–359.

innocence. Even the burning of those Templars who offered to defend the order before papal commissioners in Paris, an act that crushed effective resistance to the king among the surviving Templars, could be dressed in the mantle of legality.[70]

Although victory over phantom enemies may not seem very significant to us, to the subjects of Philip IV it may well have been very satisfying. If nothing else, it made for magnificent propaganda. Much of what rulers do is theatrical. Their acts are intended not so much to achieve real effects as to demonstrate that right order prevails in the world, that the shared universe of moral values endures.[71] Philip, in pursuing his fantastic enemies, spectacularly reaffirmed the kingdom's solidarity and restored the sacred moral order.

Philip saw himself, and was seen by his subjects, as a sacral king. In reality he was a sacral king constrained on all sides by determined enemies, recalcitrant subjects, and, paradoxically, his dynasty's very success in building administrative organs that canalized political activity through certain normatively governed institutions. However, in the realm of fantasy, he was invincible. By triumphing over chimerical enemies he could truly appear, at least for a few moments, to be that which the abbot of Cluny called him in 1294, "the leader...of the cause of God and the church and the fighter for all of Christendom."[72]

---

[70] In many ways, E.V. Walters's words about the Zulu kingdom apply equally well to early fourteenth-century France: "The conditions of legality imply that there must be a way of being innocent. If there is no path left open to avoid transgression, or if people are bound to be charged falsely with offenses they did not commit, then it is not possible to be innocent. In the terror process, no one can be secure, for the category of transgression is, in reality, abolished. Anyone may be a victim, no matter what action he chooses. Innocence is irrelevant." Walter, *Terror*, 26.

[71] Emile Durkheim, *Moral Education: A Study in the Theory and Application of the Sociology of Education*, trans. Everett K. Wilson and Herman Schnurer (New York: Free Press of Glencoe, 1961), 162. See also Clifford Geertz, *Negara: The Theatre State in Nineteenth-Century Bali* (Princeton: Princeton University Press, 1980).

[72] Strayer, "France," 308.

AFTERTHOUGHTS ON
THE ORIGINS OF EUROPEAN DISSENT

R.I. Moore

Nothing is more important to historians (*qua* historians) than that colleagues should find their conclusions worth thinking about.[1] That a first
and therefore favorite book[2] should seem after a quarter of a century
to deserve discussion of the range and quality of the essays collected
in this volume is a source of extraordinary pleasure and reassurance to
its author. Yet it must be confessed that such claims as *The Origins of
European Dissent* may have upon continuing attention are almost entirely
the fruits of my ignorance of the subject when I first approached it, and
of my consequent innocence of the conceptual and historiographical
swamps that awaited those who would rush in. I came to the study of
popular heresy in the late 1960s almost entirely without knowledge, and
correspondingly, and as it turned out very fortunately, without preconceptions. Thanks to the vagaries of the Oxford curriculum my under-
graduate education in European History had terminated at 1153, with
the death of St. Bernard of Clairvaux. I had therefore missed out on
the Albigensian crusade, and the origins and early growth of the papal
inquisition, which were at that time the only contexts in which the history of popular heresy was considered at all interesting or significant.
Nor had I noticed Bernard's expedition to the Languedoc in 1145 to
preach against Henry of Lausanne, as I would have done if I had chosen the detailed study of his life and thought which was available as
a Special Subject in my final year. I had rightly preferred that of St.
Augustine, which introduced me not only to so many things necessary

---

[1] I have to express to the contributors to this volume, and especially to Michael
Frassetto, not only my warm appreciation of their papers, but my apology for the
length of time it has taken me to prepare this response, which has benefited greatly
from the scrutiny of A.E. Redgate.

[2] R.I. Moore, *The Birth of Popular Heresy* (London: Edward Arnold, 1975, reprinted
Toronto: University of Toronto Press, 1995) and *The Origins of European Dissent* (London:
Allen Lane, 1975, 2 ed. Oxford: Basil Blackwell, 1985, reprinted Toronto: University of
Toronto Press, 1994) were prepared and written together, and effectively constitute a
single work. They are cited below as, respectively, *BPH* and *OED*.

to the medievalist, but also to the profound, benign and enduring influence of Peter Brown. My work as a graduate student was directed, as it turned out abortively, to a partial edition of the cartulary of Fontevraud under the supervision of Pierre Chaplais. I abandoned that project in 1966, but it endowed me with an invaluable introduction to the diplomatic of charters and a lasting curiosity about Robert of Arbrissel.[3]

Together these legacies shaped my future work. At a time when medieval historians—perhaps especially ecclesiastical historians—were inclined to take narrative sources much more nearly at face value than they do now, the passionate and erudite scepticism of Chaplais taught me to approach all texts with a series of questions about the circumstances, preoccupations, and motives that had given rise to them, and to doubt whether there was any simple correspondence between the assertions that they contained and objective reality. Robert of Arbrissel's activity and reputation directed my attention for the first time to the shadowy and little understood heretical preachers with whom, I had begun to realize, he had been associated by some of his critics among the higher clergy. So when my colleague at the University of Sheffield, Edward Miller, asked me to contribute a volume to a new series of medieval sources in translation the heretics offered an attractive prospect, especially since I had recently come upon Jeffrey Burton Russell's *Dissent and Reform in the Early Middle Ages*,[4] which convinced me both that there was interesting material available for the study of popular heresy before the inquisition, and that material and topic alike had yet to be properly understood. On the other hand, and fortunately for myself, I was quite unaware that A.P. Evans had begun, and Walter L. Wakefield would shortly complete, the much more comprehensive work which was published a few years later as *Heresies of the High Middle Ages*,[5] and included not only translations of almost (though not quite) all the texts that I had selected for *The Birth of Popular Heresy* but

---

[3] The cartulary is now available as *Grand Cartulaire de Fontevraud*, ed. Jean-Marc Bienvenu avec la collaboration de Robert Favreau et Georges Pon, Archives historiques de Poitou 63, (Poiters: Société des Antiquaires de l'Ouest, 2000), and the sources for Robert are translated and annotated by Bruce Venarde, *Robert of Arbrissel: A Medieval Religious Life* (Washington D.C.: Catholic University Press of America, 2003).

[4] Jeffrey Burton Russell *Dissent and Reform in the Early Middle Ages* (Berkeley and Los Angeles: University of California Press, 1965).

[5] Walter L. Wakefield and Austin P. Evans, *Heresies of the High Middle Ages* (New York: Columbia University Press, 1969). For a further collection of translated texts, with greater attention to the legal context, see Edward M. Peters, *Heresy and Authority in Medieval Europe* (Philadelphia: University of Pennsylvania Press, 1980).

a historical introduction far superior to all previous accounts. If I had not almost finished my own translations when Wakefield and Evans appeared, and become irretrievably fascinated by their implications, I would not have thought my project worth beginning.

Russell was plainly correct in his principal assertion, that the meaning of the small body of texts which constituted the primary evidence for popular heresy in the eleventh and early twelfth centuries, and the nature and significance of the heresies they described, had been radically misinterpreted. Popular heresy had appeared in western Europe at the beginning of the eleventh century, for the first time since antiquity, and was denounced sporadically but increasingly by ecclesiastical and civil authorities throughout the twelfth. The accepted opinion of the Anglophone world (which rested almost entirely on the first volume of H.C. Lea's *History of the Inquisition in the Middle Ages* and Steven Runciman's *The Medieval Manichee*[6]) explained it as the first manifestation of the Cathar heresy whose eradication was the object of the Albigensian crusade launched against the County of Toulouse in 1209, and of the papal inquisition established at Toulouse in 1233. Catharism was believed to derive from the dualist heresies of the Byzantine world, especially that preached by Bogomil in mid-tenth-century Bulgaria, and to have been disseminated in the west by missionaries from the Balkans, from c. 1000. Russell demonstrated convincingly that a critical reading of the Latin sources could not sustain this interpretation of the heresies described in western Europe up to c. 1140, but I did not think that he had come up with a satisfying alternative account of what the heretic preachers believed, and still less of why they excited popular audiences and won devoted followers. There was nothing for it but to make a virtue of my ignorance, and avoid hindsight by translating the documents in chronological order, and only after doing so reading what historians had written from and about them. This was the principle upon which I produced *The Birth of Popular Heresy*, and then *The Origins of European Dissent*, my extended commentary on the documents which I had translated.

The ignorance with which I approached my task of translation extended not only to the history and historiography of popular heresy and the contexts in which it had attracted scholarly attention, but very

---

[6] Henry Charles Lea, *A History of the Inquisition of the Middle Ages* (3 vols, New York: Harper and Brothers, 1887); Steven Runciman, *The Medieval Manichee* (Cambridge: Cambridge University Press 1947).

largely to the Catholic (including the Anglican) culture and traditions by which they had been shaped, which were quite different from those of the essentially Presbyterian culture in which I grew up. I have no taste or talent for autobiography, and have been blessed with a profoundly uninteresting life, devoid of the privations and misfortunes that usually supply the materials and inspire the masterpieces of that genre. But fellow historians are entitled to know where I am coming from. I was born in Enniskillen, Northern Ireland, in 1941. My father was a civil servant, who had grown up on a small farm in the hard 1920s and '30s, and the first in his family to reach university. My mother is the daughter of a manufacturer of linen thread, whose business, like so many, had succumbed to the depression of those decades. They met at her family church, Belfast's First Presbyterian, which was, and is, Non-Subscribing, more widely known outside Northern Ireland as Unitarian. That is to say, it was one of a group of congregations which in 1722 emerged from a division in Presbyterianism between those who were and those who were not prepared to subscribe to the Westminster Confession of Faith.[7] Unitarianism requires of its members no avowal of any religious doctrine, and no acknowledgement of any religious authority.[8] Many Catholics and evangelical Protestants hold that Unitarians are "not Christians," the former because they are not obliged to believe in the divinity of Christ, the Holy Trinity and the sacraments, the latter because they do not insist upon the divine authorship of the scriptures. But Unitarians consider themselves Christians, and derive their culture,

---

[7] The statement of (Calvinist) belief drawn up by the Westminster Assembley of Divines (1643–1649) and accepted as authoritative by the Presbyterian churches. The objection of the Non-subscribers was to its imposition, not to its content. In Belfast it was those who wished to subscribe who formed a new congregation at the point of division. T. Moore, *A History of the First Presbyterian Church Belfast, 1644–1983* (Belfast: First Presbyterian Church, 1983), 23–25.

[8] Compare: "Dissent from Church doctrine remains what it is, dissent. As such it may not be proposed or received on an equal footing with the Church's authentic teaching." (John Paul II). It was Jeffery Burton Russell's comment, "Nor can the dissidents themselves escape responsibility [for religious persecution and the injustices associated with it]. If the Church acted with lack of charity towards the dissidents, the dissidents acted with arrogance towards the Church." (*Dissent and Reform in the Early Middle Ages*, p. 257) that first startled me into thinking of writing on heresy myself: hence "in exploring the appearance of unorthodox beliefs and practices in the eleventh and twelfth centuries... we must approach it not in the spirit of alienists (whether charitable or severe) patiently accounting for irrational deviations from normality, but as historians observing the emergence of a natural, even an essential, ingredient of human development..." (*OED*, 3).

ethics and beliefs as well as their religious practices from (Protestant) Christianity and from the Bible, especially the New Testament, and its teachings. Many Unitarians possess a strong religious faith of a traditionally Christian kind, and almost all of them are firmly (which in Northern Ireland has often meant courageously) liberal in their intellectual and political outlook.

All this meant that I grew up in a Christian, but not a hierarchical, evangelical or intellectually authoritarian environment. The excellent school which I attended from the age of eleven, the Royal Belfast Academical Institution, sprang from the same liberal tradition, imposed no religious tests, and was unaggressively but unambiguously secular in its teaching and culture. Each school morning, as the law then required, began with a short, non-sectarian but Christian assembly, which included the singing of hymns, the recital of prayers, and readings from the Bible; twice a week there were lessons in "Divinity" which largely rehearsed elements of the Christian tradition; and on many Sundays I attended the services of my parents' church. I cannot, however, recall any period of my life at which it appeared to me at all probable that the fundamental assertions of the Christian faith—as for example that there was a God, that he (*sic*) had a son who assumed human form, or that he had chosen at a particular moment in history to communicate directly with a particular group of people on earth—were true. Nor, more importantly, has this ever caused me, apart from a brief period in early adolescence, the slightest anxiety or concern. Augustine was right that the real difference is not between those who believe in God and those who do not, but between those who seek religious belief and those who are indifferent to it. I belong firmly in the latter category.[9] The religious quest has never been mine, and the word "spiritual" conveys about as much to me as "harmony" might if I were entirely tone-deaf. Except to the extent (which to a medieval historian is not inconsiderable) that it has limited my understanding of the thoughts and feelings of others, that has never troubled me in the least. On the contrary, the delight which a healthy adolescent raised among God-fearing people naturally took in Gibbon's majestic scepticism, or Ferdinand Lot's dismissal of religious faith as "une maladie de l'esprit,"

---

[9] When, after graduating, I asked Peter Brown why he had paired me for Oxford-style tutorials with a monk he replied "Because you need to learn to take religion seriously." The arrangement had worked out very well, but in that respect with only partial success.

was reinforced by the brutal contrast between the role of religious confession and affiliation in the humane and tolerant circles in which I
myself grew up, and in the wider society of Northern Ireland in the
1940s and '50s. For most of my life I have considered religious belief an
obvious delusion, at best an excuse for muddled thinking and at worst a
source and sanction of every kind of evil. Only slowly, and with continuing reservations, have I come to regard it also as capable of providing
a useful and apparently even a necessary language of social harmony,
and historically a vehicle for imaginative and subtle exploration of the
human condition.

Whatever the merits of these conclusions, growing up in Northern
Ireland made it impossible to doubt the fundamental importance of
religious allegiance, belief, and practice in social life. This, together with
recognition of the puzzling centrality of religious faith to the lives and
thinking of so many people for whose abilities and intellectual integrity
I have had the highest regard, led me to the study of medieval history
and has very largely shaped my pursuit of it. It also inclined me deci-
sively against Marxism, which even in its more sophisticated versions
evades the questions raised by the ubiquity of religious conviction, solidarity, and sacrifice that are for me the most challenging and rewarding
that the historian has to confront, and against populism and nationalism, not so much the last as the first refuges of the scoundrel, the char-
latan, and the bully. Indeed I owe to Northern Ireland and those who
have made it their playground an instinctive distrust of any set of ideas
which claims special knowledge or insight for its initiates beyond what
is accessible to unaided (as distinct from untrained) human reason, or
which offers its adherents a rationale for distorting or suppressing information, or elevating their own interests above those of others who are
weaker than they are.

It sometimes happens that a book acquires a reputation for original-
ity by good luck in the timing of its publication rather than from the
intrinsic novelty of its contents. So it was with *The Origins of European Dissent.* Its main conclusions (except, perhaps, the observation that
those accused of heretical innovation were in fact often clinging to what
they knew as traditional beliefs and practices, of which more below)
were not new. The understanding of the "heretical movement" of the
eleventh and early twelfth centuries as springing from the same ideals
and impulses as the new religious orders of the same period derived
ultimately, of course, from the work of Herbert Grundmann in the

1930s.[10] As Edward Peters correctly notes above[11] I was not nearly so familiar with it as I should have been, but its conclusions in this respect were being widely assimilated by the 1960s, and had been popularized for an English readership by Christopher Brooke.[12] Grundmann had pointed to the demand for Apostolic renewal voiced by reforming and "heretical" preachers alike as the inspiration not only of the movements which they led, but of their criticism of the morals of the clergy and consequent disparagement of the authority of the church. Hence the debate initiated after World War II by Raffaello Morghen,[13] who argued that the abstinence of eleventh-century heretics and their followers from the pleasures of the flesh, which was commonly interpreted by the ecclesiastical authorities and most subsequent commentators as indicative of theological dualism, could be explained as excesses of enthusiasm in the Catholic ascetic tradition, or excessively suspicious responses to it, rather than as betraying the presence and influence of Balkan missionaries or of an organised dualist church. At the same time others, notably the East German Marxists, sought to explain popular disaffection from the Church as a result of changes that were taking place in western society, rather than of contamination by external ideas and influences.[14] The attribution of heretical movements in the West to

---

[10] Herbert Grundmann *Religiöse Bewegungen im Mittelalter* (Berlin: Ebering, 1935, repr. Darmstadt: Wissenschaftliche Buchgesellschaft, 1977), trans. Steven Rowan as *Religious Movements in the Middle Ages* (Notre Dame: University of Notre Dame Press, 1995), with an important introduction by Robert E. Lerner.

[11] Peters, above, p. 13.

[12] See especially C.N.L. Brooke, "Heresy and Religious Sentiment: 1000–1250," *Bulletin of the Institute of Historical Research* xli (1968), reprinted in C.N.L. Brooke, *Medieval Church and Society* (New York: New York University Press, 1972), 139–161.

[13] Raffaello Morghen, a series of papers from "Osservazioni critiche su alcune questione fondamentali riguardanti le origini e le carraterri delle eresie medievali," *Archivio della R. Deputazione Romana della Storia Patria* 67, (1944): 97–151, reprinted in *Medioevo Cristiano* (Bari: Laterza, 1951) to "Problèmes sur les origines de l'hérésie médiévale," *Revue historique* cccxxxvi (1966); contra, Antoine Dondaine, "L'origine de l'hérésie médiévale," *Revista di storia dell chiesa in Italia* 5 (1951): 47–78. For full references and survey, J.B. Russell, "Some Interpretations of the Origins of Medieval Heresy", *Medieval Studies* xxv (1963); R.I. Moore, "The Origins of Medieval Heresy," *History* lv (1970). On Morghen and his influence, G. Cracco, "Eresiologia in Italia tra otto e novecento," in G. Merlo, ed., *Eretici ed eresie medievali nella storiografia contemporanea: Bollettino della Società Valdesi* 174 (Turin: Torrepellice 1994), 16–38, at 31ff., and on the influence on him of the Modernist controversy, Heinrich Fichtenau, *Heretics and Scholars in the High Middle Ages 1000–1200* trans. Denise A. Kaiser (University Park, PA: Pennsylvania University Press, 1998), 119–120.

[14] E. Werner, *Pauperes Christi* (Leipzig: Koehler und Amelang, 1956); Gottfried Koch, *Frauenfrage und Ketzertum im Mittelalter* (Berlin: Akademie-Verlag, 1962); see further Wer-

indigenous causes, whether spiritual or material, was reinforced by the contemporaneous re-evaluation of Bulgarian and Byzantine Bogomilism, notably by Puech and Vaillant in France and Obolensky in England.[15] Their conclusions cast doubt both on the extent to which the teachings of Bogomil had been theologically dualist from the outset, and on the rapidity and coherence with which they were disseminated from their original foyer in tenth-century Bulgaria.

Most of this had been set out by Jeffrey Russell, though literary as well as analytical shortcomings diminished the impact of his work. These ideas also laid the foundations and provided the scaffolding for the conference convened at Royaumont in 1963 under the presidency of Jacques Le Goff, on heresy and society in pre-industrial Europe.[16] When its proceedings were published in 1968 they did a great deal to help the subject to break out of the confines of traditional religious history and to bring its interest and importance to the attention of a wider scholarly public. The times were propitious in other ways. The thawing of the Cold War in the 1960s made it easier to discuss religious change in its social context without being forced to either pole of a dichotomy between the uncompromising denial of any but undiluted spiritual and intellectual motivations on the one hand and a rigidly formulaic materialist determinism on the other, though the dichotomy remained, and remains, noticeably more assertive in North America than in Europe. The new climate of religious dialogue after Vatican II encouraged historiography to overflow the parallel and habitually non-communicating confessional channels in which it had tended to run, often corresponding to the disciplinary division between university departments of History and of Ecclesiastical History or History of Religion. By the end of the decade, for fairly obvious reasons, the interest in popular movements of every kind which had been stimulated by historians like Rodney Hilton, Christopher Hill, E.P. Thompson, Eric Hobsbawm, and George Rudé—to mention only English examples—had been widely embraced by scholars of almost all periods and regions. Norman Cohn

---

ner Maleczek, "Le ricerce eresiologiche in area germanica," in Merlo, *Eretici ed eresie*, pp. 69–73.

[15] H-C Puech and A. Vaillant, eds, *Le traité contre les Bogomiles de Cosmas le Prêtre* (Paris: Imprimerie nationale, 1945); D. Obolensky, *The Bogomils* (Cambridge, 1948); H-C Puech, "Catharisme médiévale et bogomilisme," *Accademia Nazionale dei Lincei....Atti di convegne xii, Oriente ed Occidente nel Medio Evo* (Rome, 1956).

[16] Jacques le Goff, ed., *Hérésies et sociétés dans l'Europe prè-industrielle* (Paris, La Haye, 1968).

had already pointed out their significance for medievalists as early as 1956, in a book at first more noticed by sociologists than by historians.[17] Christopher Brooke, probably the most admired of the younger generation of English medievalists, regularly drew attention to popular religion in general, and heresy in particular.[18] The extent to which the new approaches were "in the air" is demonstrated by the fact that when I became interested in popular heresy Robert Lerner had already—unknown to me—been working for some years on the Heresy of the Free Spirit.[19] The introduction to his book, published in 1972, set out with much deeper learning and sharper analysis than I could have deployed essentially the same conclusions that I had reached about the ways in which the assertions of inquisitors and others about connections between those accused of heresy, as well as the nature of the accusations, should be read. Malcolm Lambert, again unknown to me until both of us were almost finished, had also been working for several years on his *Medieval Heresy*.[20] Its publication in 1975 at last put the subject securely on the teaching map, while giving the greater part of its attention to the thirteenth century and after. In short, to the undeserved good fortune of its author, *The Origins of European Dissent* presented ideas whose time had come.

As it turned out, the main conclusions of *The Origins of European Dissent* contained, with varying degrees of explicitness, the agenda for the remainder of my career as a medievalist. The one which interested me least, but which has proved stubbornly difficult to leave behind, was that I agreed with those who maintained that western heresy was indigenous, and not attributable directly or indirectly to imported Bogomilism. Dismissal of the hypothesis of external contamination naturally entailed a search for alternative explanations of the appearance, nature and appeal of religious dissent, which has remained at the heart of my work and curiosity. These were, and will remain, questions that

---

[17] Norman Cohn, *The Pursuit of the Millennium* (London: Secker and Warburg, 1957).

[18] E.g. C.N.L. Brooke *Europe in the Central Middle Ages* (London: Longmans, Green, 1964), 329–350—in marked contrast to, for example, R.W. Southern, who scarcely mentioned popular heresy anywhere in his work.

[19] Robert E. Lerner, *The Heresy of the Free Spirit* (Berkeley and Los Angeles: University of California Press, 1972).

[20] Malcolm Lambert, *Medieval Heresy from Bogomil to Hus* (London: E. Arnold, 1977). The second part of the title was dropped in later editions, the author having been convinced by the skeptics in the debate mentioned above.

cannot be approached directly, but only through the record created, directly and indirectly, by the accusers. Their accounts were seldom simple summaries of the evidence that they obtained at first hand from those suspected of heresy or from other witnesses. It did not always seem that they had listened carefully to what they were told. Rather, they had a certain tendency to assume that they already knew what they were confronted with, to highlight what confirmed their expectations and discount what did not, and to see what they did not approve of as the result of the wicked machinations of outsiders, rather than as responses to any shortcomings in the Church's discharge of its responsibilities. As a junior faculty member in the late 1960s it did not appear to me either that such a habit of mind was particularly surprising in senior office-holders of hierarchically organised institutions, or that it invariably assisted them to reach accurate conclusions about the motivation and convictions of those who challenged their authority. Nevertheless, it was a question that became increasingly insistent in my later work why sophisticated and intelligent men, as most of them were, should so persistently have exaggerated the threat by which they were confronted. That question became even more pressing when it began to dawn on me that it was by no means only when heresy was at issue that they did so. Conversely, the accused often seemed surprised to be told that the beliefs which they professed were novelties in conflict with the teaching of the church, and they were sometimes quite content to accept correction. In some cases at least the surprise appeared perfectly genuine: I did not think the people arraigned at Arras in 1024 were disingenuous in protesting that "they believed that the sum of Christian salvation could consist in nothing but what the bishop had set out."[21] This not only reinforced my curiosity about the sensitivities of the authorities but raised another question: who were the innovators? And, conversely, if the accused, before interrogation, had been neither good Catholics, as defined by the bishop, nor heretics of whatever kind he had suspected, what had they really believed, and why? The first of those questions, who the real innovators were, has coloured everything that I have written since 1977 on the eleventh and twelfth centuries; the second I consider the largest and most interesting piece of unfinished business that remains to me. Both questions have been taken up in a number of ways in the present volume.

---

[21] *BPH.* 18; cf. *OED*, 9–18.

The first of the issues mentioned above, the extent of Bogomil influence in the eleventh-century west and its bearing on the "origins"[22] of medieval heresy, has remained stubbornly controversial. There is no logically necessary connection between the questions whether manifestations of popular heresy should be attributed, on the one hand, to material or to spiritual causes, and on the other to developments within western Europe or to influences from without. Nevertheless, such a correlation had been taken for granted in the debates of the 1950s and '60s. There was also a difference of methodology, as well as of ideology, between the protagonists. Morghen and those who agreed with him regarded "neo-Manichaeism" as a construct of modern scholarship. They pointed out that none of the eleventh-century sources contained anything like a complete description of a dualist creed or practice. The modern diagnosis of "Manichaeism"—a term used only by Ademar of Chabannes and Anselm of Liège among eleventh-century writers—was based on the advocacy by the accused of particular points, such as abstention from sex and meat, which were interpreted and generalised by observers who were conditioned by their reading of St Paul's prophecy of the last times, and by Augustine's description of the Manichaeism of his youth. For Morghen and others a more probable source of such austerity, and of criticism of the short-fallings of the tenth-century church and its ministers, than wandering missionaries from the Balkans was the example of monks or hermits inspired by late Carolingian neoplatonism, in rebellion against the laxity of traditional Benedictine observance.[23] Many, though by no means all, who took that view also looked to resentment of increasing social differentiation and economic exploitation as a source of hostility to ecclesiastical authority and those who wielded it.

On the other hand, the greatest scholar of heresy of his generation, if not of the twentieth century, Antoine Dondaine O.P., maintained that all the essential attributes of Bogomilism were noted in the western sources, though fragmentarily, and that these scattered revelations were

---

[22] Marc Bloch's caution against the ambiguity of this word, with its meretricious invitation to "confuse ancestry with explanation," is particularly pertinent in the discussion of religion, as he noted, and *a fortiori* of heresy: Marc Bloch, *The Historian's Craft*, trans. Peter Putnam, (Manchester: Manchester University Press, 1954), pp. 32–35. Even so, my use of it in the title of *OED* was deliberate, if foolhardy.

[23] A point insufficiently remembered in much subsequent discussion, and superbly developed by Giorgio Cracco, "Riforma ed eresia in momenti della cultura Europea tra X e XI secolo", *Rivista di storia e letteratura religiosa* vii (1971), 411–477.

connected by the invisible links of a dualist movement (though not, in Dondaine's view, a dualist church[24])—that what the sources revealed, in Christopher Brooke's vivid paraphrase, was "a variety of aspects of a Bogomil iceberg."[25] By the 1970s the more sceptical view was almost universally preferred, but an extreme statement of the older position—far more extreme than Dondaine's—may be found in an influential textbook, Jean-Pierre Poly and Eric Bournazel's *The Feudal Transformation*, where with the aid of a variety of ingenious maps almost every reference to heresy in western Europe in the eleventh and twelfth centuries is assimilated to a vast conspiracy directed from Mont-Aimé in Champagne, for which there is not a scrap of contemporary evidence worth the name.[26] Those who care to pursue the matter will have to do so without the assistance of Poly and Bournazel's otherwise generous bibliography, which neglects to note many of the places in which their readings of almost every text to which they refer had been rebutted, and many will think refuted, by earlier work.[27]

---

[24] "Catharism is often spoken of as *a* religion, as a spiritual body hierarchically organized; it has even been discussed whether there was a Cathar pope, a supreme head of the sect. This is a grave historical error. There were *dualist sects*, as much in the East as in Lombardy, which had no more in common than a more or less related doctrinal legacy." (Dondaine's italics, my translation.) Antoine Dondaine, "L'hiérachie cathare en Italie: I, Le *de heresi catharorum;* II. Le *tractatus de hereticis* d'Anselme d'Alexandrie O.P.", *Archivum Fratrum Preadicatorum* xix (1949), xx (1950), reprinted in Antoine Dondaine *Les hérésies et l'Inquisition XIIe.-XIIIe.* siècles (Aldershot: Variorum 1990), at I 292–293. It is this which I have primarily in mind when I "question the validity of the term Cathar Church" (Hamilton, above, p. 111). Certainly the term is open to many further objections, including those so vigorously stated by Pegg in this volume (227–239), but this is the fundamental distinction. If it was good enough for Dondaine it is good enough for me.

[25] "Heresy and Religious Sentiment," above n. 11, p. 120.

[26] Jean-Pierre Poly and Eric Bournazel, trans. C. Higgitt, *The Feudal Transformation 900–1200* (New York: Holmes and Meier, 1991, from *La mutation féodale x–xii siécles*, Paris: Press universitaires de France, 1980), 272–309, a wonderfully erudite and quite perverse discussion. On Mont-Aimé cf. Barber, above p. 119; as Barber comments, to connect even the reference to Mont-Aimé by the canons of Liège in 1145 with the conflagration of 1239 is speculative; to extend the connection to Liutard of Vertus shortly after 1000 (Poly and Bournazel, p. 276) is to descend from speculation to fantasy.

[27] For references see in addition to the works mentioned in notes 12 and 16 above and *OED*, 139–167 and notes, R.I. Moore, "Heresy, Repression and Social Change in the Age of Gregorian Reform," in Scott L. Waugh and Peter D. Diehl eds., *Christendom and its Discontents* (Cambridge: Cambridge University Press, 1996), 19–46, and for a fuller and more restrained restatement of the gnostic tradition from the point of view of an expert on the eastern churches see Y. Stoyanov, *The Other God. Dualist Religions from Antiquity to the Cathar Heresy* (New Haven and London: Yale University Press, 2000).

In its essentials the debate has scarcely changed. The arguments of Frassetto, Callahan, and Hamilton in this volume, though enhanced by freshly discovered materials and penetrating new insights, in large part recapitulate those of Dondaine in favour of accepting, by and large, that the eleventh-century authorities upon whom we rely knew a Manichee when they saw one, and hence that they were correct in detecting the presence, and increasing organisation and influence, of the emissaries of a dualist movement which had originated in the Balkans. Yet for all the vivid and circumstantial wealth of Ademar's concerns about the heretics against whom he preached, the information that he gives informs us directly only about his own anxieties and perceptions. The old questions, first, to what extent those perceptions were founded on experience and observation rather than on preconception, and second, to the extent that they were so, how far Ademar interpreted what he observed correctly, remain. Ademar has emerged in recent years as one of the most fascinating and puzzling writers of the entire medieval period, and the study of his thought which is promised by Callahan and Frassetto will provide a remarkable perspective on medieval Christianity at a critical moment of its formation. As Frassetto's paper in this collection points out, the vividness and completeness with which he anticipates the range of anxieties and insecurities about the Church and its enemies that would seize his successors in the high Middle Ages is particularly striking. In the present argument, nevertheless, his editors are no more able than was Dondaine to point to a single identifiable Bogomil in the west before those who were burned at Cologne in 1143.[28]

My own rejection of "neo-manichaeism" as a description of eleventh-century heresy, and of its implications that all or most of the reported episodes were connected with each other and directly inspired by ideas and emissaries from the east, was in part the result of reviewing the arguments already advanced by others, as I had done in my first, and somewhat naïve, published paper in the field.[29] It was also, and more importantly, because I had read the sources roughly in chronological order,[30] innocent of the comprehensive account of Cathar doc-

---

[28] Possible indications of Bogomil colonies at Verona and Turin before c. 1047 are considered-but not accepted-by Fichtenau, *Heretics and Scholars*, 113, in a subtle and historiographically informative discussion of this issue, pp. 105–123.

[29] Above, n. 13.

[30] My naiveté in reading and translating in the order of the dates usually attributed to the episodes of "heresy" they described, rather than that in which the texts were

trine and organization subsequently composed, and imposed, by commentators and inquisitors from Eckbert of Schönau onwards. Consequently, I had no predisposition to attach any more significance to those aspects of the reported "heresies" that might seem to anticipate points of Cathar doctrine or organisation than to those that did not. This chronological reading convinced me that fragmentary though the reports were, they showed quite clearly that these early "heresies" differed greatly from one another in doctrinal content and social context, at least until the 1140s. They often shared certain general tendencies typical of their time, of course—most obviously, an unsurprisingly low opinion of the morals of the clergy and its pretensions to holiness—but while each of them made sense when placed in its particular context of time and place, so far as that could be done, they could be forced into a common pattern only by selecting certain features of each, and ignoring what were often the most striking as well as the most individual parts of the accounts. Hence the conclusion of *The Origins of European Dissent* that the handful of reports of heresy in the first half of the eleventh century described no single movement or tendency, and had in common only that "they signalled the changes [in religious mentalities and social tensions] that were on the way."[31]

This is, perhaps, a less vacuous observation than it may seem at first glance. It summarized an impression which has been consistently reinforced by what we have learned since, namely that while the disjointed and fragmentary accounts of seemingly very various episodes are difficult both to interpret in themselves and to weave into a pattern, all of them suggest in one way or another some kind of reaction or response to change. Georges Duby's "feudal revolution" is now under fierce and damaging attack from several quarters[32] as exaggerating the

---

produced, is exposed by several of the papers collected in Monique Zerner, ed. *l'hérésie? Discours polémiques et pouvoirs avant l'inquisition* (Nice: Centre d'études médiévales, Faculté des lettres, arts et sciences humaines, Université de Nice Sophia-Antipolis 1998), now the indispensable starting point for any study of twelfth-century heresy. But even if I had known better I would, in the early 1970s, have had no practicable alternative.

[31] *OED*, 45.

[32] Led by Dominique Barthélemy, *La mutation de l'an mil, a-t-elle eu lieu* (Paris: Fayard, 1997); see most recently, Stephen D. White, "Tenth-Century Courts at Mâcon and the Perils of Structuralist History: Re-reading Burgundian Judicial Institutions," in Warren C. Brown and Piotr Gorecki eds., *Conflict in Medieval Europe: Changing Perspectives on Society and Culture* (Aldershot: Variorum, 2003), 37–38; Frederic L. Cheyette, "Some Reflections on Violence, Reconciliation and the 'Feudal Revolution,'" ibid. pp. 242–263; "Georges

pace and depth of social change in the decades around the millennium, and the extent to which a new social and cultural order—the
European *ancien régime*—was put in place at that point. It is easy to for-
get that until Duby's account became widely accepted, in the 1970s,
the early eleventh century was generally treated, like the tenth, as a
sort of no man's land between the brief splendor of the Carolingian
Empire at its height and the real beginning of medieval, or European
history with (according to taste) the Investiture Conflict, the Crusades,
the Commercial Revolution, the Revival of Monarchy or the Twelfth-
century Renaissance. In consequence, for most of the twentieth century
not only textbooks and lecture courses but monographs and thematic
studies were at least as much inclined to take their starting point somewhere near 1100 as they now do a hundred years earlier. *The Origins of
European Dissent* was written in this tradition. Siegel's close examination
in this volume of the heretics of Monforte and their world shows how
they have been made more readily understandable by the greater inte-
gration of the history of the eleventh century with that of the twelfth
and beyond which has been achieved in the last quarter-century. His
vivid and circumstantial account of the conditions in which attacks on
clerical prestige and authority arose reaffirms the view that it is by reference to the changes at work within European society, in cultural and
religious as well as in economic and social development, rather than
to external influence, that accusations of heresy are best understood.
Conversely, for those who regard the appearance of popular heresy
as reflecting a co-ordinated movement of conscious repudiation of the
Church, however inspired, its disappearance in the second half of the
eleventh century, when the Church was sounding its claims so loudly
is puzzling. This is not a problem for those who see it largely as an
expression of the same ideals and discontents that drove papal policy from Leo IX to Urban II. Ecclesiastically, the demand for reform
was continuous, but expressions and accusations of "dualist" tendencies
were not. Socially, the resistance of "heretics" to tithes, baptism, the
Eucharist, matrimony, the cross, and church building shows "heresy"
as occasionally directed against the foundations of the new social order
that was in the course of aggressive construction in these decades. It
also shows, however, enough common ground, and common enemies,
between those who appear in retrospect as "heretics" and "reformers"

to obscure for a time the profound differences of value and loyalty that divided them.[33]

Since the persistence of the suspicion of Bogomil influence behind the appearance of popular heresy in the eleventh century is not attributable solely to the perverse incapacity of fellow scholars to appreciate the irresistible force of the arguments that have persuaded me the debate will rumble on. But the importance we attach to the difference is much less than it used to be. Hamilton "would not wish to support the traditional view that all heresies found in western Europe from 1000 to 1050 were manifestations of dualism." He is, however, quite as much entitled to consider that modern research reinforces his suggestion that "a whole range of Byzantine influences might have entered the West" as Siegel or I might claim for our social interpretation. For Hamilton it would be "unnecessarily dogmatic to rule out the possibility," which "it is not [Siegel's] intention to dismiss outright ... of Bogomil teaching forming the basis for practice and practices and beliefs of western heresies".[34] The argument will continue, since it remains a matter of taste whether it is better to avoid "unnecessary dogmatism" or the multiplication of superfluous entities. Some of us might be more surprised than others by compelling evidence of a Bogomil presence in the eleventh-century west, but it would not make much difference to how we describe the first manifestations of dissent from the teaching and practices of the Roman Church, or account for its appeal.

A truce can be called, then, in the battle of the Bogomils, but the Cathar wars show no sign of abating. They are being fought around very much the same methodological issues. That there were dualists from the Byzantine world, or their converts, in western Europe after 1143, and that some of them at least were proselytizing, cannot reasonably be doubted, except by impugning either the authenticity or the essential accuracy of Eberwin of Steinfeld's famous letter to Bernard of Clairvaux about events of that year.[35] So far as I know nobody has ever questioned it on either count, and I am aware of no basis for doing so.[36] Eberwin describes the interrogation in Cologne not of one group

---

[33] *OED*, 71–81; R.I. Moore, *The First European Revolution* (*FER*) (Oxford: Blackwell Publishers, 2001), especially at pp. 55–64, 101–111; see further below, pp. 366–368.

[34] Above, pp. 98, 98, 98, 45 respectively; similarly, *OED*. p. 166.

[35] *BPH*, 74–78.

[36] But see now Uwe Brunn, "L'hérésie dans l'archévêche de Cologne (1100–1233)," *Heresis* 38 (2004): 183–190.

of heretics but of two, who had brought themselves to the attention of the authorities by publicly quarrelling with each other. Two spokesmen of one group, namely "one who was called their bishop with his companion," claimed that "their heresy had been hidden until now ever since the time of the martyrs, and persisted in Greece and other lands." They described in some detail beliefs and practices which corresponded closely to those of the Bogomils as described by Cosmas the Priest (soon after 972) and later Byzantine writers, and their sect was divided, as the Cathars would be, between the initiates (*electi*) through whom alone its rituals could be carried out and the sect perpetuated, and the simple believers (*auditores*). The bishop and his companion went to the stake "and endured the torment of the flames not merely courageously but joyfully." The diffusion of their sect in the Rhineland and the development of their teachings during the next twenty years may be traced quite closely in the sermons of Eckbert of Schönau (1163–1167), which are still much less familiar than they ought to be.[37] It was this development, I concluded in *The Origins of European Dissent*, which produced the faith known in western Europe as Catharism.[38] Henceforth such people appeared more frequently, spread more widely, and established themselves with varying degrees of permanence in many places. Working backwards from the thirteenth-century inquisitors' manuals, Dondaine's masterly study of the Cathar hierarchy in Italy established an account of the dissemination and organisation of their heresy upon which all subsequent narratives, including that of *The Origins of European Dissent*, are founded,[39] although—of course—it remains open to dispute in many particulars, and can be amplified in others. Barber's paper in this volume offers the most complete survey to date of the surviving indications of the process at work in northern France, while Hamilton follows the details of Cathar organisation and teaching in the Languedoc into the thirteenth century and beyond.

Who were the Cathars? A simple enough question, but differing answers to it will be found to lurk behind much disagreement both about particular incidents and groups of people and about the nature of popular heresy in the high middle ages and the reasons for its persecu-

---

[37] *PL* 195, col. 11–102. A modern edition and translation are very much to be desired.

[38] *OED*, 172–182.

[39] Above, n. 24. The conclusions are summarized at IV 264–278, but this necessarily highlights some of the more dated parts of it.

tion. To begin with, self-evidently, not the followers of Valdès of Lyons, the founder of the other great organized heresy of the high Middle Ages, habitually bracketed with the Cathars by the inquisitors, though in fact the two were bitter enemies.[40] Self-evidently, not the followers or adherents of many native evangelists of varying degrees of radicalism, such as the people described by Eberwin as quarrelling with the dualists in Cologne, or the associates of Lambert le Bègue of Liège,[41] or the spiritual Franciscans. These exclusions may seem too obvious to be worth stating, but apart from the fact that its treatment, or lack of treatment, of these groups is the greatest defect of *The Origins of European Dissent*, to mention them is to remind ourselves that the history of heresy, still more of dissent, in this period is by no means to be equated with that of the Cathars. As Mark Pegg points out so trenchantly in this volume, too many modern historians use the word "Cathar" a great deal more freely than it was used in the twelfth century.[42] For example, both Hamilton and Barber go further than taking the source too much at face-value when they use the term to describe the people who were tried at Oxford in 1165,[43] for William of Newburgh, the author of by far the most detailed and very hostile account, says of them that they "answered correctly on the nature of Christ."[44] That is to say, they accepted that God had assumed human flesh. This contradicts a logical concomitant of dualism, which all the inquisitorial sources insist

---

[40] For recent surveys of the considerable body of modern work on the Waldensians, Gabriel Audisio, *The Waldensian Dissent: Persecution and Survival c. 1170–c. 1570* (Cambridge: Cambridge University Press, 1999) and, more critical, Evan Cameron, *Waldenses: Rejections of Holy Church in Medieval Europe* (Oxford: Blackwell Publishers, 2000). Michel Rubellin, "Au temps où Valdès n'était pas hérétique: hypothèse sur la rôle de Valdès à Lyon", in Zerner, *Inventer l'hérésie?* 193–218 is one of the most dramatic revisions of received knowledge in recent years.

[41] Walter Simons, *Cities of Ladies: Beguine Communities in the Low Countries, 1200–1565* (Philadelphia: University of Pennsylvania Press, 2001), 24–34, with important corrections to *BPH* and *OED*.

[42] Pegg, above p. 229.

[43] Above, pp. 102 and 126. Gervase of Tilbury's story about dualism at Reims in the 1170s should also be omitted from Barber's account (as from *OED*, 183–184), having been thoroughly exposed by Ed Peters as "a tissue of rhetorical and literary embellishment filled out with conventional and generalised descriptions of Publican beliefs": Edward Peters, *The Magician, the With and the Law* (Philadelphia: University of Pennsylvania Press, 1978), 35–39.

[44] *BPH*, 83. William of Newburgh was writing in the 1190s—and the tendency to stereotype the ideas of those accused of dualist heresy would have increased rather than diminished in the interval—but probably had his information from the excellently informed Roger of Hoveden.

was a fundamental tenet of Cathar teaching, that Christ's assumption of human flesh was an illusion.[45] Whatever the Oxford *populicani* were, they were not Cathars. This is hardly problematic in a Europe teeming with groups of variously motivated and self-taught religious enthusiasts. Among them the term Cathar should be reserved for people whose beliefs and organisation corresponded to those described by Eckbert of Schönau, not least because his observations were based on direct encounters over a lengthy period (and, in general, are not difficult to distinguish from what he took from Augustine), and initially at least in circumstances in which the heretics debated freely and were not subject to coercion.

For Eckbert, as for the inquisitors whose treatises his sermons anticipate in a number of ways, "Cathar" meant one who had received the *consolamentum*, and he thought of such people as actively engaged in the dissemination and ministration of the faith, "willing to cross sea and desert to win a Cathar."[46] Most of us ordinarily, and reasonably, extend the term to include the "believers" who accepted such teaching and ministration, so that the term "perfected Cathar", strictly a tautology, has a useful place in the historian's vocabulary. These details apart, however, the questions remain, what was the relationship between the missionary movement (or movements) and the "heresies" discovered, alleged and reported in the century or so after Eberwin's letter? Were those who became Cathar believers converted from Catholicism, or from other groups, sects, or heresies, which became absorbed into the ranks of the Cathars? How far did the authors of our texts or their informants report what really happened or make it up, consciously or unconsciously, because it expressed the anxieties or misapprehensions, or suited the interests, of the authorities involved or of the authors themselves? The balance of probabilities in particular cases, often hotly debated, is less relevant to the present purpose than the general observation that the question "who were the Cathars?" points beyond theological niceties to the relationship between those who preach a religion, especially when they are far from their native land, and those who lis-

---

[45] Nevertheless, that Eckbert of Schönau reports their docetist teaching briefly and as something he has learnt only recently, after twenty years' acquaintance with the heretics, is a salutary reminder that logical rigor is not always a safe guide to what people actually believed or said. It also leaves open the possibility that the group who came to England had originated among those observed by Eckbert in the Rhineland at some point before they embraced docetism—but there is no particular reason to think so.

[46] *BPH*, 92.

ten to them. In this respect, ironically enough, the inquisitors were not altogether wrong in assuming certain parallels between the perspectives and ambitions of the leaders of the Cathars and their own. At any rate, as Hamilton's paper above brings out, they shared a natural tendency to maximize their estimate of the extent to which Cathar preaching, accurately and enthusiastically received, was the agent primarily responsible for causing and disseminating "heresy."

With Catharism—some of whose corpus of legends and commentaries reached the west in written form perhaps before the end of the twelfth century, in the shape of the *Interrogatio Iohannis*[47]—as with Catholicism the relationship between the literate elite and ordinary believers is therefore both crucial and problematic, and until fairly recently little considered. It was natural that the inquisitors should have attached great importance to the doctrinal and mythological content of the heresies, just as it is natural that modern historians similarly learned and intellectually oriented should follow them in doing so. What the teachings and myths meant to the ordinary believers, and whether the Cathars were really the source of the deviations from Catholic fidelity which the bishops and friars found in the countryside of the Languedoc, are quite different questions. Since the 1970s the anthropological turn has taught medievalists to consider popular religion not merely as what the church taught the people, but as the systems of belief actually held and ritual actually practised in the "little community,"[48] with particular attention to how and in whom holiness was recognised and the uses to which it was put. Carol Lansing's brilliant study of *Power and Purity* in thirteenth-century Orvieto,[49] for example, showed that the influence of the heretics in the city depended not on their systems of

---

[47] Edina Bozoky, *Le livre secret des cathares* (Paris: Beauchesne, 1980).

[48] I use the terms "great" and "little" community, originally coined by Robert Redfield and in his usage open to some objections which need not concern us here, to describe respectively the upper and lower portions of Ernest Gellner's diagram of the agro-literate society to which Peters refers above, p. 17 (cf. Ernest Gellner, *Nations and Nationalism*, (Oxford: Blackwell, 1983), 9–11). It should be remembered that essential characteristics of the producing communities which constituted the latter were that they were socially similar, not being sharply differentiated internally, but largely isolated from each other and therefore culturally idiosyncratic; the great community, conversely, is defined by its possession of a common, literate culture, not simply by political power or economic privilege, and is characterized by very precise definition and expression of the differences of rank and function between its component groups.

[49] Carol Lansing, *Power and Purity. Cathar Heresy in Medieval Italy* (New York and Oxford: Oxford University Press, 1998).

thought, but on the spiritual prestige of their leaders and the ways in which particular teachings and practices supported believers in coping with the dilemmas of everyday life. Mark Pegg, in *The Corruption of Angels*[50] and in this volume, conducts what amounts to a field study of the villages of the Lauragais, and finds their devotion and practice so remote from the intellectual constructs of the inquisitors and their historians that he is ready to doubt altogether the connection between the Balkans and the Languedoc. Before these issues and their implications can be pursued further, however, it is necessary to turn again to the question of the relationship between the content of our sources and the circumstances which produced them, and hence from the victims to the persecutors, and the reasons for their activity.

Behind almost all the conflicts of interpretation which have been touched upon in this discussion lies a deceptively simple difference between historians: whether in reading our sources we pay more attention to the similarities that they reveal between those whom they describe, or to the differences. It is, in effect, the distinction between reading the texts with and against the grain. The sources seek similarity, and betray difference. It was not only natural but almost inevitable that those who encountered popular heresy—and before the thirteenth century, as far as we know, very few did so on more than one occasion—should seek to make sense of it by comparing what they saw and heard with recorded experience, and in the first instance with St. Paul's warning of the heretics who would come in the last times, and the descriptions of the great heresies of antiquity by the Fathers of the Church. In any case, if the heresies were to be correctly identified, and the threat they presented to the Faith assessed and countered, it was the similarities that mattered: the vagaries and eccentricities of particular groups, so revealing to the mundane curiosity of the modern historian, were neither here nor there. Beyond that, it is only to be expected that churchmen should have noted with most concern the objections to Catholicism which bore most directly on their own preoccupations— that dedicated men sincerely anxious and active to secure the veneration of the cross and of the Eucharist, the baptism of infants, marriage in church, confession to priests, the performance of penance, the payment of tithes and the generous support of soaringly ambitious build-

---

[50] Mark Gregory Pegg, *The Corruption of Angels: The Great Inquisition of 1245–1246* (Princeton: Princeton University Press, 2001).

ing programs, should have noted resistance on these points with alarm corresponding to their own commitment to them. It is equally unsurprising that those whom they questioned perceived as novelties not the customary routines and practices with which they were familiar, however scandalous to the reformers, but rather the very points which the reformers themselves were pressing with growing determination.

All of this made the interrogation of those suspected of heresy, and the recording of their examination, a self-fulfilling process, reinforcing the expectations and preconceptions of the interrogators, and constructing a stereotypical description of the heretic and of heretical behavior. Neither process nor stereotype arose, in the first place, from a zeal for persecution, though they tended both to foment the zeal and to facilitate the persecution. Until around the middle of the twelfth century the church and its prelates, like the savage animal in the French zoo, defended itself when attacked, more often with surprise than anger. Before that time the popular heresy which is so interesting and seems so portentous to us actually aroused very little interest beyond the places in which it occurred. Only the affair at Orléans in 1022, the first burnings since antiquity, arising from a major scandal at the royal court, is mentioned in more than a tiny handful of local sources. When those accused of heresy were treated with violence it was lay people, of varying status and with many motives, rather than the clergy, who insisted on it.[51] Change is noticeable in the 1130s and early '40s, when heresy began to be perceived as more than a local problem, and bigger guns than ever before were deployed against it, in the shape of Peter the Venerable and Bernard of Clairvaux.[52] As so often the change is registered in the career of Henry of Lausanne. Orderic Vitalis does not

---

[51] E.g., as at Orléans in 1022, Milan in 1028, Goslar in 1052, Cambrai in 1076, Soissons in 1114, St. Gilles du Gard in 1139, Liége in 1135 and 1145, Cologne in 1143. R.H. Bautier, "L'hérésie d'Orléans et le mouvement intellectuel au debut du xie siècle," *Enseignement et vie intellectuelle, IXe–XVIe siècles: Actes du 95e. congrés des sociétés savantes (Reims, 1970), Section philologique et historique,* (Paris: Bibliothèque nationale, 1975): I, 63–88 remains the essential analysis; among many other discussions note especially Brian Stock, *The Implications of Literacy: Written Language and Models of Interpretation in the Eleventh and Twelfth Centuries* (Princeton: Princeton University Press, 1983), 106–120; on Monforte, Stock, *Implications of Literacy,* 139–145, Fichtenau, *Heretics and Scholars,* 41–46, and Siegel above, pp. 43–72; on Goslar, Fichtenau, 27–28. For the others see R.I. Moore, "Popular Heresy and Popular Violence, 1022–1179," in *Studies in Church History 21,* ed. W.J. Sheils, *Toleration and Persecution* (Oxford: Blackwell Publishers, 1984), 43–50.

[52] On the context of this change see especially Dominique Iogna-Prat, *Order and Exclusion,* trans. Graham Robert Edwards (Ithaca, NY: Cornell University Press, 2001),

mention him, though St. Evroult could hardly have failed to hear of his exploits in 1116 at Le Mans, less than 100 km. away,[53] but three decades later Bernard denounced him in letters that would reverberate through Christendom, and in 1145 pursued him through the Languedoc, on the mission which in so many ways anticipated later developments.

The signs of a decisive movement in the direction of systematic persecution appeared in the 1160s. Capital punishment was visited not only on the leaders of convicted groups but on their followers, to the distress of those who saw a young girl burned at Cologne in 1163, though not of any recorded witness at Oxford two years later, when "more than thirty people both men and women ... simple and illiterate people, uncultivated peasants, Germans by race and language ...were driven into the intolerable cold of winter and died in misery."[54] These were manifestations of the new, proactive strategy against heresy demanded by the Council of Tours in 1163, whose edict against the Cathars (here for the first time called Albigenses) said to be spreading from the region of Toulouse foresaw that they would conceal themselves in secret places, from which they must be rooted out. The campaign thus inaugurated, which culminated in the papally sponsored mission to Toulouse in 1178, was prompted directly by the determination of Henry II to revenge himself on Louis VII, who in 1159 had frustrated the greatest military campaign of Henry's reign by interposing himself between Henry and the Count of Toulouse. Louis had thus placed Henry in the position of being able to pursue his war against Raymond only at the unacceptable cost of attacking his lord, and therefore declaring himself an enemy of all lordship. But a lord who could be represented as a protector of heretics would be unable to repeat that stratagem. So, by contrast with the position of 1159, not only Louis but Raymond V himself, however unwillingly, were constrained to co-operate with the mission of 1178. This in its turn laid both the ideological and the procedural foundations for the depiction of the County of Toulouse as a land torn

---

99–261 and Constant Mews, "The Council of Sens (1141): Abelard, Bernard and the Fear of Social Upheaval," *Speculum* 77 (2002): 342–382.

[53] Today it is straight down N138; the route was probably the same in the twelfth century. Orderic was interested in "reforming" activity generally, reporting sympathetically, for instance, on the preaching of Bernard of Tiron and Vitalis of Mortain: Marjorie Chibnall ed., *The Ecclesiastical History of Orderic Vitalis* IV (Oxford: Clarendon Press, 1973), viii. 27, 328–333. His silence on Henry is noted by Chibnall, *The World of Orderic Vitalis*, (Oxford: Clarendon Press, 1984), 163–165.

[54] *BPH*, 88–89, 83–84, where the Oxford trial is mistakenly dated c. 1163.

by heresy and disorder which led through the Third Lateran Council to the series of denunciations and manoeuvres that culminated in the proclamation of the Albigensian crusade.[55] The extent to which the preparation and justification of that venture moulded, both consciously and unconsciously, the character and content of the surviving sources for popular heresy in the twelfth century is the central though by no means the only thread of the series of fundamental studies conducted by a group of scholars led by Monique Zerner, and published under the devastating and sufficient title, *Inventer l'hérésie?*[56]

Marvin's thorough reassessment in this volume of the massacre at Béziers and its historiography suggests that the stereotyping, as heretics and supporters of heretics, of those who resisted the crusaders rationalised the absence of restraint on the part of the victors. He is perfectly correct, at the same time, to point to the border between heresy and orthodoxy as a typical locus of particularly ruthless mass killings. In this respect it was akin to other sorts of frontier, such as that between Christianity and Islam—including the frontier between the privileged and the unprivileged, for, as Marvin also points out, Catholic knights were not conspicuously merciful towards plebeian co-religionists in similar circumstances. A notorious function of stereotyping, of course, is precisely to dehumanize its victims, and correspondingly to erode the inhibitions of their attackers. It follows that increasing the number and sharpening the definition of social boundaries, internal and external, both heightens vigilance at them and intensifies conflict across them. Such differentiation was, of course, inseparable from the transformation of European society in the twelfth century, described with particular brilliance by John Gillingham in respect of the construction of ethnicity, and by Dominique Iogna Prat in relation to that of religious and cultural frontiers.[57]

Heresy is by definition the refusal of a demand for the acknowledgement of religious authority; much confusion in its historiography might have been avoided if everybody who wrote about it had remembered

---

[55] R.I. Moore, "Les albigeois d'après les chroniques angevines", Colloque Centre d'études cathares: La Croisade contre les Albigeois, Carcassonne, October 2002, in press.

[56] *Inventer l'hérésie? Discours polémiques et pouvoirs avant l'inquisition* Collection du centre d'études médiévales de Nice, 2 (Nice: Centre d'études médiévales, Faculté des lettres, arts et sciences humaines, Université de Nice Sophia-Antipolis, 1998).

[57] John Gillingham, "The Beginnings of English Imperialism," *Journal of Historical Sociology* 5/4 (1992): 392–409; Iogna Prat, *Order and Exclusion*, passim.

that logically the demand must precede the refusal. So long as scholars accepted that the belief of bishops or others that they were newly confronted by heresy—that is, by conscious and deliberate rejection of the doctrines, disciplines and authority of the Church—was objectively correct their vigilance against it did not require much explanation beyond the conventional supposition that with the progress of reform such persons tended to become more conscientious in the discharge of their duties. Conversely, the conclusion of *The Origins of European Dissent* that in the twelfth century "heresy" and still more novelty were constructed to so very great and increasing an extent in the minds of the accusers raised the question why the churchmen should at this time have been prone—and markedly more prone than their predecessors for several centuries past—to exaggerate the threat represented by the generally not very formidable sectaries whom they came across, or prey to anxieties which were not obviously founded in reality.

This is the reason why the remainder of my scholarly life has been increasingly dominated, as Edward Peters articulates in his perceptive contribution to this book, by the phenomenon of persecution. The preoccupation was fuelled by the gradual realization that the same mental processes which invented heresy could invent other deviations as well. While translating the texts in *The Birth of Popular Heresy* I had noticed how frequently the image of leprosy was used in anti-heretical polemic, which drew my attention to close parallels in the perception and treatment of the two conditions in this period.[58] After finishing *The Origins of European Dissent* I began to see that accusations very similar to those directed against heretics were also made against Jews (as Lerner had already noted[59]) and against male homosexuals. In this respect the work of John Boswell was particularly stimulating,[60] and pointed me towards the view that persecution must be regarded as a phenomenon in its own right, and not simply as a reaction to the behavior, teaching or just the presence of its victims. Indeed, the coincidences of chronology, rhetoric, and actual treatment deployed against very diverse categories of persons classified as threatening Christian society suggested that sometimes at least the victims had very little to do with it: perse-

---

[58] R.I. Moore, "Heresy as Disease," W. Lourdaux and D. Verhelst, eds., *The Concept of Heresy in the Middle Ages*, *Medievalia Lovanensia*, Series I, Studia IV (Louvain: University Press, 1976), 1–11.

[59] *Heresy of the Free Spirit*, 3–4.

[60] John Boswell, *Christianity, Social Tolerance and Homosexuality* (Chicago: University of Chicago Press, 1980), especially at 269–302.

cution appeared to have become an end in itself, in some sense even a structural necessity to European society, during the twelfth and thirteen centuries, and to have remained so. This is the argument that was worked out in *The Formation of a Persecuting Society*, and elaborated in a subsequent paper.[61] I ought to have made it clearer, however, that I was not saying, and did not mean to imply, that this constituted in any sense a complete or general explanation of subsequent persecutions in Europe.[62] Persecution in itself is not, of course, a peculiarly European phenomenon, and while all persecutions have their particular causes, contexts, and courses they can also have a great deal in common. Both points are illustrated by many fine studies, such as Philip Kuhn's fascinating and entertaining account of the Chinese witch-hunt of 1768, following rumours that all over the Empire sorcerers were surreptitiously clipping off men's pigtails.[63] What has made Europe different is not the nature or causes of particular persecutions since the thirteenth century, but their scale and number, and the variety of their ostensible objects, so that the phenomenon of persecution itself has seemed to be inseparable from the development of European society and institutions. This suggests to me a distinction similar to that used by historians of slavery, between societies in which slavery is practised, but is of relatively limited importance—"societies with slavery," very numerous in history—and those in which slavery is fundamental to the economy and therefore also to social institutions, including high culture—"slave societies," of which there have been only a handful of examples.

The conclusion of *The Formation of a Persecuting Society*, not anticipated when I began work on the book, was that the initiative for persecution, both of heresy and of Jews, to say nothing of others, came neither from the Church nor from the people, as had generally been

---

[61] R.I. Moore *The Formation of a Persecuting Society: Power and Deviance in Western Europe, 950–1250* (Oxford & New York: Basil Blackwell, 1987); "A la naissance d'une société persécutrice: les clercs, les Cathares et la formation de l'Europe," in *La persécution du catharisme, xiie.-xive. siècles* Actes de la 6e. session d'histoire médiévale du Centre nationale d'études cathares, September 1993 (Carcassone: Centres d'Etudes Cathares, 1996), 11–37. The argument is placed much more fully in context and considerably refined, though not radically revised, in *FER*, 146–180.

[62] Hence almost the only comment in David Nirenberg's wonderful *Communities of Violence* (Princeton: Princeton University Press, 1996) with which I disagree is that quoted by Peters above, p. 14, to the effect that Nirenberg thought his conclusions at variance with mine.

[63] Philip A. Kuhn, *Soulstealers: The Chinese Sorcery Scare of 1768* (Cambridge MA: Harvard University Press, 1990).

assumed, but from the newly emerging educated elite, the *clerici* and *magistri* who flocked to the courts of princes and prelates and carried through the "twelfth-century revolution in government." In this way my two chief historical interests unexpectedly came together, for as the pupil of R.H.C. Davis and V.H. Galbraith I had learned to respect the clerks and administrators of western Europe in the high Middle Ages as a principal formative influence in medieval society. The question why the identification, and if necessary invention, of objects for persecution should have seemed necessary or desirable to men whose energy, ingenuity, and idealism I greatly admired largely accounts for the focus of *The First European Revolution* on their formation, circumstances and character.

In *The Formation of a Persecuting Society* I argued that the process of the construction and pursuit of minorities provided a mechanism whereby clerks who competed so desperately for position and influence at court were enabled both to consolidate their own claims against their rivals and to advance the interests of their masters by increasing the power of lordship to penetrate the defences of local communities against external intervention. James Givens' paper in this volume presents an original and important refinement of that suggestion, reminding us once again how much medievalists can learn from those who have had the opportunity of studying segmentary societies at first hand. Above all he underlines how little we can hope to understand the behavior of kings and their ministers without remembering the glaring contradiction between the height of their legitimate as well as their illegitimate ambitions and the means at their disposal for realising them. For Philip IV and his servants, the disparities in their real power to achieve their goals in different theatres of action remained both baffling and frustrating. A century and a half of brilliantly successful state-building had not produced a dependable answer to Walter Map's question, "How is our king to control thousands of thousands when we poor lords can scarcely control the few men that we have?"[64]

The pursuit of the persecutors carried me a long way from what I had considered the most interesting question to emerge from *The Origins of European Dissent*, and from the realization that the protagonists of my texts—mostly bishops or abbots on the one hand, laymen of vary-

---

[64] Walter Map, *de nugis curialium*, ed. and trans. M.R. James, C.N.L. Brooke and R.A.B. Mynors, (Oxford: Clarendon Press, 1983), 222.

ing but often quite modest standing on the other—had quite different notions of what constituted tradition and what innovation. If the beliefs and practices which aroused the suspicion of the authorities were not recently imported by the emissaries of a foreign heresy, what was their source, and if, as their votaries believed, they were traditional, what was the nature of the traditions in question? Edward Peters' appraisal above of my "travels in the agro-literate polity" shows why I have now come full circle, as it were, to return to this question. He describes with great clarity the connections between the formation of a persecuting society and that of a new, cosmopolitan, clerical elite. The transformation of European society in the long twelfth century was rooted, as he puts it, in "the material ability on the part of smaller and smaller geograph-ical areas to support more and more layers of elites on their own."[65] This is the process which economists call intensive growth. In con-trast to extensive growth, which merely replicates an economy and the social structures it supports across wider and wider territories, inten-sive growth changes social relations because it increases the surplus of disposable wealth in relation to the size of the population. This, in Europe, was not a once-for-all transformation, but a continuing, dialec-tical process. Thus, in the architectural example that I used to illus-trate this point, to which Peters refers, more complex technology and a more articulate aesthetic gave the Gothic style of the twelfth century markedly greater uniformity and a correspondingly more metropolitan character than the Romanesque which it superseded. Yet Gothic also continued to develop within itself the rich variety of styles and forms of expression to which Peters finds Konigsberger alluding, although I still think that their variations were related, on the whole, more closely to chronology than to geography, whereas the variations of Romanesque had been very markedly, and from the outset, expressive of regional styles and traditions.[66]

Intensification entails not only social but also political and cultural change. It is inherently destabilizing. Both the increase of productivity and the collection of the resultant surplus require—certainly, they did in medieval Europe—very considerable coercion and regulation of the

---

[65] Above, p. 18.

[66] *FER*, 121, Peters, above p. 19. Peters is entirely correct in his suspicion that if I had been familiar with Konigsberger's discussion I would have borrowed the example of the bell founder, which offers a perfect illustration of circumstances that I wanted to describe.

cultivators, and therefore the creation of a new body of institutions and a new class of petty officials and middlemen. The generation of new wealth enhances local power, which simultaneously attracts and threatens the metropolitan authority. This creates requirements for the means of intervention and for a rationale for intervening, both of which must be supplied by the clerical elite. Naturally, the local powers resist, and to maintain their position seek in their turn legitimacy and the capacity for further intensification. In other world civilizations the periodic attempts of the central power to intervene regularly and effectively at the local level have generally been short-lived, frustrated by the difficulty of penetrating the dense fabric of local solidarity and hegemony,[67] but in Latin Europe after the eleventh century, though the balance of advantage rested with the nobles in many regions and for long periods, kings and their ministers never entirely gave up the struggle. It is a simplification, but not a falsification, to say that the emergence in the nineteenth century of modern social and economic structures, and of the modern state, represented their final victory.

The seismic conflicts which marked the course of the enduring tension between locally based and centralising power are registered in the familiar themes of the grand narrative of European history—the Investiture Contest, Church and State, Feudal Monarchy, The Rise of the Towns and so on. They arose, in one way or another, from the rivalries created within the great community by intensive growth, and reflected them. The element common to all the innumerable guises in which "reform," both sacred and secular, appeared in the twelfth century was the desire of a wider community to impose its values on and assert its control over a more restricted one. Wherever we have sufficient information to follow closely one of the innumerable disputes over the reform of a cathedral church, as famously at Milan in the 1050s and '6os, (and without suggesting that this is necessarily a complete explanation in particular cases) it resolves into the question whether the resources of the diocese are to remain under the exclusive control of the regional nobility, or to be placed at the disposal of the representative of a wider, outside power—the great community—which is represented

---

[67] Cf John Hall, *Powers and Liberties* (Oxford: Blackwell, 1985), who also discusses this point in terms of Gellner's model of the agro-literate polity. I was not conscious of being greatly impressed by Hall's analysis when it was published, but the extent to which my own resembles it nearly twenty years later suggests that I must have learned more from it than I realized at the time.

by the critics of an unreformed bishop, as at Milan, or the allies of
a reforming one, as at Bordeaux in the 1140s or Lyons in the 1170s.[68]
Henry II's vigorous and imaginative application of the *inquisitio* to the
enforcement of order in the English shires is the most familiar example,
but only one of many, of the same phenomenon in a secular context.
At the parish level the conflict was even more universal, and more fundamental, because this was the frontier between the privileged and the
producers, between the great and the little communities.[69] Since economic growth and all that flowed from it depended on the subordination, or at least the more effective exploitation, of the productive population, the question who was to control the power which flowed from
increased production ultimately depended on the maintenance of order
in small communities. In this religious leadership played an indispensable role, and a great deal might hang on whether it was to be exercised
by a representative of the community or of an external power. Hence
the confrontations between bishops and those whom they accused of
heresy amounted, in very many cases, to demands for the subordination of the little community to the great, and heresy itself became one
of the mechanisms—there were plenty of others—by which the leaders of the little community could be identified, and if necessary isolated
and disciplined.

No individual illustrates these tensions and difficulties better than
the man who first drew my attention to popular heresy, Robert of
Arbrissel, a leader of the little community who committed himself—
converted as he might have said—to the great, and spent his entire
life trying to reconcile the conflict of personal loyalties that resulted.
This was not a matter of class in the Marxist sense. As a member of
a priestly dynasty Robert was part of the elite of the small world into
which he was born. He abjured that position to embrace the values and
aspirations of the wider world, the great community. He was recruited
by Archbishop Sylvester de la Guèrche as archpriest of the diocese
of Rennes, with a mandate to make its priests give up their wives,
presenting them thereby with the choice between allegiance to their

---

[68] Bordeaux: the conflict resolved by Bernard in 1145 (*BPH*, 42); Lyons: Rubellin,
above n. 40.

[69] The significance of the First European Revolution itself, as I understand it,
lay precisely in the success of the newly formed great community, or high culture,
constituted by the tripartite elite of those who prayed, fought, and worked (that is, the
bourgeoisie, not the peasantry) in establishing itself securely in command of the agro-
literate polity which was Latin Christendom, and was becoming Europe.

families, communities and traditional structures on one hand and their bishop and his Church on the other. It is not surprising that failure led to breakdown, and a retreat to the forest, from which he emerged as a hermit-preacher, more committed than ever to the values of reform— and correspondingly and excoriatingly critical of fellow clerks who were lax in their lives or half-hearted in the cause.[70]

These were the tensions that made a wild-eyed, skin-clad hot gospeller the founder of one of the richest and most aristocratic convents in Christendom—and made his successors bury him not in the pauper's grave he had asked for, but before the altar of the mighty basilica that arose from, if it did not altogether commemorate, his achievements. We do not know when or why Robert first embraced the great community which was asserting itself so vigorously in his lifetime, but his biographer implies that it had something to do with his period as a student in Paris in the 1070s, during the pontificate of Gregory VII. It is not an unusual choice for a student to make—indeed for many that is the whole point of being a student. But it was the choice that Henry of Lausanne refused, in confrontation with Robert's friend and supporter, Hildebert of Lavardin, bishop of Le Mans. Henry appeared at Le Mans in 1116, the year of Robert's death, very much as Robert had appeared at many cities in his time, as a holy man come to inveigh against the sins of the world and the wicked. At Le Mans that meant attacking the morals and corruption of the clergy, which is as much as to say their connections and place in local society, as Robert had done so often. But while Henry emerged from his stay at Le Mans in clear and stark defiance of the bishop's authority, and entered the historical record as a heresiarch, Robert had remained an obedient son of the church throughout his career, though frequently it seems by the slenderest of margins, and it was his opponents who were characterised pejoratively. Or to put it otherwise, although Henry's memory continued to be cherished by the people of Le Mans, it was his enemies, and Hildebert's admirers, like Robert's, who wrote the history.[71]

---

[70] See especially Baldri of Dol's *Life*, chaps. 7–12, in Venarde (above, n. 3), 10–13, and the letter of Marbod of Rennes, ibid. at pp. 96–98. The speculation is my own, but Baldri, at p. 13, does describe Robert as being "an implacable enemy at war with himself alone."

[71] *BPH*, 33–39; cf. R.I. Moore, "Heresy and the Making of Literacy, c. 1000–1150," Peter Biller and Anne Hudson eds., *Heresy and Literacy in the Middle Ages* (Cambridge: Cambridge University Press, 1994), 19 37.

In Claire Taylor's meticulous account in this volume of religious conflict in the Agenais in the twelfth century, Robert of Arbrissel and
Henry of Lausanne illustrate some of the most important and elu-
sive implications of the developing tensions between the great and
little communities. She describes five occasions in the twelfth century when heterodoxy in the region was detected and denounced.[72] In
1114 Robert preached there against "an otherwise unidentified sect."
In 1145 Bernard of Clairvaux, in pursuit of Henry, complained that
the region was infested by many heresies. Before 1150 Abbot Hervé of
Déols described as "Manichaeans" and "Agenais" a "sect"—his word—
who opposed marriage and meat-eating; c. 1155 Bishop Elie de Castillon asked a brother prelate to help him restore the lapsed faith of
the people of Gontaud, a few miles to the north; and five years after
that the bishop of Périgueux attacked the nearby castle of Gavau-
dan, on the ground that it was infested by heresy. Here is a variety
of grounds which to representatives of the large community justified
intervention in the religious affairs of small ones. It is a list, of course,
which would be manna to those who, eagerly anticipating the years of
crusade and inquisition, smell a Cathar under every unrumpled bed.
Taylor does nothing of the kind, but it seems fair, even so, to ask to
what extent our reading of these descriptions is a function of our own
processes of classification. Precisely what is implied by accepting the
categorisation by each of these authority figures of those whom they
attacked as "sects" or "heretics"? Even supposing their perfect sincerity and disinterestedness–which we may certainly do at least in the
case of Robert of Abrissel, whose own Catholicism had been unfairly
impugned by those embarrassed by the vigour of his attacks on clerical
morals—were they not making an assumption which we ought to question, that in the Agenais there had once existed a correct, uncorrupted
Catholicism whose perversion they sought to explain by attributing it to
the malevolent intrusion of sectaries or heretics? And ought we not to
consider the alternative, that it was they, the authors or inspirers of our
sources, who were the outsiders, and in their minds rather than in the
earlier history of the communities in question, that the vision of pristine
Catholic orthodoxy and fidelity was to be found?

This is precisely the question which is raised by Mark Pegg in *The
Corruption of Angels*, and in this volume by his redoubtable assault on

---

[72] Above, pp. 139–194.

the conventional description of the religion of the countryside of the Languedoc as Catharism, which he sees as a construct of modern scholarship as well as of the inquisitors. Even those—it seems a safe bet that there will be some—who do not follow him so far as to question its very connection with the Bogomils must be impressed by the thoroughness with which he is able to demonstrate that in the eyes of their followers the religion of the *good men* had very little to do with dualist theology. What it was really about was communal leadership earned by and practised through personal austerity, which signified disinterestedness and therefore trustworthiness, and the sanctification of neighborly respect and support. In this his findings are strikingly in harmony with those of Rene Weis for Montaillou half a century later,[73] except—and it is an interesting exception—that Pegg's subjects (or their interrogators) do not seem to attach such desperate importance to deathbed consolation as those of Weis. Carol Lansing had reached similar conclusions in respect of the very different context of Orvieto, where "only in the imaginations of anti-Catholic polemicists did the Italian cathars effectively create an anti-church, with a defined membership and an institutional and sacramental structure parallel to Rome," and heretical allegiance was founded on the belief that "because the perfects were *boni homines,* good men, salvation was in them and not in the clergy of the Catholic Church".[74] In this volume Susan Taylor Snyder shows that this was also the case in Bologna at the end of the century. Both Lansing and Pegg had noted that one consequence of the fact that popular belief was vested in the character and conduct of individuals rather than in systems of doctrine was to undermine the differences between Cathars and Catholics in day to day observance and piety. In quite another way Lansing's Riperando, in this volume, cocking a snook at our perhaps over-rigid conceptions of what constitutes intellectual or spiritual respectablity, also subverts the notion that in the little community religious idiosyncracy was always symptomatic of faction or division. Snyder is able not only to bring fascinatingly vivid and circumstantial detail to that observation, but to show that for her subjects at least the readiness of ordinary Cathar believers to share Catholic religious practices and occasions is attributable not to ignorance, but to a conscious willingness to grant practical holiness and the maintenance

---

[73] René Weis, *The Yellow Cross* (London: Viking, 2000), a work whose readability should not be allowed to obscure the depth and acuteness of its analysis.

[74] Lansing, *Power and Purity*, pp. 7, 11.

of sociability priority over theological considerations.[75] She takes us beyond the implication of all these studies that the religious differences between Catholics and heretics did not always cause or reflect intolerable social divisions or tensions, to contemplate the remarkable possibility that some people at least were deliberately prepared to use the body of common values and modes of communication embodied in traditional religious practices to counter the divisions caused or expressed by the theological conflicts of their respective leaders.

Which leaves the question, what was the source and nature of the traditional practices and values to which, it may appear, at least some of the little communities of Europe clung so resolutely while their superiors fought over the number of their principles? So we return to the texts and their grain. Like that of every great struggle, the history of the "reform" of the church between the age of Gregory VII and that of Innocent III, which is nothing less than the history of the creation of Catholic Europe, was written by the victors. Bringing the little community safely under the wing of the great was the work of doughty bishops and saintly preachers. Their heroic endeavors could be glowingly recorded in chronicles and *vitae*. But the failures of this mighty effort—and it has to be said that in proportion to the successes there were not very many of them—made more taxing demands on their historians. It was necessary to discredit those who had obstructed the good work, and to show that resistance to the advance of the great community could only result from the dissemination of the forces of evil.

The positive aspect of this construction of memory, the story of how the spread of heresy among the people grew slowly but inexorably into a menace that threatened to undermine Christendom itself and had to be heroically countered and overthrown, is now well known. Scholars have labored long, and with some success, to understand its telling and its part in our history, as well as to disentangle the fragments of truth which it certainly contains from the dazzlingly seductive nightmare of whose reality the makers of Europe so thoroughly persuaded themselves. But there is also a negative aspect, which we must struggle to discern in the shadows of the grand narrative—and it is one of the very grandest—that is our inheritance from the high Middle Ages. The story of the religion of the little community, of the many versions of

---

[75] Above, pp. 241–251.

Christianity which grew and flourished between the age of conversion and that of reform (both, of course, terms of the greatest chronological imprecision), has vanished almost beyond recall. Conversion, of necessity, had generally been a flexible business, capable of accommodating, as Gregory the Great famously advised Augustine of Canterbury, a great deal in the way of customary practice, not to mention customary leadership, so long as the essentials of Christianity were acknowledged.[76] Reform, as we have been reminded so often in these pages, was anything but flexible. Confronted by its demands small communities could surrender or resist. Their former customs must be abandoned and forgotten (at least as far as the written record was concerned— writing being the ultimate marker and the ultimate weapon of the great community[77]) as superstition or corruption, unless they were to be condemned as heresy.[78] Either way, they were consigned to oblivion, from which some fragment wedged stubbornly in the grain of the texts can occasionally be rescued. In recent years great progress has been made in uncovering the dynamics and modes of operation of the religion of the people of Europe in the centuries on either side of the millennium not as a reflection of what the church hoped they would believe, but as a revelation of how the little community could be energized and mobilized in defense, though often unavailing, of its own values and aspirations.[79]

This is the context in which "the birth of popular heresy" and "the formation of a persecuting society" must now be placed. As all the

---

[76] Bede, *Historia Ecclesiastica* I, 27, trans. B. Colgrave, in Judith McClure and Roger Collins, *The Ecclesiastical History of the English People* (Oxford: Clarendon Press, 1994), 29–54.

[77] Pertinent examples include Julia M.H. Smith, "Oral and Written: Saints, Miracles and Relics in Brittany, c. 850–1250," *Speculum* 65 (1990), 309–343; Kathleen Ashby and Pamela Sheingorn, *Writing Faith: Text, Sign and History on the Miracles of Sainte Foy* (Chicago: University of Chicago Press, 1999). More generally understanding of popular religion, including popular heresy, has been immensely enriched by Brian Stock, *The Implications of Literacy*, and Rosamund McKitterick, ed., *The Uses of Literacy in Early Medieval Europe* (Cambridge: Cambridge University Press, 1990).

[78] Compare the very similar comments of Richard Fletcher, *The Conversion of Europe* (London: HarperCollins, 1997), 389–390, 461–479.

[79] For examples, Patrick Geary, *Living with the Dead in the Middle Ages* (Ithaca, NY: Cornell University Press 1994); Geoffrey Koziol, *Begging Pardon and Favor: Ritual and Political Order in Early Medieval France* (Ithaca and London: Cornell University Press, 1992); Lester K. Little, *Benedictine Maledictions: Liturgical Cursing in Romanesque France* (Ithaca and London: Cornell University Press, 1993); R.I. Moore, "Between Sanctity and Superstition: Saints and their Miracles in the Age of Revolution," in Miri Rubin,

contributors to this volume demonstrate, in their different ways, the beliefs and practices of those who were identified as heretics are a central chapter of that story. A few years ago Patrick Geary argued that the wholesale destruction of the memory of a former world was inseparable from the eleventh- and twelfth-century reconstruction of European society.[80] He wrote of the great community, the world of the noble families and their institutions, but the same is also true for the little community. Among its spokesmen, and the custodians of its memory, were the *good men* and women whose influence rulers must either command or destroy. Until we understand what they stood for and why we will not properly have grasped the origins of European dissent.

---

ed., *The Work of Jacques Le Goff and the Challenges of Medieval History*, (Woodbridge: Boydell Press, 1997).

   [80] Patrick Geary, *Phantoms of Remembrance* (Princeton: Princeton University Press, 1994).

INDEX

Studies in the History
of Christian Traditions

·(formerly Studies in the History of Christian Thought)

EDITED BY ROBERT J. BAST

96. IZBICKI, T.M. and BELLITTO, C.M. (eds.). *Reform and Renewal in the Middle Ages and the Renaissance.* Studies in Honor of Louis Pascoe, S. J. 2000

97. KELLY, D. *The Conspiracy of Allusion.* Description, Rewriting, and Authorship from Macrobius to Medieval Romance. 1999

98. MARRONE, S.P. *The Light of Thy Countenance.* Science and Knowledge of God in the Thirteenth Century. 2 volumes. 1. A Doctrine of Divine Illumination. 2. God at the Core of Cognition. 2001

99. HOWSON, B.H. *Erroneous and Schismatical Opinions.* The Question of Orthodoxy regarding the Theology of Hanserd Knollys (c. 1599-169)). 2001

100. ASSELT, W.J. VAN. *The Federal Theology of Johannes Cocceius (1603-1669).* 2001

101. CELENZA, C.S. *Piety and Pythagoras in Renaissance Florence the* Symbolum Nesianum. 2001

102. DAM, H.-J. VAN (ed.), *Hugo Grotius, De imperio summarum potestatum circa sacra.* Critical Edition with Introduction, English translation and Commentary. 2 volumes. 2001

103. BAGGE, S. *Kings, Politics, and the Right Order of the World in German Historiography c. 950-1150.* 2002

104. STEIGER, J.A. *Fünf Zentralthemen der Theologie Luthers und seiner Erben.* Communicatio – Imago – Figura – Maria – Exempla. Mit Edition zweier christologischer Frühschriften Johann Gerhards. 2002

105. IZBICKI, T.M. and BELLITTO, C.M. (eds.). *Nicholas of Cusa and his Age: Intellect and Spirituality.* Essays Dedicated to the Memory of F. Edward Cranz, Thomas P. McTighe and Charles Trinkaus. 2002

106. HASCHER-BURGER, U. *Gesungene Innigkeit.* Studien zu einer Musikhandschrift der Devotio moderna (Utrecht, Universiteitsbibliotheek, MS 16 H 94, olim B 113). Mit einer Edition der Gesänge. 2002

107. BOLLIGER, D. *Infiniti Contemplatio.* Grundzüge der Scotus- und Scotismusrezeption im Werk Huldrych Zwinglis. 2003

108. CLARK, F. *The 'Gregorian' Dialogues and the Origins of Benedictine Monasticism.* 2002

109. ELM, E. *Die Macht der Weisheit.* Das Bild des Bischofs in der *Vita Augustini* des Possidius und andere spätantiken und frühmittelalterlichen Bischofsviten. 2003

110. BAST, R.J. (ed.). *The Reformation of Faith in the Context of Late Medieval Theology and Piety.* Essays by Berndt Hamm. 2004.

111. HEERING, J.P. *Hugo Grotius as Apologist for the Christian Religion.* A Study of his Work De Veritate Religionis Christianae (1640). Translated by J.C. Grayson. 2004.

112. LIM, P.C.-H. *In Pursuit of Purity, Unity, and Liberty.* Richard Baxter's Puritan Ecclesiology in its Seventeenth-Century Context. 2004.

113. CONNORS, R. and GOW, A.C. (eds.). *Anglo-American Millennialism, from Milton to the Millerites.* 2004.

114. ZINGUER, I. and YARDENI, M. (eds.). *Les Deux Réformes Chrétiennes.* Propagation et Diffusion. 2004.

115. JAMES, F.A. III (ed.). *Peter Martyr Vermigli and the European Reformations:* Semper Reformanda. 2004.

116. STROLL, M. *Calixtus II (1119-1124).* A Pope Born to Rule. 2004.

117. ROEST, B. *Franciscan Literature of Religious Instruction before the Council of Trent.* 2004.

118. WANNENMACHER, J.E. *Hermeneutik der Heilsgeschichte.* De septem sigillis und die sieben Siegel im Werk Joachims von Fiore. 2004.

119. THOMPSON, N. *Eucharistic Sacrifice and Patristic Tradition in the Theology of Martin Bucer, 1534-1546.* 2005.

120. VAN DER KOOI, C. *As in a Mirror. John Calvin and Karl Barth on Knowing God.* A Diptych. 2005.

121. STEIGER, J.A. *Medizinische Theologie.* Christus medicus und theologia medicinalis bei Martin Luther und im Luthertum der Barockzeit. 2005.

122. GIAKALIS, A. *Images of the Divine.* The Theology of Icons at the Seventh Ecumenical Council – Revised Edition. With a Foreword by Henry Chadwick. 2005.

123. HEFFERNAN, T.J. and BURMAN, T.E. (eds.). *Scripture and Pluralism.* Reading the Bible in the Religiously Plural Worlds of the Middle Ages and Renaissance. Papers Presented at the First Annual Symposium of the Marco Institute for Medieval and Renaissance Studies at the University of Tennessee, Knoxville, February 21-22, 2002. 2005.

124. LITZ, G., MUNZERT, H. and LIEBENBERG, R. (eds.). *Frömmigkeit – Theologie – Frömmigkeitstheologie – Contributions to European Church History.*

125. FERREIRO, A. *Simon Magus in Patristic, Medieval and Early Modern Traditions.* 2005.

126. GOODWIN, D.L. *"Take Hold of the Robe of a Jew".* Herbert of Bosham's Christian Hebraism. 2006.

127. HOLDER, R.W. *John Calvin and the Grounding of Interpretation.* Calvin's First Commentaries. 2006.

128. REILLY, D.J. *The Art of Reform in Eleventh-Century Flanders.* Gerard of Cambrai, Richard of Saint-Vanne and the Saint-Vaast Bible. 2006.

129. FRASSETTO, M. (ed.). *Heresy and the Persecuting Society in the Middle Ages.* Essays on the Work of R.I. Moore. 2006.

Prospectus available on request

BRILL — P.O.B. 9000 — 2300 PA LEIDEN — THE NETHERLANDS

317